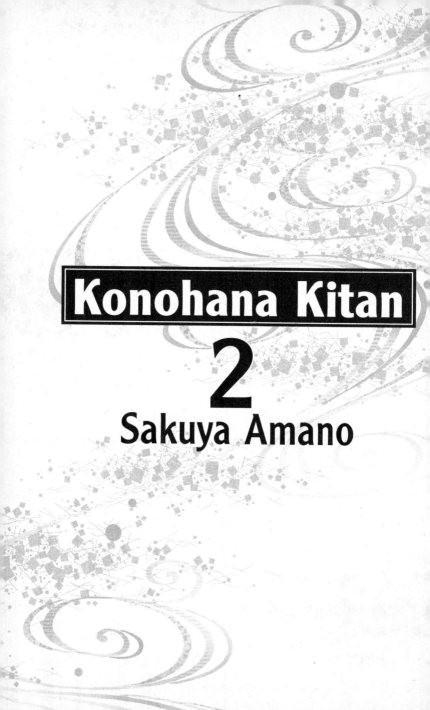

Konohana Kitan

2

Sakuya Amano

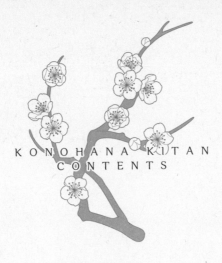

K O N O H A N A   K I T A N
C O N T E N T S

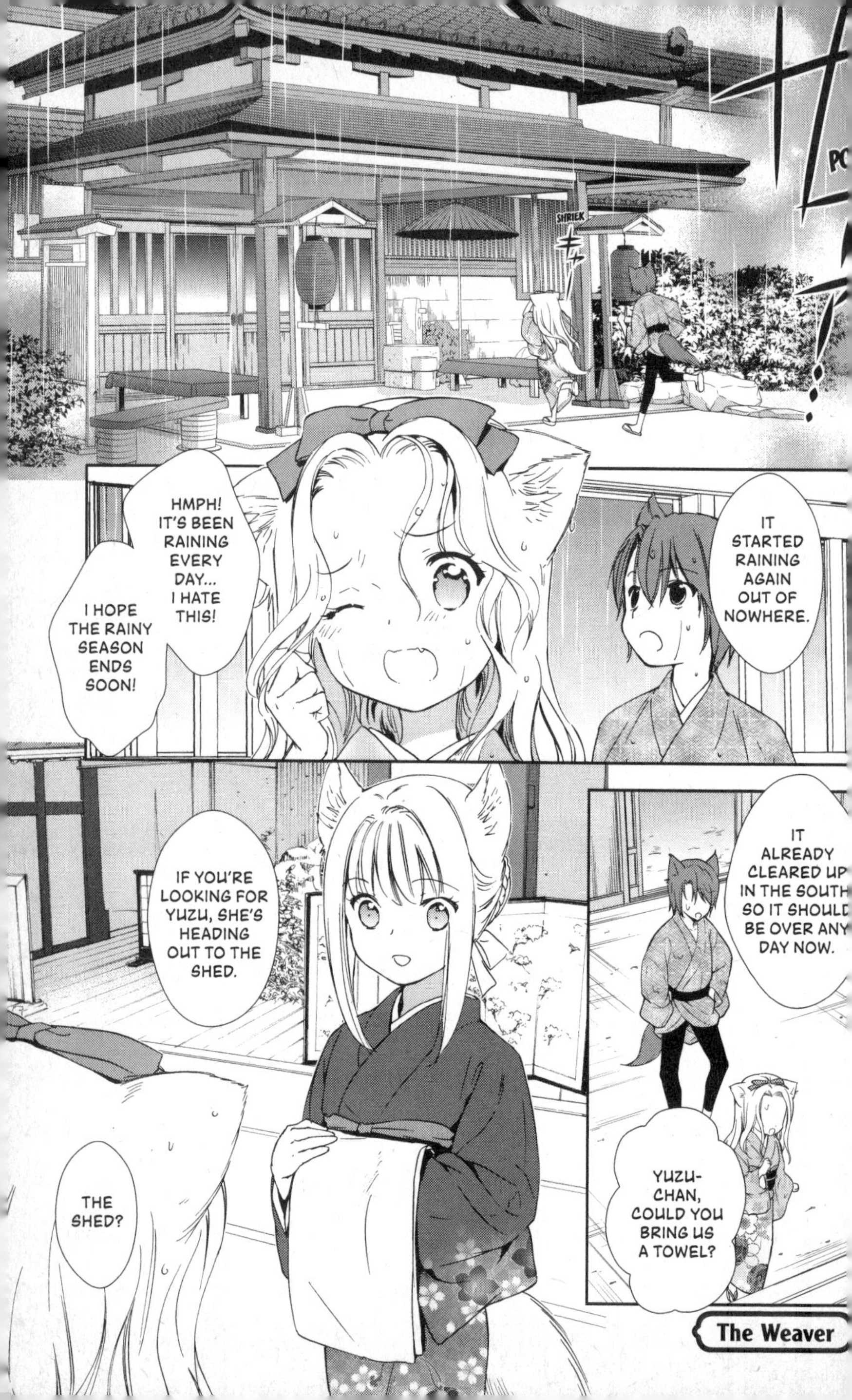
SHRIEK
IT STARTED RAINING AGAIN OUT OF NOWHERE.
HMPH! IT'S BEEN RAINING EVERY DAY... I HATE THIS!
I HOPE THE RAINY SEASON ENDS SOON!
IT ALREADY CLEARED UP IN THE SOUTH SO IT SHOULD BE OVER ANY DAY NOW.
YUZU-CHAN, COULD YOU BRING US A TOWEL?
IF YOU'RE LOOKING FOR YUZU, SHE'S HEADING OUT TO THE SHED.
THE SHED?
The Weaver

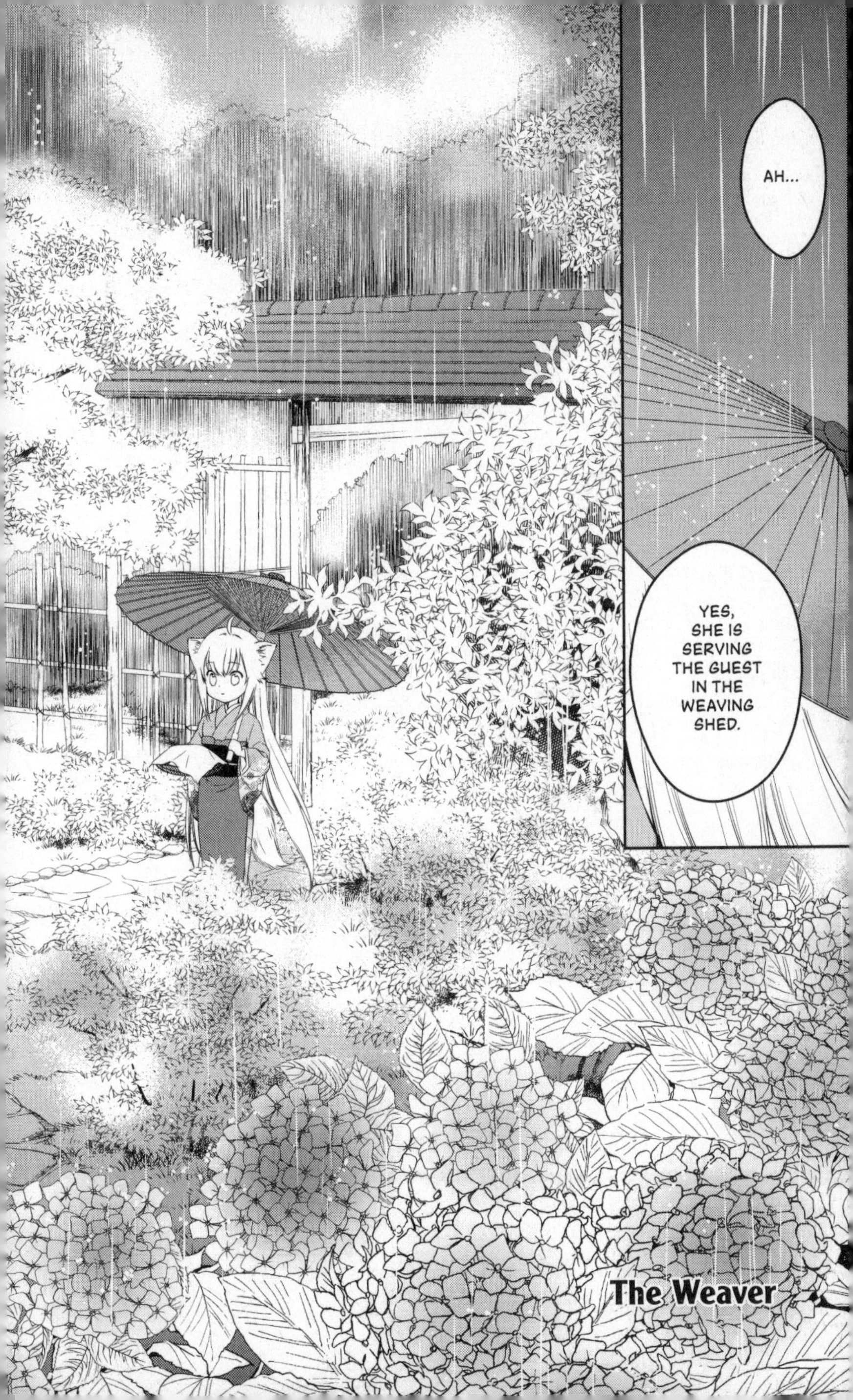
AH...
YES, SHE IS SERVING THE GUEST IN THE WEAVING SHED.
The Weaver

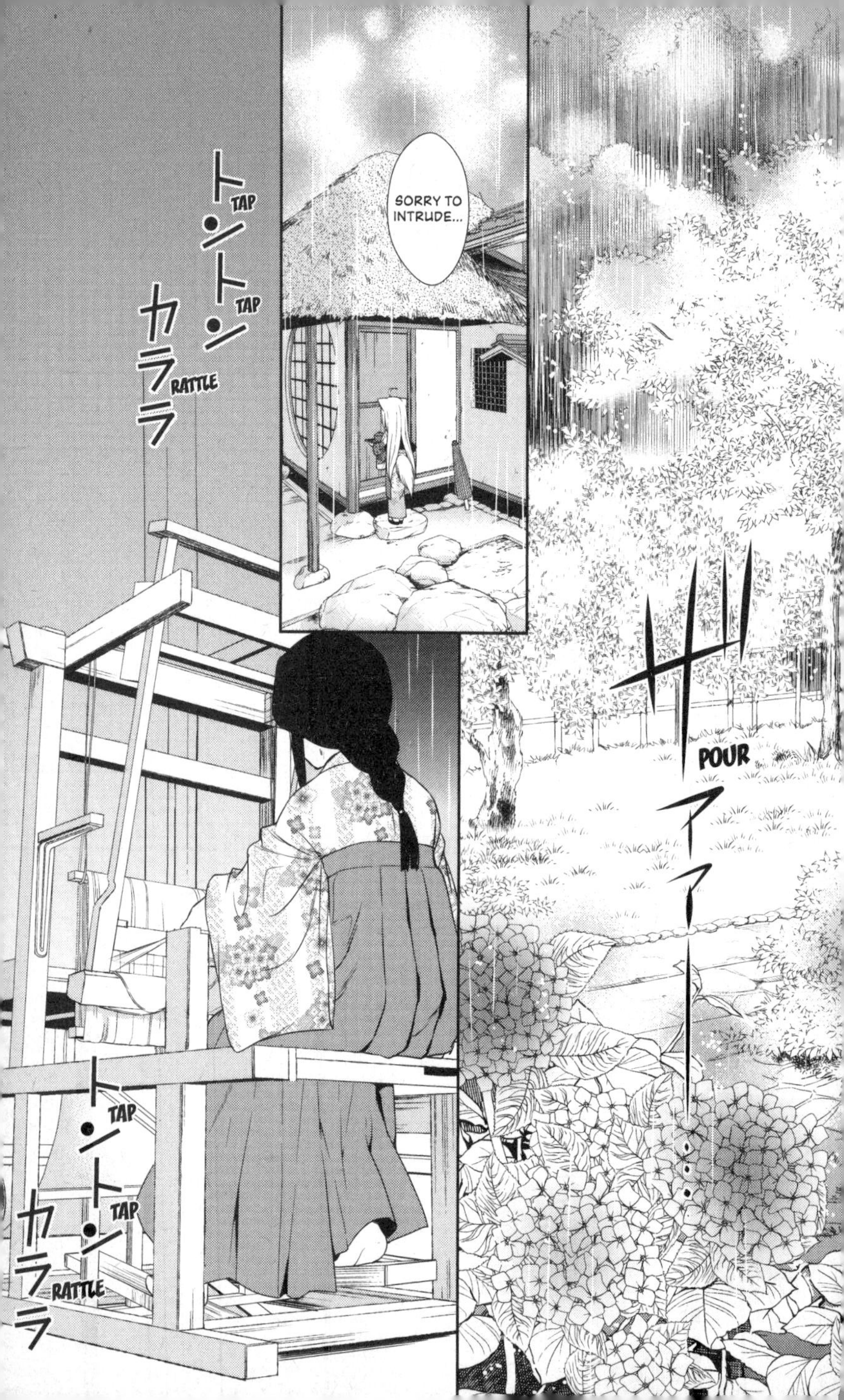
ザアアー…
POUR
SORRY TO INTRUDE...
トントンカララ
TAP
TAP
RATTLE
トントンカララ
TAP
TAP
RATTLE

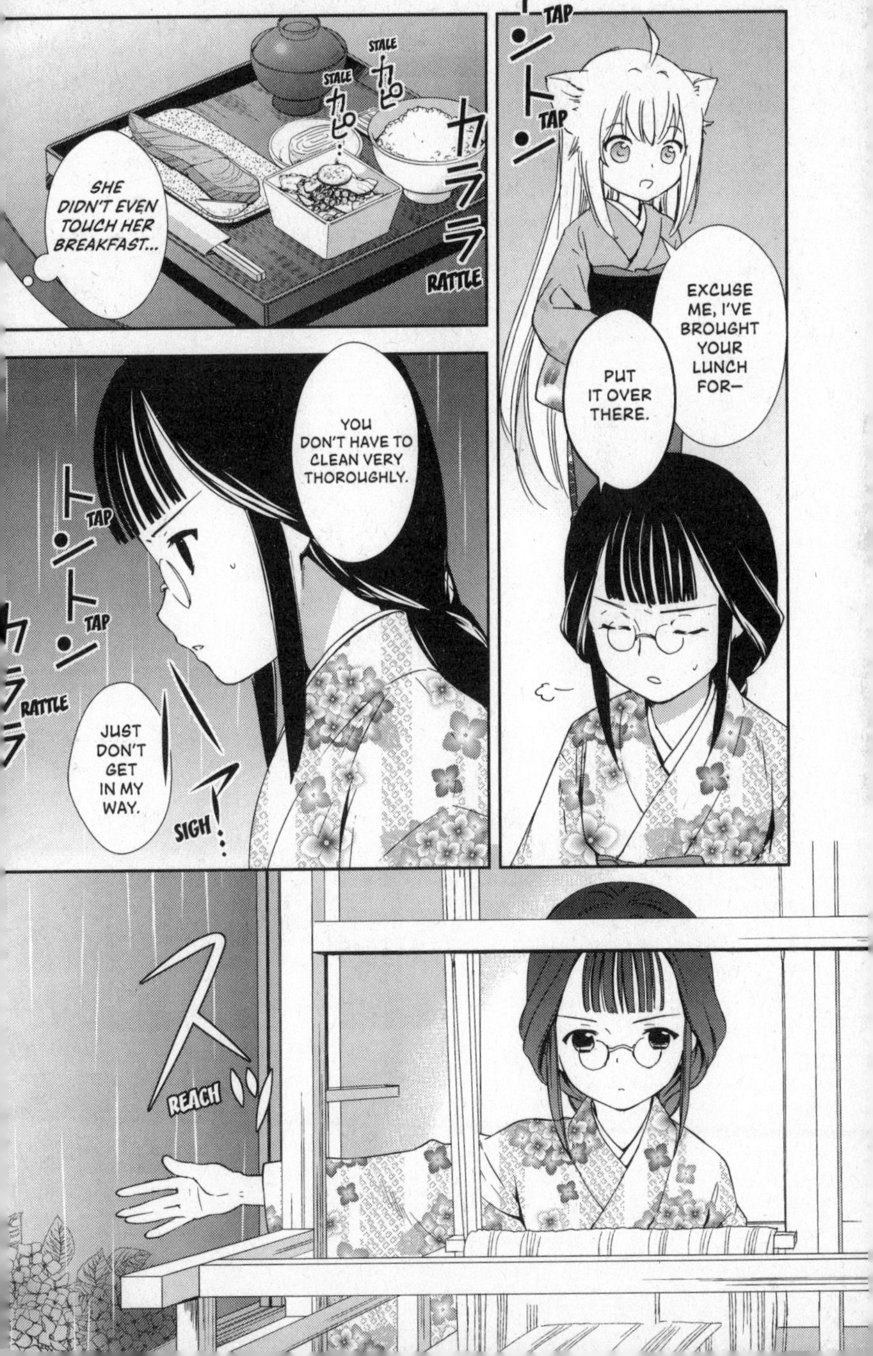
TAP
TAP
EXCUSE ME, I'VE BROUGHT YOUR LUNCH FOR—
PUT IT OVER THERE.
RATTLE
STALE
STALE
SHE DIDN'T EVEN TOUCH HER BREAKFAST...
YOU DON'T HAVE TO CLEAN VERY THOROUGHLY.
TAP
TAP
RATTLE
SIGH
JUST DON'T GET IN MY WAY.
REACH

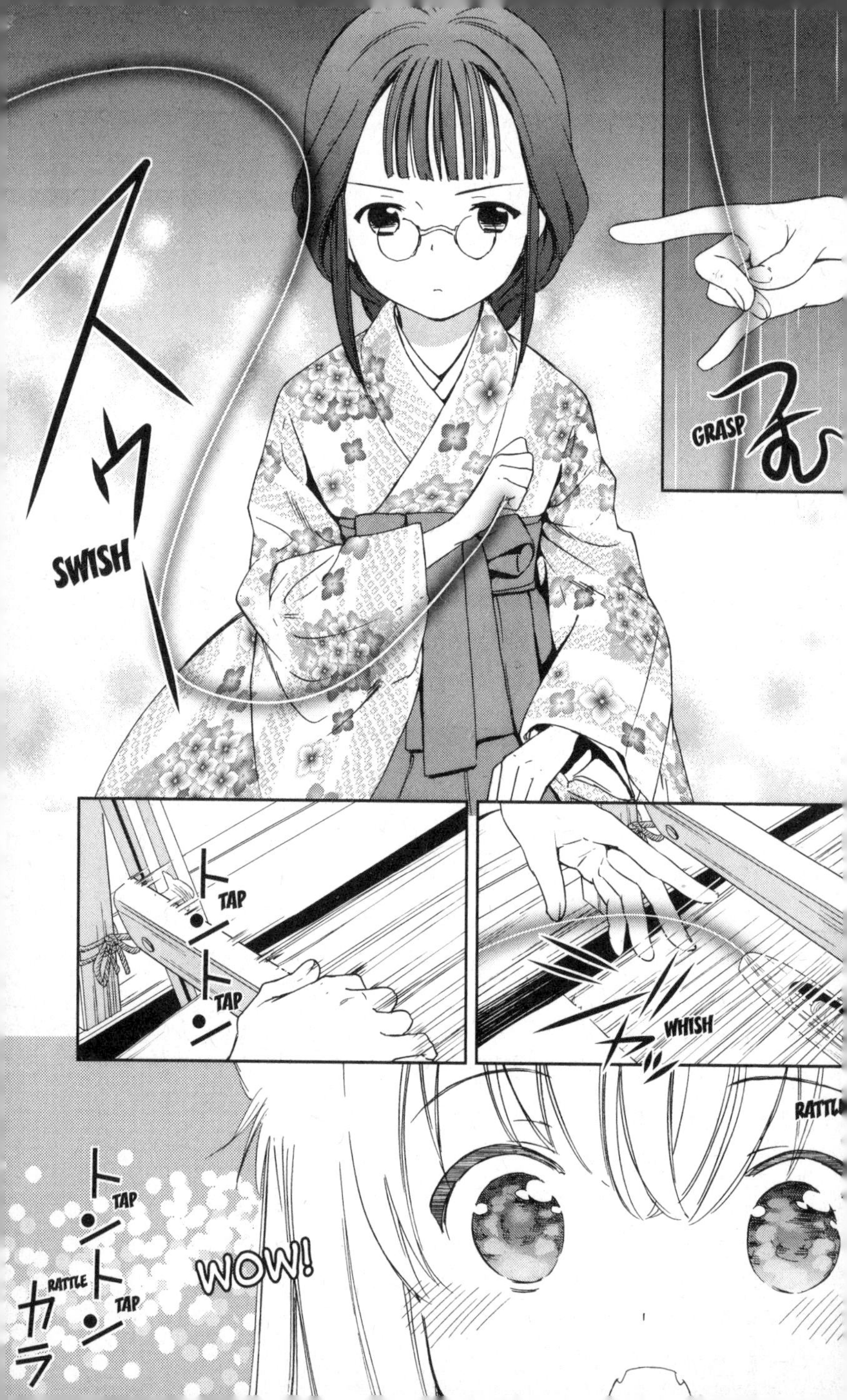

GRASP
SWISH
WHISH
TAP
TAP
RATTLE
WOW!
TAP
TAP
RATTLE

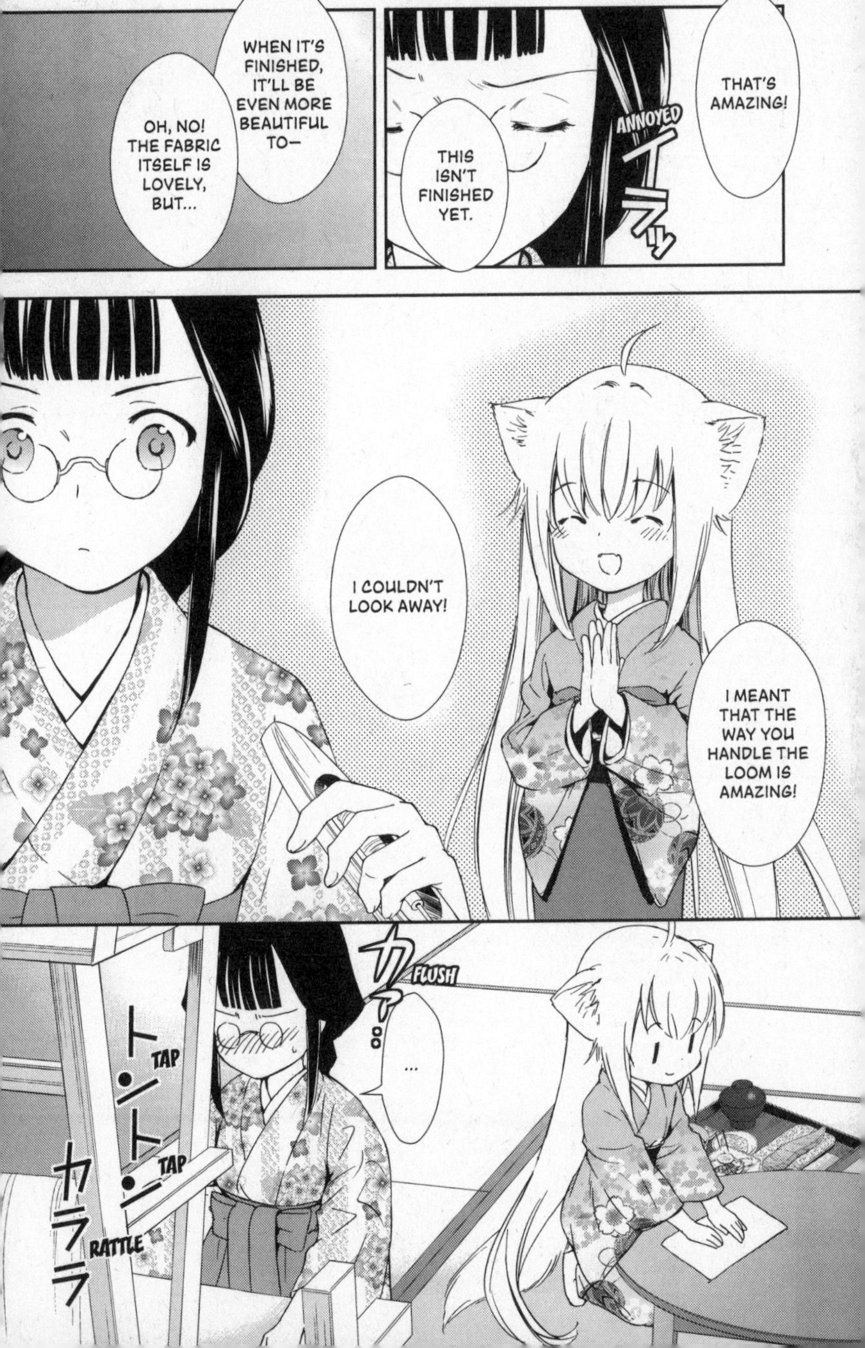
THAT'S AMAZING!
ANNOYED
THIS ISN'T FINISHED YET.
WHEN IT'S FINISHED, IT'LL BE EVEN MORE BEAUTIFUL TO—
OH, NO! THE FABRIC ITSELF IS LOVELY, BUT...
I MEANT THAT THE WAY YOU HANDLE THE LOOM IS AMAZING!
I COULDN'T LOOK AWAY!
FLUSH
...
TAP
TAP
RATTLE

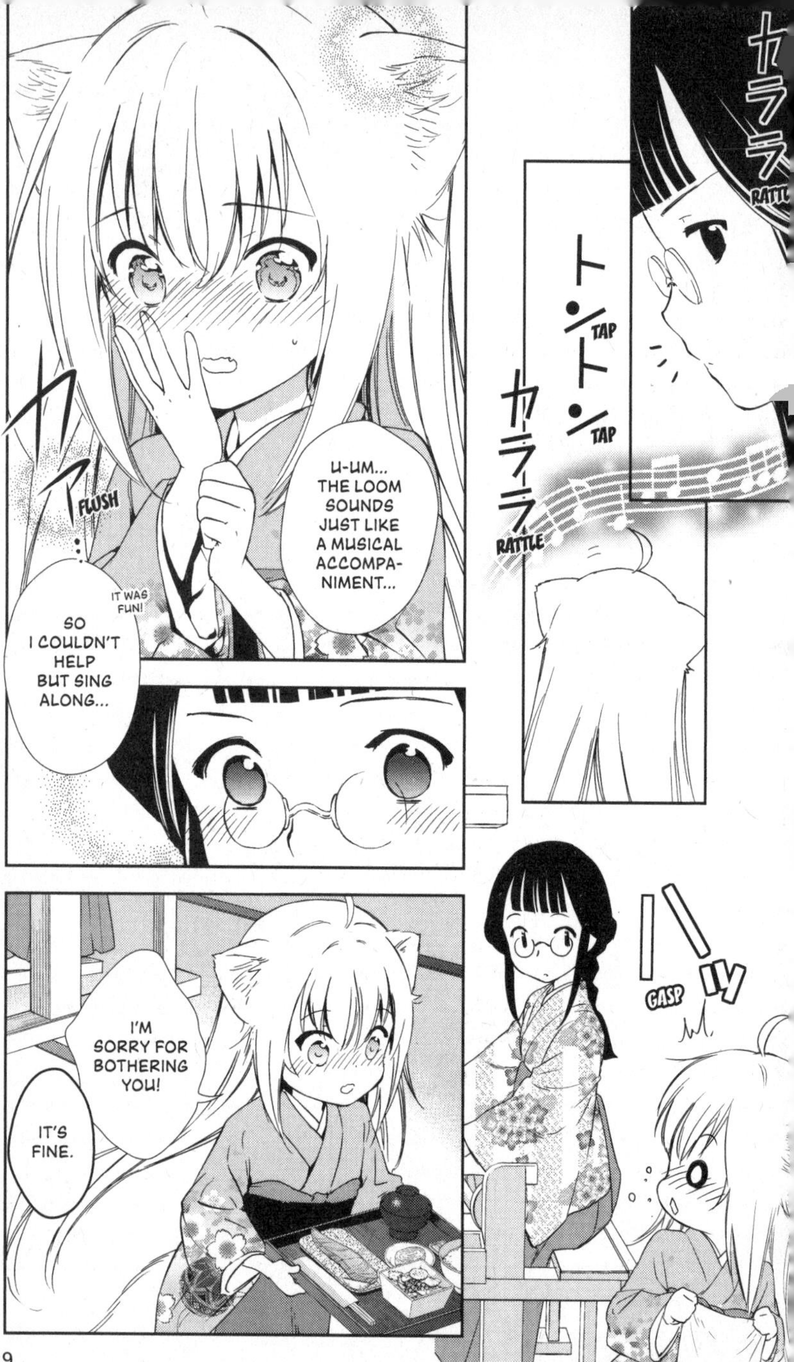

カラ
RATTLE
トントン
TAP
TAP
カララ
RATTLE
U-UM... THE LOOM SOUNDS JUST LIKE A MUSICAL ACCOMPANIMENT...
カァ
FLUSH
IT WAS FUN!
SO I COULDN'T HELP BUT SING ALONG...
ハッ
GASP
I'M SORRY FOR BOTHERING YOU!
IT'S FINE.

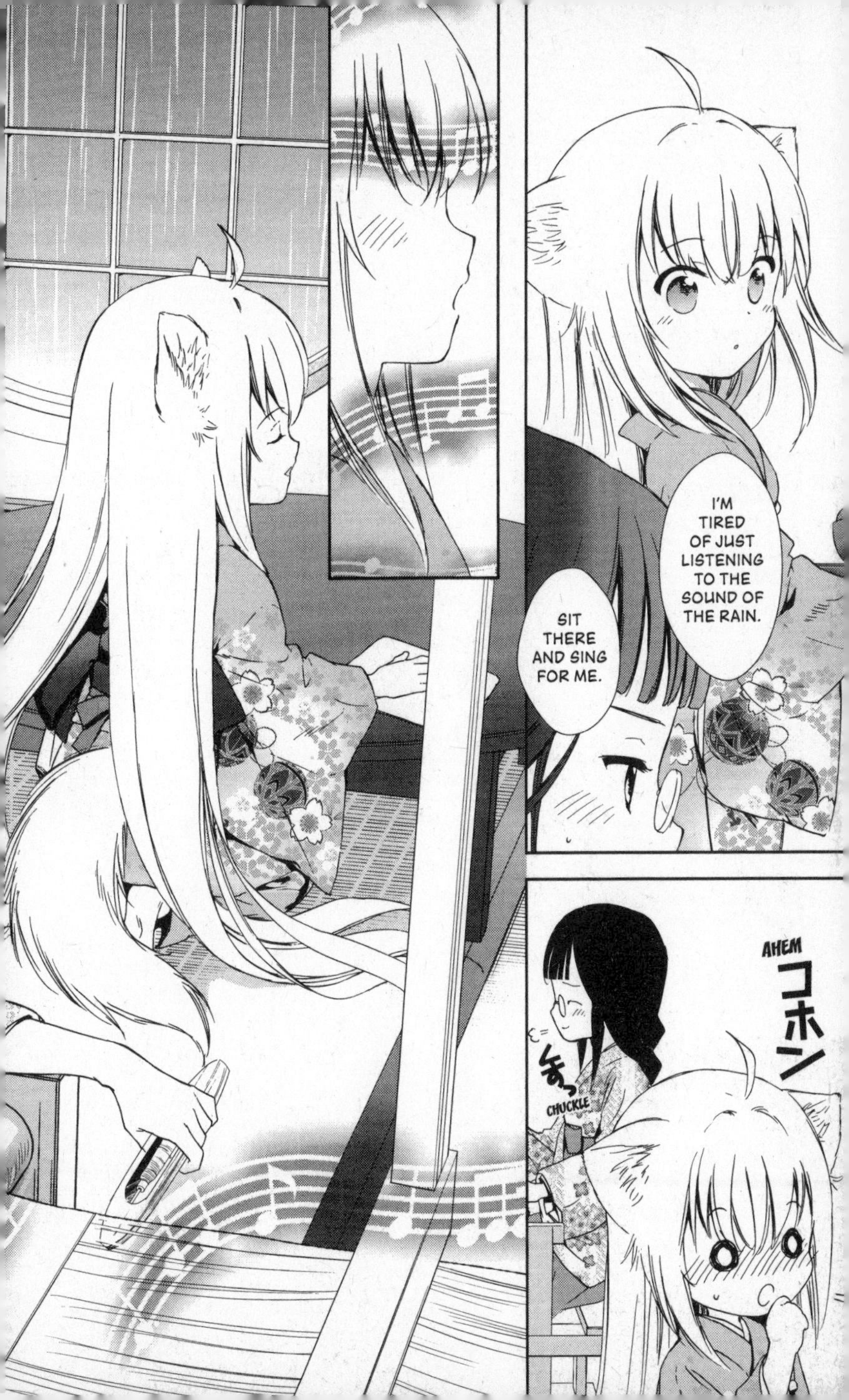
I'M TIRED OF JUST LISTENING TO THE SOUND OF THE RAIN.
SIT THERE AND SING FOR ME.
AHEM
コホン
CHUCKLE

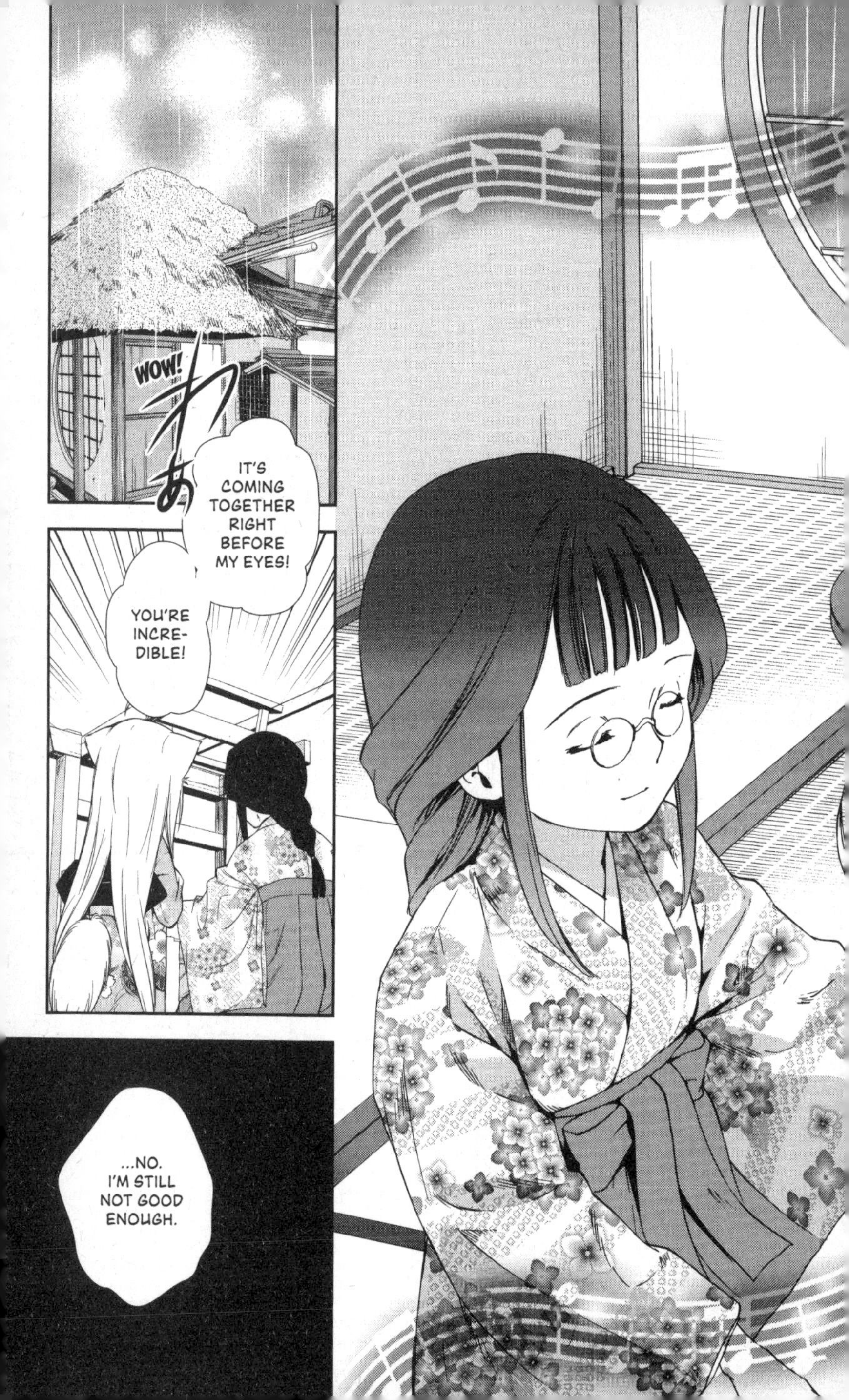
WOW!
IT'S COMING TOGETHER RIGHT BEFORE MY EYES!
YOU'RE INCREDIBLE!
...NO. I'M STILL NOT GOOD ENOUGH.

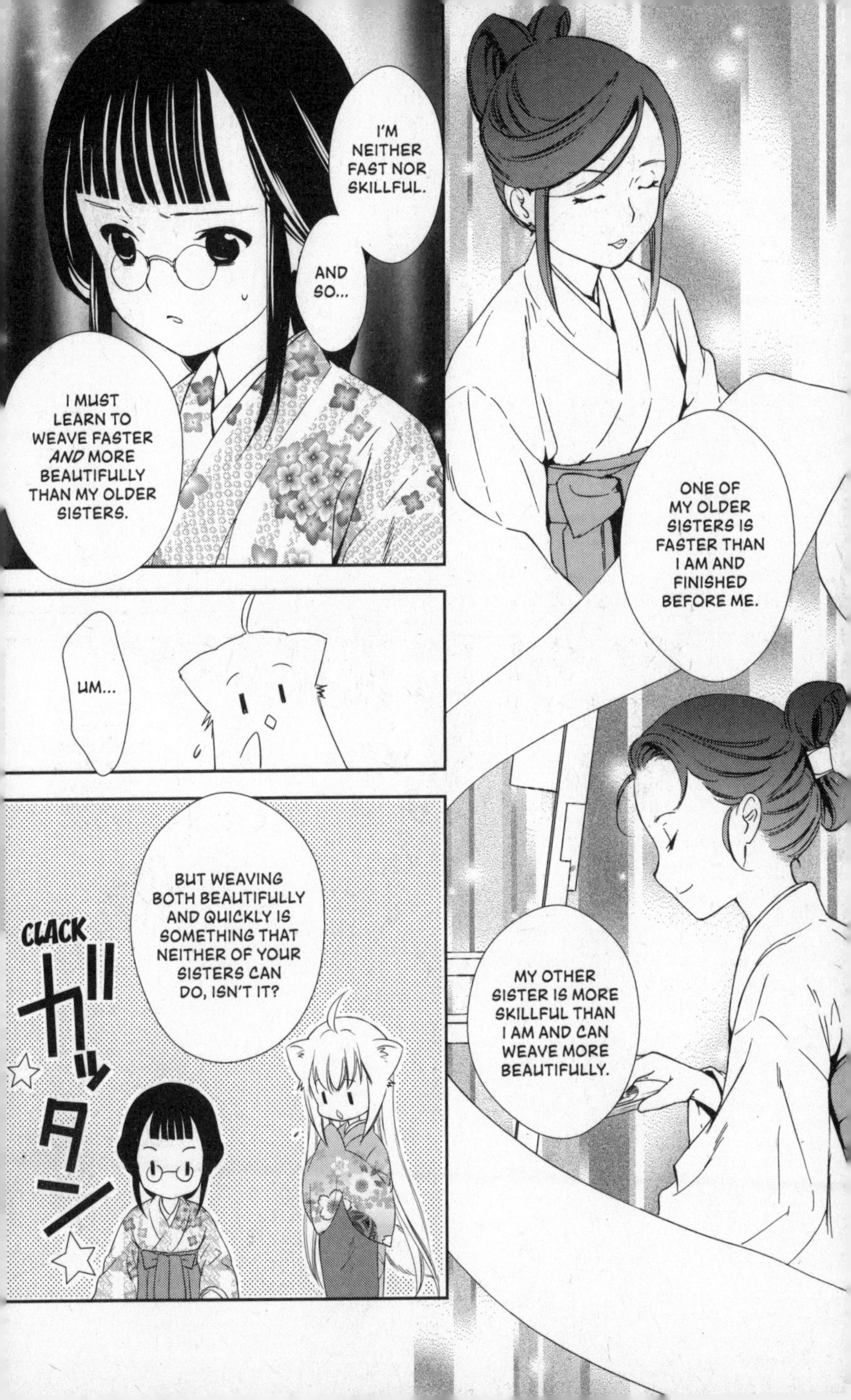
ONE OF MY OLDER SISTERS IS FASTER THAN I AM AND FINISHED BEFORE ME.
MY OTHER SISTER IS MORE SKILLFUL THAN I AM AND CAN WEAVE MORE BEAUTIFULLY.
I'M NEITHER FAST NOR SKILLFUL.
AND SO...
I MUST LEARN TO WEAVE FASTER *AND* MORE BEAUTIFULLY THAN MY OLDER SISTERS.
UM...
BUT WEAVING BOTH BEAUTIFULLY AND QUICKLY IS SOMETHING THAT NEITHER OF YOUR SISTERS CAN DO, ISN'T IT?
CLACK
カッタン

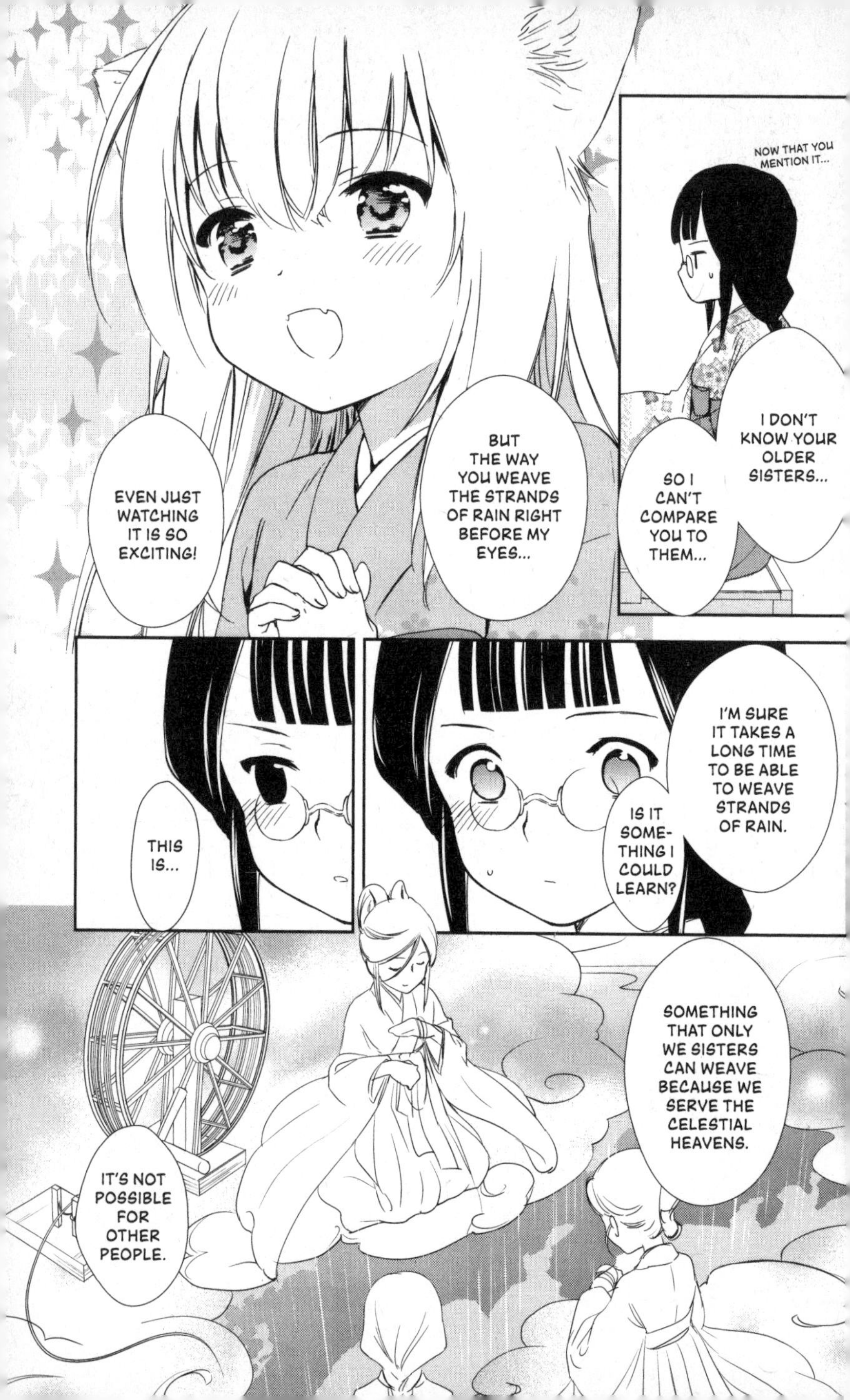
NOW THAT YOU MENTION IT...
I DON'T KNOW YOUR OLDER SISTERS...
SO I CAN'T COMPARE YOU TO THEM...
BUT THE WAY YOU WEAVE THE STRANDS OF RAIN RIGHT BEFORE MY EYES...
EVEN JUST WATCHING IT IS SO EXCITING!
I'M SURE IT TAKES A LONG TIME TO BE ABLE TO WEAVE STRANDS OF RAIN.
IS IT SOME-THING I COULD LEARN?
THIS IS...
SOMETHING THAT ONLY WE SISTERS CAN WEAVE BECAUSE WE SERVE THE CELESTIAL HEAVENS.
IT'S NOT POSSIBLE FOR OTHER PEOPLE.

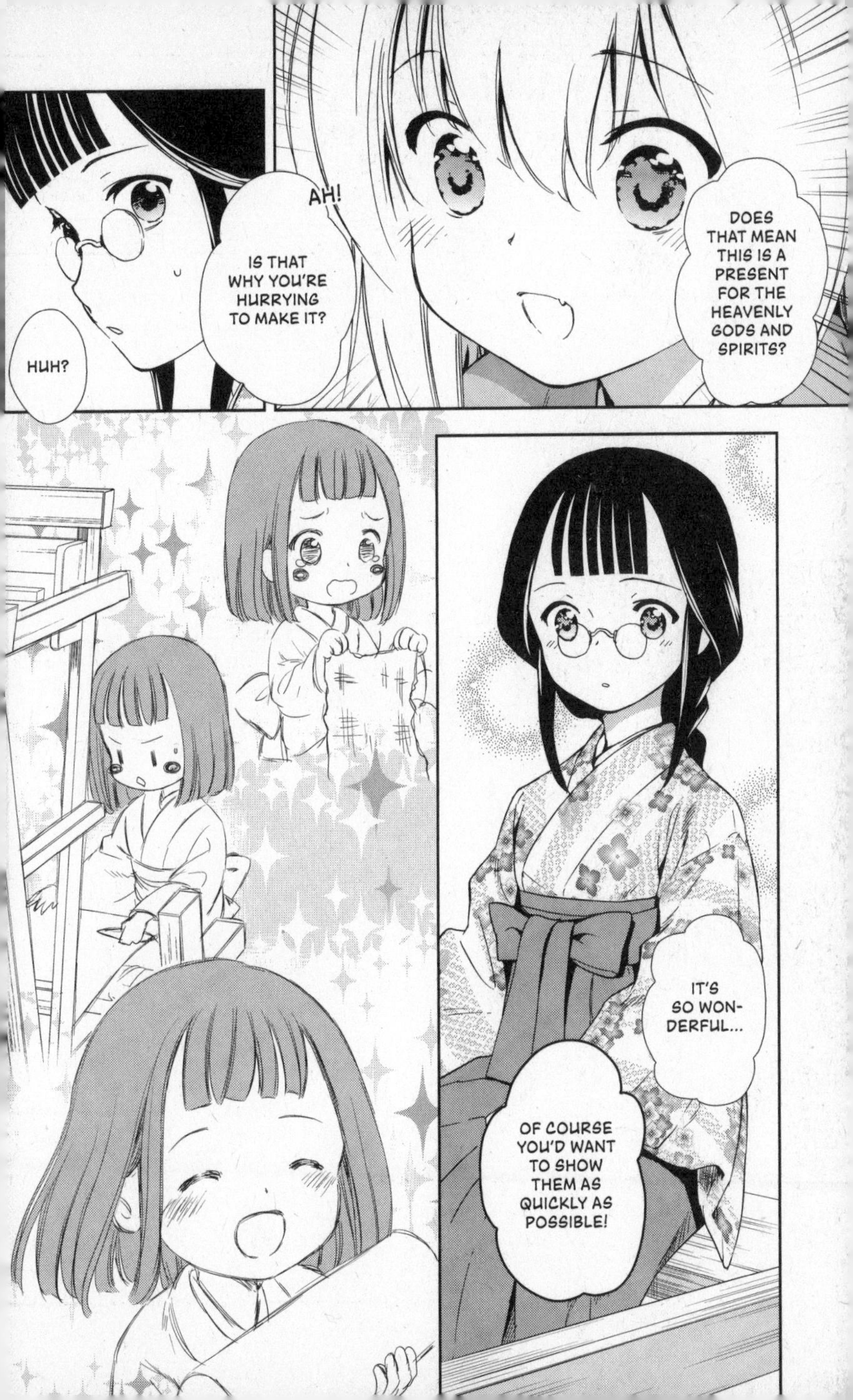
AH!
DOES THAT MEAN THIS IS A PRESENT FOR THE HEAVENLY GODS AND SPIRITS?
IS THAT WHY YOU'RE HURRYING TO MAKE IT?
HUH?
IT'S SO WON-DERFUL...
OF COURSE YOU'D WANT TO SHOW THEM AS QUICKLY AS POSSIBLE!

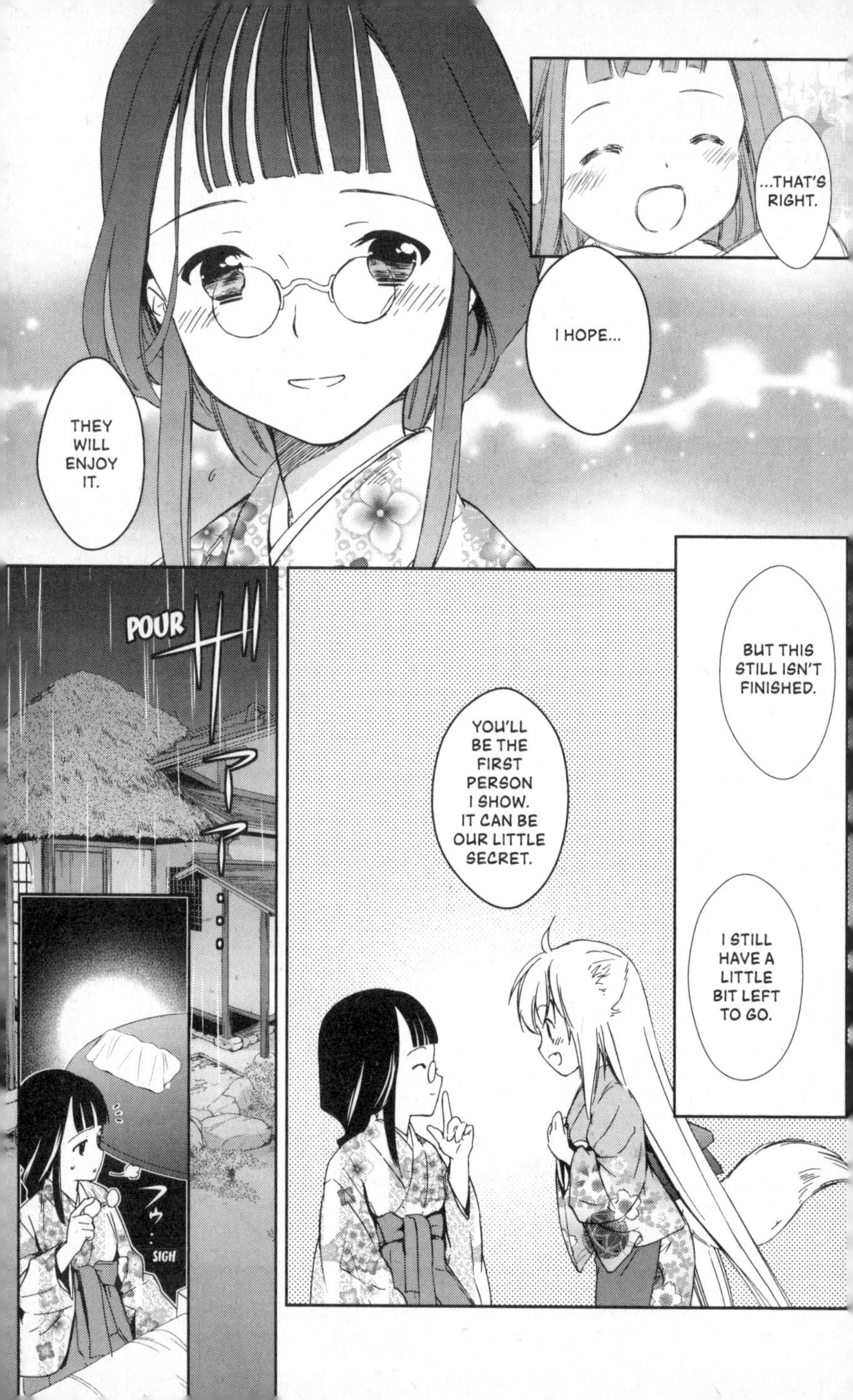

...THAT'S RIGHT.
I HOPE...
THEY WILL ENJOY IT.
BUT THIS STILL ISN'T FINISHED.
I STILL HAVE A LITTLE BIT LEFT TO GO.
YOU'LL BE THE FIRST PERSON I SHOW. IT CAN BE OUR LITTLE SECRET.
POUR
SIGH

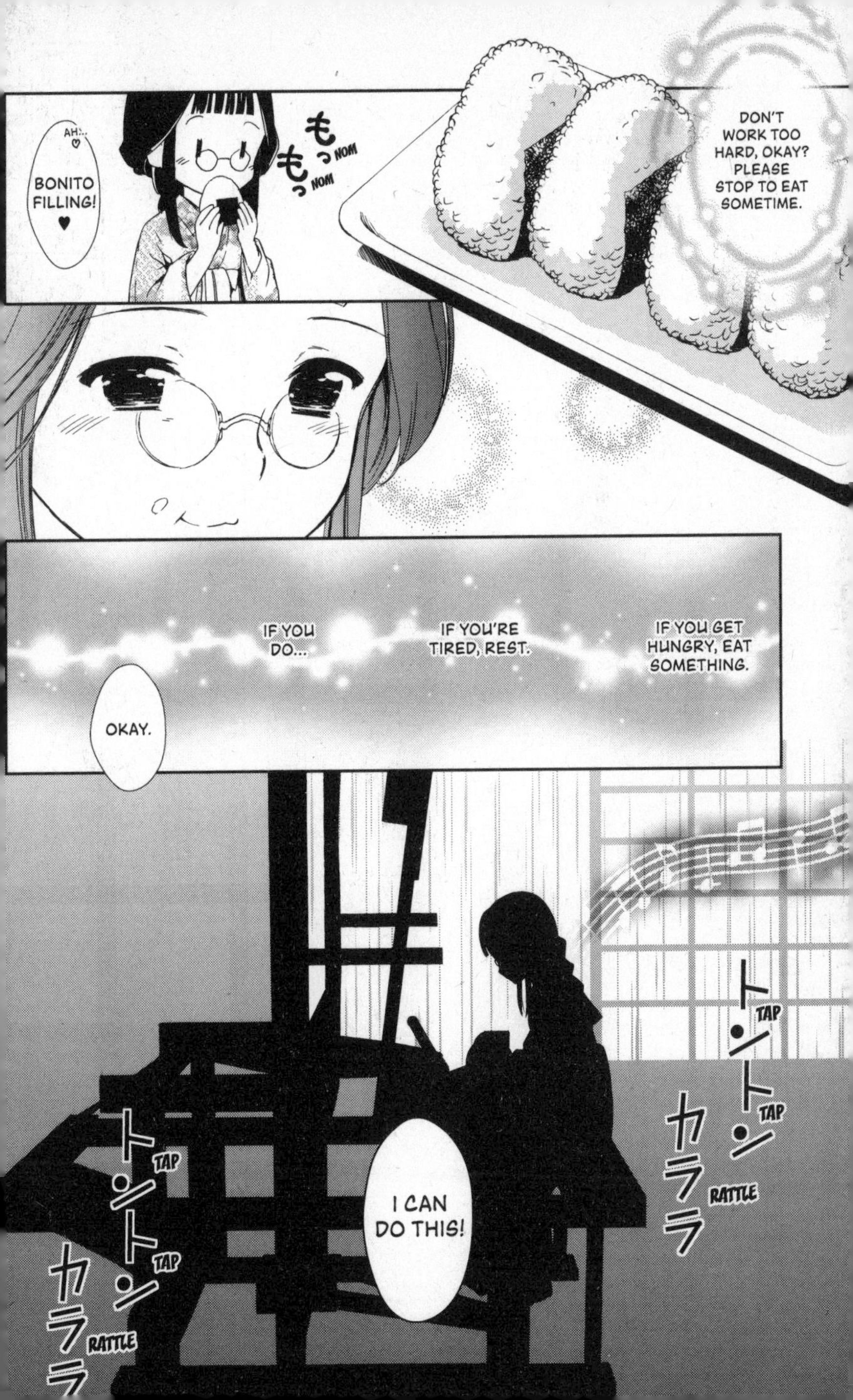
DON'T WORK TOO HARD, OKAY? PLEASE STOP TO EAT SOMETIME.
もっ NOM もっ NOM
AH... ♡
BONITO FILLING! ♥
IF YOU GET HUNGRY, EAT SOMETHING.
IF YOU'RE TIRED, REST.
IF YOU DO...
OKAY.
トン TAP トン TAP カララ RATTLE
I CAN DO THIS!
トン TAP トン TAP カララ RATTLE

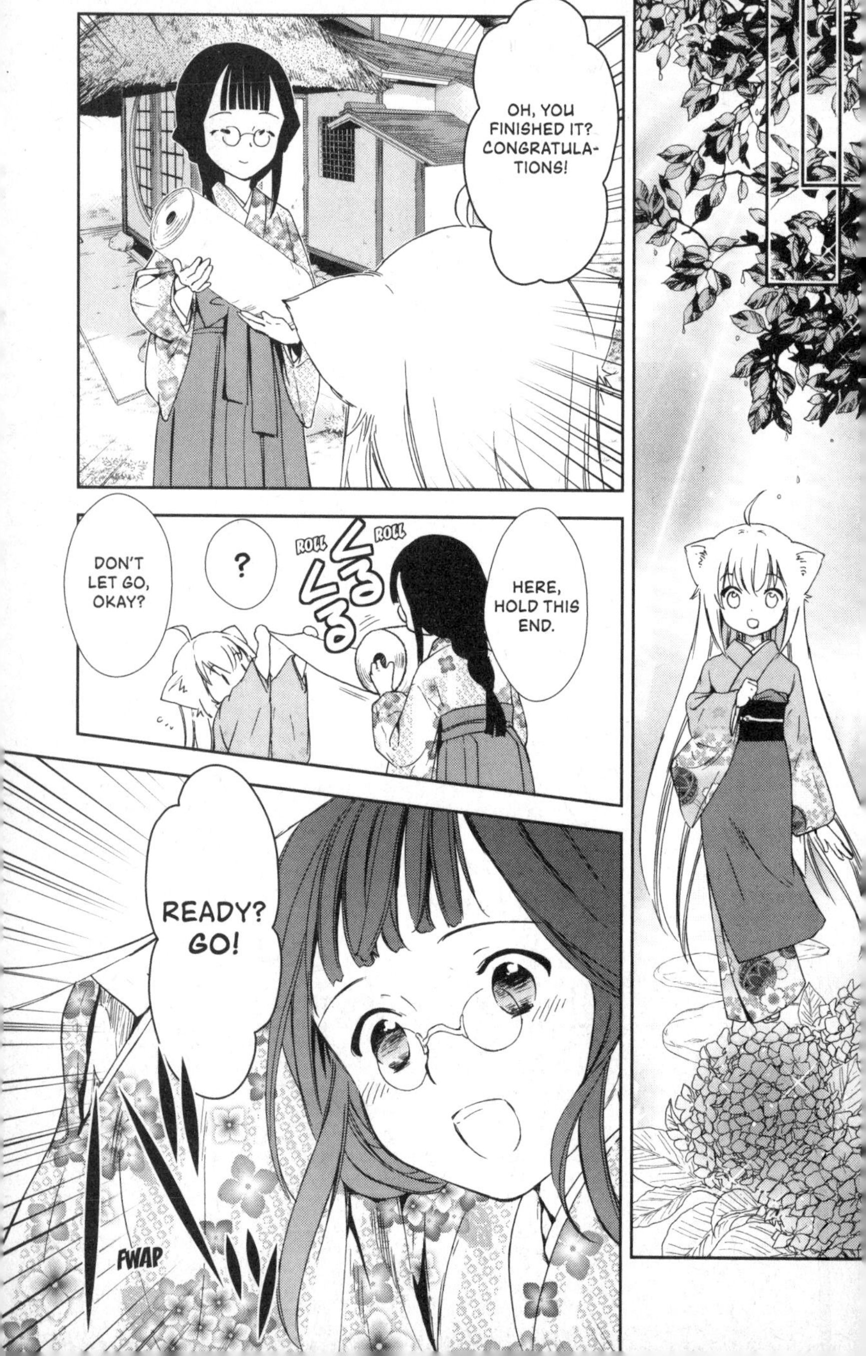
OH, YOU FINISHED IT? CONGRATULA-TIONS!
HERE, HOLD THIS END.
ROLL
くるくる
ROLL
?
DON'T LET GO, OKAY?
READY? GO!
FWAP

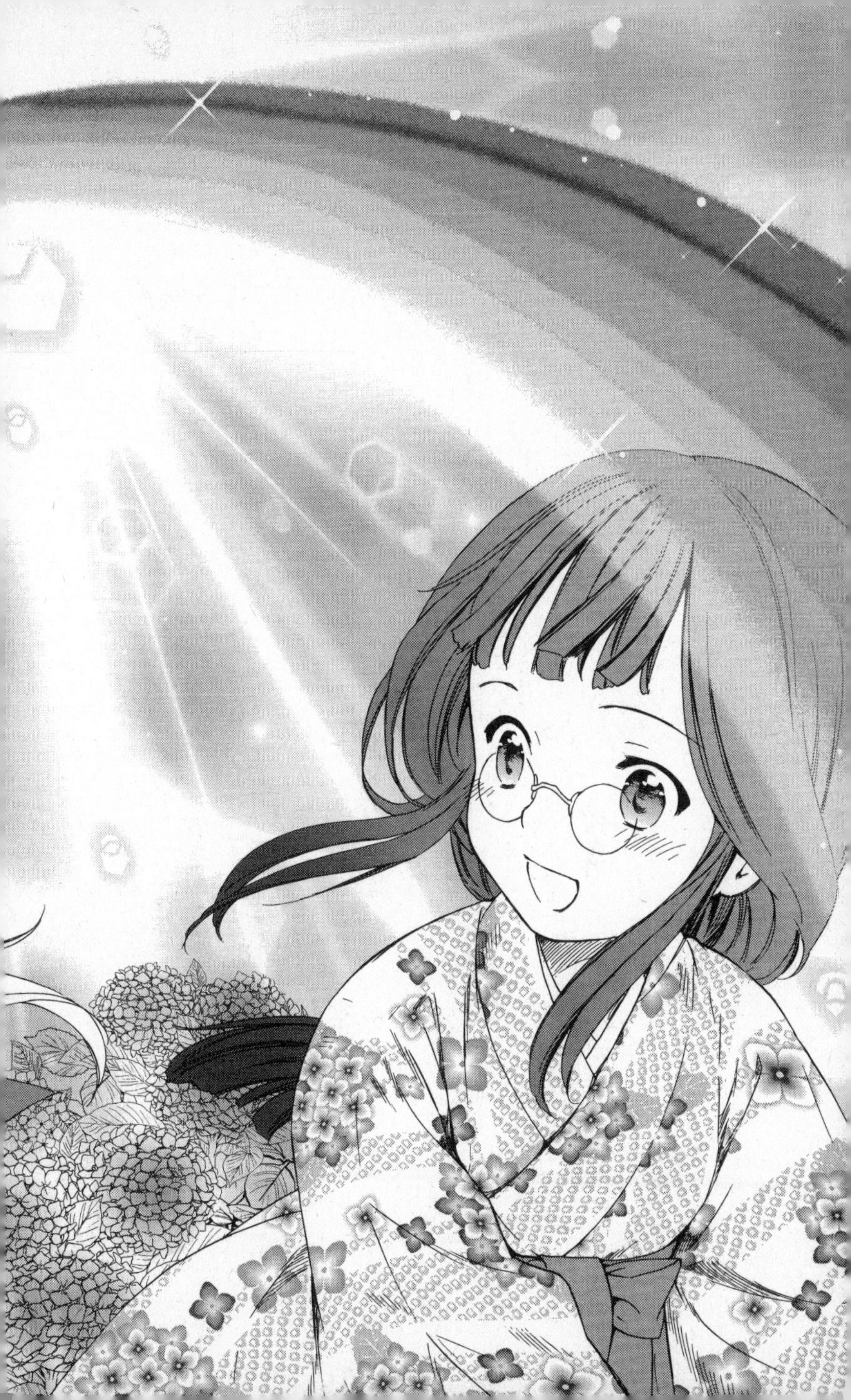

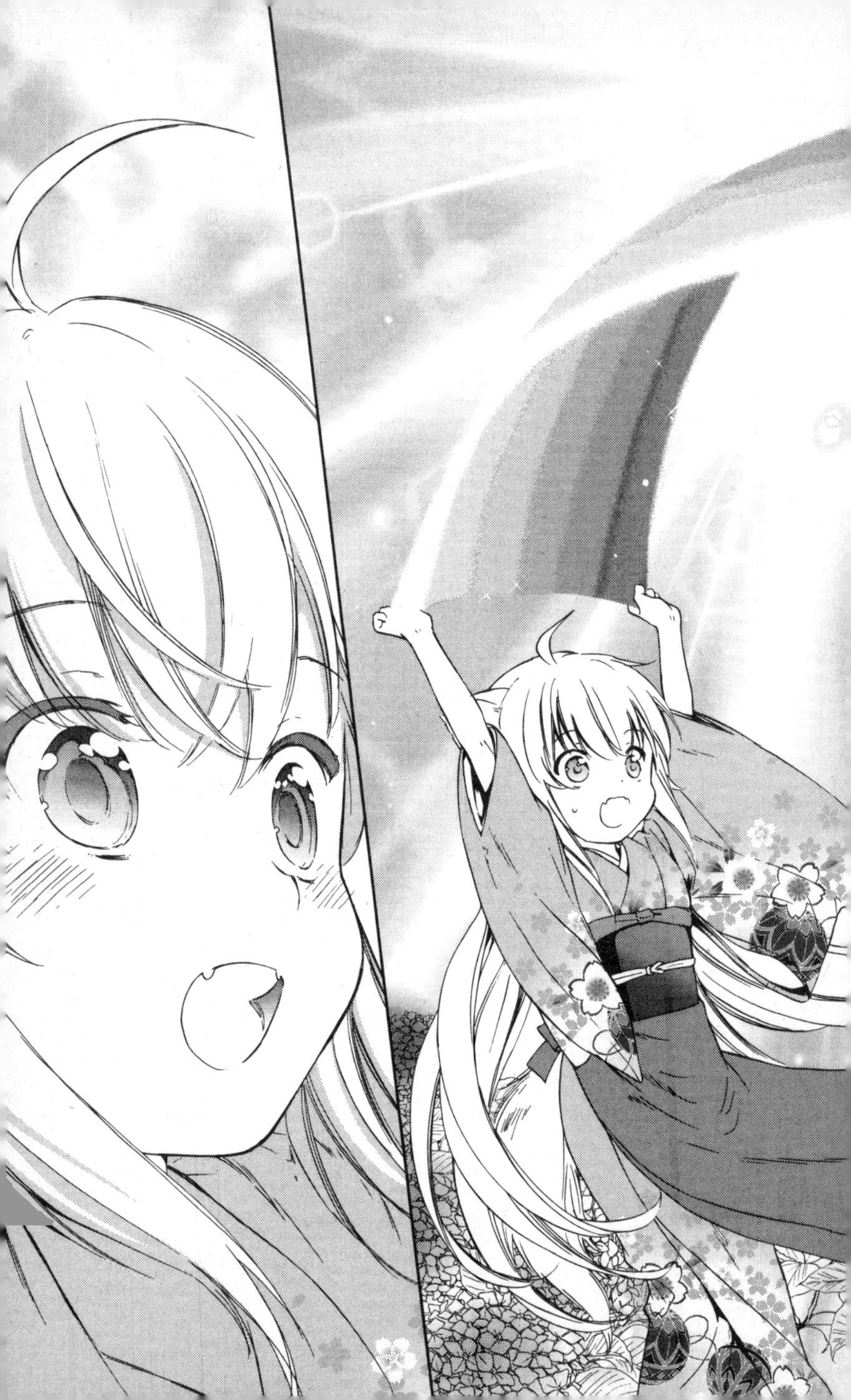

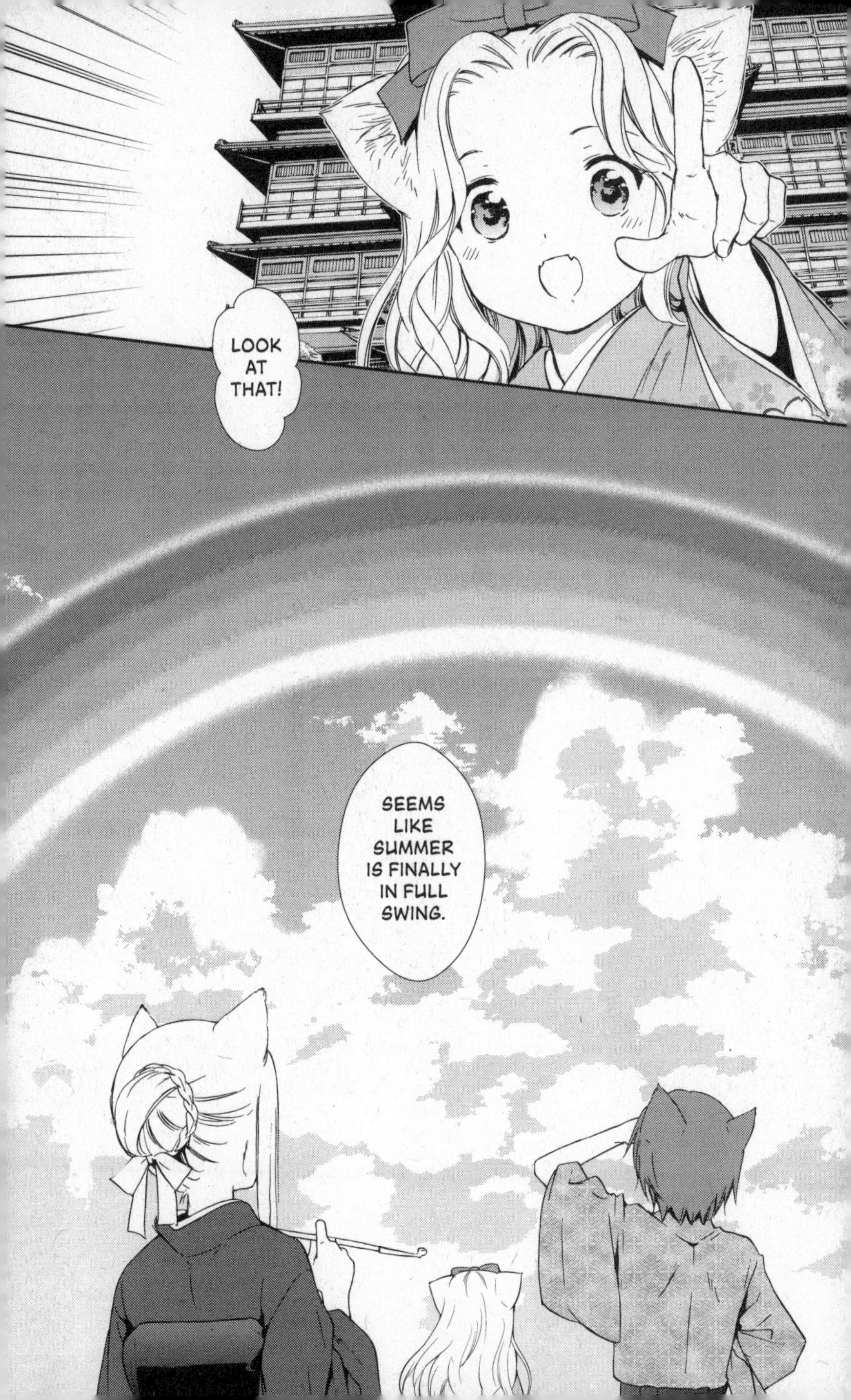
LOOK AT THAT!
SEEMS LIKE SUMMER IS FINALLY IN FULL SWING.

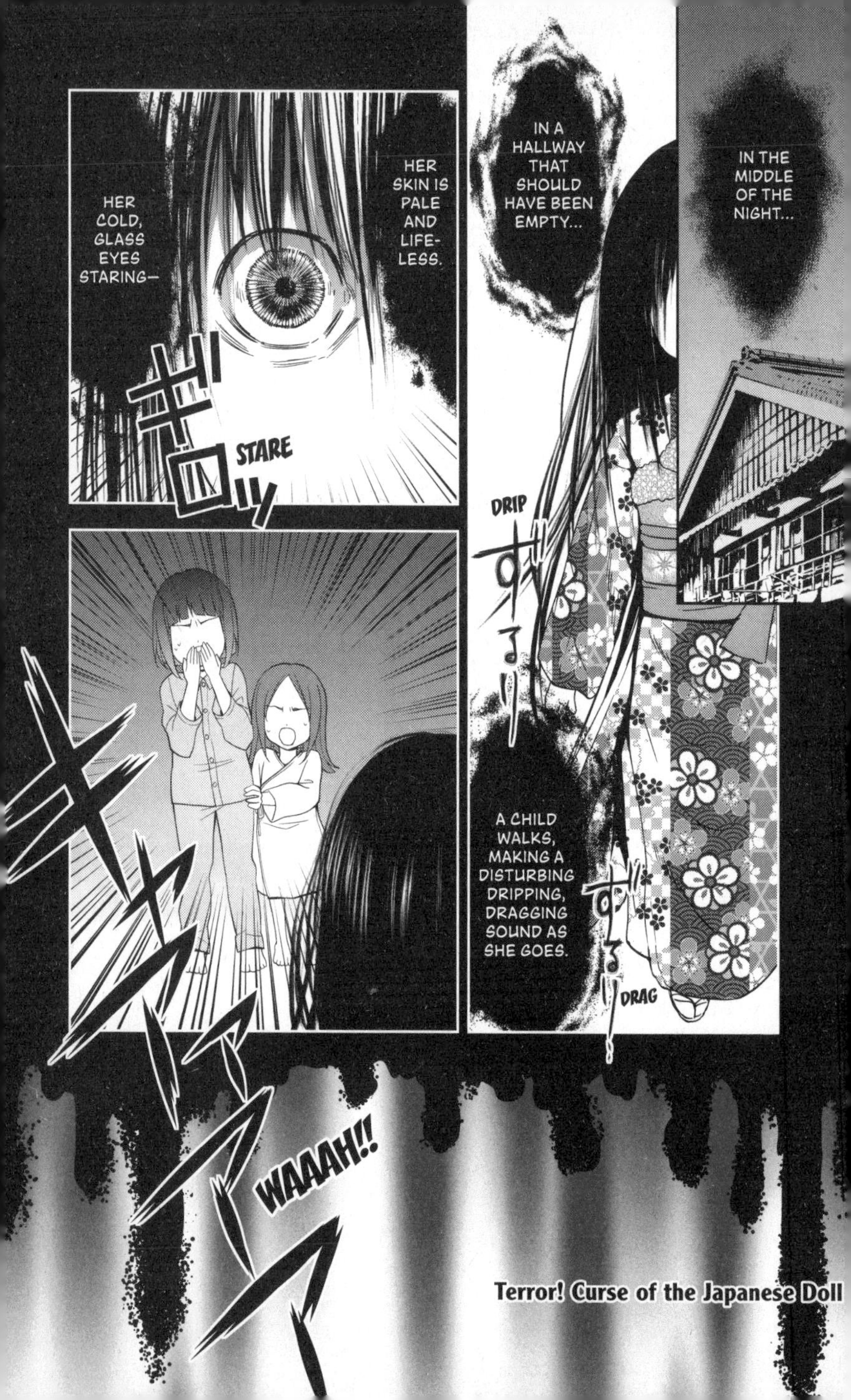
IN THE MIDDLE OF THE NIGHT...
IN A HALLWAY THAT SHOULD HAVE BEEN EMPTY...
DRIP
A CHILD WALKS, MAKING A DISTURBING DRIPPING, DRAGGING SOUND AS SHE GOES.
DRAG
HER SKIN IS PALE AND LIFE-LESS.
HER COLD, GLASS EYES STARING—
STARE
WAAAH!!
Terror! Curse of the Japanese Doll

Terror! Curse of the Japanese Doll

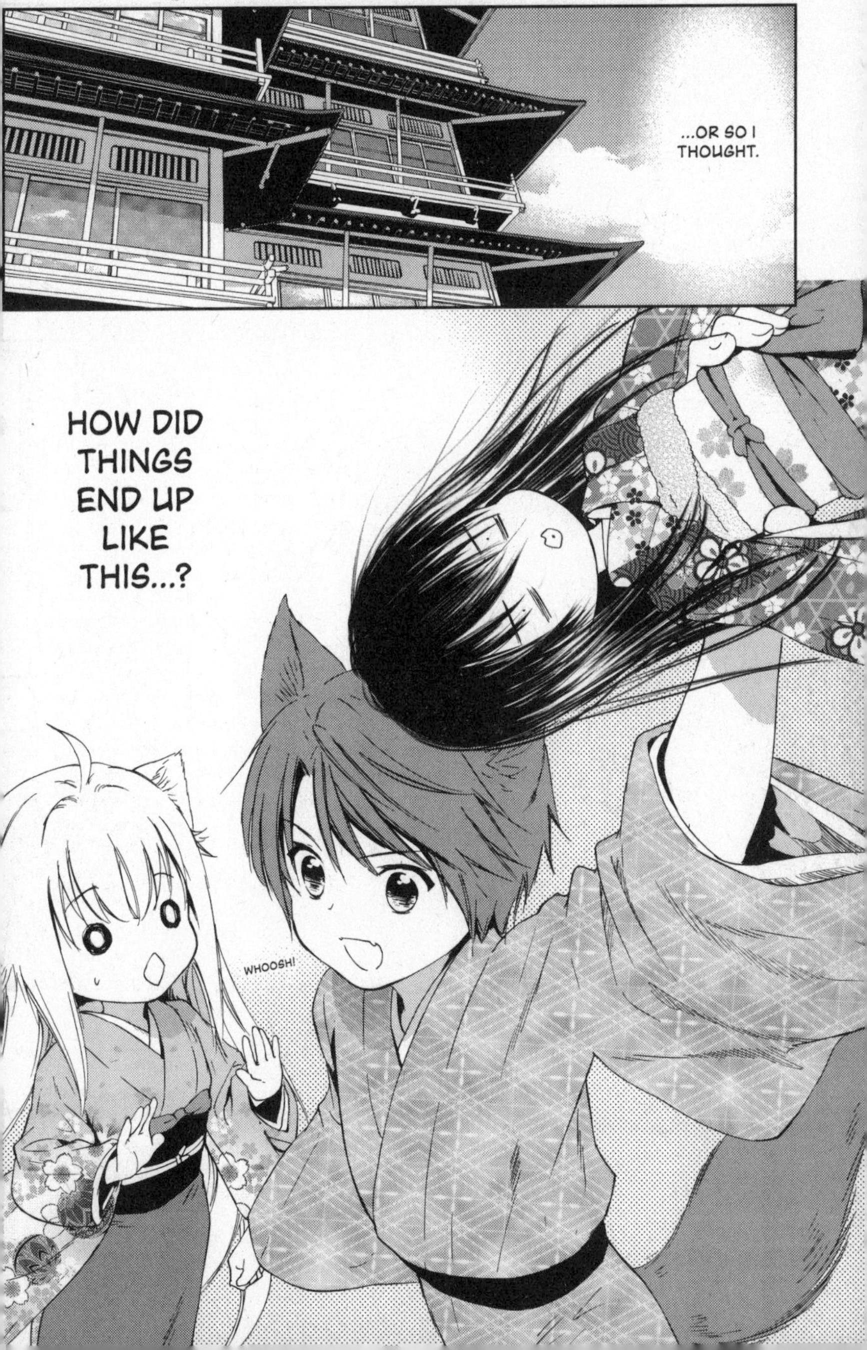

...OR SO I THOUGHT.
HOW DID THINGS END UP LIKE THIS...?
WHOOSH!

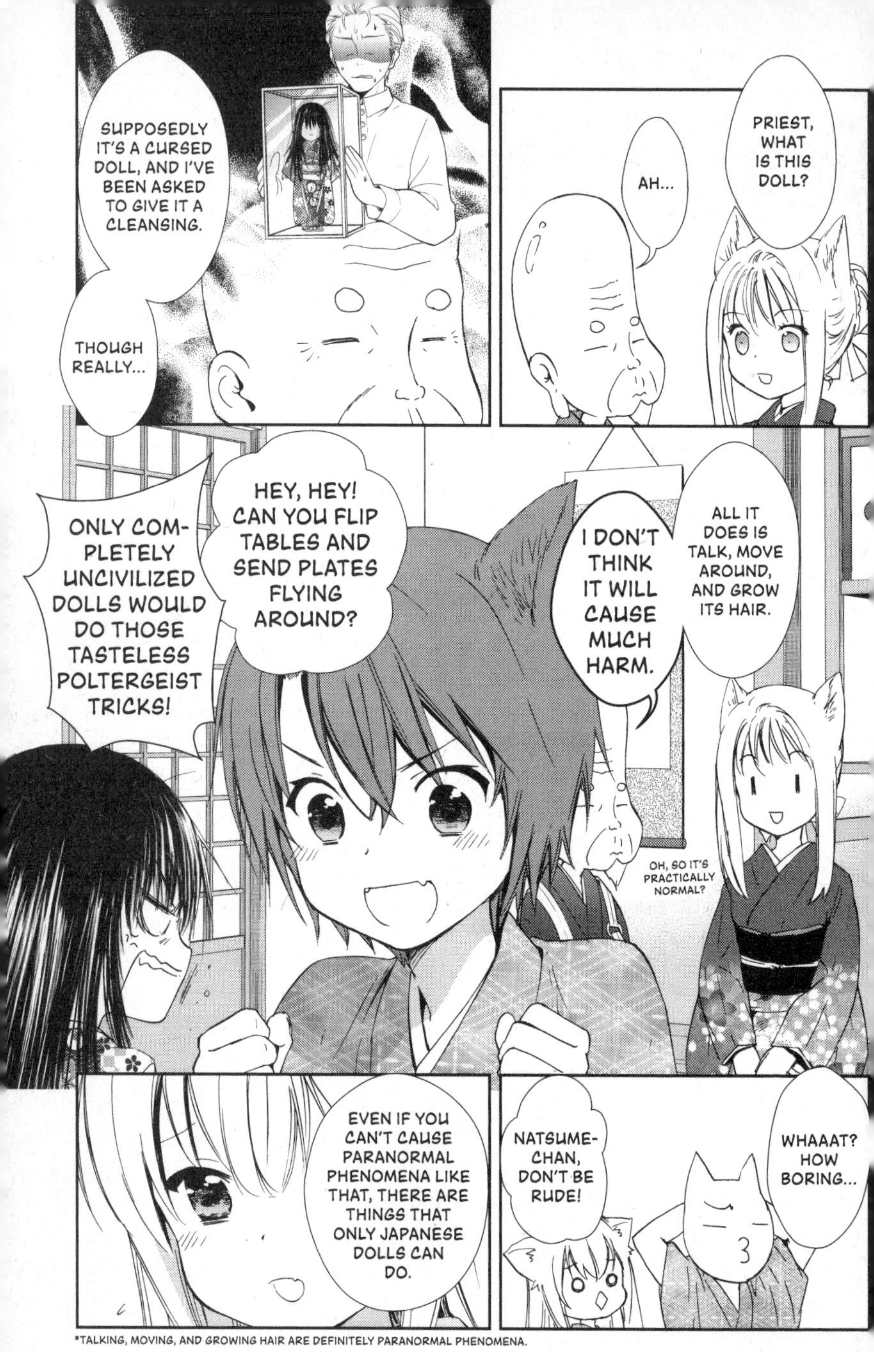
PRIEST, WHAT IS THIS DOLL?
AH...
SUPPOSEDLY IT'S A CURSED DOLL, AND I'VE BEEN ASKED TO GIVE IT A CLEANSING.
THOUGH REALLY...
ALL IT DOES IS TALK, MOVE AROUND, AND GROW ITS HAIR.
I DON'T THINK IT WILL CAUSE MUCH HARM.
OH, SO IT'S PRACTICALLY NORMAL?
HEY, HEY! CAN YOU FLIP TABLES AND SEND PLATES FLYING AROUND?
ONLY COMPLETELY UNCIVILIZED DOLLS WOULD DO THOSE TASTELESS POLTERGEIST TRICKS!
WHAAAT? HOW BORING...
NATSUME-CHAN, DON'T BE RUDE!
EVEN IF YOU CAN'T CAUSE PARANORMAL PHENOMENA LIKE THAT, THERE ARE THINGS THAT ONLY JAPANESE DOLLS CAN DO.

*TALKING, MOVING, AND GROWING HAIR ARE DEFINITELY PARANORMAL PHENOMENA.

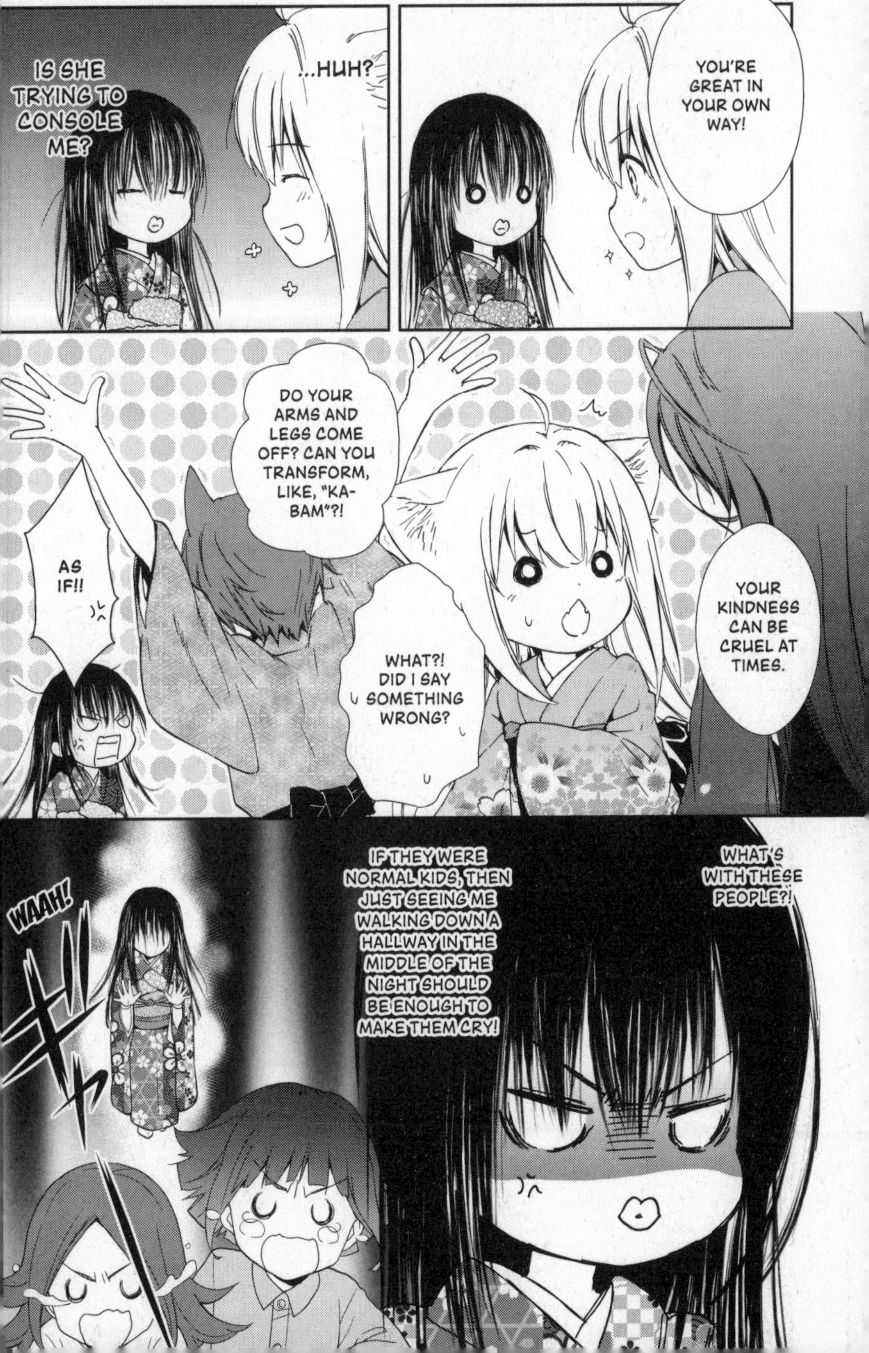
YOU'RE GREAT IN YOUR OWN WAY!
...HUH?
IS SHE TRYING TO CONSOLE ME?
DO YOUR ARMS AND LEGS COME OFF? CAN YOU TRANSFORM, LIKE, "KA-BAM"?!
AS IF!!
WHAT?! DID I SAY SOMETHING WRONG?
YOUR KINDNESS CAN BE CRUEL AT TIMES.
WHAT'S WITH THESE PEOPLE?!
IF THEY WERE NORMAL KIDS, THEN JUST SEEING ME WALKING DOWN A HALLWAY IN THE MIDDLE OF THE NIGHT SHOULD BE ENOUGH TO MAKE THEM CRY!
WAAH!

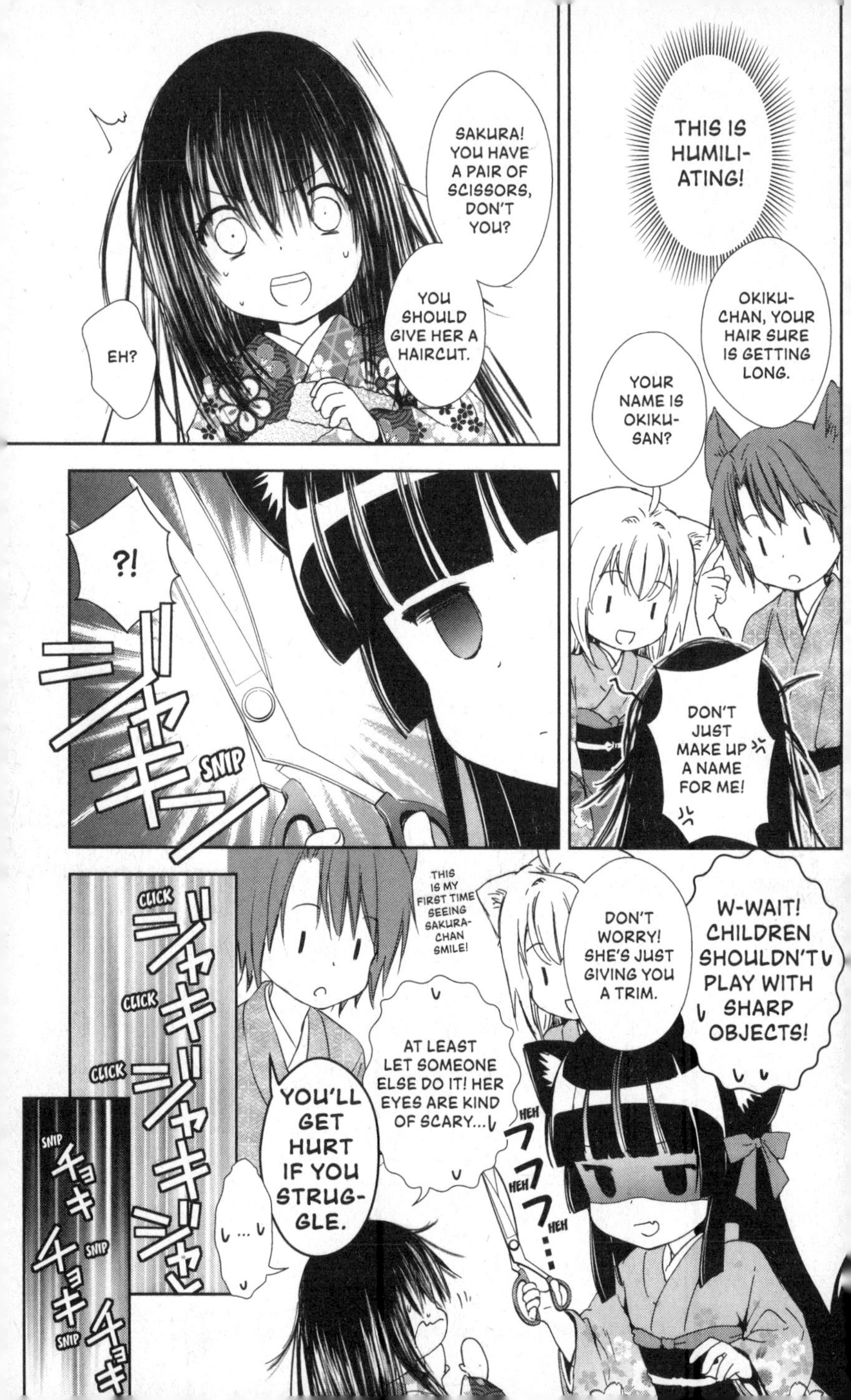
THIS IS HUMILIATING!
OKIKU-CHAN, YOUR HAIR SURE IS GETTING LONG.
YOUR NAME IS OKIKU-SAN?
DON'T JUST MAKE UP A NAME FOR ME!
SAKURA! YOU HAVE A PAIR OF SCISSORS, DON'T YOU?
YOU SHOULD GIVE HER A HAIRCUT.
EH?
?!
ジャキーン
SNIP
W-WAIT! CHILDREN SHOULDN'T PLAY WITH SHARP OBJECTS!
DON'T WORRY! SHE'S JUST GIVING YOU A TRIM.
THIS IS MY FIRST TIME SEEING SAKURA-CHAN SMILE!
AT LEAST LET SOMEONE ELSE DO IT! HER EYES ARE KIND OF SCARY...
フフフ...
HEH HEH HEH
YOU'LL GET HURT IF YOU STRUGGLE.
...
ジャキジャキジャキ
CLICK CLICK CLICK
チョキチョキチョキ
SNIP SNIP SNIP

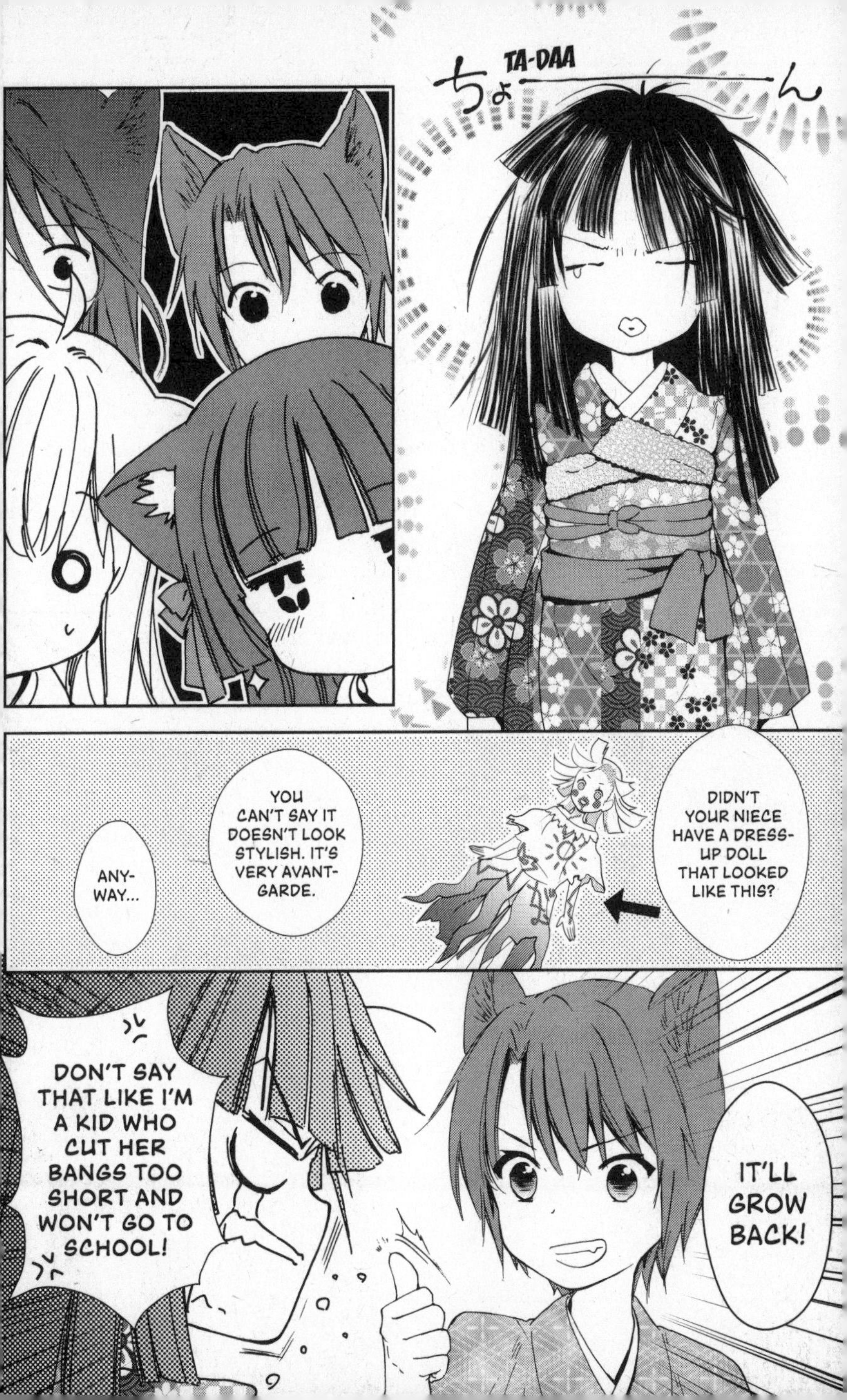
TA-DAA
ちょーん
DIDN'T YOUR NIECE HAVE A DRESS-UP DOLL THAT LOOKED LIKE THIS?
YOU CAN'T SAY IT DOESN'T LOOK STYLISH. IT'S VERY AVANT-GARDE.
ANY-WAY...
IT'LL GROW BACK!
DON'T SAY THAT LIKE I'M A KID WHO CUT HER BANGS TOO SHORT AND WON'T GO TO SCHOOL!

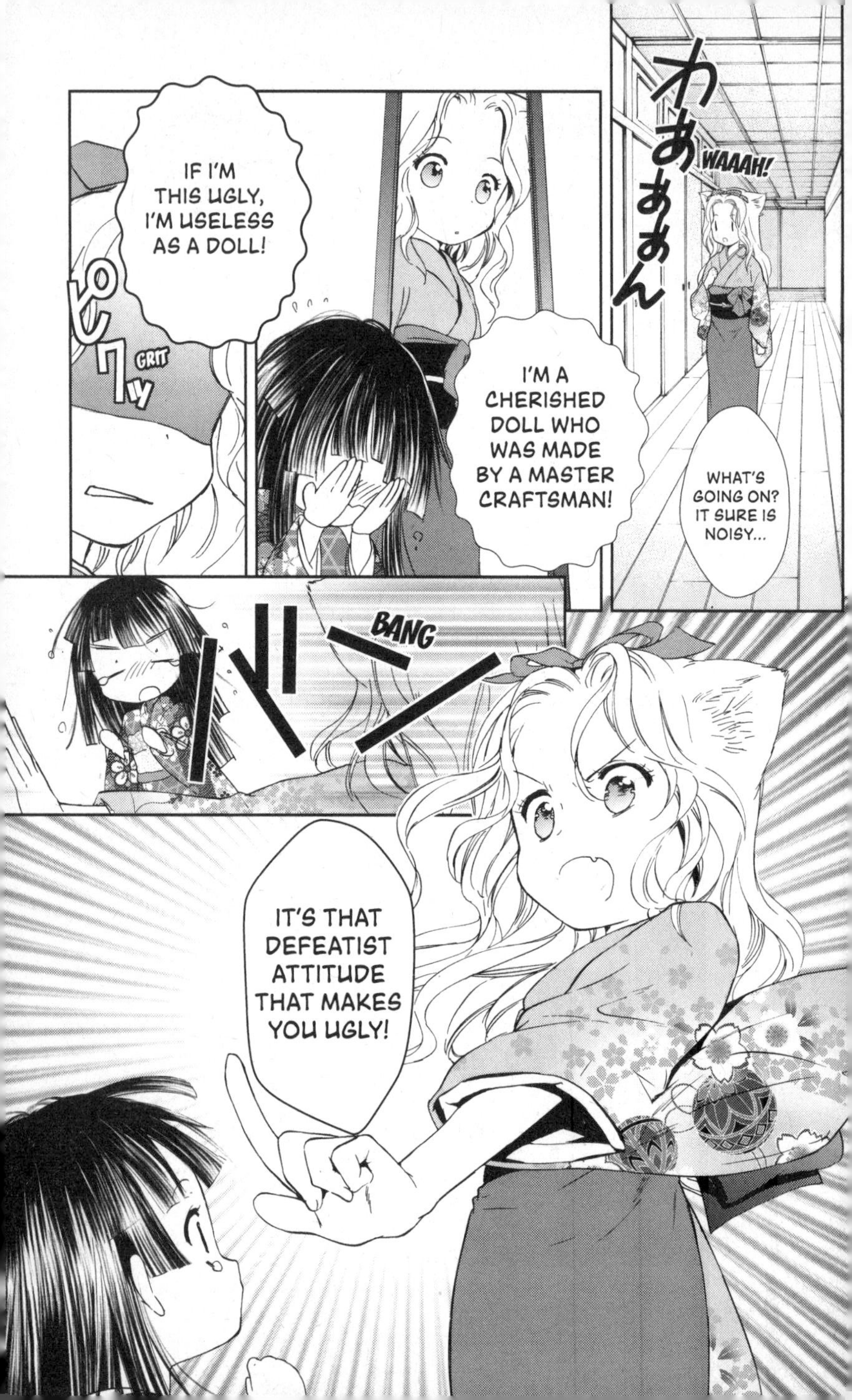
わあああん
WAAAH!
WHAT'S GOING ON? IT SURE IS NOISY...
I'M A CHERISHED DOLL WHO WAS MADE BY A MASTER CRAFTSMAN!
IF I'M THIS UGLY, I'M USELESS AS A DOLL!
ぴクッ
GRIT
バン
BANG
IT'S THAT DEFEATIST ATTITUDE THAT MAKES YOU UGLY!

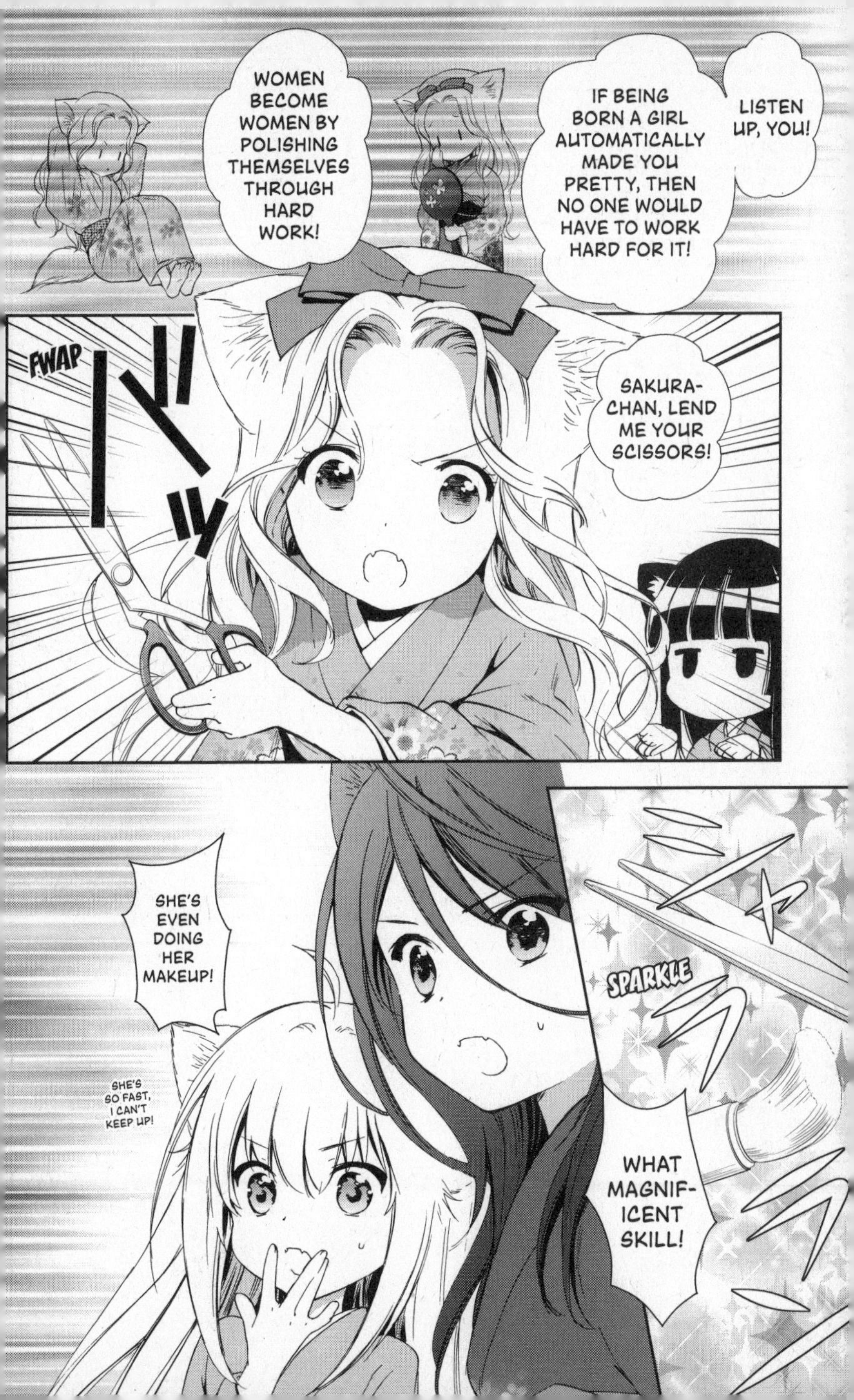
LISTEN UP, YOU!
IF BEING BORN A GIRL AUTOMATICALLY MADE YOU PRETTY, THEN NO ONE WOULD HAVE TO WORK HARD FOR IT!
WOMEN BECOME WOMEN BY POLISHING THEMSELVES THROUGH HARD WORK!
SAKURA-CHAN, LEND ME YOUR SCISSORS!
FWAP
SPARKLE
WHAT MAGNIFICENT SKILL!
SHE'S EVEN DOING HER MAKEUP!
SHE'S SO FAST, I CAN'T KEEP UP!

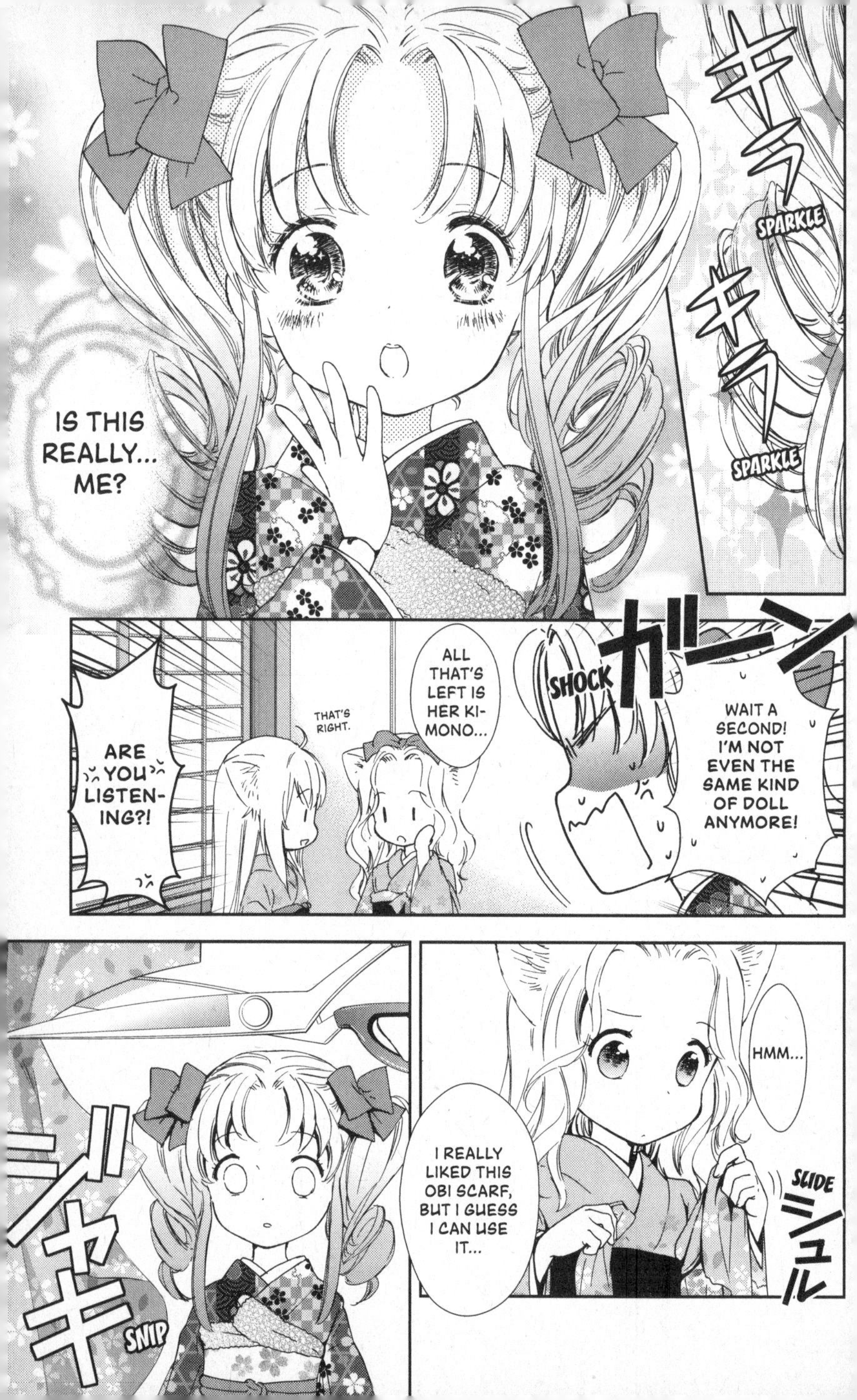

キラ
SPARKLE
キラ
SPARKLE
IS THIS REALLY... ME?
ガーン
SHOCK
WAIT A SECOND! I'M NOT EVEN THE SAME KIND OF DOLL ANYMORE!
ALL THAT'S LEFT IS HER KI-MONO...
THAT'S RIGHT.
ARE YOU LISTEN-ING?!
HMM...
I REALLY LIKED THIS OBI SCARF, BUT I GUESS I CAN USE IT...
シュル
SLIDE
ジャキ
SNIP

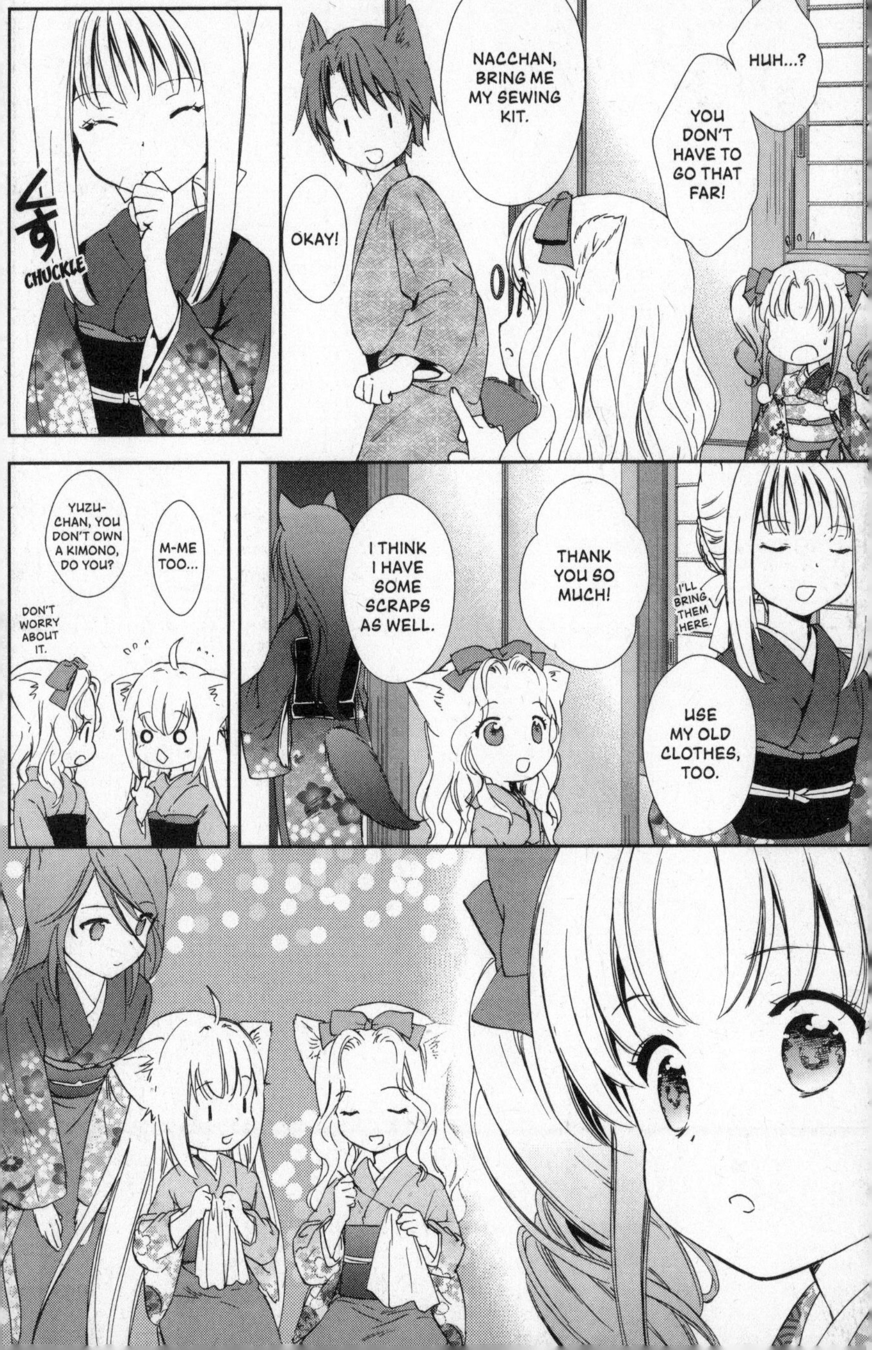
HUH...?
YOU DON'T HAVE TO GO THAT FAR!
NACCHAN, BRING ME MY SEWING KIT.
OKAY!
くす
CHUCKLE
USE MY OLD CLOTHES, TOO.
I'LL BRING THEM HERE.
I THINK I HAVE SOME SCRAPS AS WELL.
THANK YOU SO MUCH!
YUZU-CHAN, YOU DON'T OWN A KIMONO, DO YOU?
M-ME TOO...
DON'T WORRY ABOUT IT.

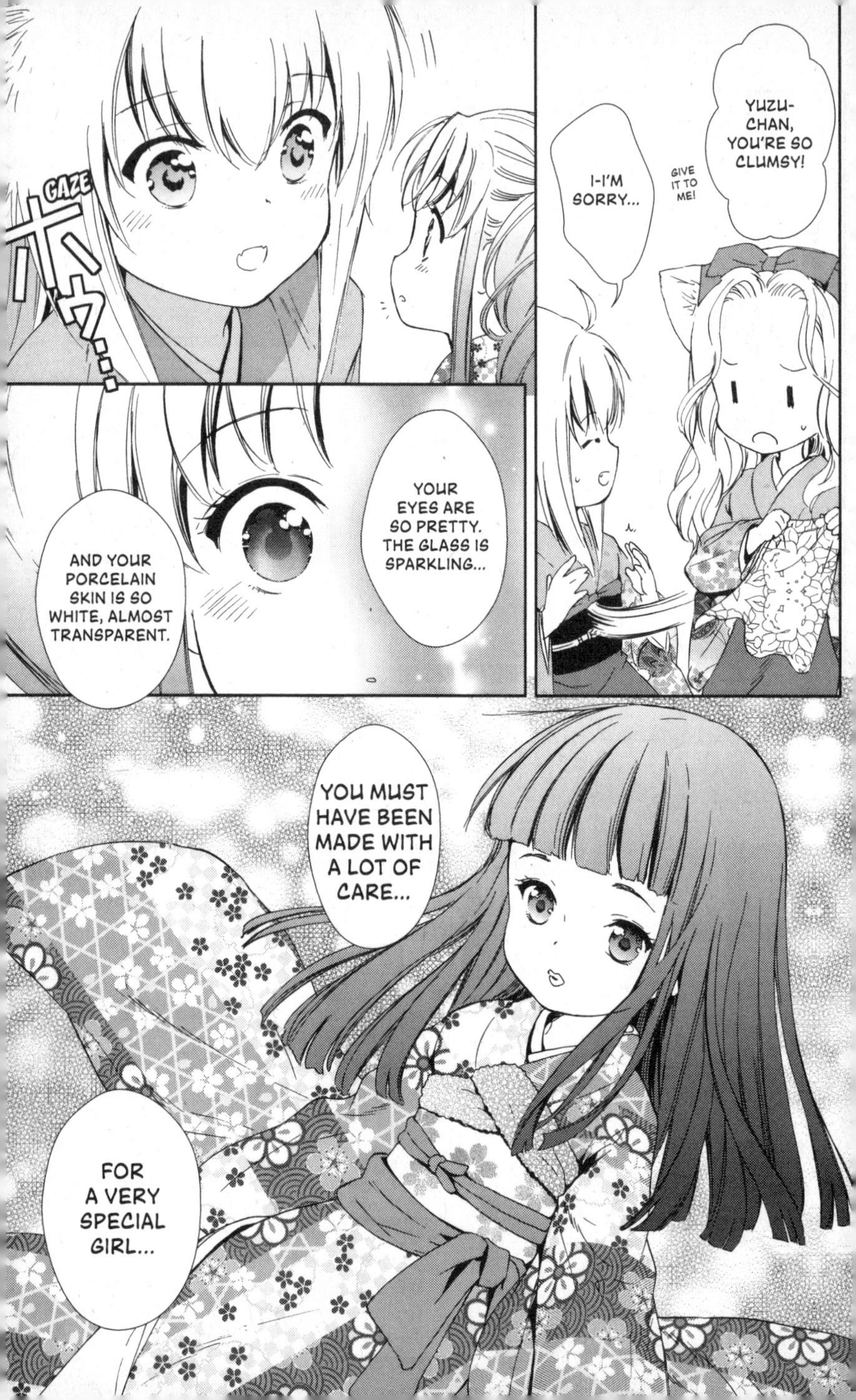
YUZU-CHAN, YOU'RE SO CLUMSY!
GIVE IT TO ME!
I-I'M SORRY...
GAZE
YOUR EYES ARE SO PRETTY. THE GLASS IS SPARKLING...
AND YOUR PORCELAIN SKIN IS SO WHITE, ALMOST TRANSPARENT.
YOU MUST HAVE BEEN MADE WITH A LOT OF CARE...
FOR A VERY SPECIAL GIRL...

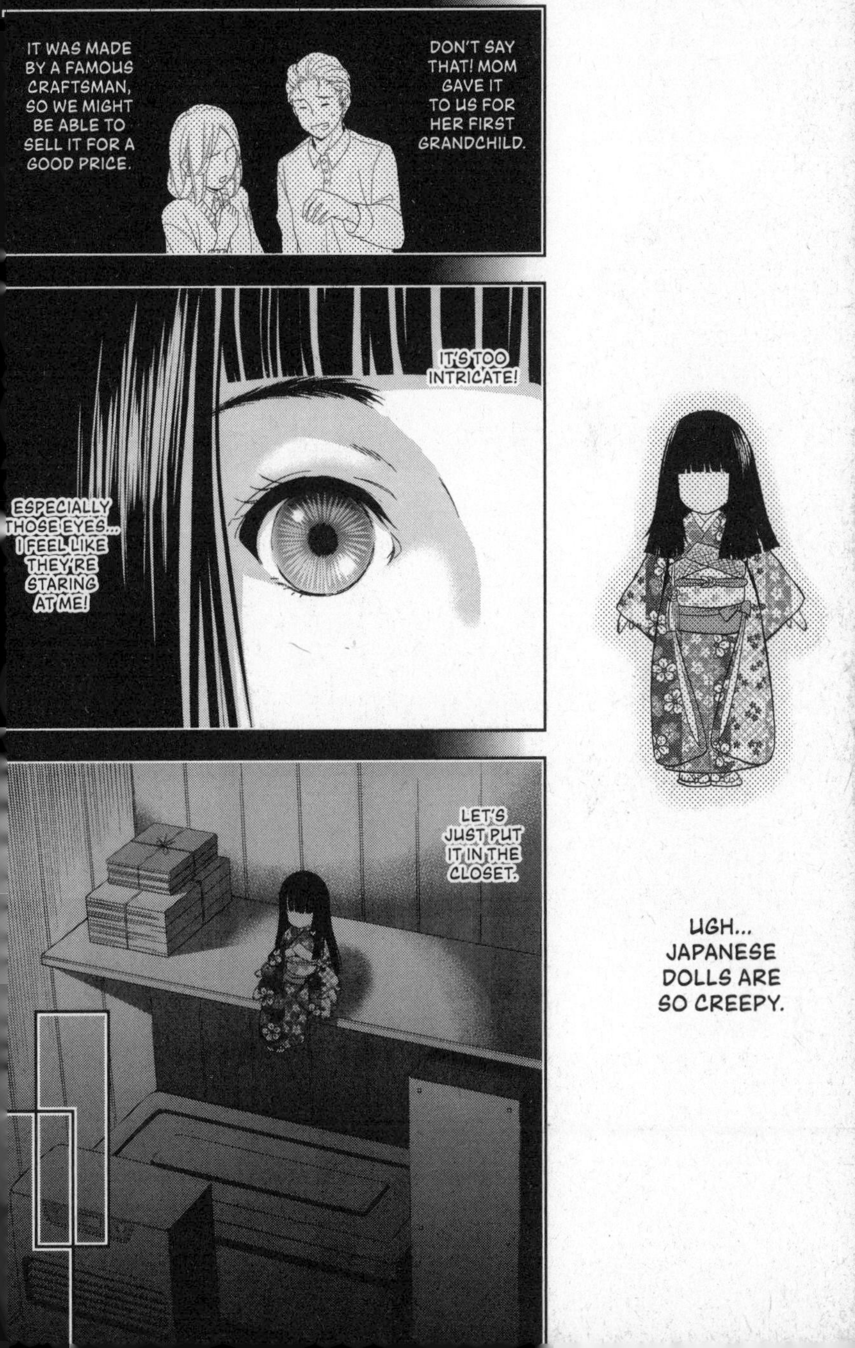
UGH... JAPANESE DOLLS ARE SO CREEPY.
DON'T SAY THAT! MOM GAVE IT TO US FOR HER FIRST GRANDCHILD.
IT WAS MADE BY A FAMOUS CRAFTSMAN, SO WE MIGHT BE ABLE TO SELL IT FOR A GOOD PRICE.
IT'S TOO INTRICATE!
ESPECIALLY THOSE EYES... I FEEL LIKE THEY'RE STARING AT ME!
LET'S JUST PUT IT IN THE CLOSET.

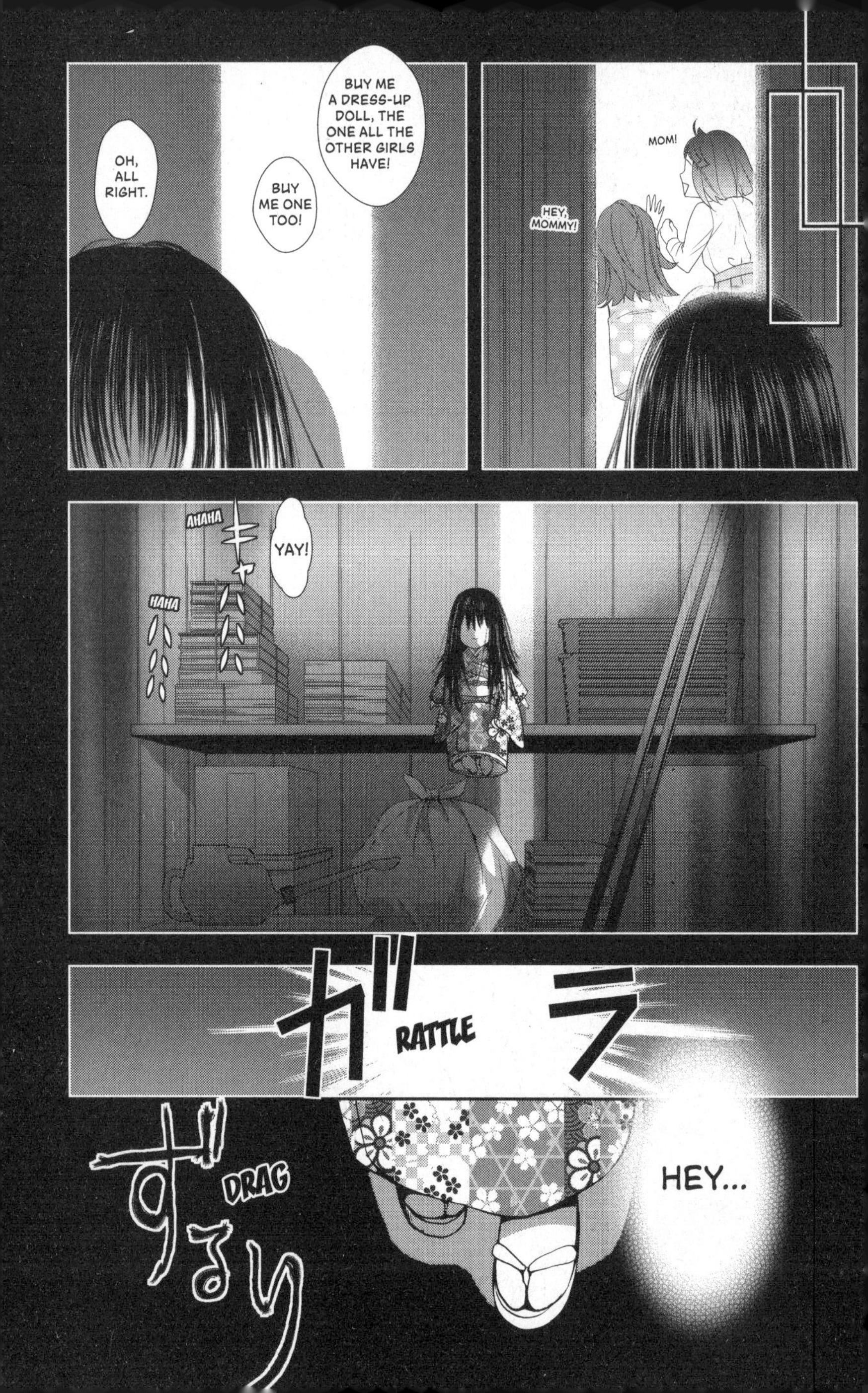
MOM!
HEY, MOMMY!
BUY ME A DRESS-UP DOLL, THE ONE ALL THE OTHER GIRLS HAVE!
BUY ME ONE TOO!
OH, ALL RIGHT.
YAY!
AHAHA
HAHA
ガラ
RATTLE
HEY...
ずるり
DRAG

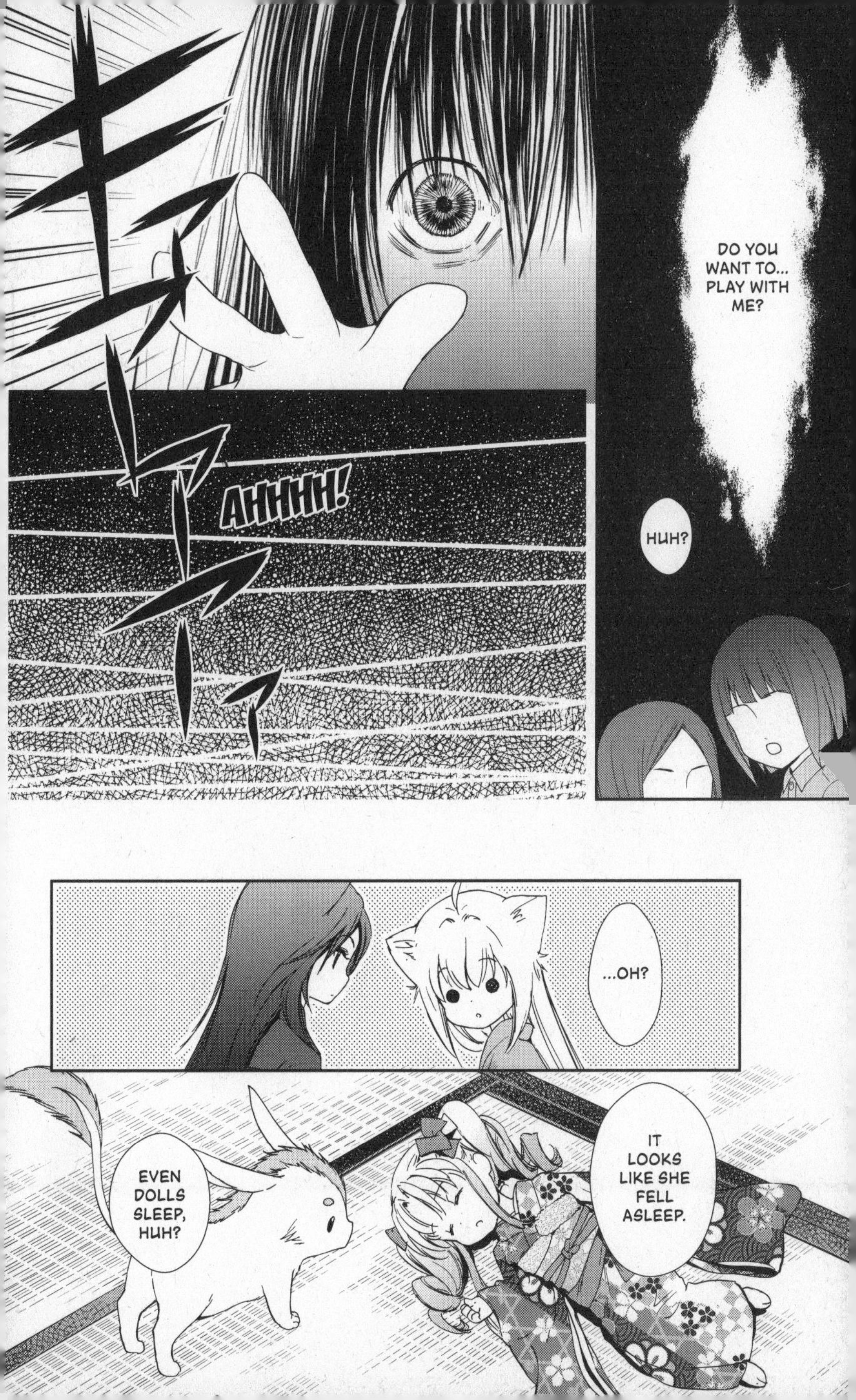
DO YOU WANT TO... PLAY WITH ME?
HUH?
AHHHH!
...OH?
IT LOOKS LIKE SHE FELL ASLEEP.
EVEN DOLLS SLEEP, HUH?

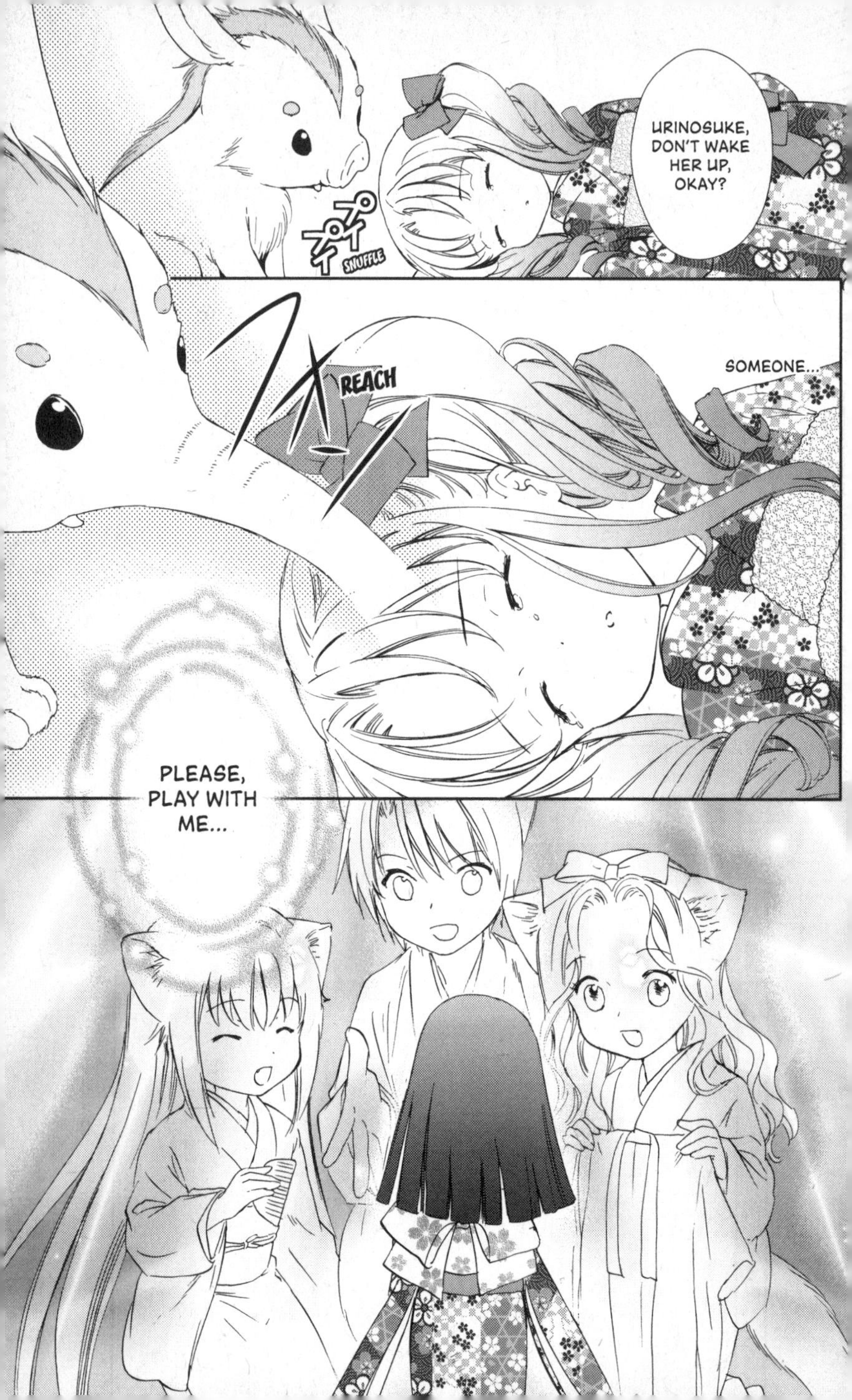
URINOSUKE, DON'T WAKE HER UP, OKAY?
プイ プイ
SNUFFLE
SOMEONE...
REACH
PLEASE, PLAY WITH ME...

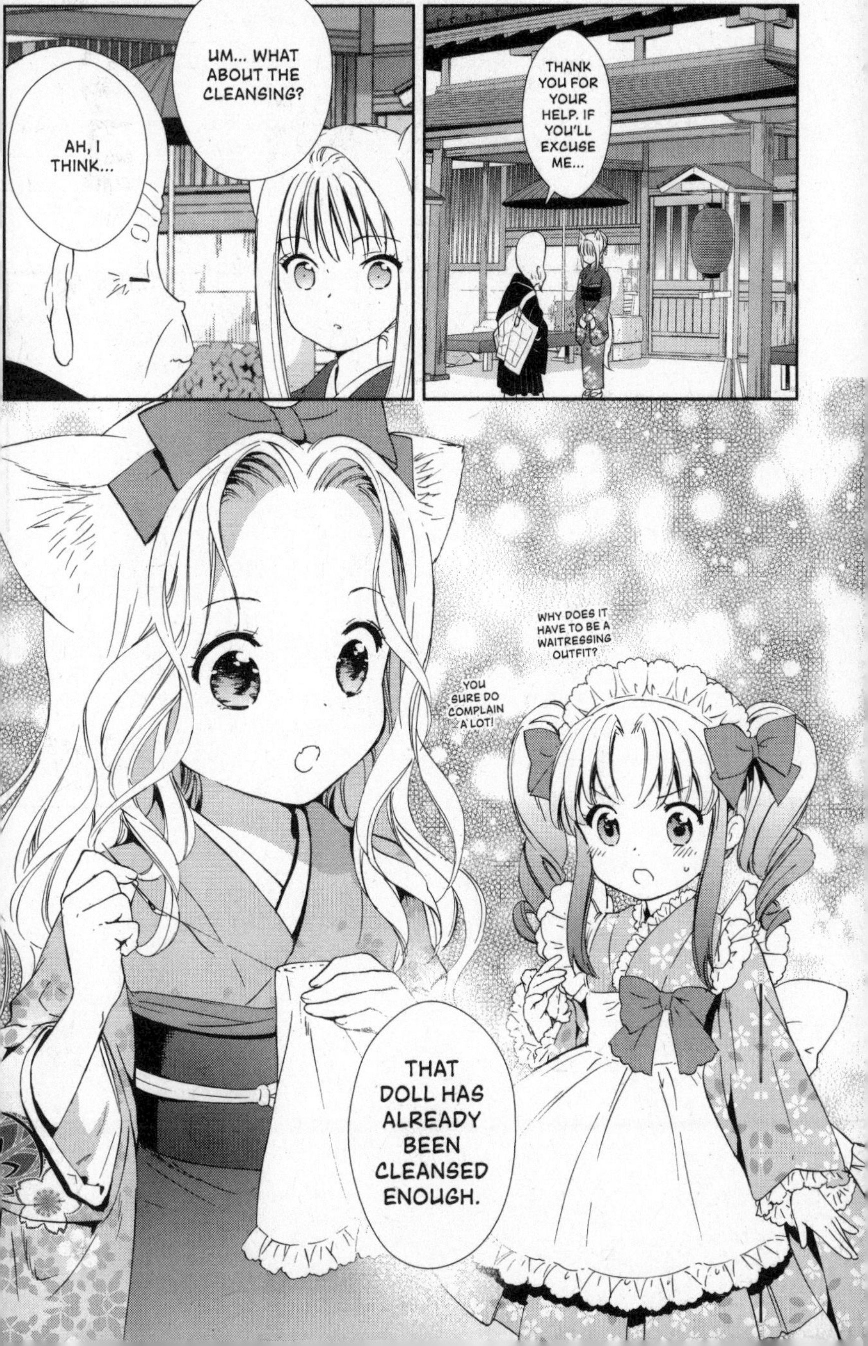
THANK YOU FOR YOUR HELP. IF YOU'LL EXCUSE ME...
UM... WHAT ABOUT THE CLEANSING?
AH, I THINK...
WHY DOES IT HAVE TO BE A WAITRESSING OUTFIT?
YOU SURE DO COMPLAIN A LOT!
THAT DOLL HAS ALREADY BEEN CLEANSED ENOUGH.

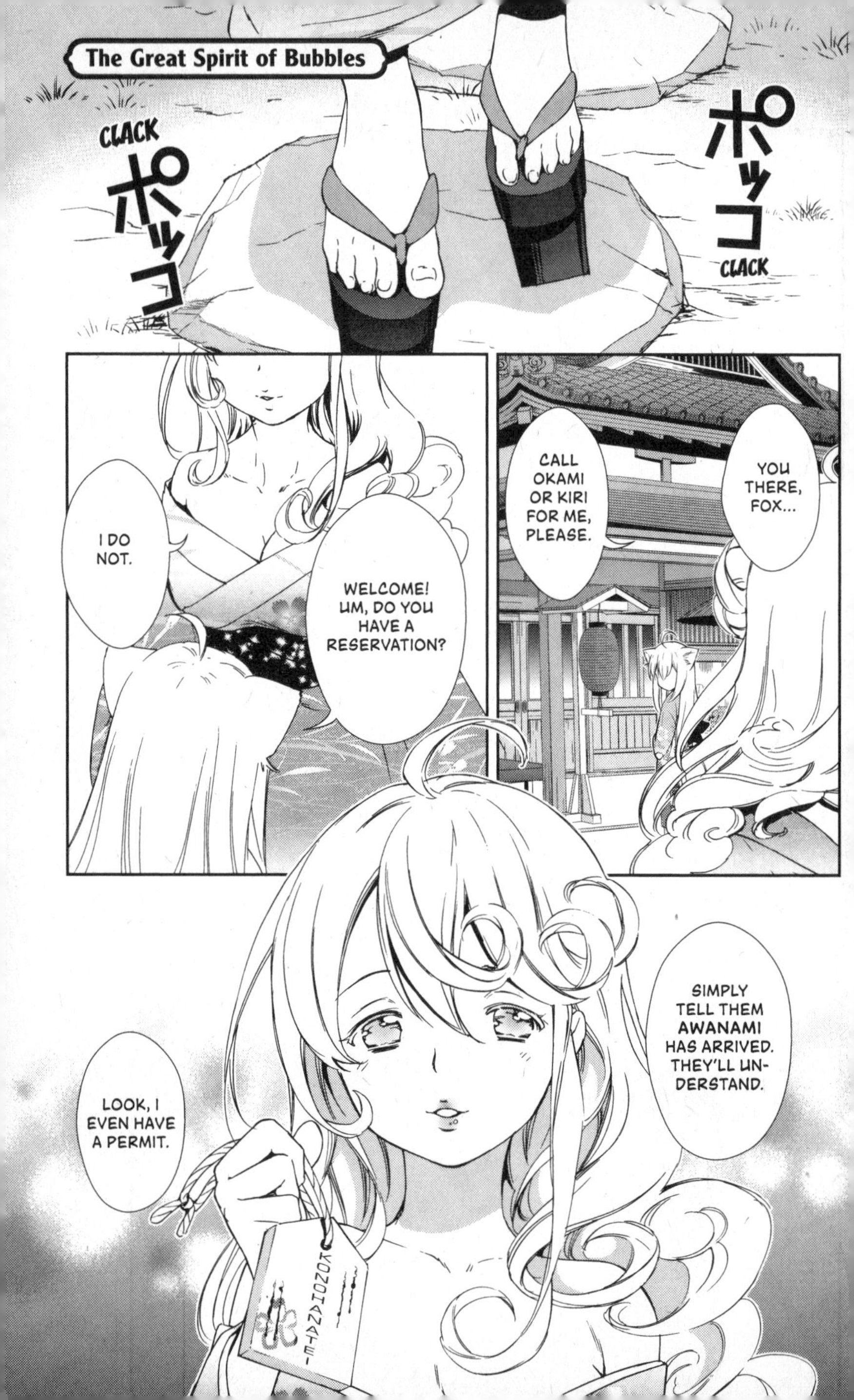
The Great Spirit of Bubbles
ポッコ
CLACK
CLACK
ポッコ
YOU THERE, FOX...
CALL OKAMI OR KIRI FOR ME, PLEASE.
WELCOME! UM, DO YOU HAVE A RESERVATION?
I DO NOT.
SIMPLY TELL THEM AWANAMI HAS ARRIVED. THEY'LL UN-DERSTAND.
LOOK, I EVEN HAVE A PERMIT.
KONOHANATEI

The Great Spirit of Bubbles

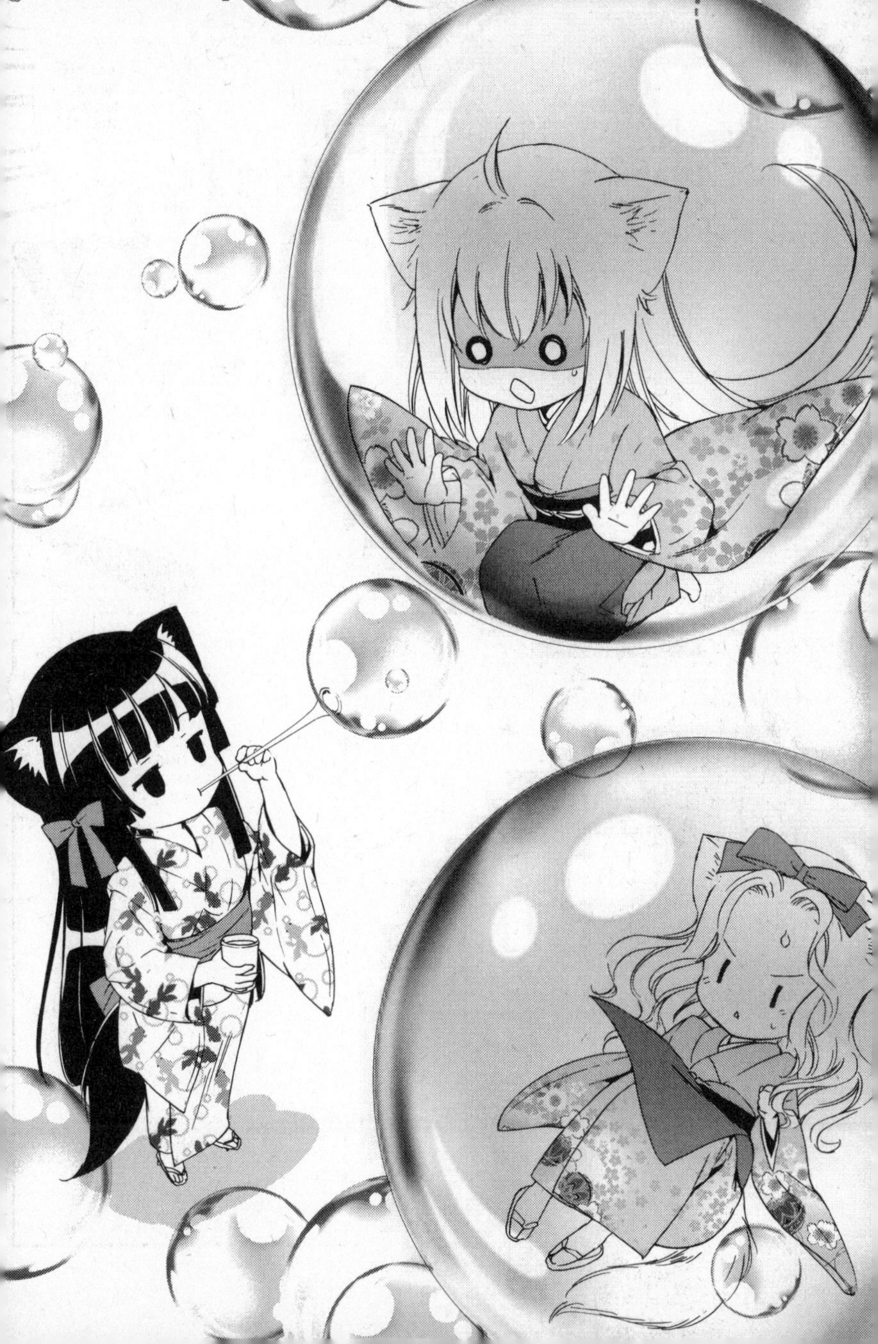

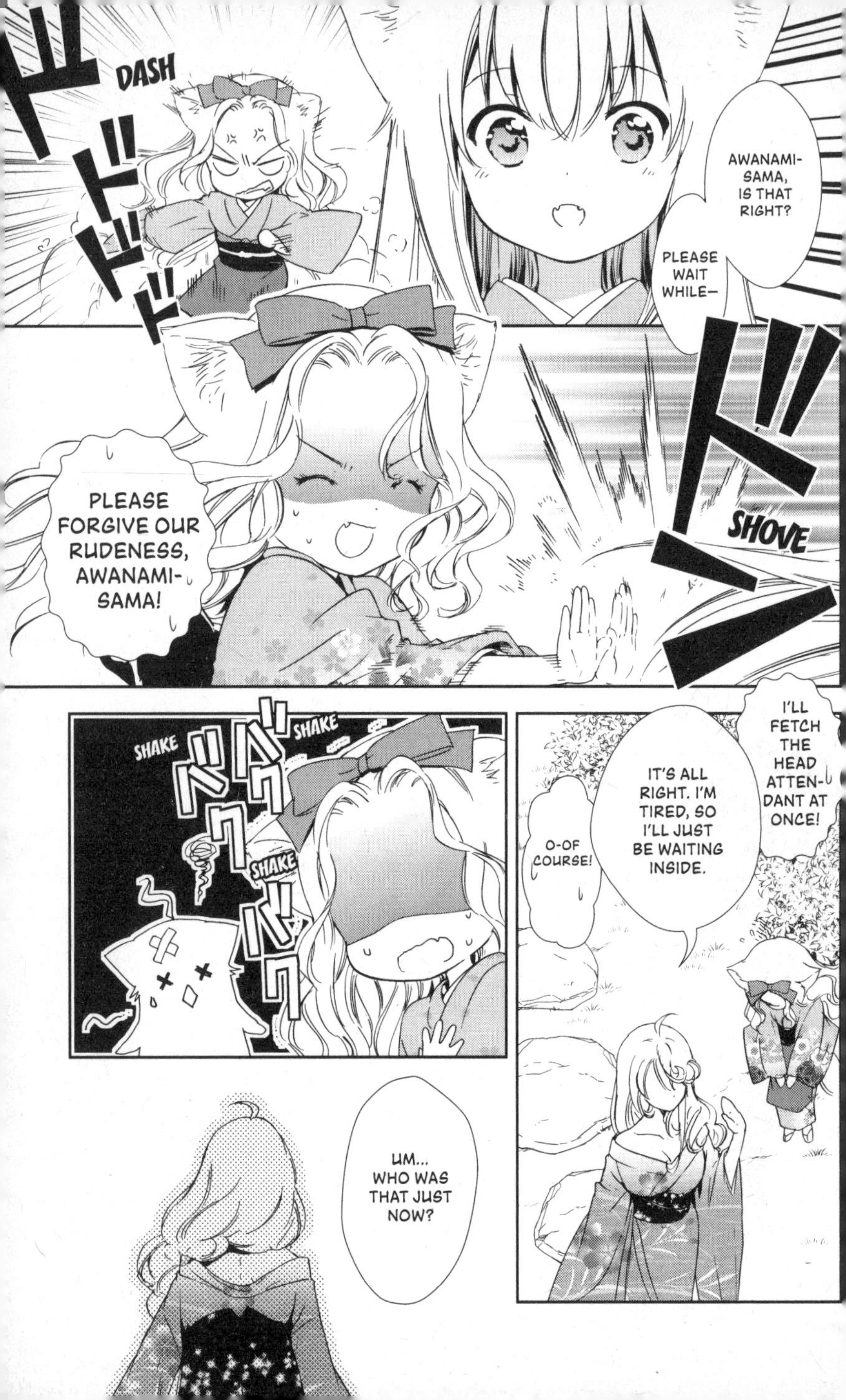
AWANAMI-SAMA, IS THAT RIGHT?
PLEASE WAIT WHILE—
DASH
SHOVE
PLEASE FORGIVE OUR RUDENESS, AWANAMI-SAMA!
I'LL FETCH THE HEAD ATTENDANT AT ONCE!
IT'S ALL RIGHT. I'M TIRED, SO I'LL JUST BE WAITING INSIDE.
O-OF COURSE!
SHAKE
SHAKE
SHAKE
UM... WHO WAS THAT JUST NOW?

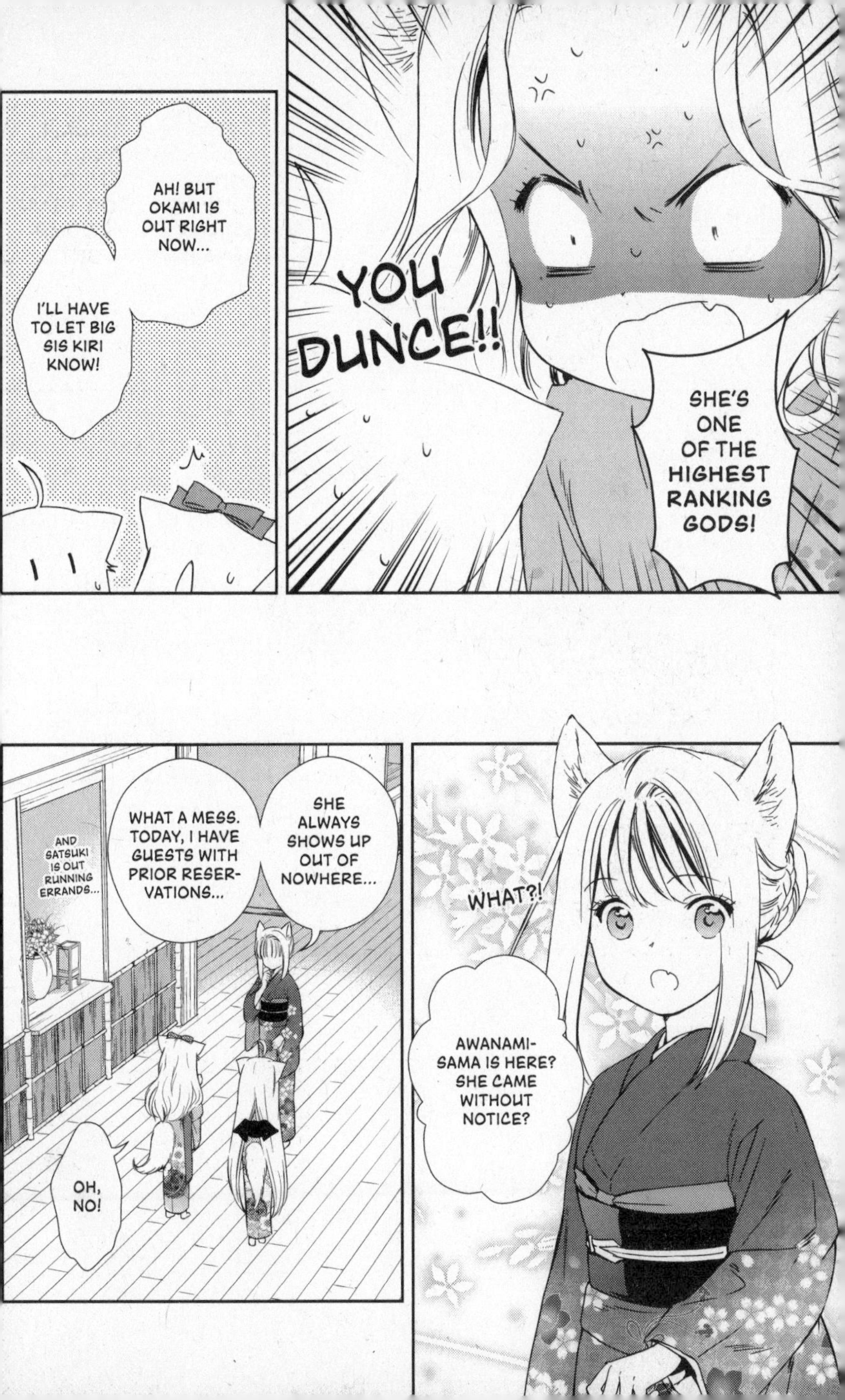
YOU DUNCE!!
SHE'S ONE OF THE HIGHEST RANKING GODS!
AH! BUT OKAMI IS OUT RIGHT NOW...
I'LL HAVE TO LET BIG SIS KIRI KNOW!
WHAT?!
AWANAMI-SAMA IS HERE? SHE CAME WITHOUT NOTICE?
SHE ALWAYS SHOWS UP OUT OF NOWHERE...
WHAT A MESS. TODAY, I HAVE GUESTS WITH PRIOR RESER-VATIONS...
AND SATSUKI IS OUT RUNNING ERRANDS...
OH, NO!

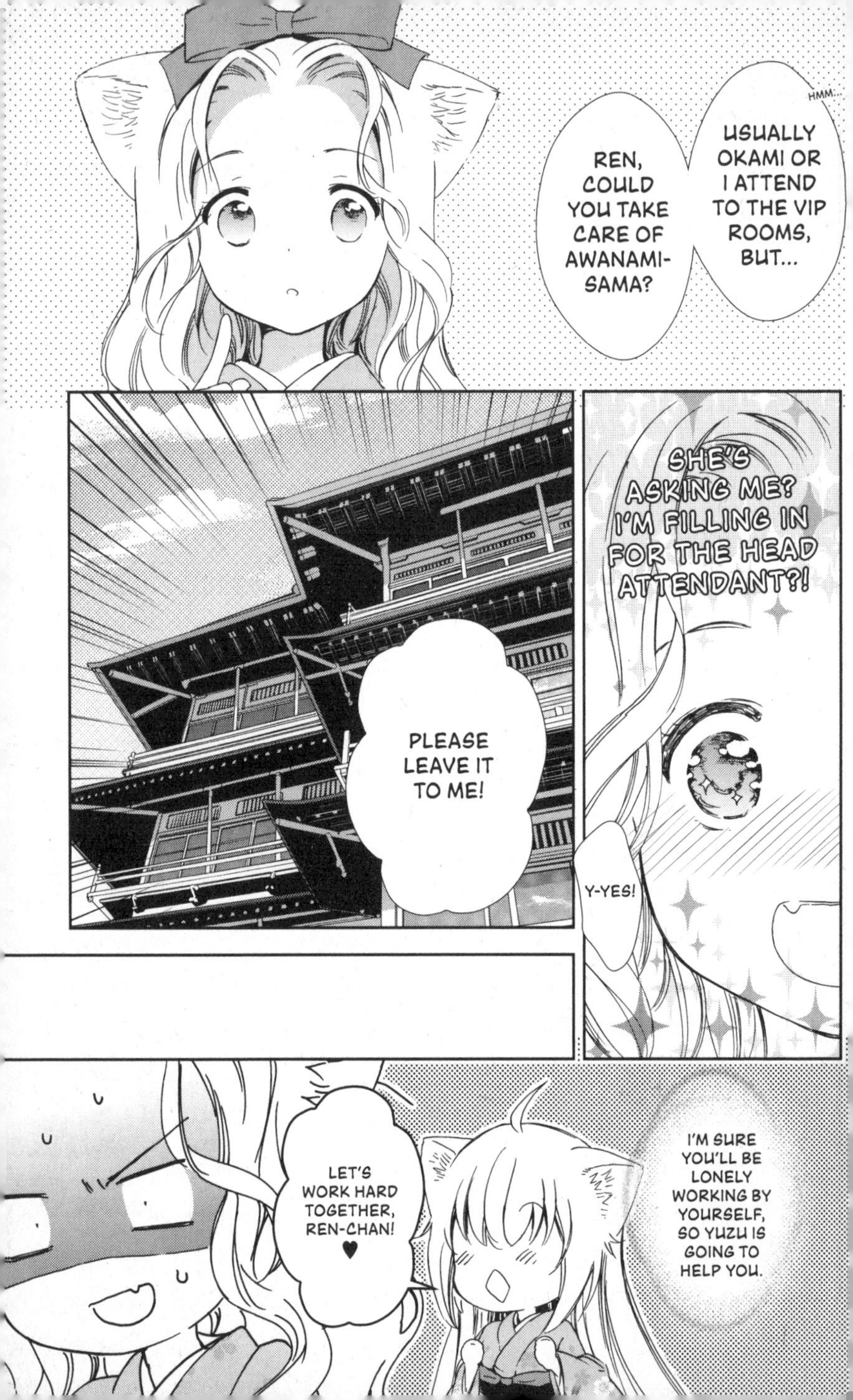
HMM...
USUALLY OKAMI OR I ATTEND TO THE VIP ROOMS, BUT...
REN, COULD YOU TAKE CARE OF AWANAMI-SAMA?
SHE'S ASKING ME? I'M FILLING IN FOR THE HEAD ATTENDANT?!
Y-YES!
PLEASE LEAVE IT TO ME!
I'M SURE YOU'LL BE LONELY WORKING BY YOURSELF, SO YUZU IS GOING TO HELP YOU.
LET'S WORK HARD TOGETHER, REN-CHAN! ♥

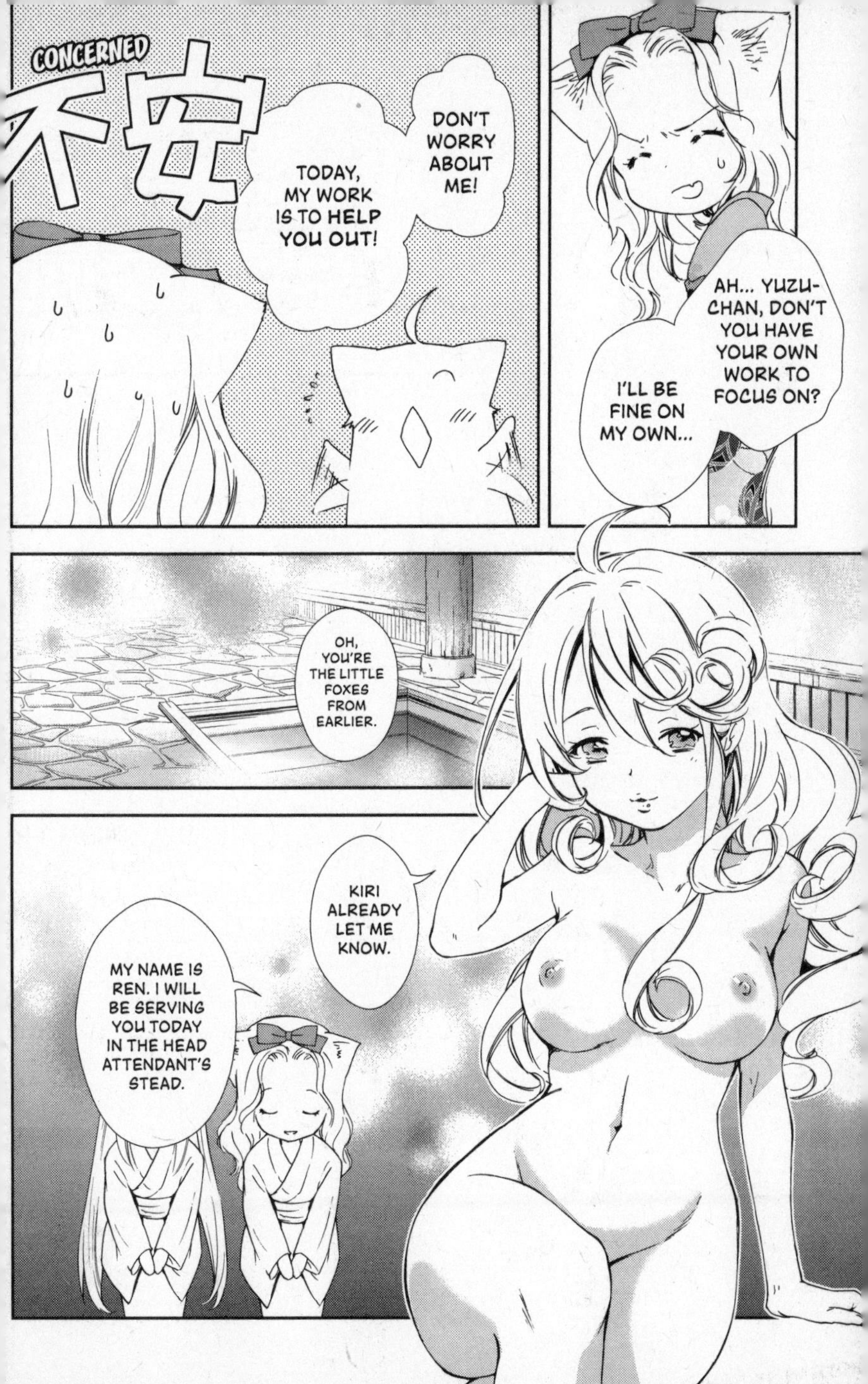
AH... YUZU-CHAN, DON'T YOU HAVE YOUR OWN WORK TO FOCUS ON?
I'LL BE FINE ON MY OWN...
CONCERNED
不安
DON'T WORRY ABOUT ME!
TODAY, MY WORK IS TO HELP YOU OUT!
OH, YOU'RE THE LITTLE FOXES FROM EARLIER.
KIRI ALREADY LET ME KNOW.
MY NAME IS REN. I WILL BE SERVING YOU TODAY IN THE HEAD ATTENDANT'S STEAD.

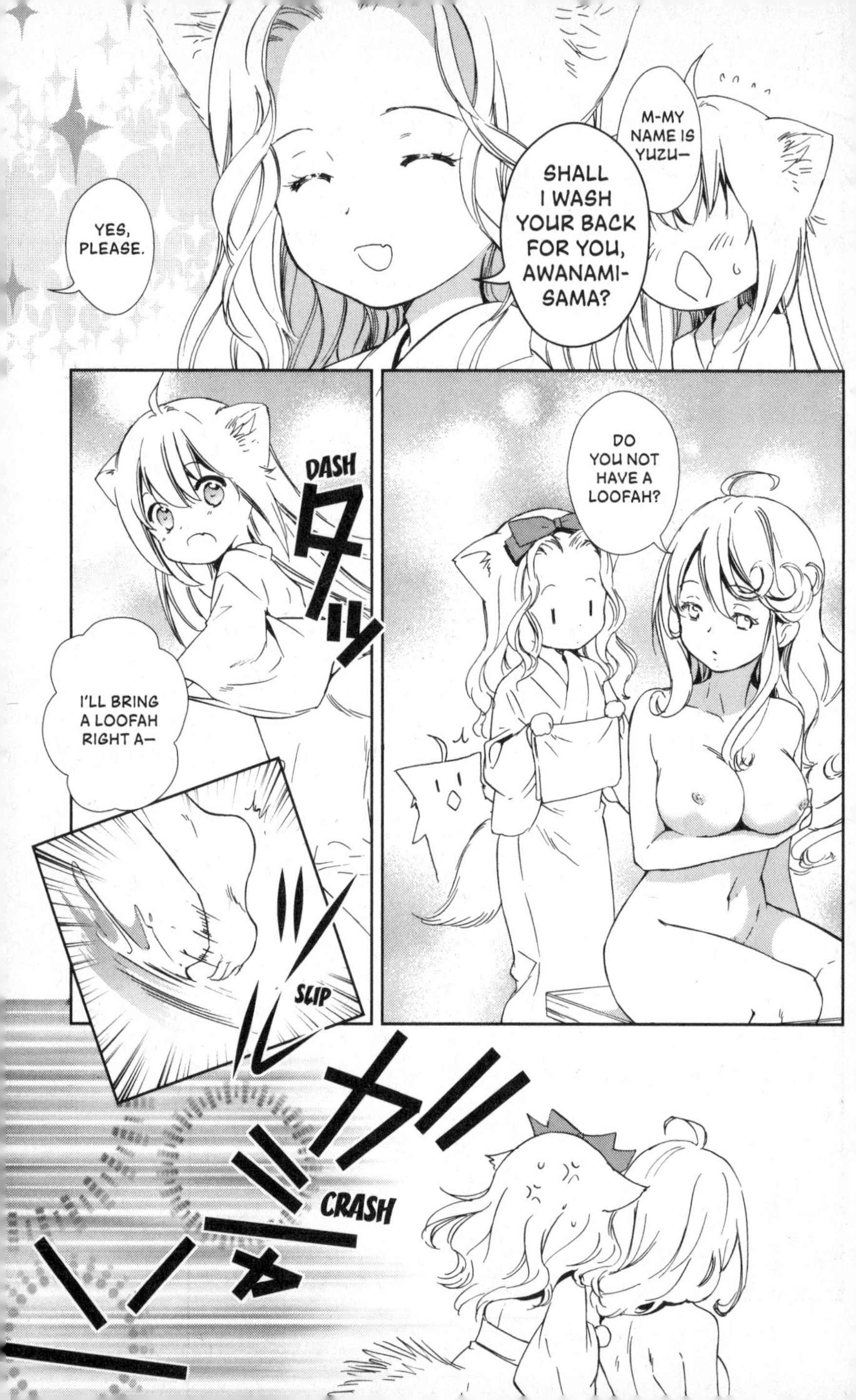
M-MY NAME IS YUZU—
SHALL I WASH YOUR BACK FOR YOU, AWANAMI-SAMA?
YES, PLEASE.
DO YOU NOT HAVE A LOOFAH?
DASH
I'LL BRING A LOOFAH RIGHT A—
SLIP
CRASH

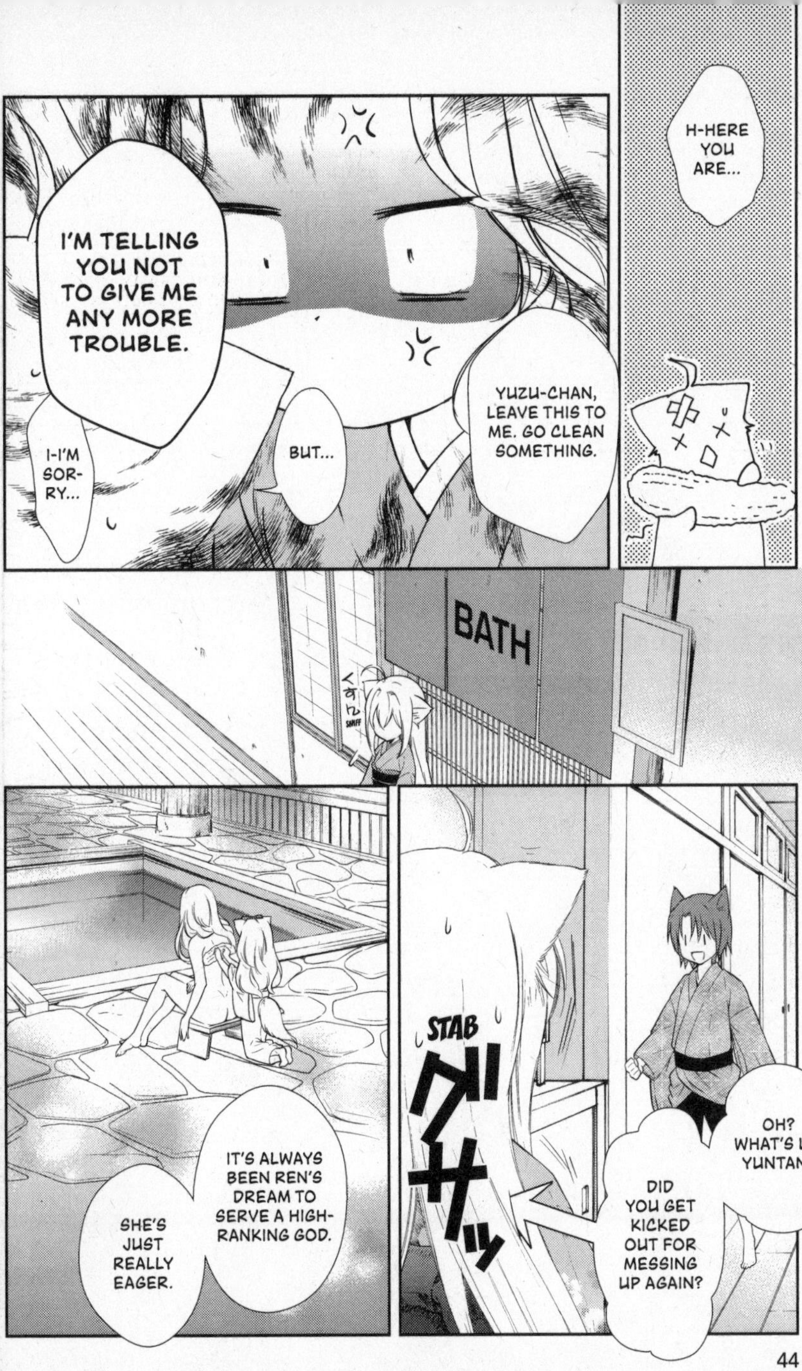
H-HERE YOU ARE...
YUZU-CHAN, LEAVE THIS TO ME. GO CLEAN SOMETHING.
BUT...
I'M TELLING YOU NOT TO GIVE ME ANY MORE TROUBLE.
I-I'M SORRY...
BATH
SNIFF
OH? WHAT'S UP, YUNTAN?
DID YOU GET KICKED OUT FOR MESSING UP AGAIN?
STAB
IT'S ALWAYS BEEN REN'S DREAM TO SERVE A HIGH-RANKING GOD.
SHE'S JUST REALLY EAGER.

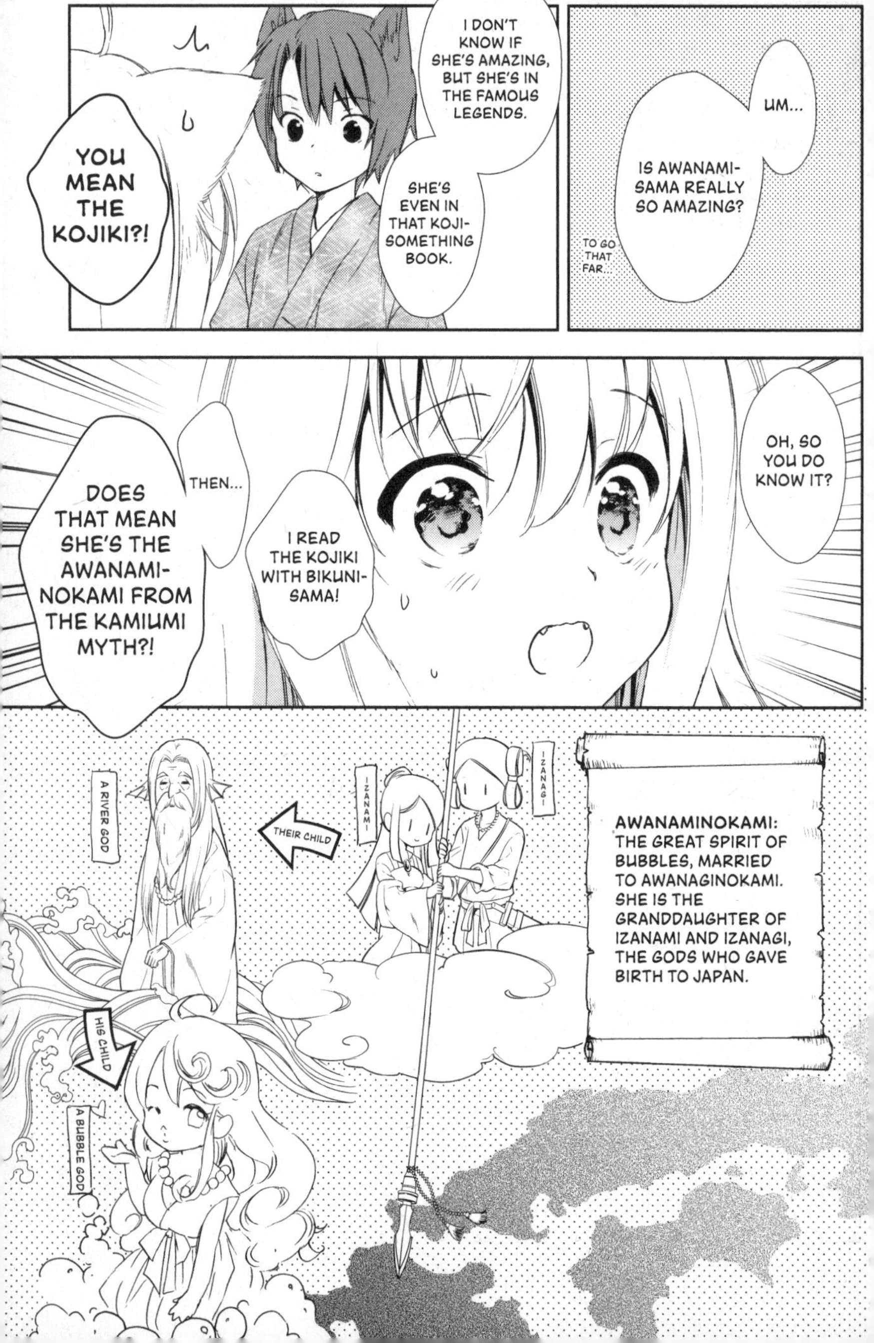
UM...
IS AWANAMI-SAMA REALLY SO AMAZING?
TO GO THAT FAR...
I DON'T KNOW IF SHE'S AMAZING, BUT SHE'S IN THE FAMOUS LEGENDS.
SHE'S EVEN IN THAT KOJI-SOMETHING BOOK.
YOU MEAN THE KOJIKI?!
OH, SO YOU DO KNOW IT?
I READ THE KOJIKI WITH BIKUNI-SAMA!
THEN...
DOES THAT MEAN SHE'S THE AWANAMI-NOKAMI FROM THE KAMIUMI MYTH?!
AWANAMINOKAMI: THE GREAT SPIRIT OF BUBBLES, MARRIED TO AWANAGINOKAMI. SHE IS THE GRANDDAUGHTER OF IZANAMI AND IZANAGI, THE GODS WHO GAVE BIRTH TO JAPAN.
IZANAGI
IZANAMI
THEIR CHILD
A RIVER GOD
HIS CHILD
A BUBBLE GOD

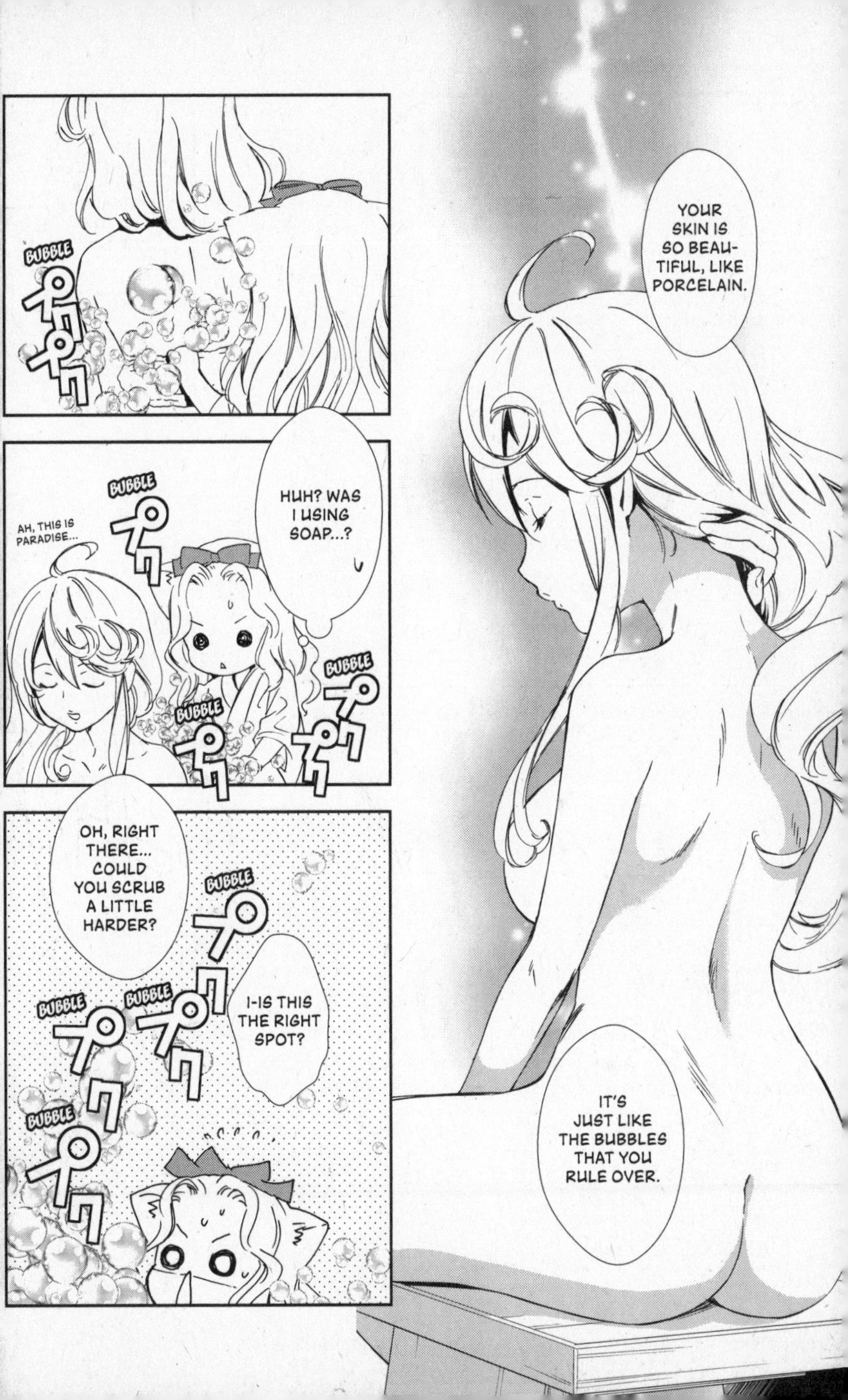
YOUR SKIN IS SO BEAU-TIFUL, LIKE PORCELAIN.
IT'S JUST LIKE THE BUBBLES THAT YOU RULE OVER.
BUBBLE
HUH? WAS I USING SOAP...?
BUBBLE
AH, THIS IS PARADISE...
BUBBLE
BUBBLE
OH, RIGHT THERE... COULD YOU SCRUB A LITTLE HARDER?
BUBBLE
I-IS THIS THE RIGHT SPOT?
BUBBLE
BUBBLE
BUBBLE

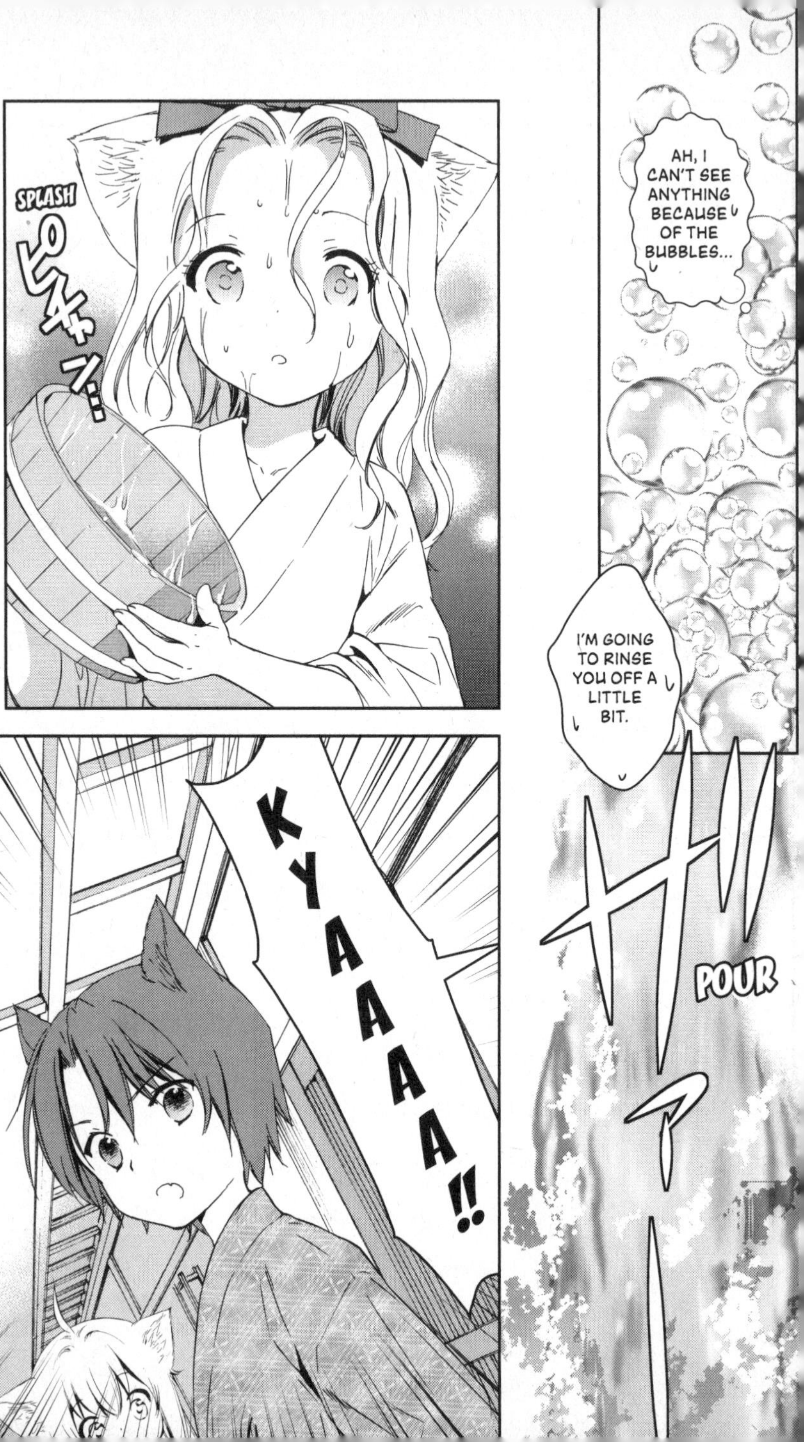
AH, I CAN'T SEE ANYTHING BECAUSE OF THE BUBBLES...
I'M GOING TO RINSE YOU OFF A LITTLE BIT.
SPLASH
POUR
KYAAAAA!!

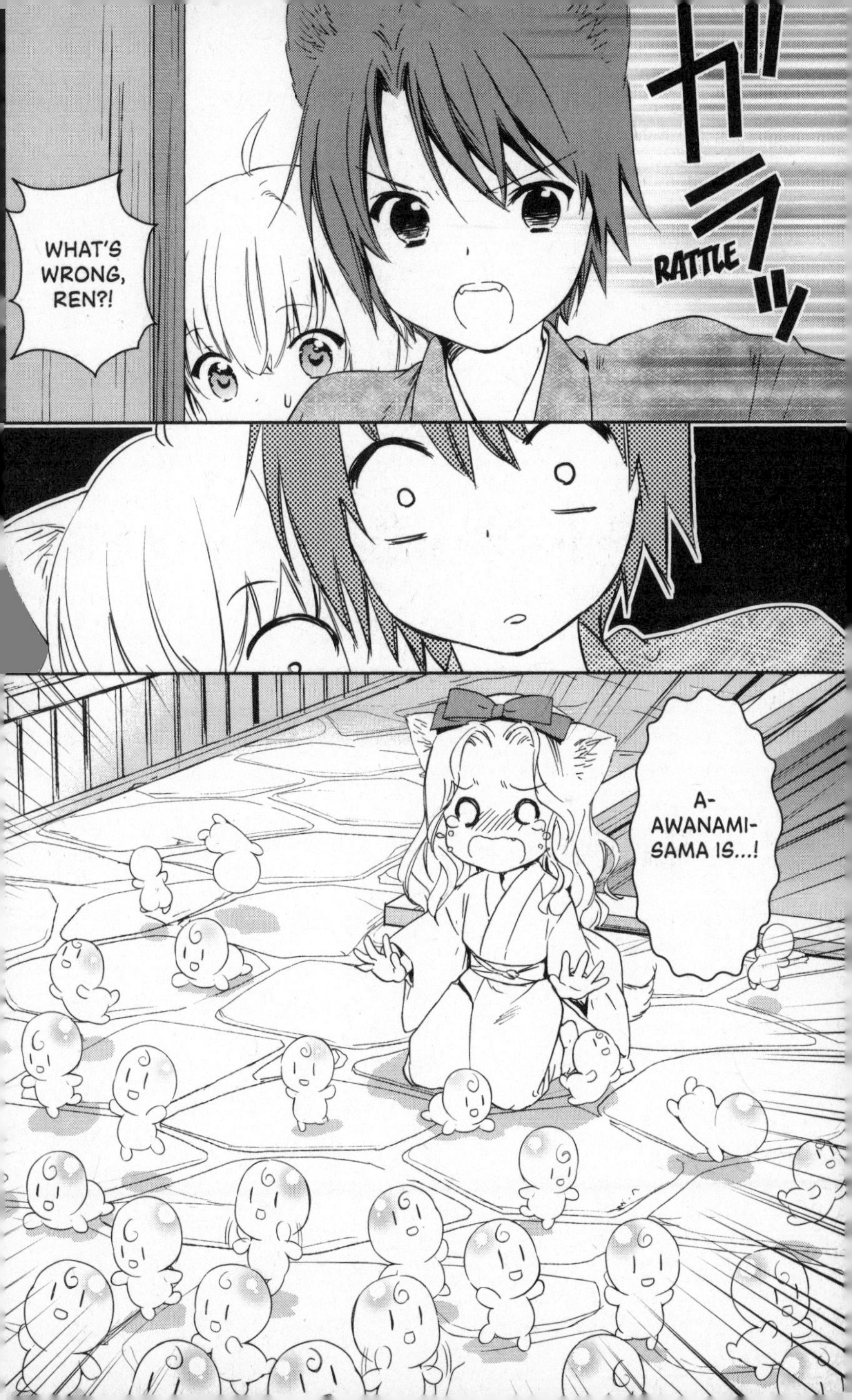
ガラッ
RATTLE
WHAT'S WRONG, REN?!
A- AWANAMI-SAMA IS...!

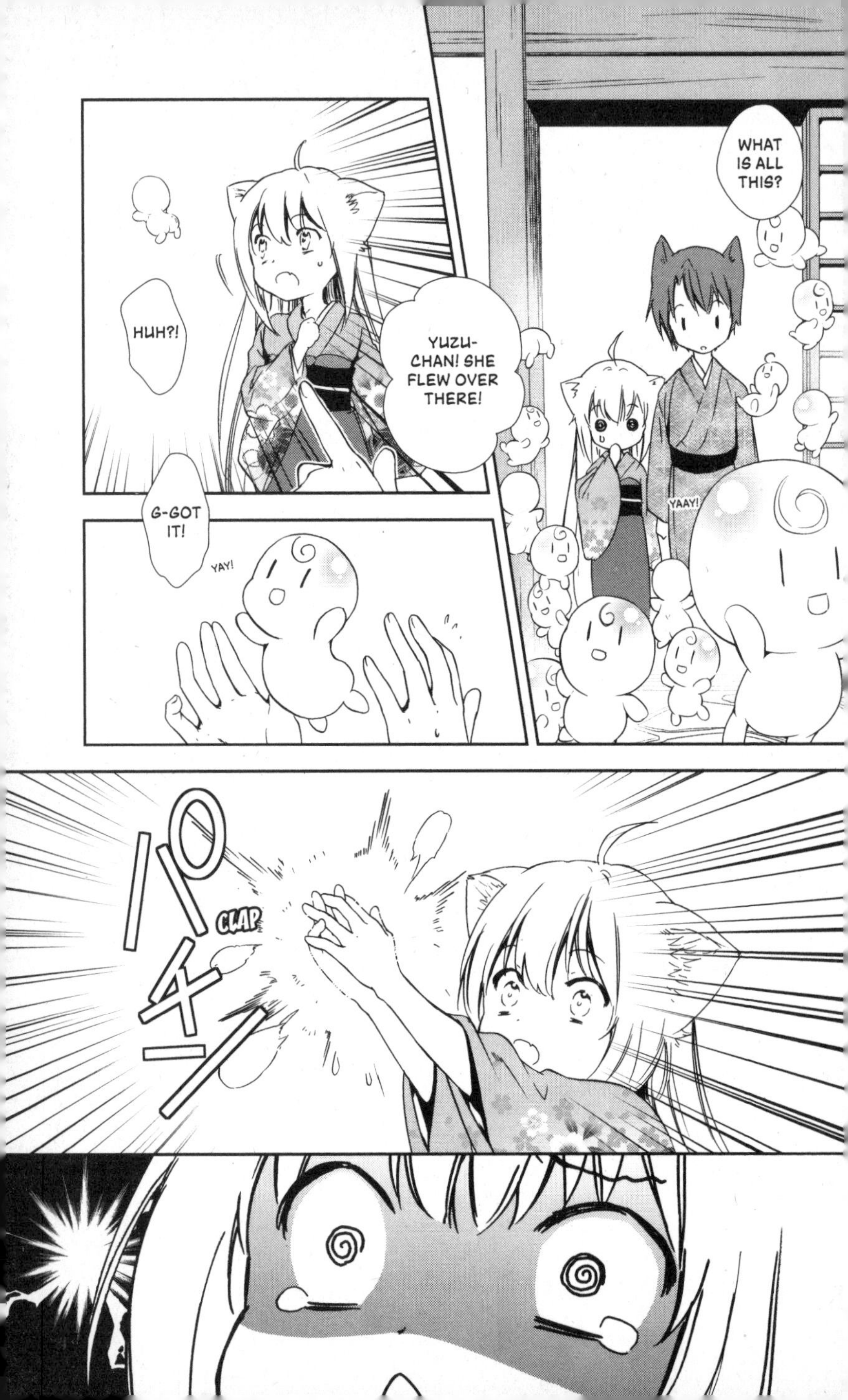
WHAT IS ALL THIS?
YAAY!
YUZU-CHAN! SHE FLEW OVER THERE!
HUH?!
G-GOT IT!
YAY!
CLAP

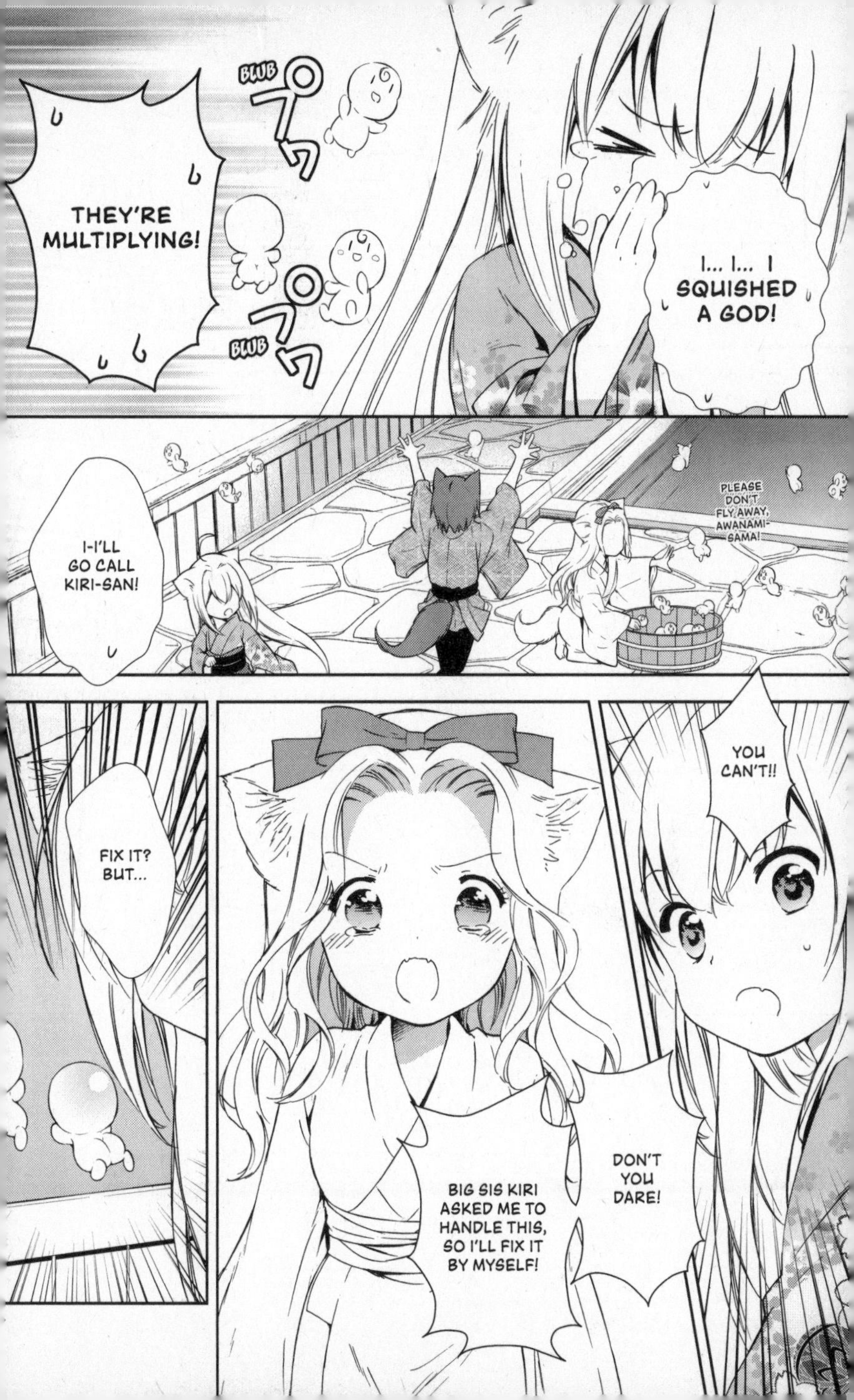
I... I... I SQUISHED A GOD!
BLUB
THEY'RE MULTIPLYING!
BLUB
PLEASE DON'T FLY AWAY, AWANAMI-SAMA!
I-I'LL GO CALL KIRI-SAN!
YOU CAN'T!!
DON'T YOU DARE!
BIG SIS KIRI ASKED ME TO HANDLE THIS, SO I'LL FIX IT BY MYSELF!
FIX IT? BUT...

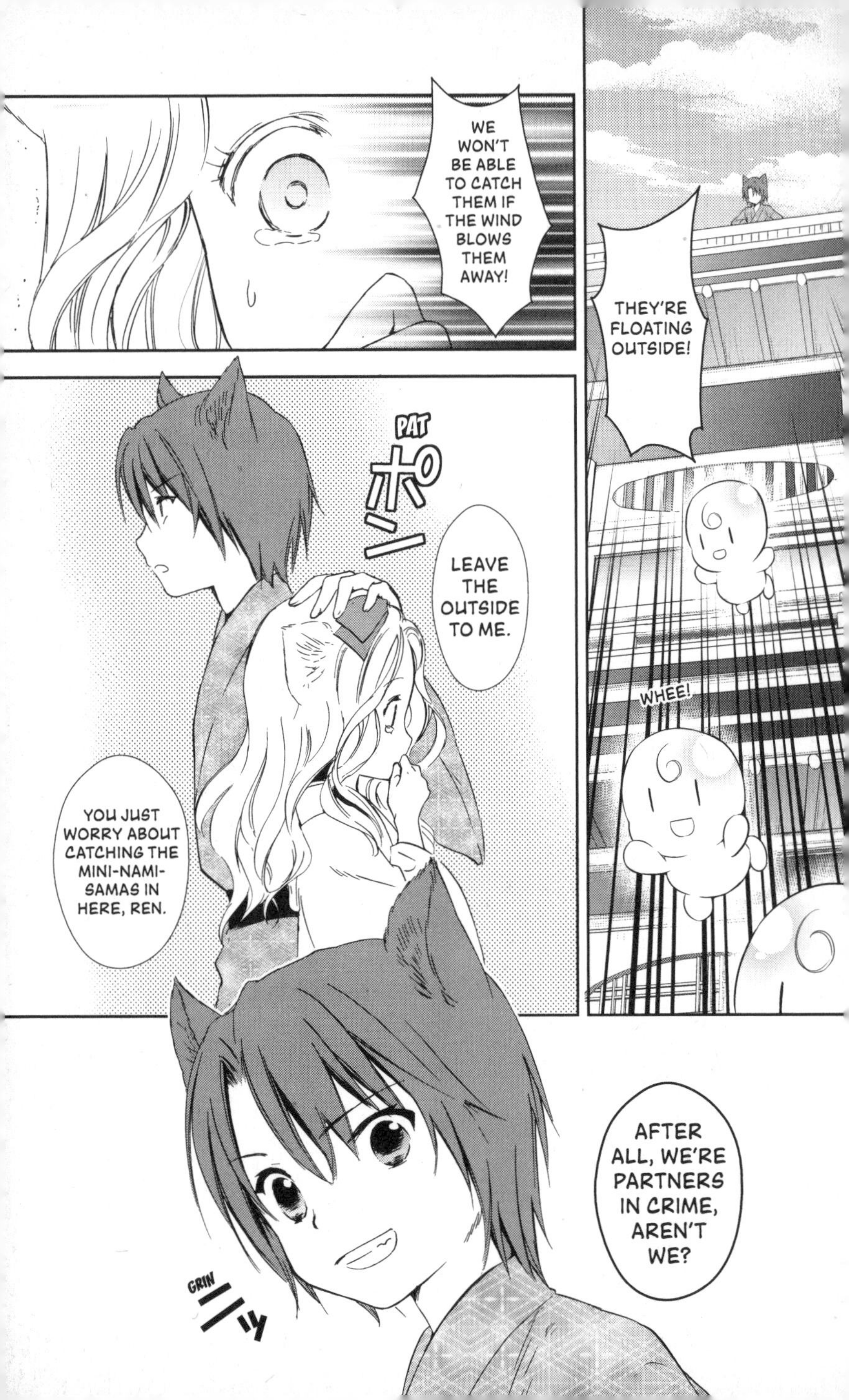
THEY'RE FLOATING OUTSIDE!
WHEE!
WE WON'T BE ABLE TO CATCH THEM IF THE WIND BLOWS THEM AWAY!
PAT
LEAVE THE OUTSIDE TO ME.
YOU JUST WORRY ABOUT CATCHING THE MINI-NAMI-SAMAS IN HERE, REN.
AFTER ALL, WE'RE PARTNERS IN CRIME, AREN'T WE?
GRIN

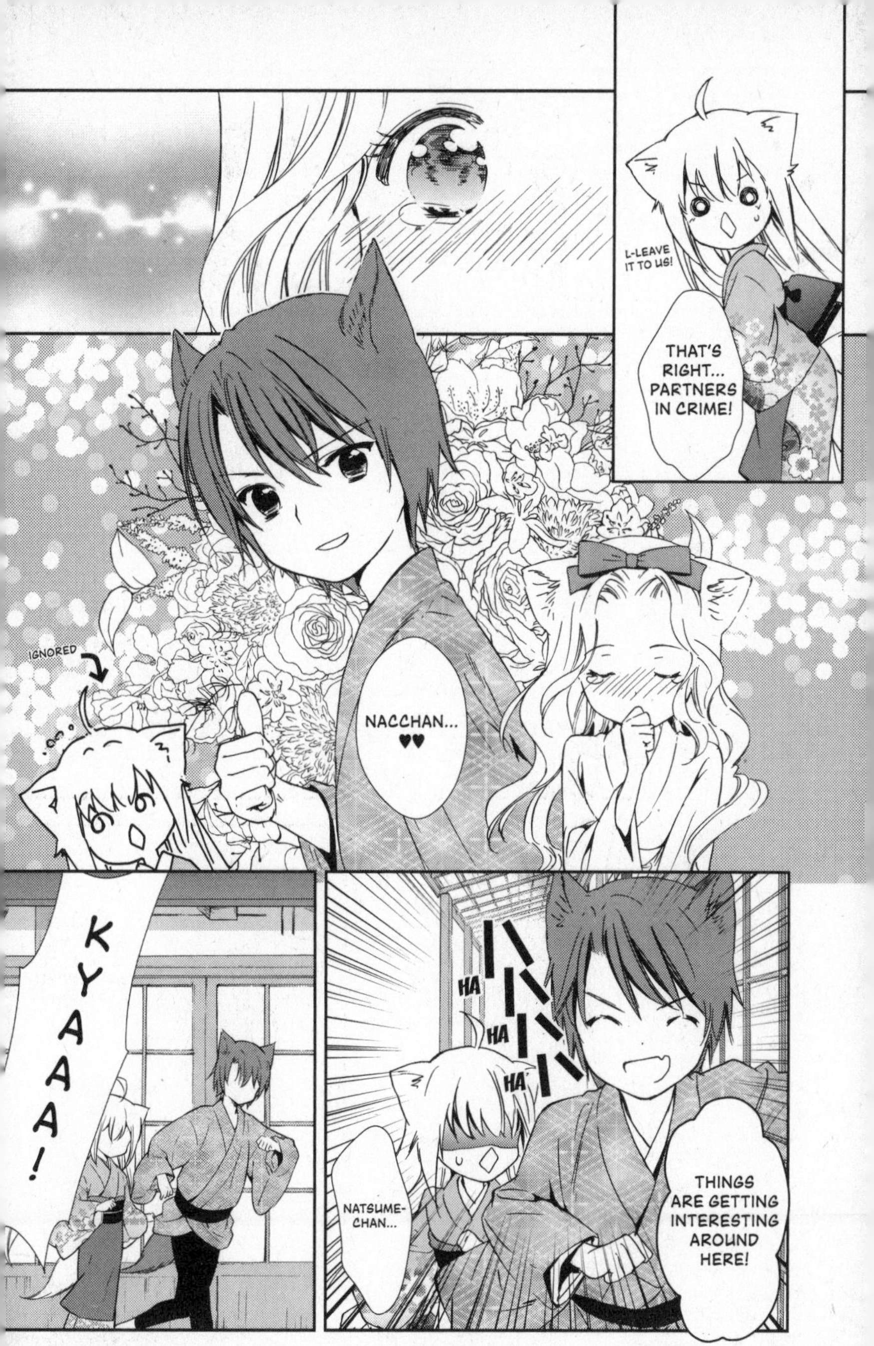
L-LEAVE IT TO US!
THAT'S RIGHT... PARTNERS IN CRIME!
NACCHAN... ♥♥
IGNORED
HA HA HA
THINGS ARE GETTING INTERESTING AROUND HERE!
NATSUME-CHAN...
KYAAAA!

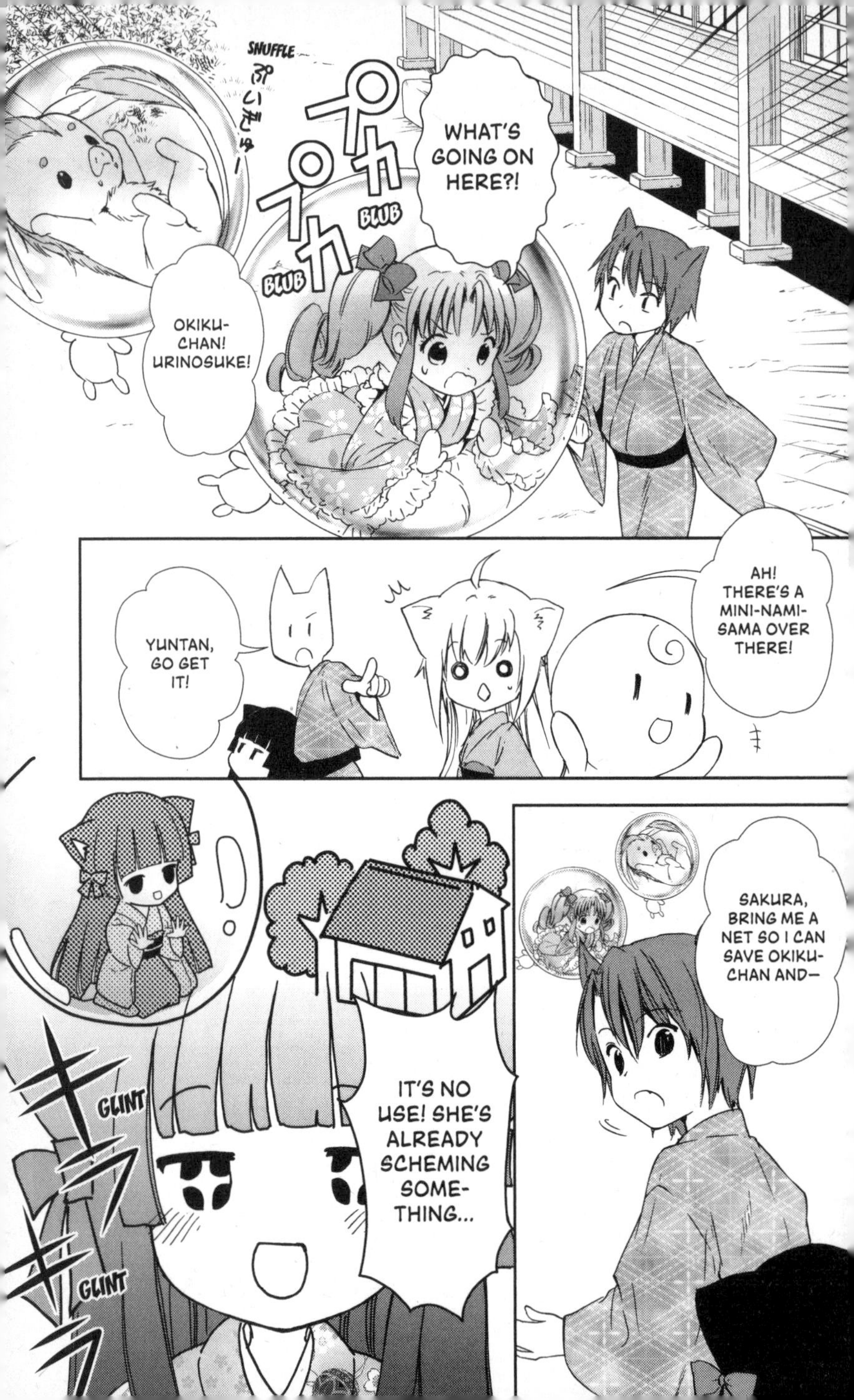
WHAT'S GOING ON HERE?!
BLUB
BLUB
SNUFFLE
OKIKU-CHAN! URINOSUKE!
AH! THERE'S A MINI-NAMI-SAMA OVER THERE!
YUNTAN, GO GET IT!
SAKURA, BRING ME A NET SO I CAN SAVE OKIKU-CHAN AND—
GLINT
GLINT
IT'S NO USE! SHE'S ALREADY SCHEMING SOME-THING...

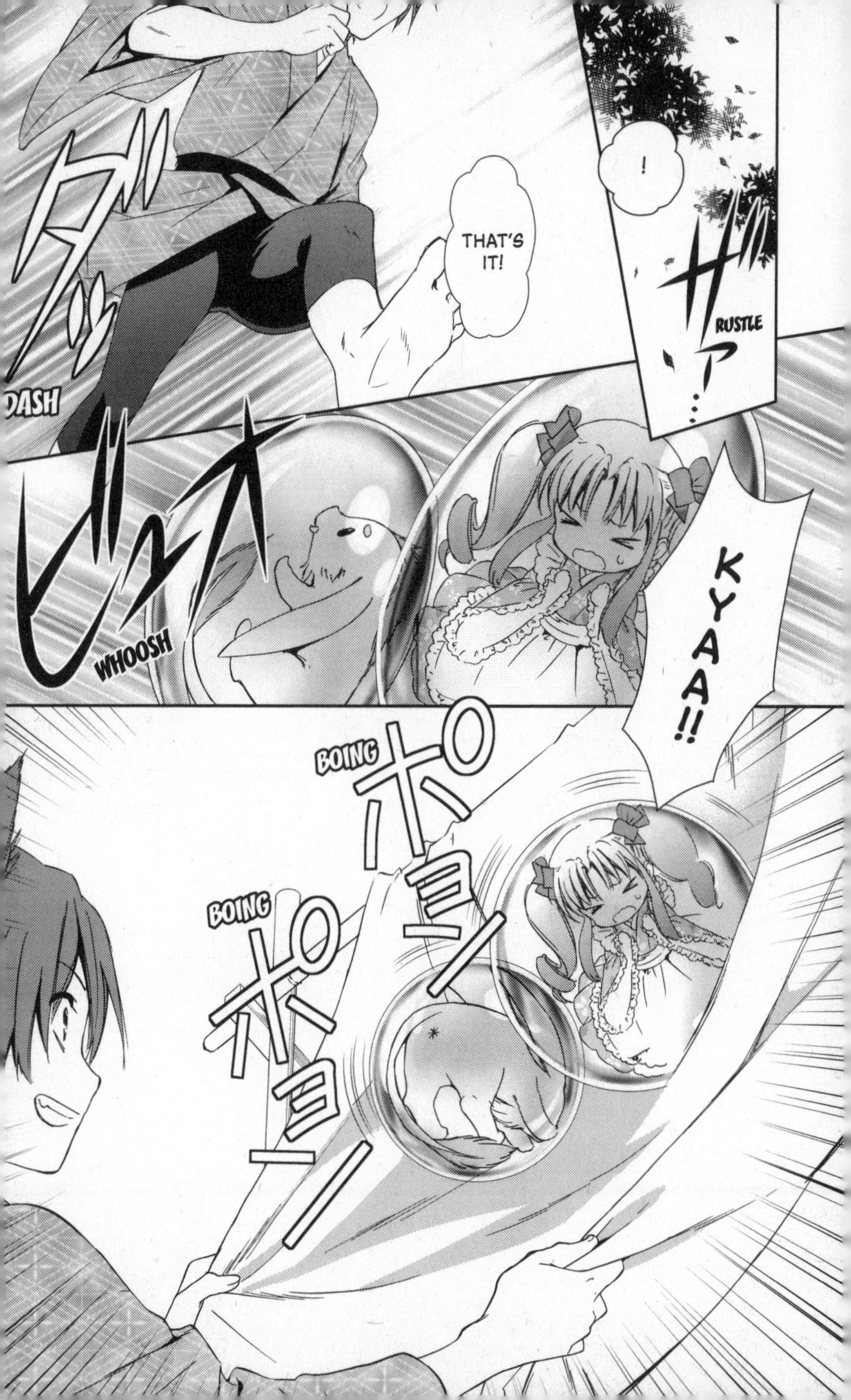
!
RUSTLE
THAT'S IT!
DASH
KYAA!!
WHOOSH
BOING
BOING

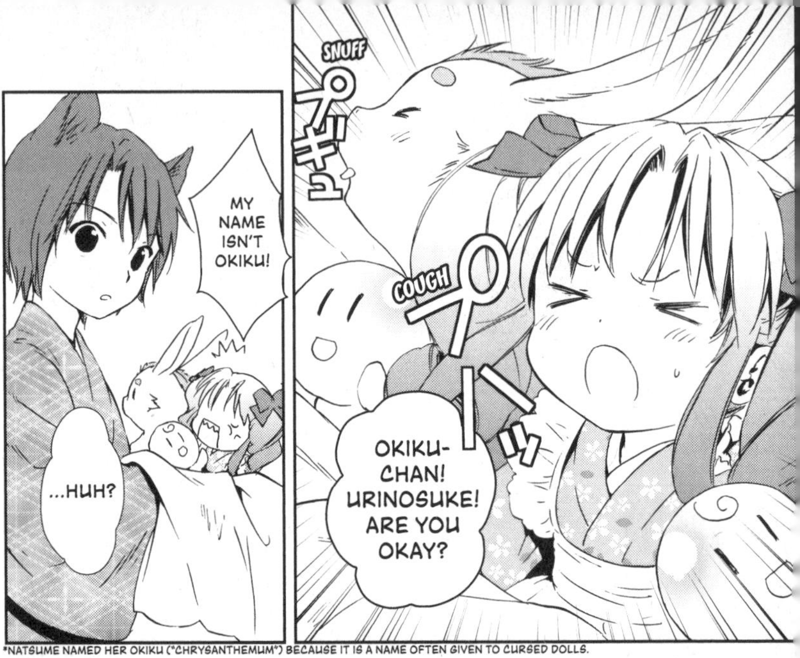
SNUFF
COUGH
OKIKU-CHAN! URINOSUKE! ARE YOU OKAY?
MY NAME ISN'T OKIKU!
...HUH?

*NATSUME NAMED HER OKIKU ("CHRYSANTHEMUM") BECAUSE IT IS A NAME OFTEN GIVEN TO CURSED DOLLS.

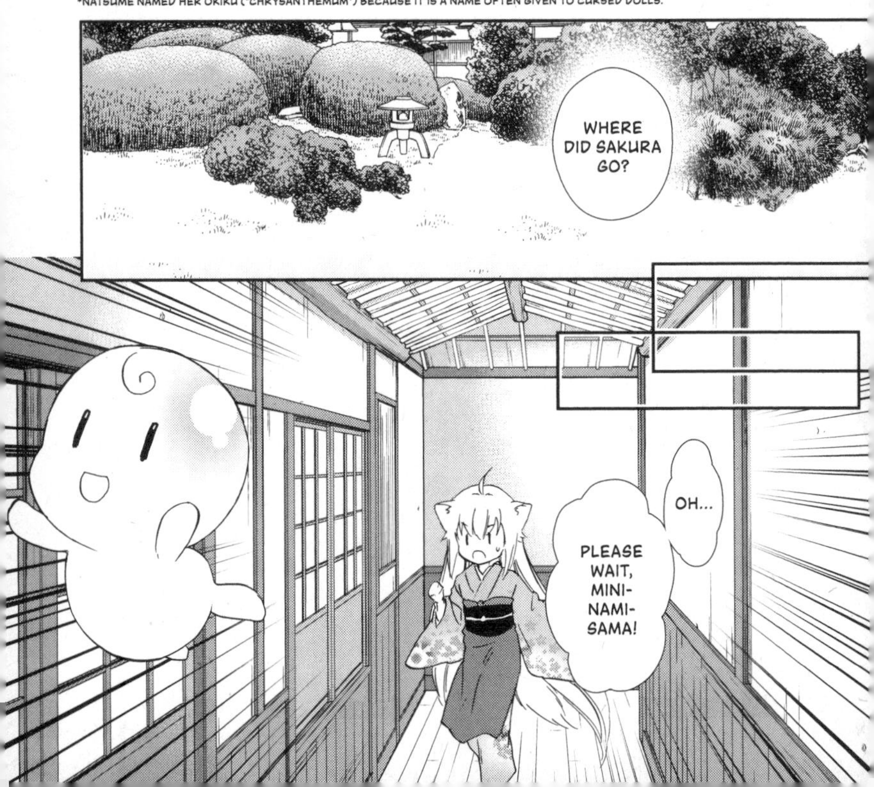
WHERE DID SAKURA GO?
OH...
PLEASE WAIT, MINI-NAMI-SAMA!

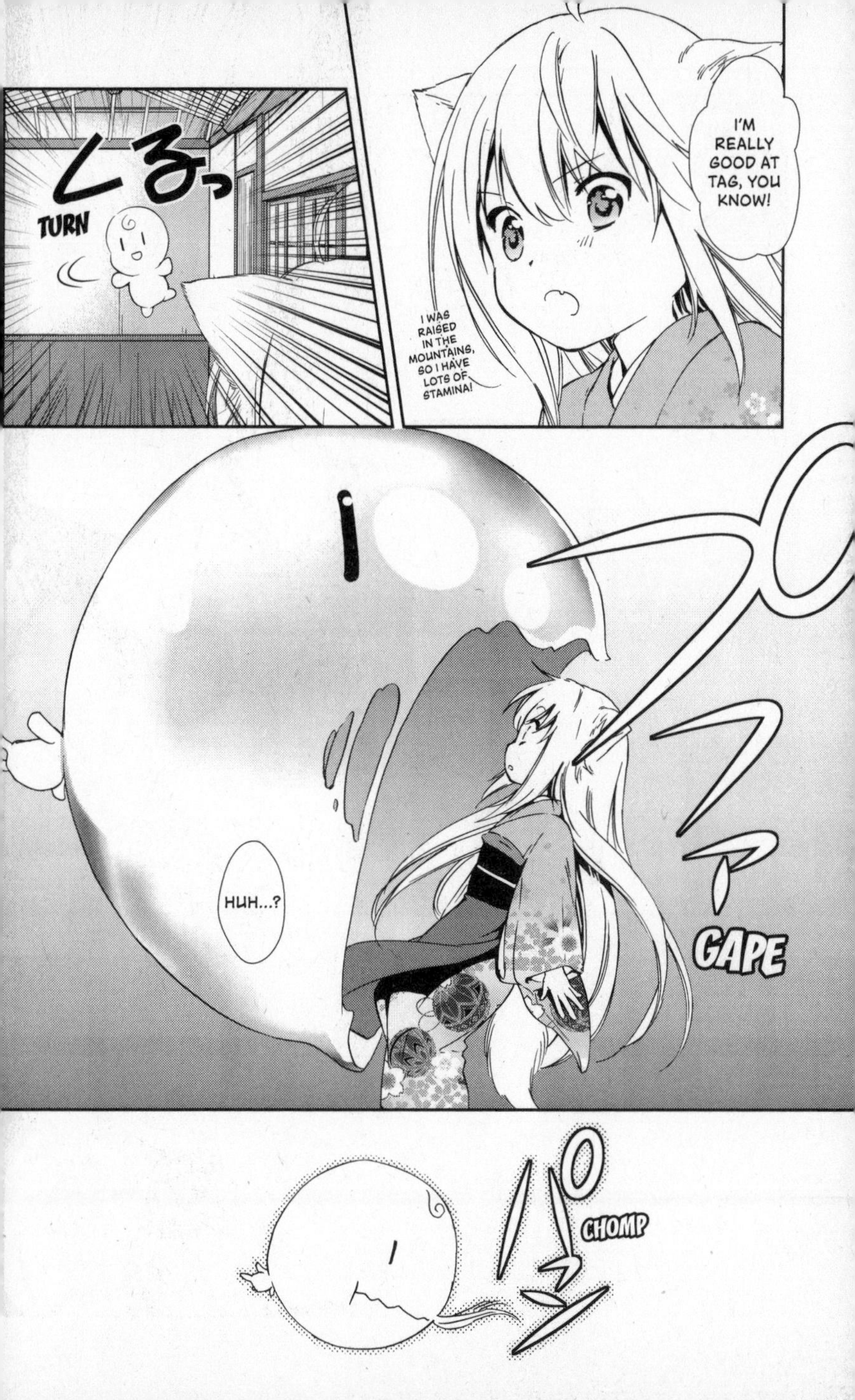
I'M REALLY GOOD AT TAG, YOU KNOW!
I WAS RAISED IN THE MOUNTAINS, SO I HAVE LOTS OF STAMINA!
くるっ
TURN
GAPE
HUH...?
CHOMP

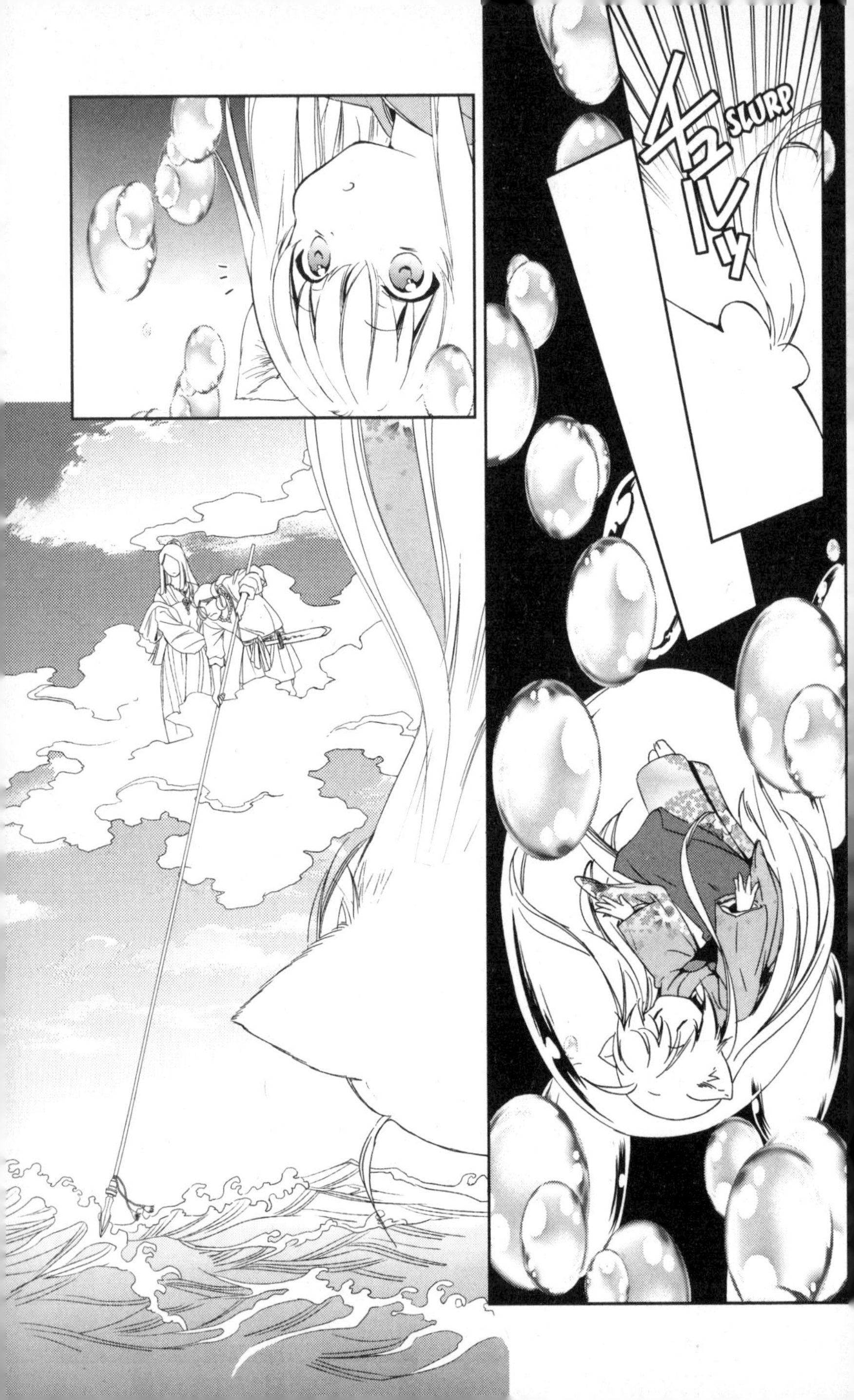
SLURP

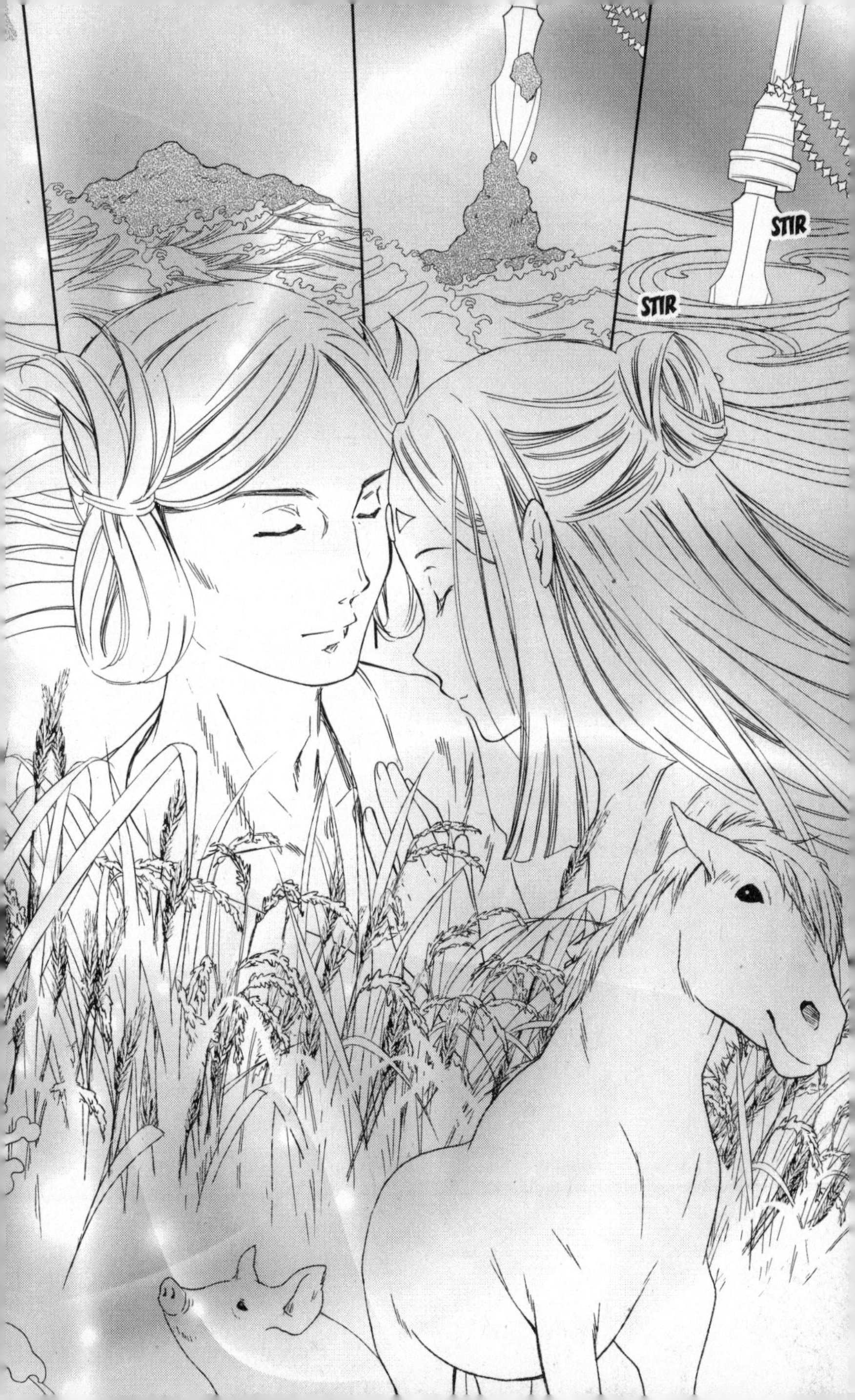
STIR
STIR

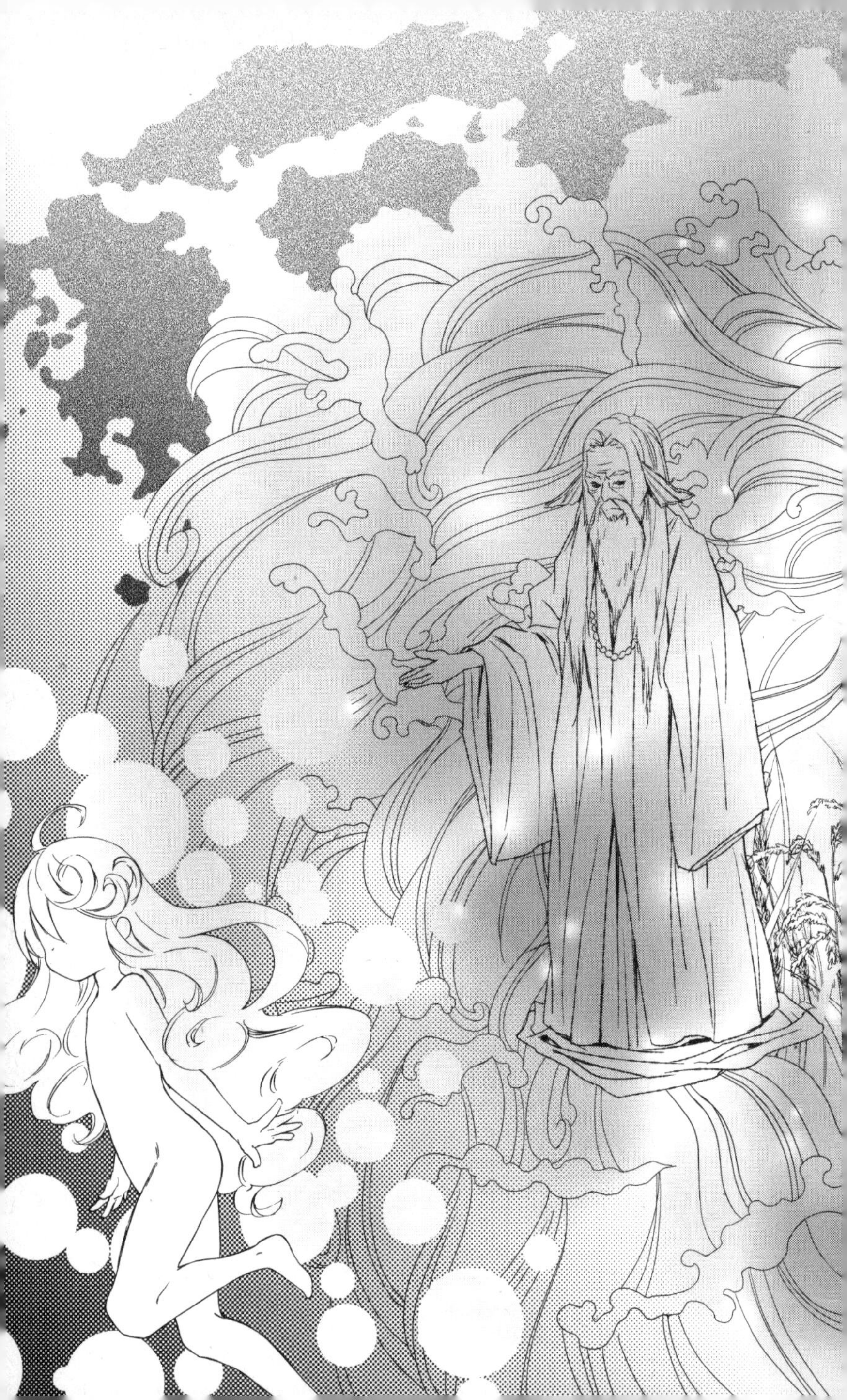

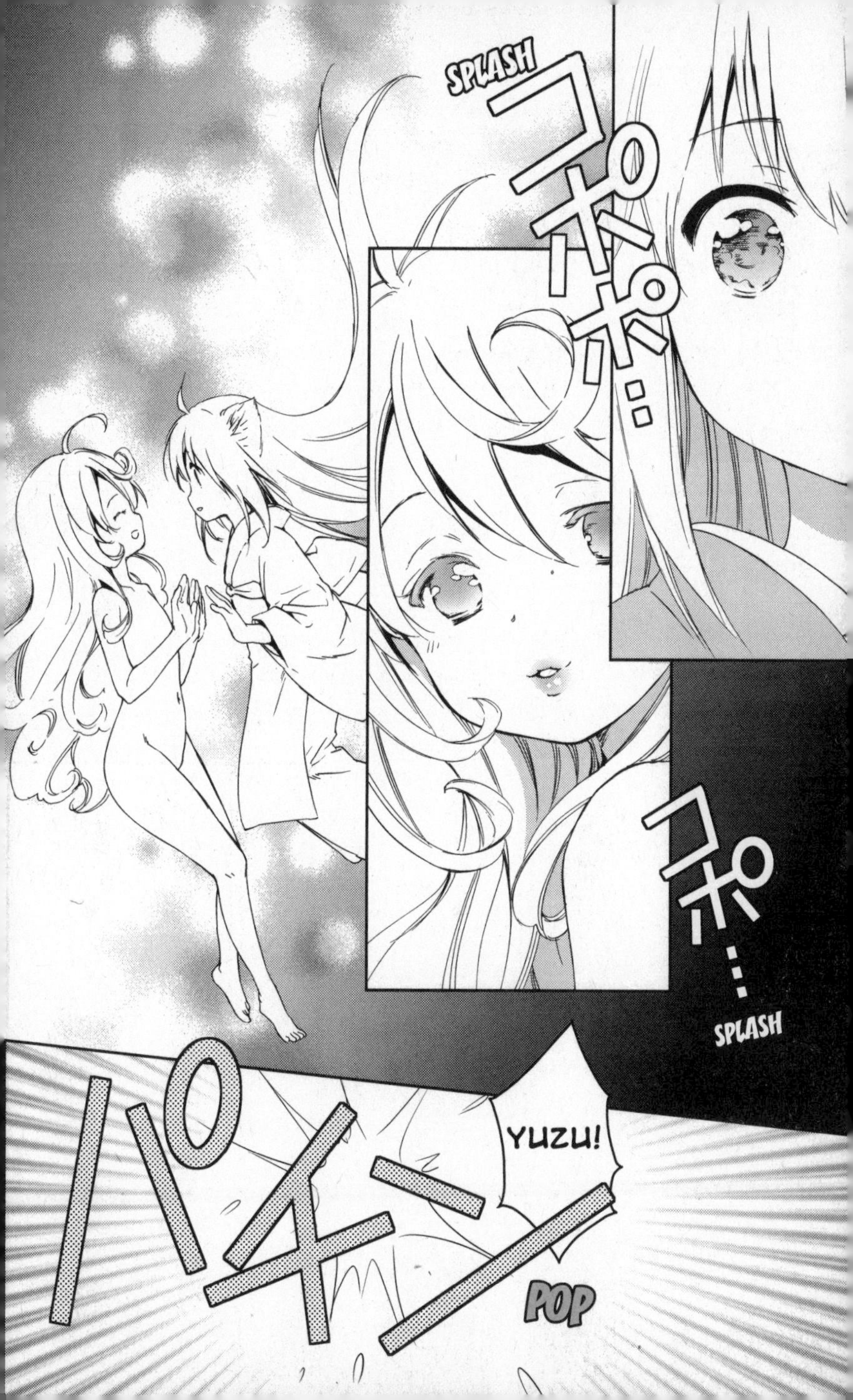
SPLASH
コポポ‥
コポ…
SPLASH
YUZU!
パイー
POP

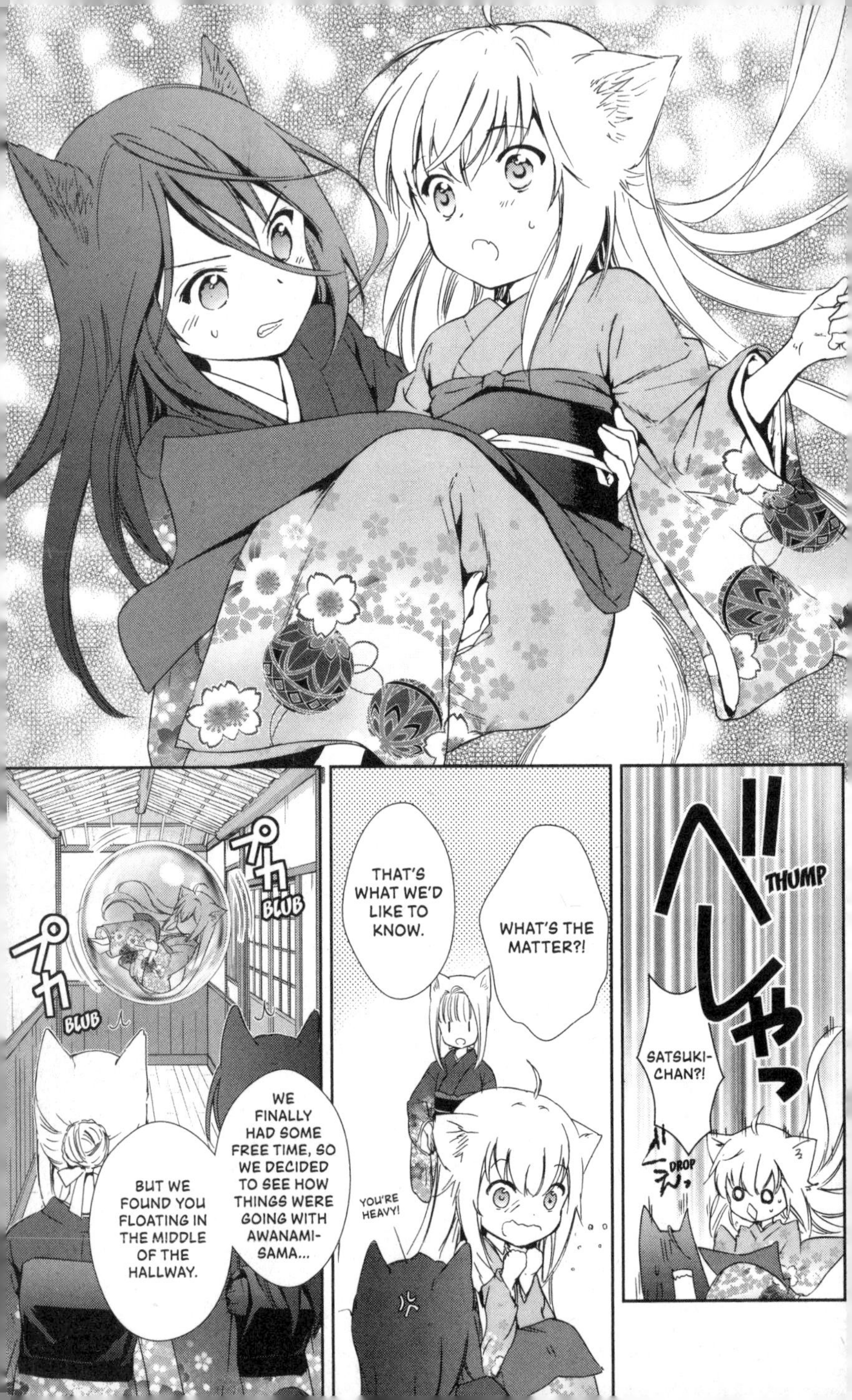
THUMP
SATSUKI-CHAN?!
DROP
WHAT'S THE MATTER?!
THAT'S WHAT WE'D LIKE TO KNOW.
YOU'RE HEAVY!
BLUB
BLUB
WE FINALLY HAD SOME FREE TIME, SO WE DECIDED TO SEE HOW THINGS WERE GOING WITH AWANAMI-SAMA...
BUT WE FOUND YOU FLOATING IN THE MIDDLE OF THE HALLWAY.

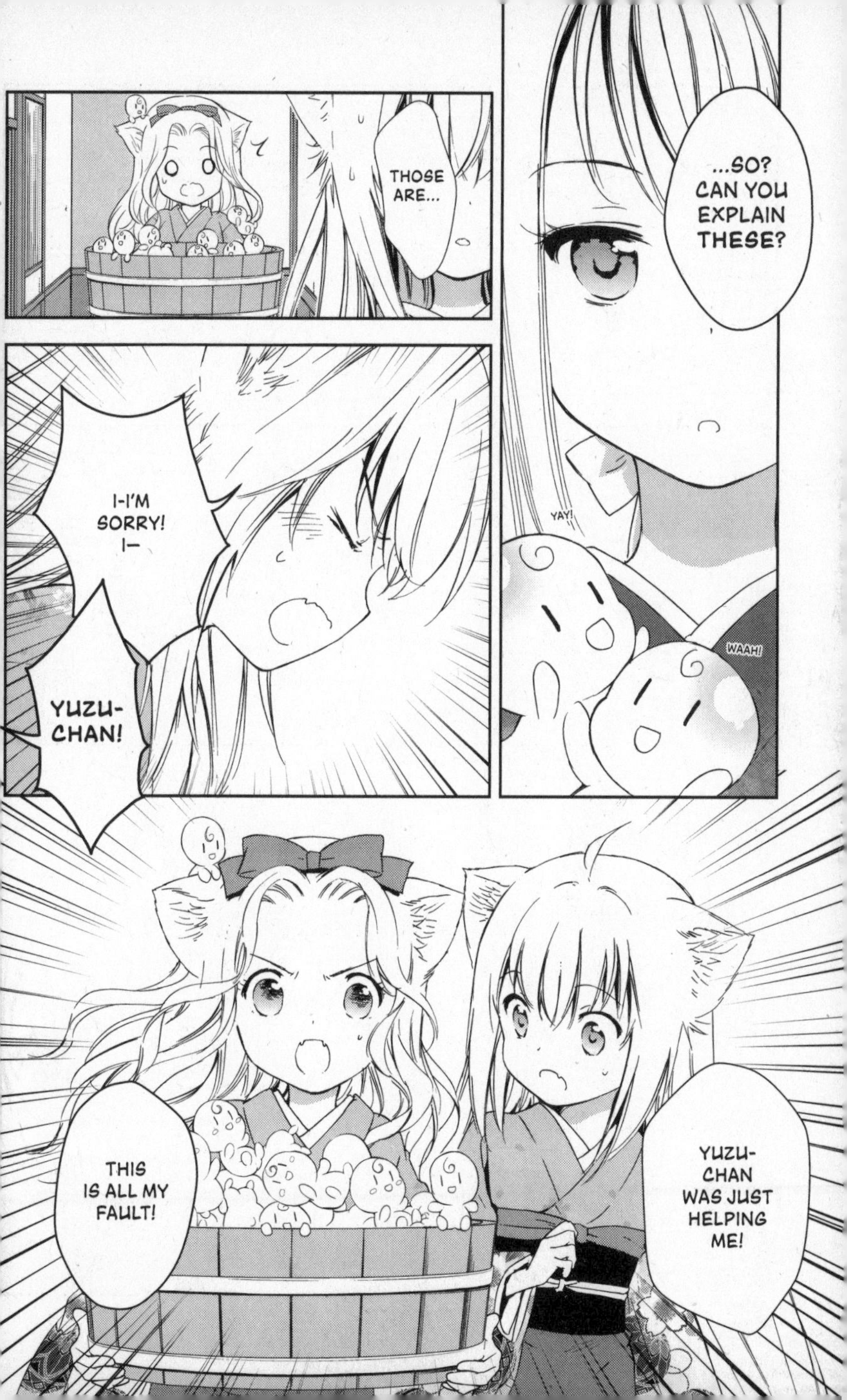

...SO? CAN YOU EXPLAIN THESE?
YAY!
WAAH!
THOSE ARE...
I-I'M SORRY! I—
YUZU-CHAN!
YUZU-CHAN WAS JUST HELPING ME!
THIS IS ALL MY FAULT!

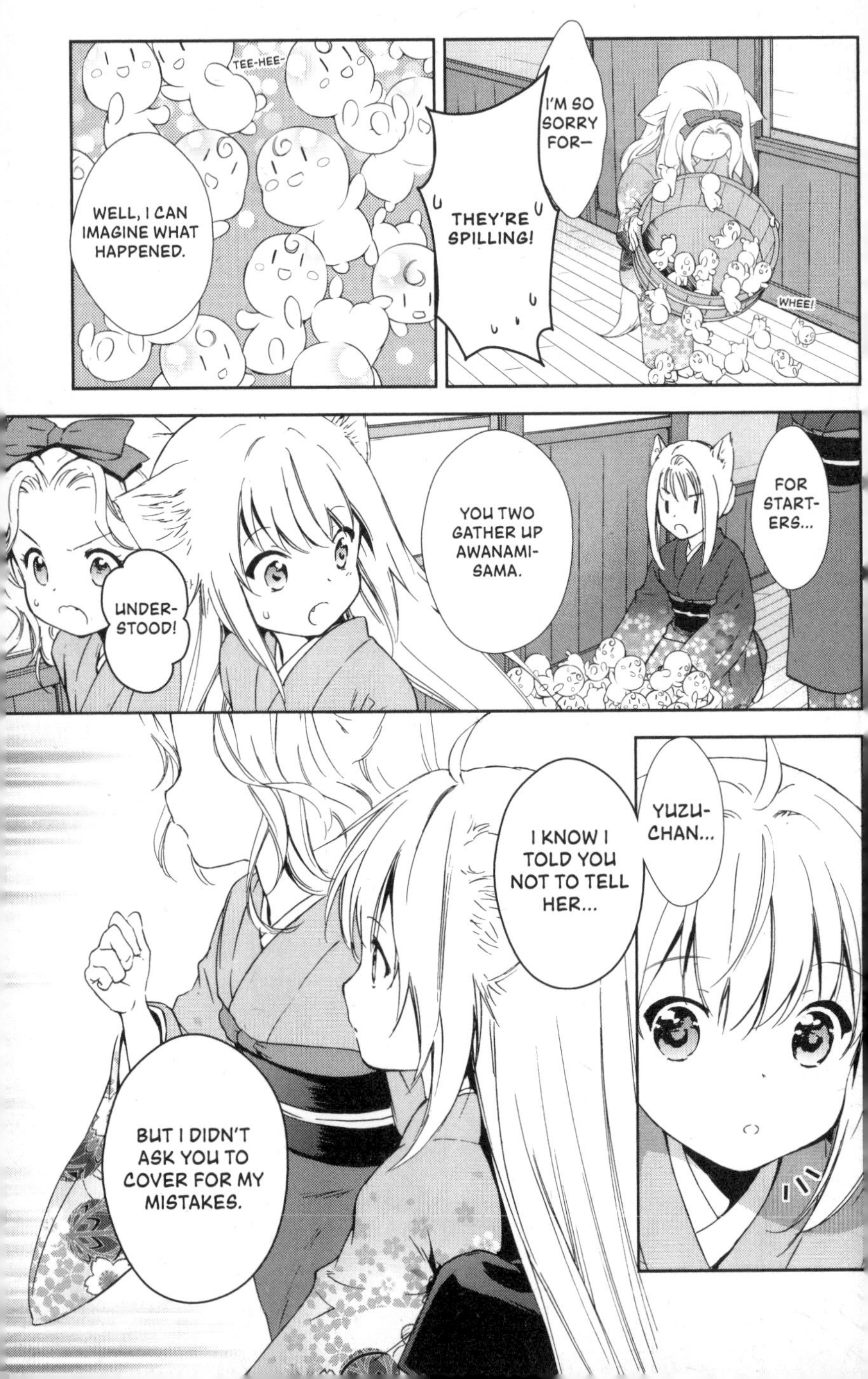
I'M SO SORRY FOR—
THEY'RE SPILLING!
WHEE!
TEE-HEE-
WELL, I CAN IMAGINE WHAT HAPPENED.
FOR STARTERS...
YOU TWO GATHER UP AWANAMI-SAMA.
UNDERSTOOD!
YUZU-CHAN...
I KNOW I TOLD YOU NOT TO TELL HER...
BUT I DIDN'T ASK YOU TO COVER FOR MY MISTAKES.

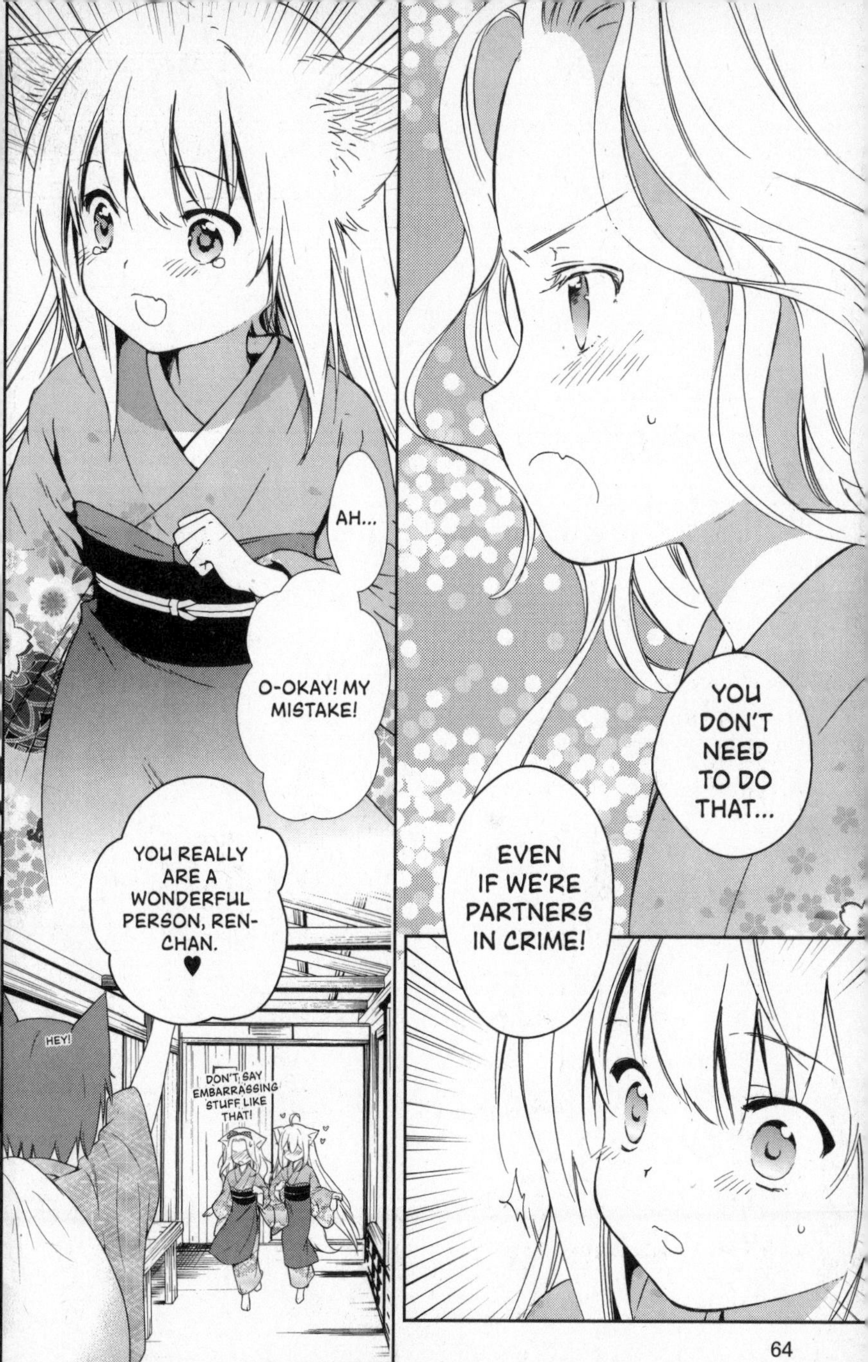
YOU DON'T NEED TO DO THAT...
EVEN IF WE'RE PARTNERS IN CRIME!
AH...
O-OKAY! MY MISTAKE!
YOU REALLY ARE A WONDERFUL PERSON, REN-CHAN. ♥
HEY!
DON'T SAY EMBARRASSING STUFF LIKE THAT!

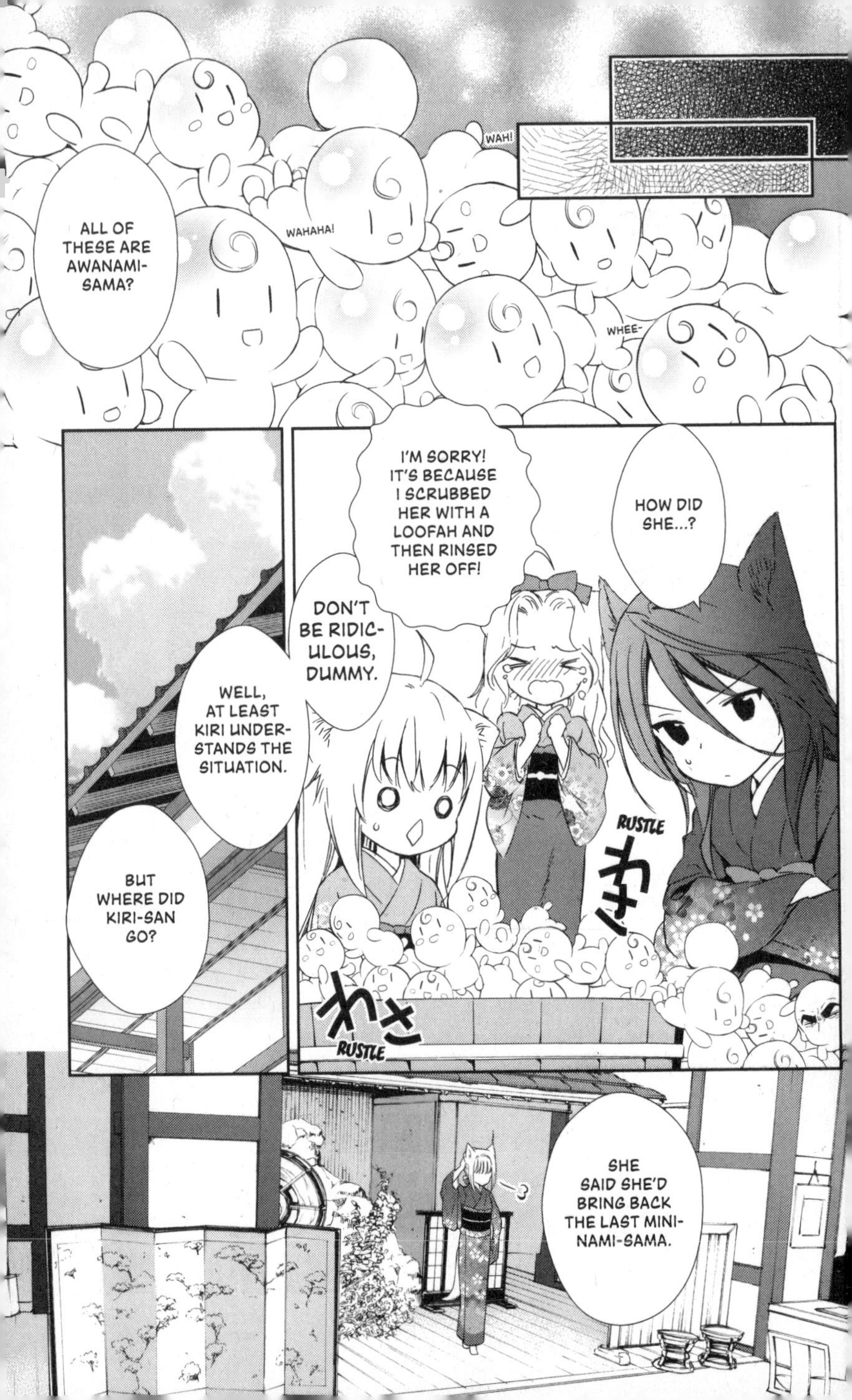
WAH!
WAHAHA!
ALL OF THESE ARE AWANAMI-SAMA?
WHEE-
HOW DID SHE...?
I'M SORRY! IT'S BECAUSE I SCRUBBED HER WITH A LOOFAH AND THEN RINSED HER OFF!
DON'T BE RIDIC-ULOUS, DUMMY.
WELL, AT LEAST KIRI UNDER-STANDS THE SITUATION.
RUSTLE
RUSTLE
BUT WHERE DID KIRI-SAN GO?
SHE SAID SHE'D BRING BACK THE LAST MINI-NAMI-SAMA.

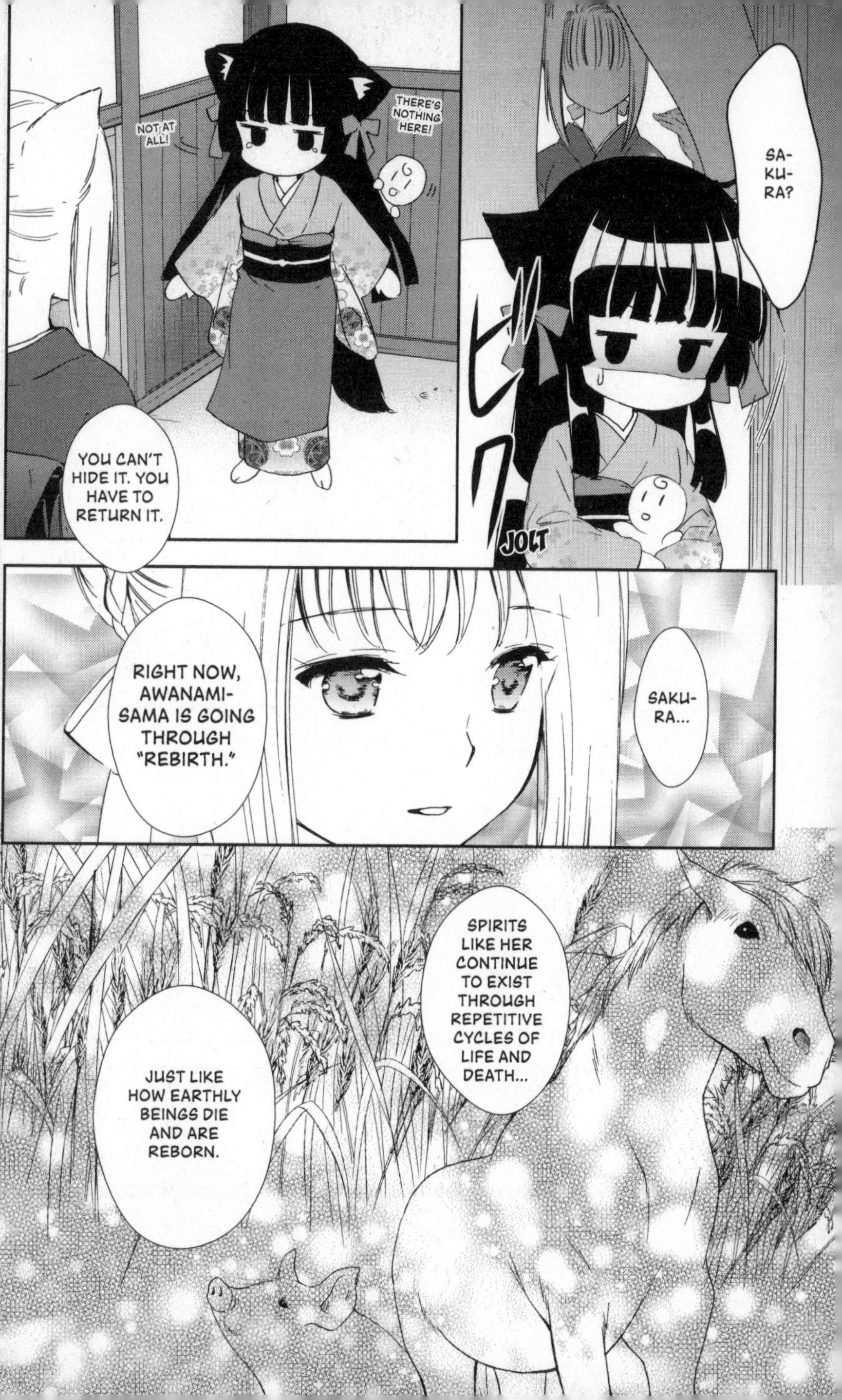
SA-KU-RA?
JOLT
THERE'S NOTHING HERE!
NOT AT ALL!
YOU CAN'T HIDE IT. YOU HAVE TO RETURN IT.
SAKU-RA...
RIGHT NOW, AWANAMI-SAMA IS GOING THROUGH "REBIRTH."
SPIRITS LIKE HER CONTINUE TO EXIST THROUGH REPETITIVE CYCLES OF LIFE AND DEATH...
JUST LIKE HOW EARTHLY BEINGS DIE AND ARE REBORN.

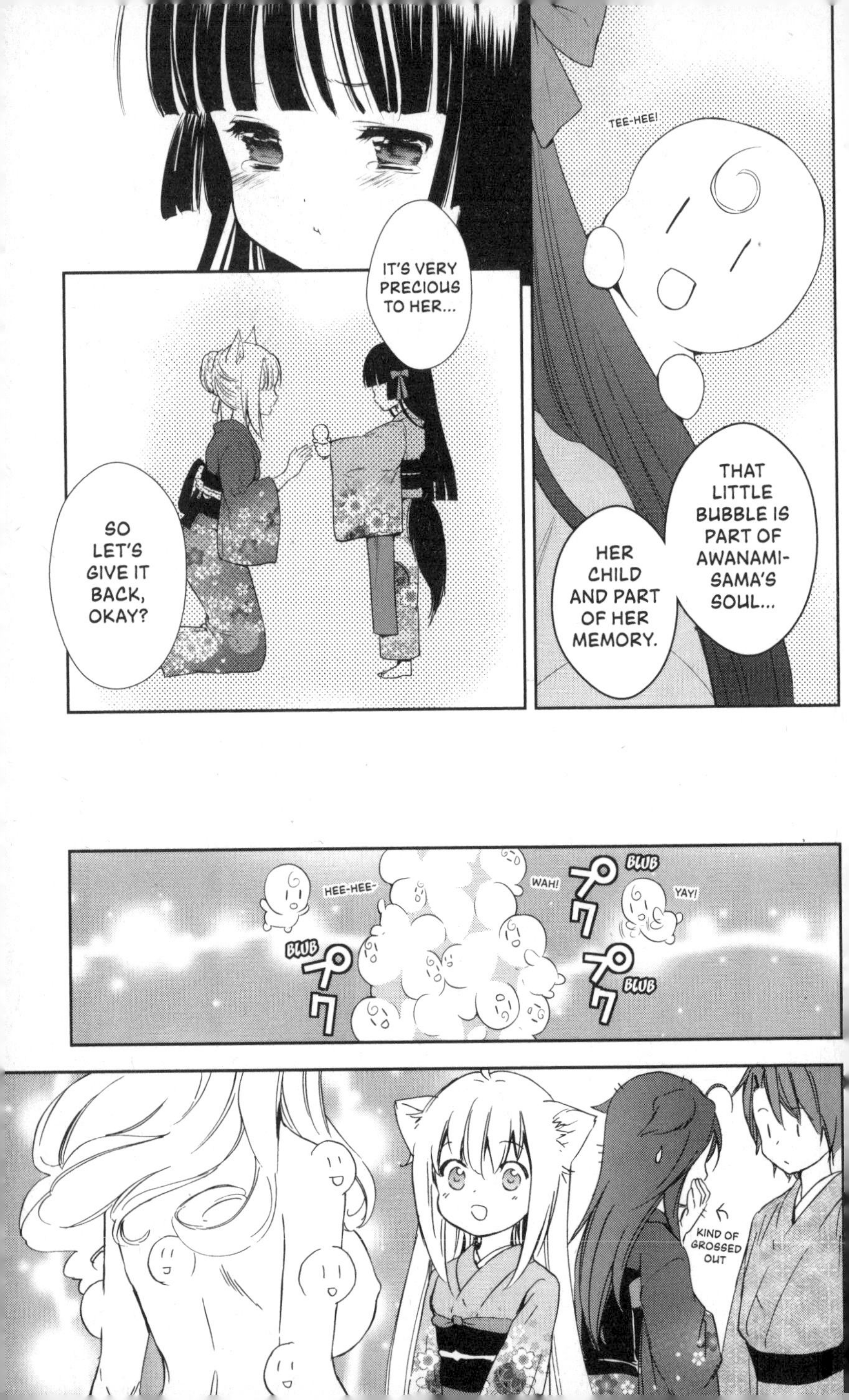
TEE-HEE!
THAT LITTLE BUBBLE IS PART OF AWANAMI-SAMA'S SOUL...
HER CHILD AND PART OF HER MEMORY.
IT'S VERY PRECIOUS TO HER...
SO LET'S GIVE IT BACK, OKAY?
YAY!
BLUB
WAH!
BLUB
HEE-HEE-
BLUB
KIND OF GROSSED OUT

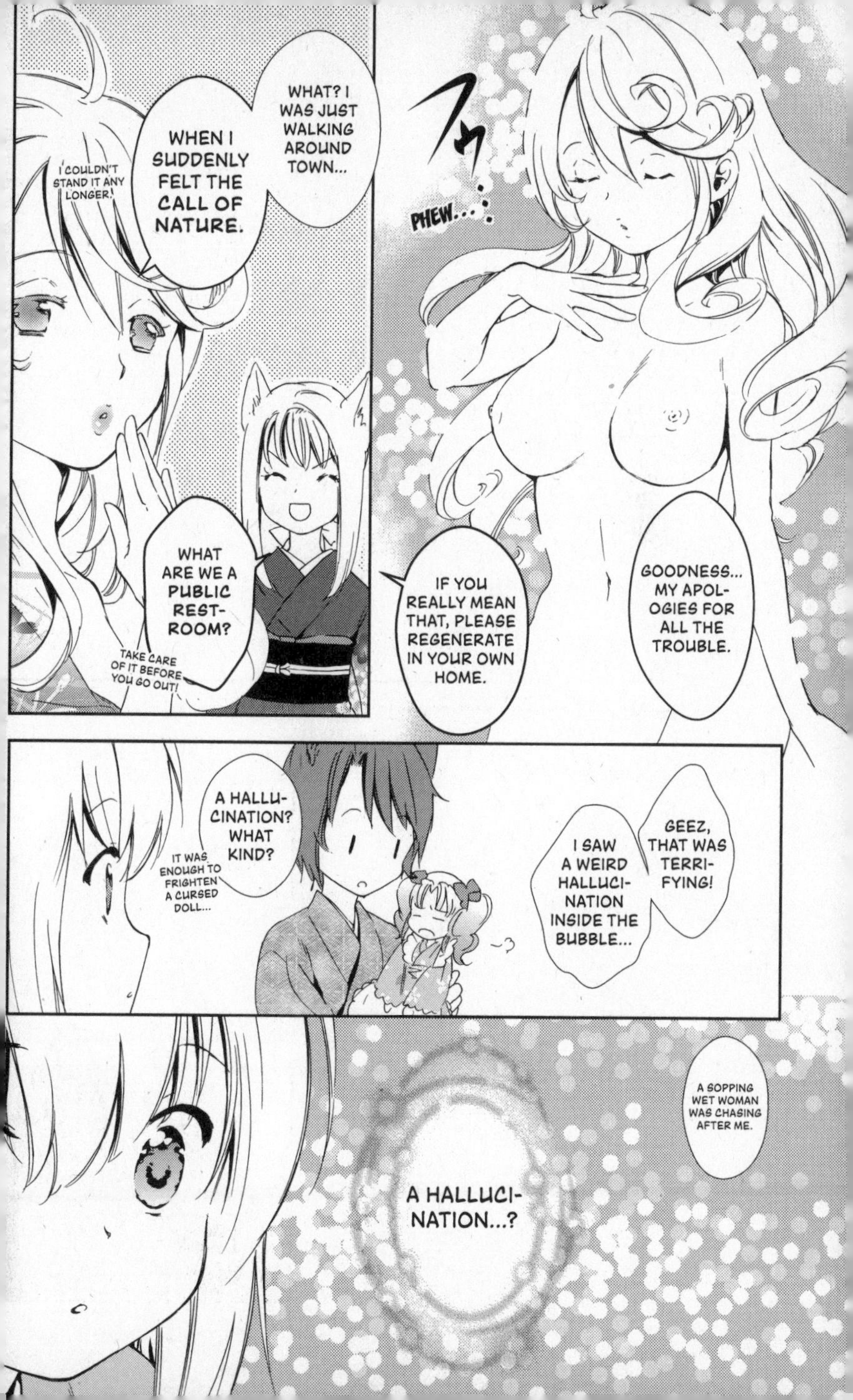
PHEW...
GOODNESS... MY APOLOGIES FOR ALL THE TROUBLE.
IF YOU REALLY MEAN THAT, PLEASE REGENERATE IN YOUR OWN HOME.
WHAT? I WAS JUST WALKING AROUND TOWN...
WHEN I SUDDENLY FELT THE CALL OF NATURE.
I COULDN'T STAND IT ANY LONGER!
WHAT ARE WE A PUBLIC REST-ROOM?
TAKE CARE OF IT BEFORE YOU GO OUT!
GEEZ, THAT WAS TERRI-FYING!
I SAW A WEIRD HALLUCI-NATION INSIDE THE BUBBLE...
A HALLU-CINATION? WHAT KIND?
IT WAS ENOUGH TO FRIGHTEN A CURSED DOLL...
A SOPPING WET WOMAN WAS CHASING AFTER ME.
A HALLUCI-NATION...?

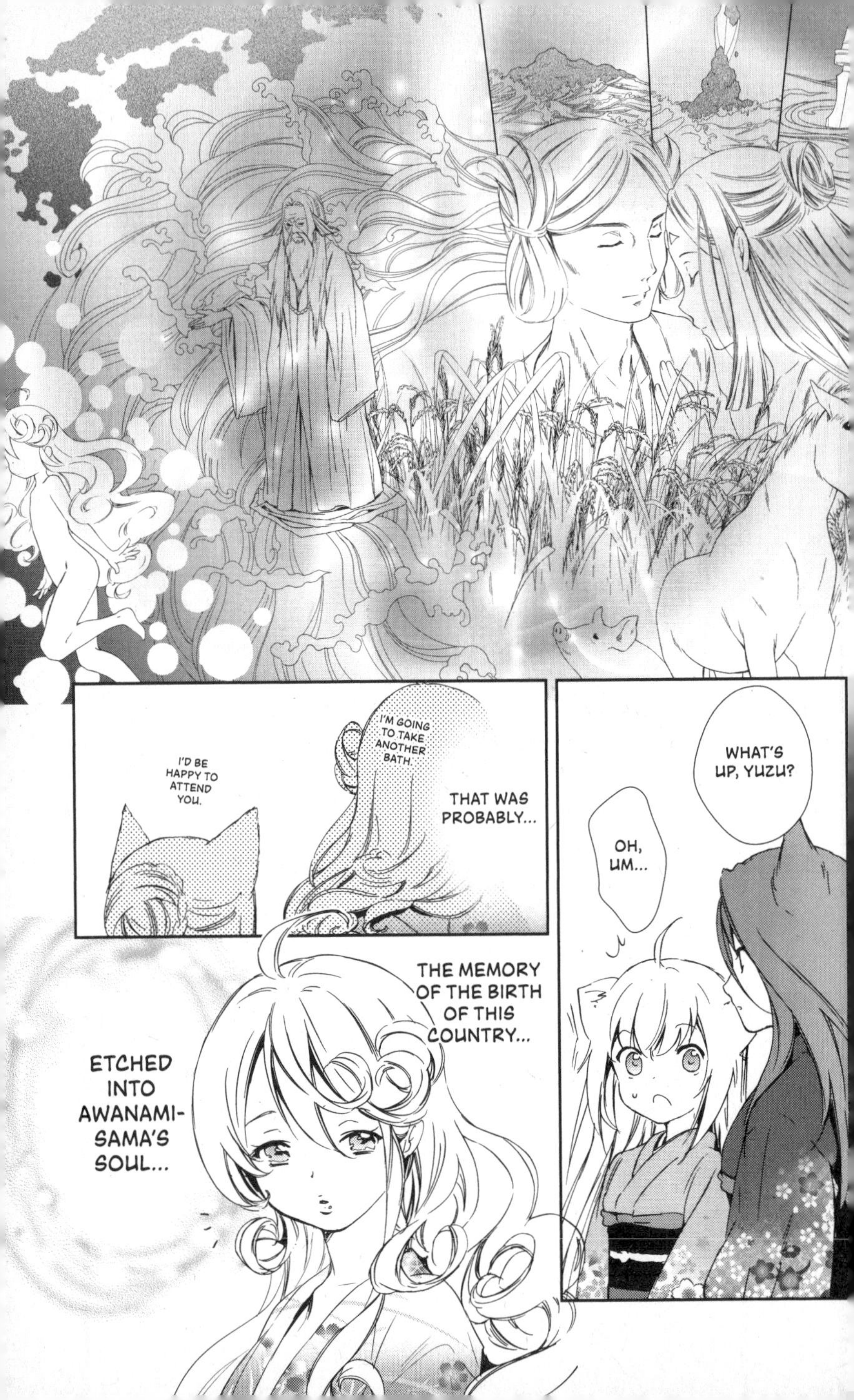
WHAT'S UP, YUZU?
OH, UM...
I'M GOING TO TAKE ANOTHER BATH.
I'D BE HAPPY TO ATTEND YOU.
THAT WAS PROBABLY...
THE MEMORY OF THE BIRTH OF THIS COUNTRY...
ETCHED INTO AWANAMI-SAMA'S SOUL...

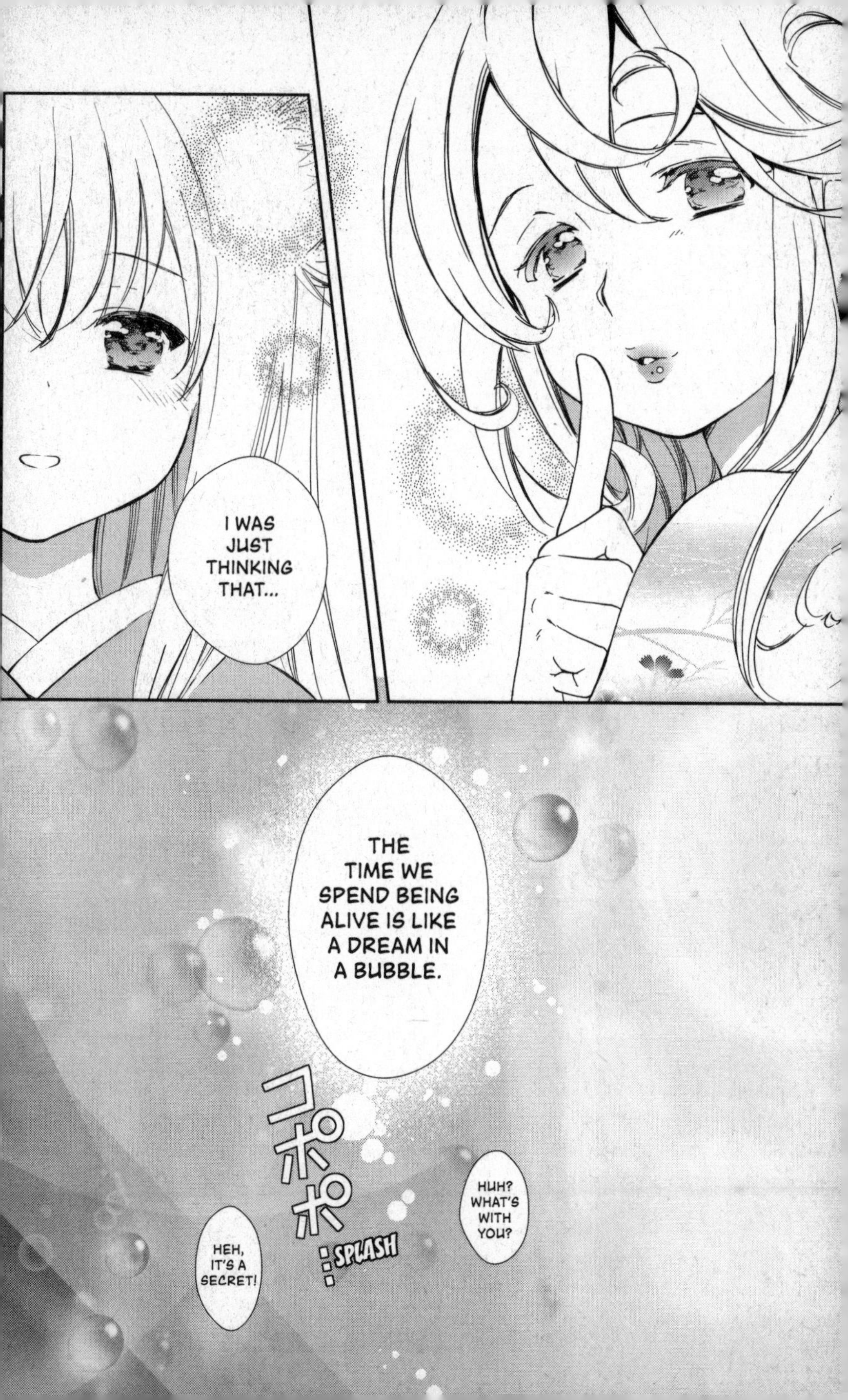
I WAS JUST THINKING THAT...
THE TIME WE SPEND BEING ALIVE IS LIKE A DREAM IN A BUBBLE.
コポポ
SPLASH
HUH? WHAT'S WITH YOU?
HEH, IT'S A SECRET!

KONOHANA KITAN

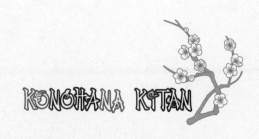

The Sound of Waves

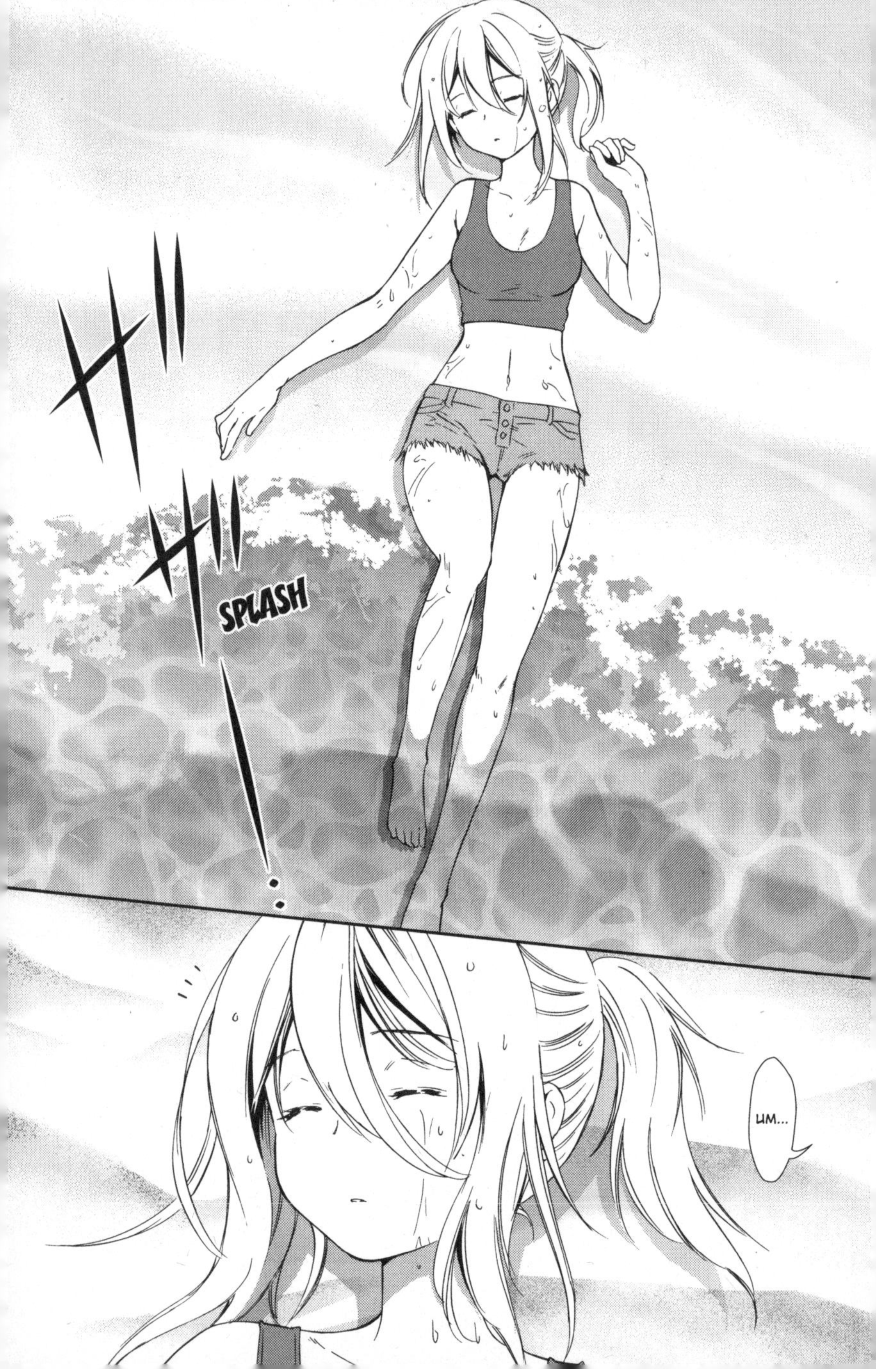
SPLASH
UM...

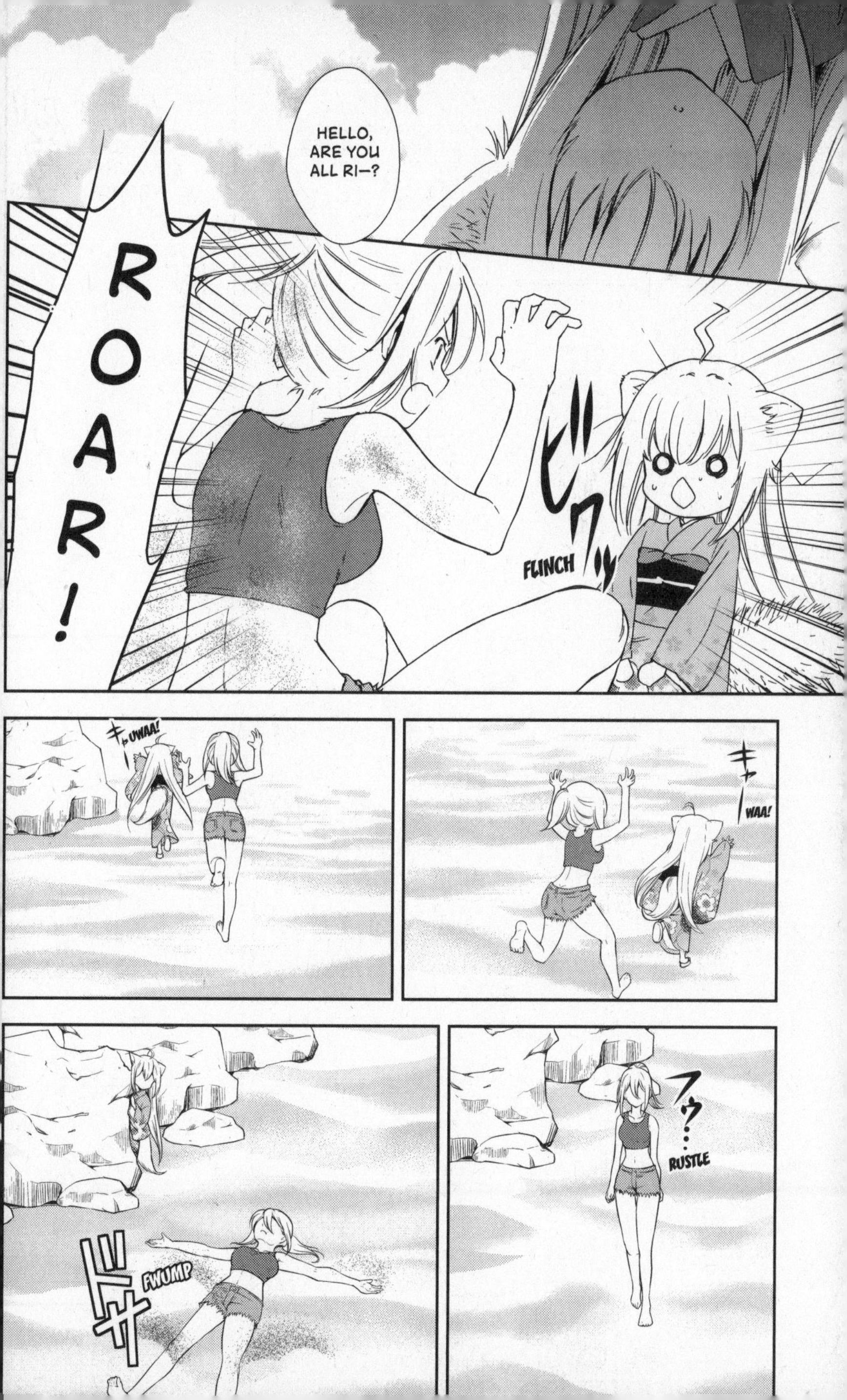
HELLO, ARE YOU ALL RI—?
ROAR!
FLINCH
WAA!
UWAA!
RUSTLE
FWUMP

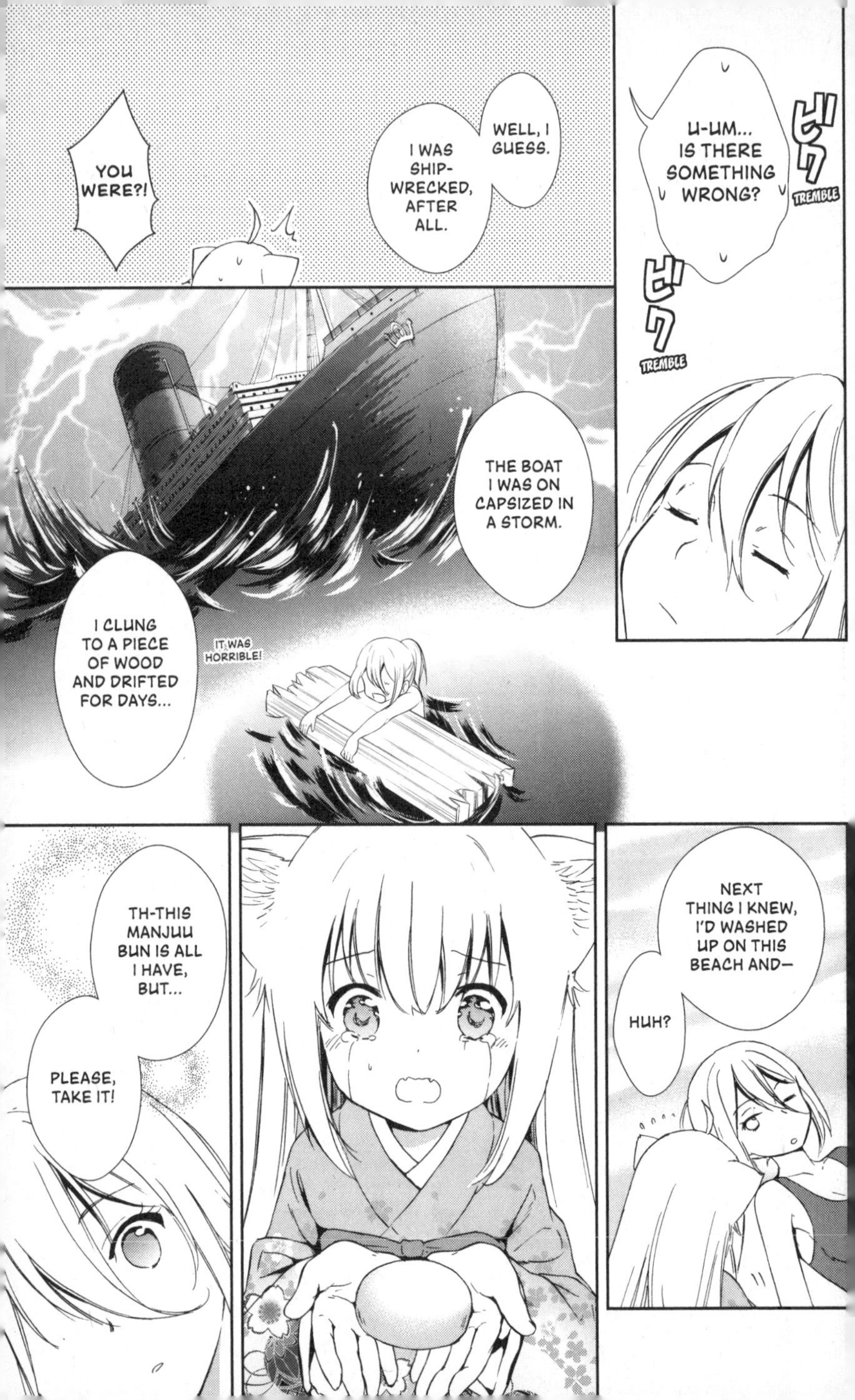
U-UM... IS THERE SOMETHING WRONG?
TREMBLE
TREMBLE
WELL, I GUESS.
I WAS SHIP-WRECKED, AFTER ALL.
YOU WERE?!
THE BOAT I WAS ON CAPSIZED IN A STORM.
I CLUNG TO A PIECE OF WOOD AND DRIFTED FOR DAYS...
IT WAS HORRIBLE!
NEXT THING I KNEW, I'D WASHED UP ON THIS BEACH AND—
HUH?
TH-THIS MANJUU BUN IS ALL I HAVE, BUT...
PLEASE, TAKE IT!

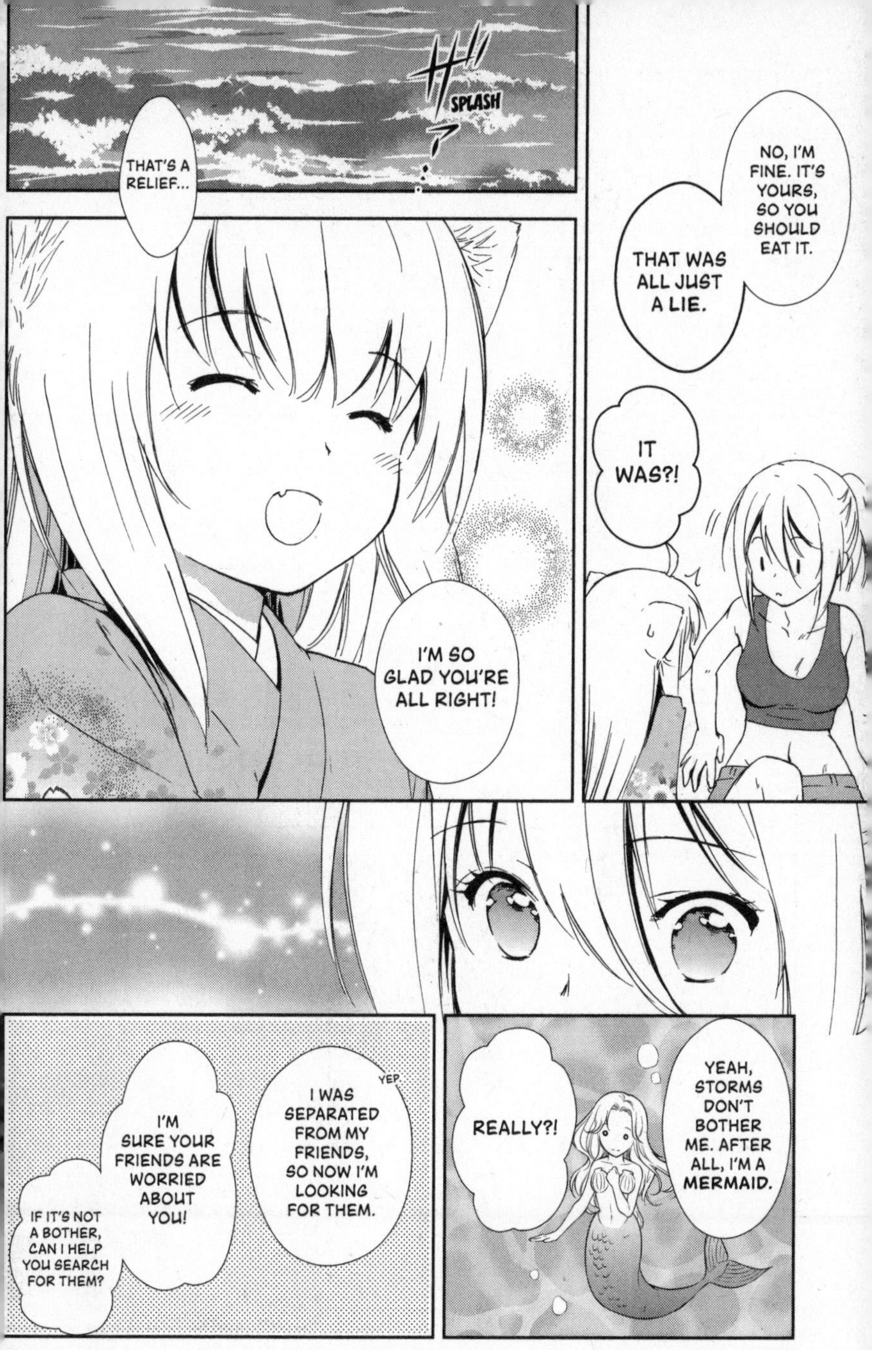
NO, I'M FINE. IT'S YOURS, SO YOU SHOULD EAT IT.
THAT WAS ALL JUST A LIE.
IT WAS?!
SPLASH
THAT'S A RELIEF...
I'M SO GLAD YOU'RE ALL RIGHT!
YEAH, STORMS DON'T BOTHER ME. AFTER ALL, I'M A MERMAID.
REALLY?!
YEP.
I WAS SEPARATED FROM MY FRIENDS, SO NOW I'M LOOKING FOR THEM.
I'M SURE YOUR FRIENDS ARE WORRIED ABOUT YOU!
IF IT'S NOT A BOTHER, CAN I HELP YOU SEARCH FOR THEM?

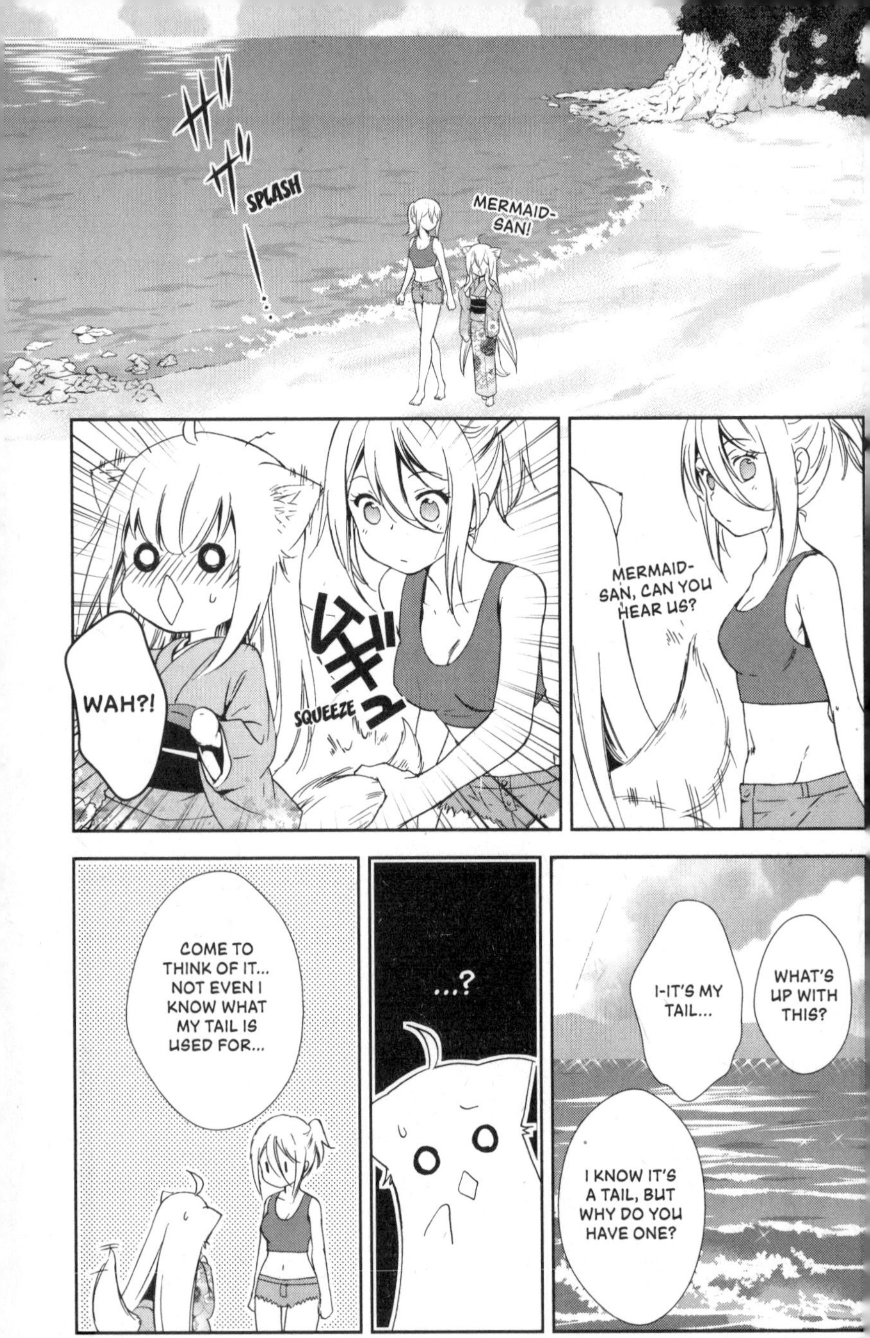
MERMAID-SAN!
SPLASH
MERMAID-SAN, CAN YOU HEAR US?
SQUEEZE
WAH?!
WHAT'S UP WITH THIS?
I-IT'S MY TAIL...
I KNOW IT'S A TAIL, BUT WHY DO YOU HAVE ONE?
...?
COME TO THINK OF IT... NOT EVEN I KNOW WHAT MY TAIL IS USED FOR...

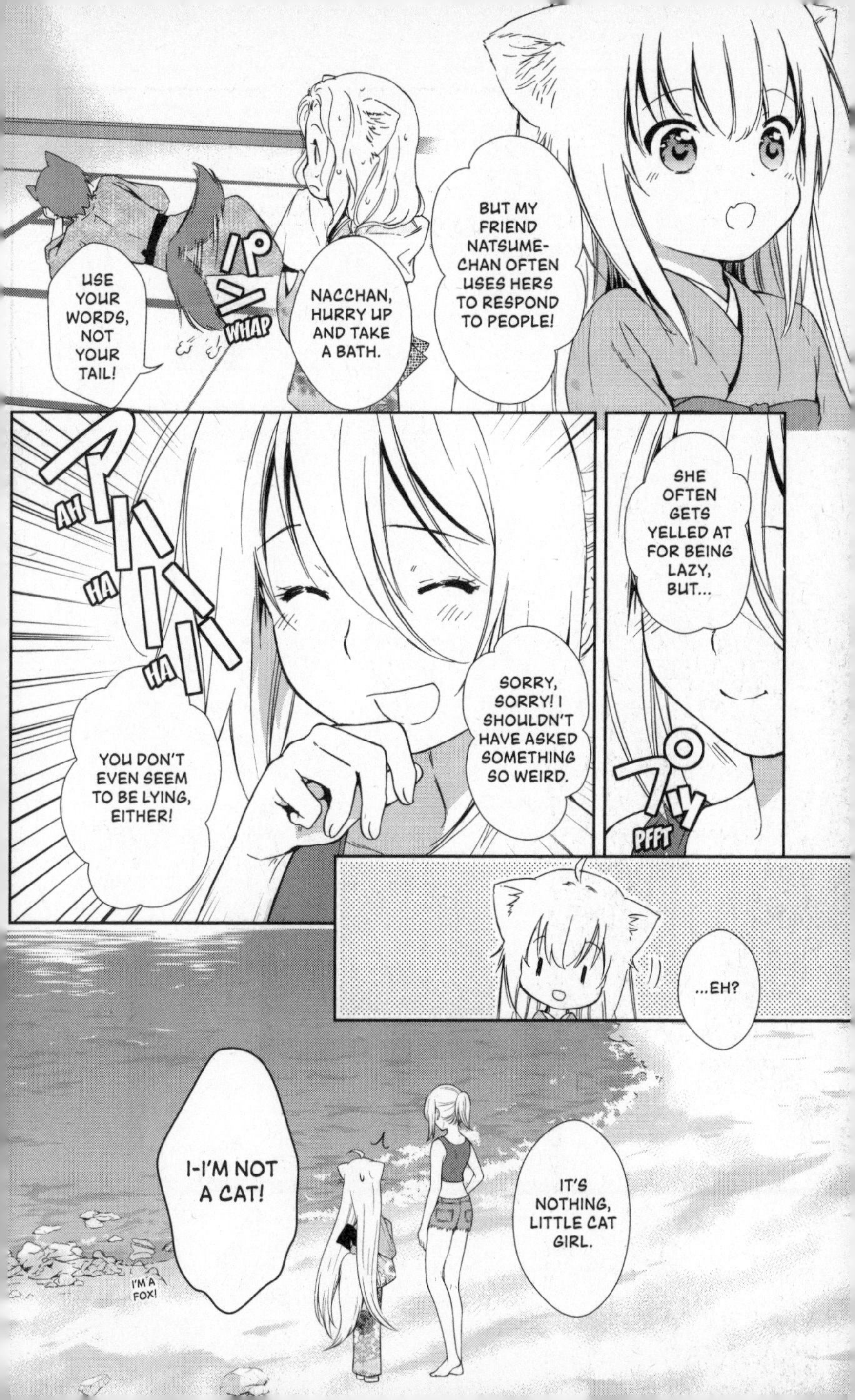

BUT MY FRIEND NATSUME-CHAN OFTEN USES HERS TO RESPOND TO PEOPLE!
NACCHAN, HURRY UP AND TAKE A BATH.
WHAP
USE YOUR WORDS, NOT YOUR TAIL!
SHE OFTEN GETS YELLED AT FOR BEING LAZY, BUT...
PFFT
AH HA HA
SORRY, SORRY! I SHOULDN'T HAVE ASKED SOMETHING SO WEIRD.
YOU DON'T EVEN SEEM TO BE LYING, EITHER!
...EH?
IT'S NOTHING, LITTLE CAT GIRL.
I-I'M NOT A CAT!
I'M A FOX!

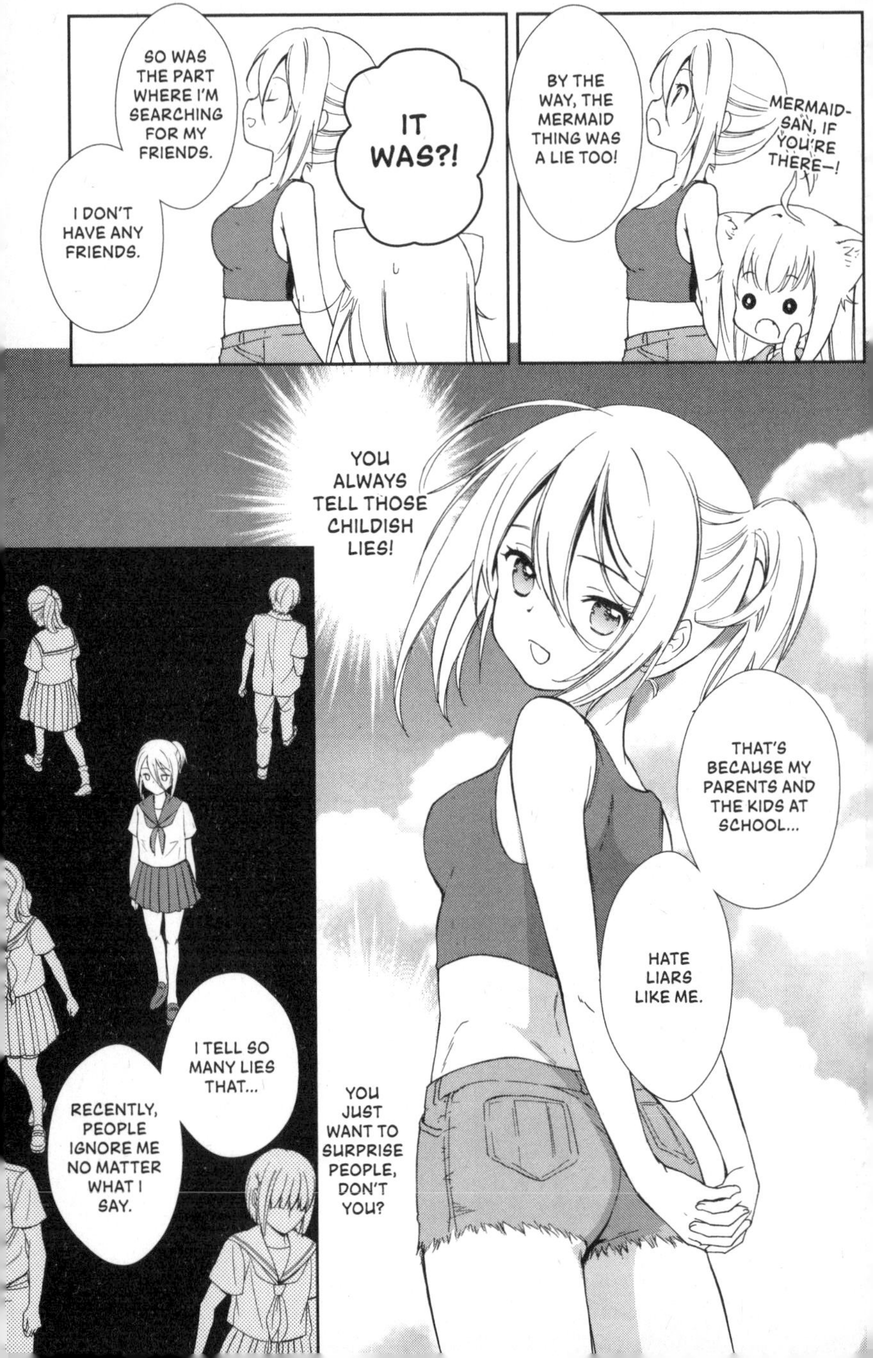
MERMAID-SAN, IF YOU'RE THERE—!
BY THE WAY, THE MERMAID THING WAS A LIE TOO!
IT WAS?!
SO WAS THE PART WHERE I'M SEARCHING FOR MY FRIENDS.
I DON'T HAVE ANY FRIENDS.
YOU ALWAYS TELL THOSE CHILDISH LIES!
THAT'S BECAUSE MY PARENTS AND THE KIDS AT SCHOOL...
HATE LIARS LIKE ME.
YOU JUST WANT TO SURPRISE PEOPLE, DON'T YOU?
I TELL SO MANY LIES THAT...
RECENTLY, PEOPLE IGNORE ME NO MATTER WHAT I SAY.

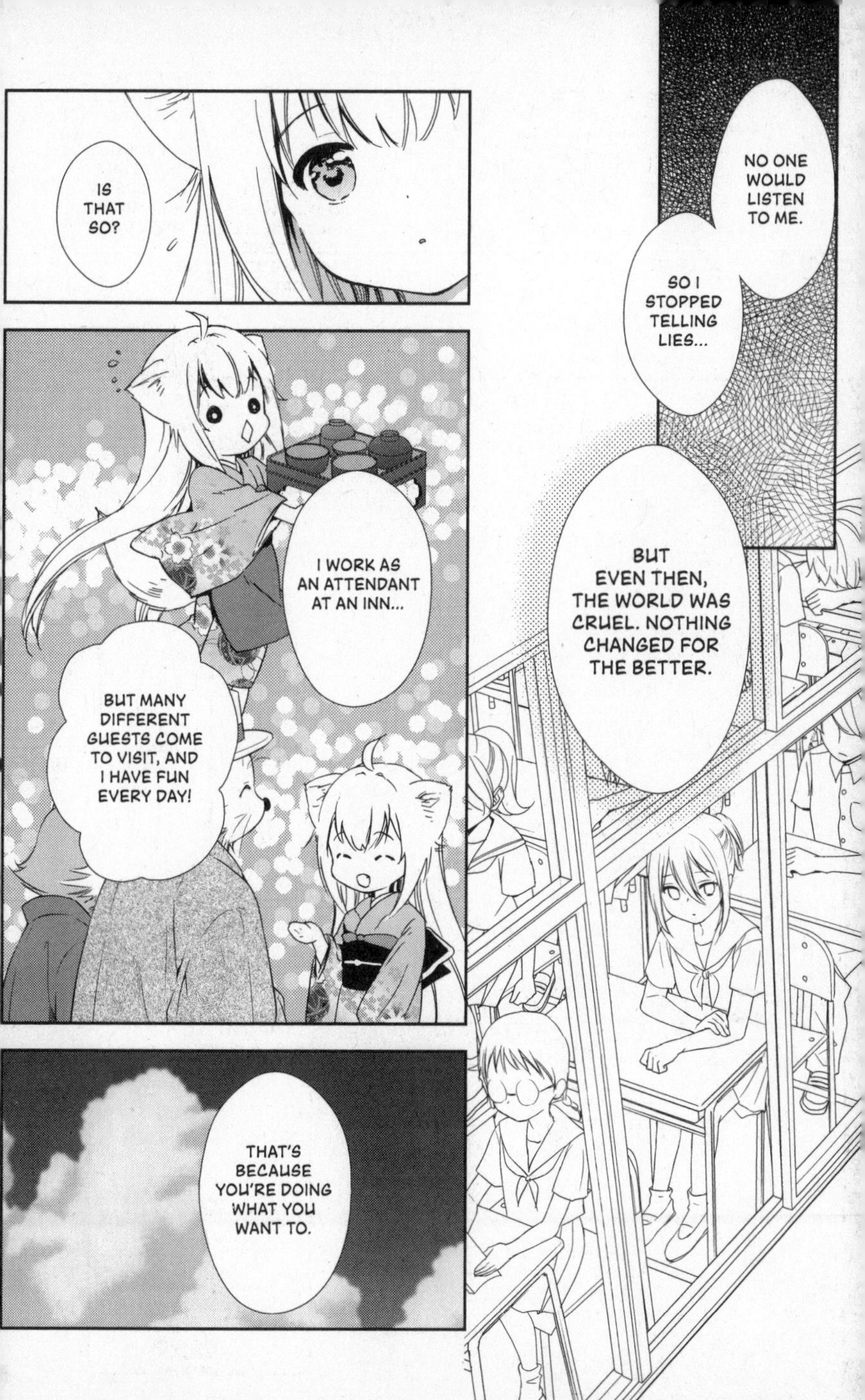
NO ONE WOULD LISTEN TO ME.
SO I STOPPED TELLING LIES...
BUT EVEN THEN, THE WORLD WAS CRUEL. NOTHING CHANGED FOR THE BETTER.
IS THAT SO?
I WORK AS AN ATTENDANT AT AN INN...
BUT MANY DIFFERENT GUESTS COME TO VISIT, AND I HAVE FUN EVERY DAY!
THAT'S BECAUSE YOU'RE DOING WHAT YOU WANT TO.

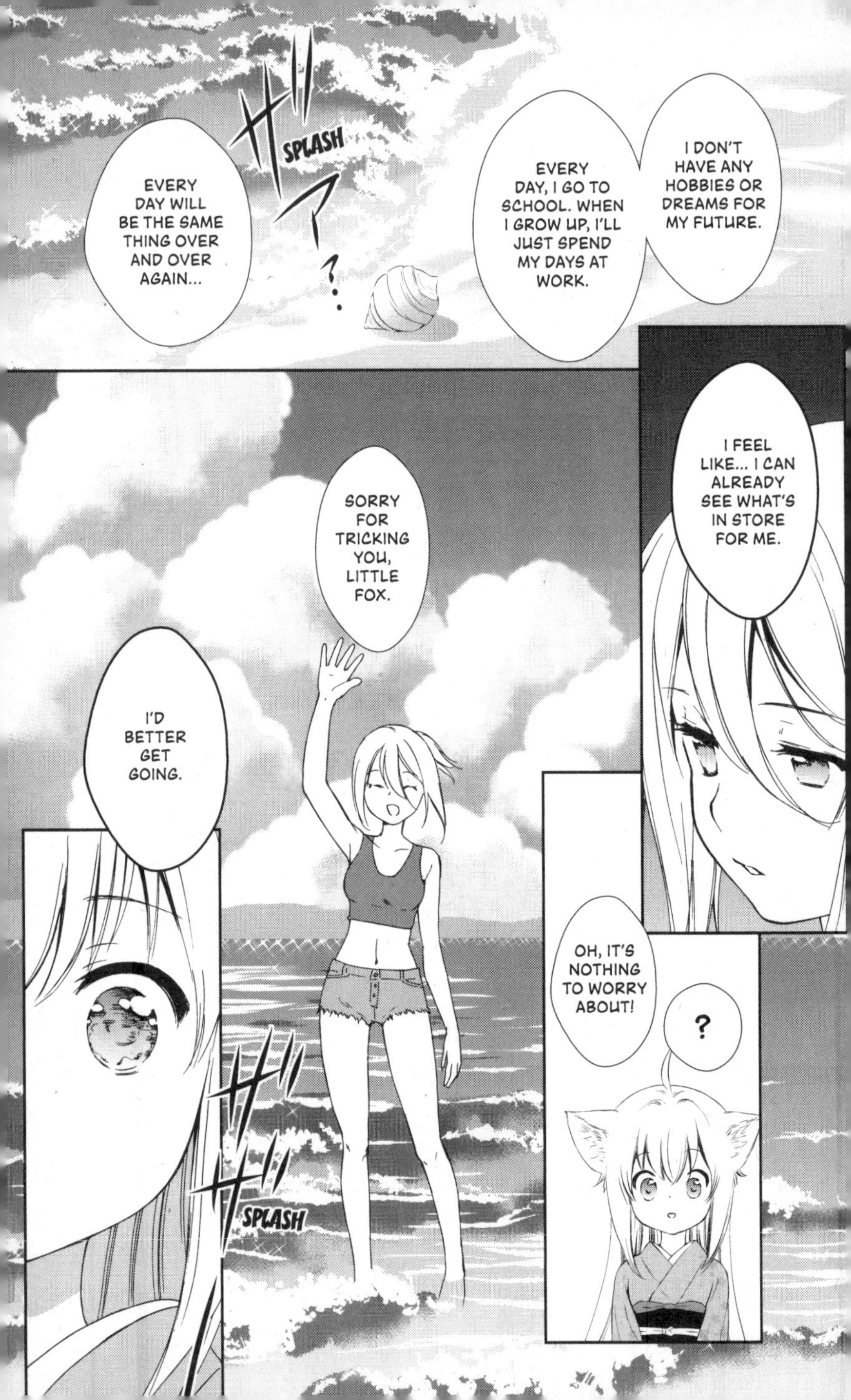
I DON'T HAVE ANY HOBBIES OR DREAMS FOR MY FUTURE.
EVERY DAY, I GO TO SCHOOL. WHEN I GROW UP, I'LL JUST SPEND MY DAYS AT WORK.
SPLASH
EVERY DAY WILL BE THE SAME THING OVER AND OVER AGAIN...
?..
I FEEL LIKE... I CAN ALREADY SEE WHAT'S IN STORE FOR ME.
SORRY FOR TRICKING YOU, LITTLE FOX.
I'D BETTER GET GOING.
OH, IT'S NOTHING TO WORRY ABOUT!
?
SPLASH

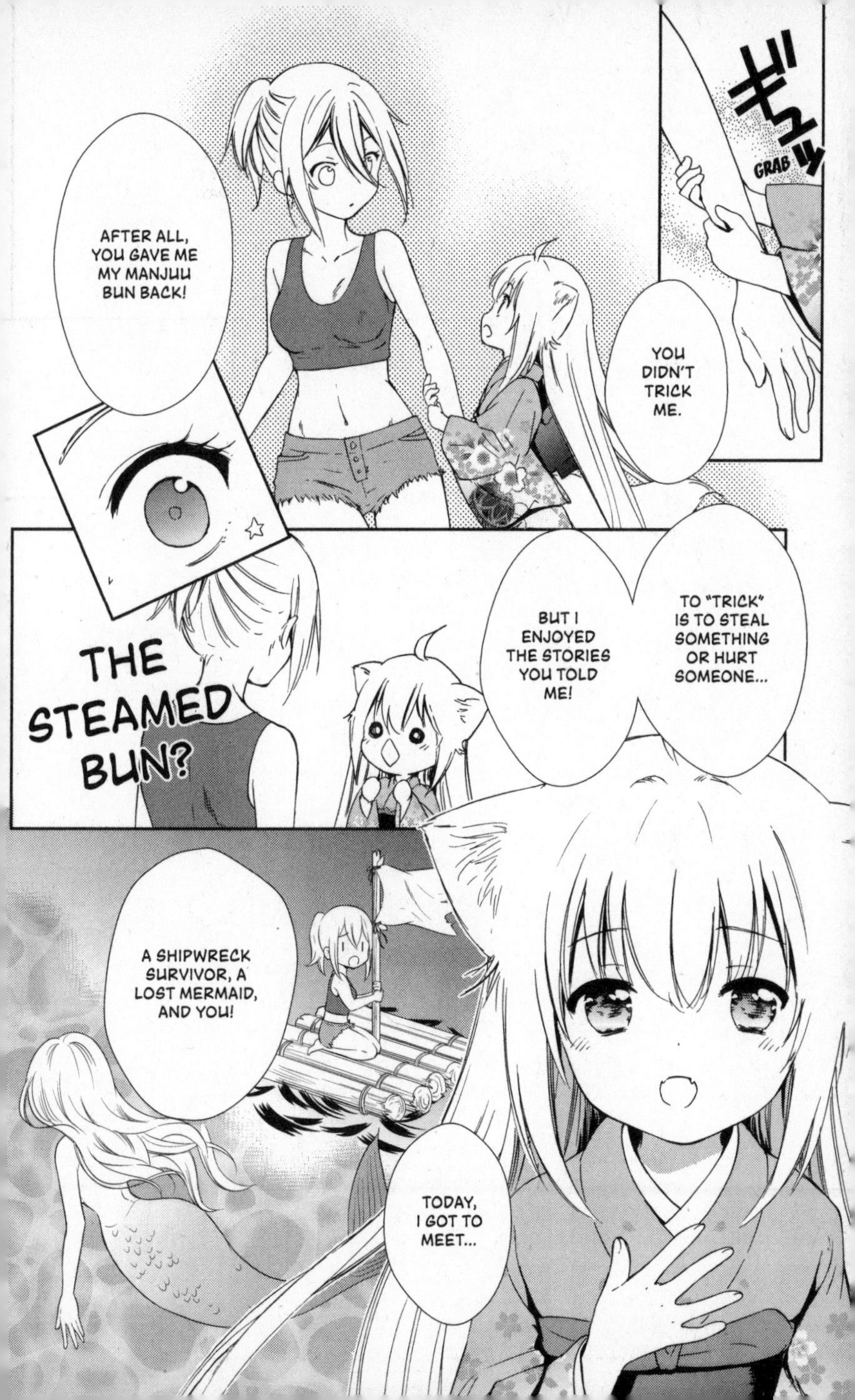

ギュッ
GRAB
YOU DIDN'T TRICK ME.
AFTER ALL, YOU GAVE ME MY MANJUU BUN BACK!
THE STEAMED BUN?
TO "TRICK" IS TO STEAL SOMETHING OR HURT SOMEONE...
BUT I ENJOYED THE STORIES YOU TOLD ME!
TODAY, I GOT TO MEET...
A SHIPWRECK SURVIVOR, A LOST MERMAID, AND YOU!

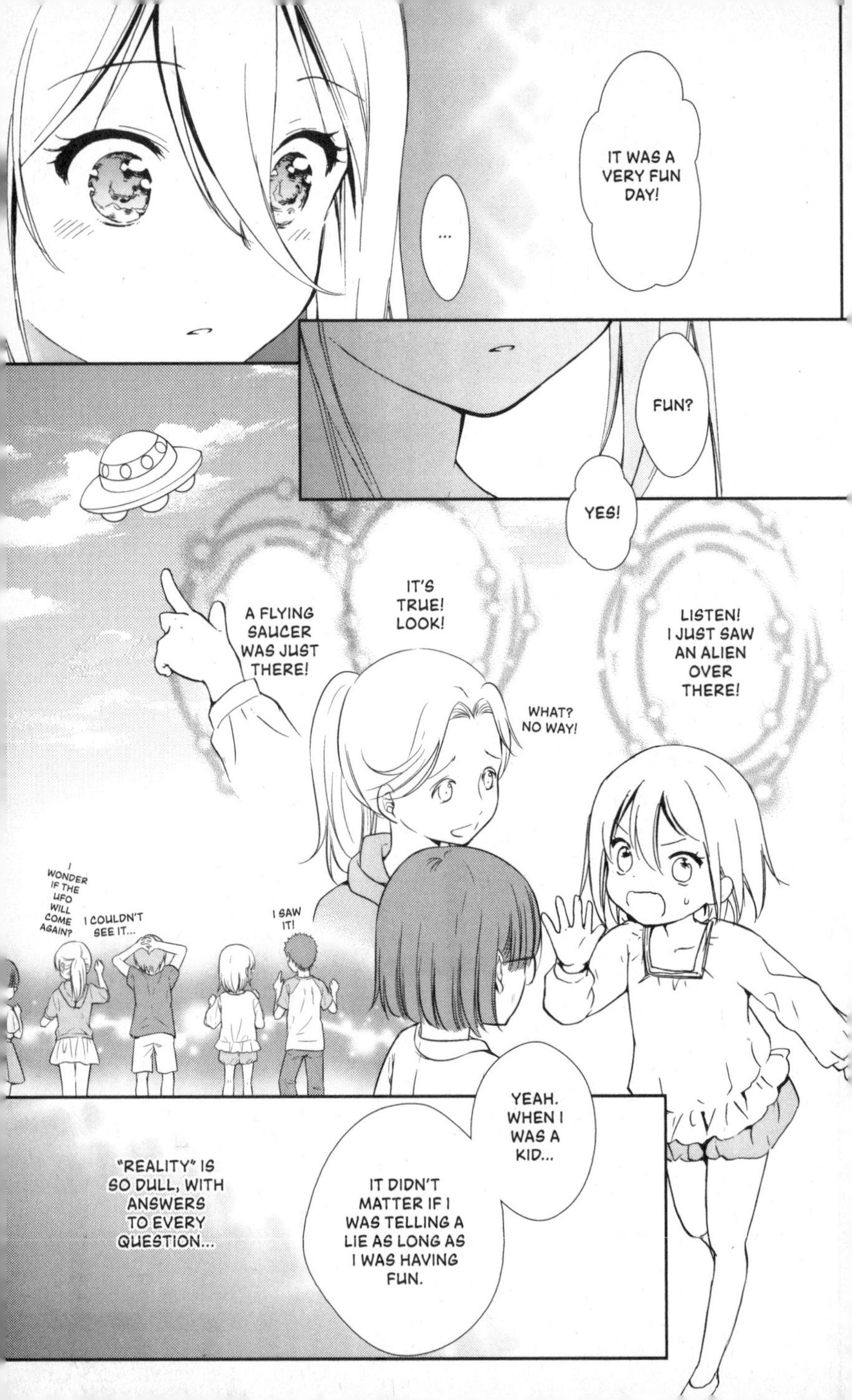
IT WAS A VERY FUN DAY!
...
FUN?
YES!
LISTEN! I JUST SAW AN ALIEN OVER THERE!
WHAT? NO WAY!
IT'S TRUE! LOOK!
A FLYING SAUCER WAS JUST THERE!
I SAW IT!
I COULDN'T SEE IT...
I WONDER IF THE UFO WILL COME AGAIN?
YEAH. WHEN I WAS A KID...
IT DIDN'T MATTER IF I WAS TELLING A LIE AS LONG AS I WAS HAVING FUN.
"REALITY" IS SO DULL, WITH ANSWERS TO EVERY QUESTION...

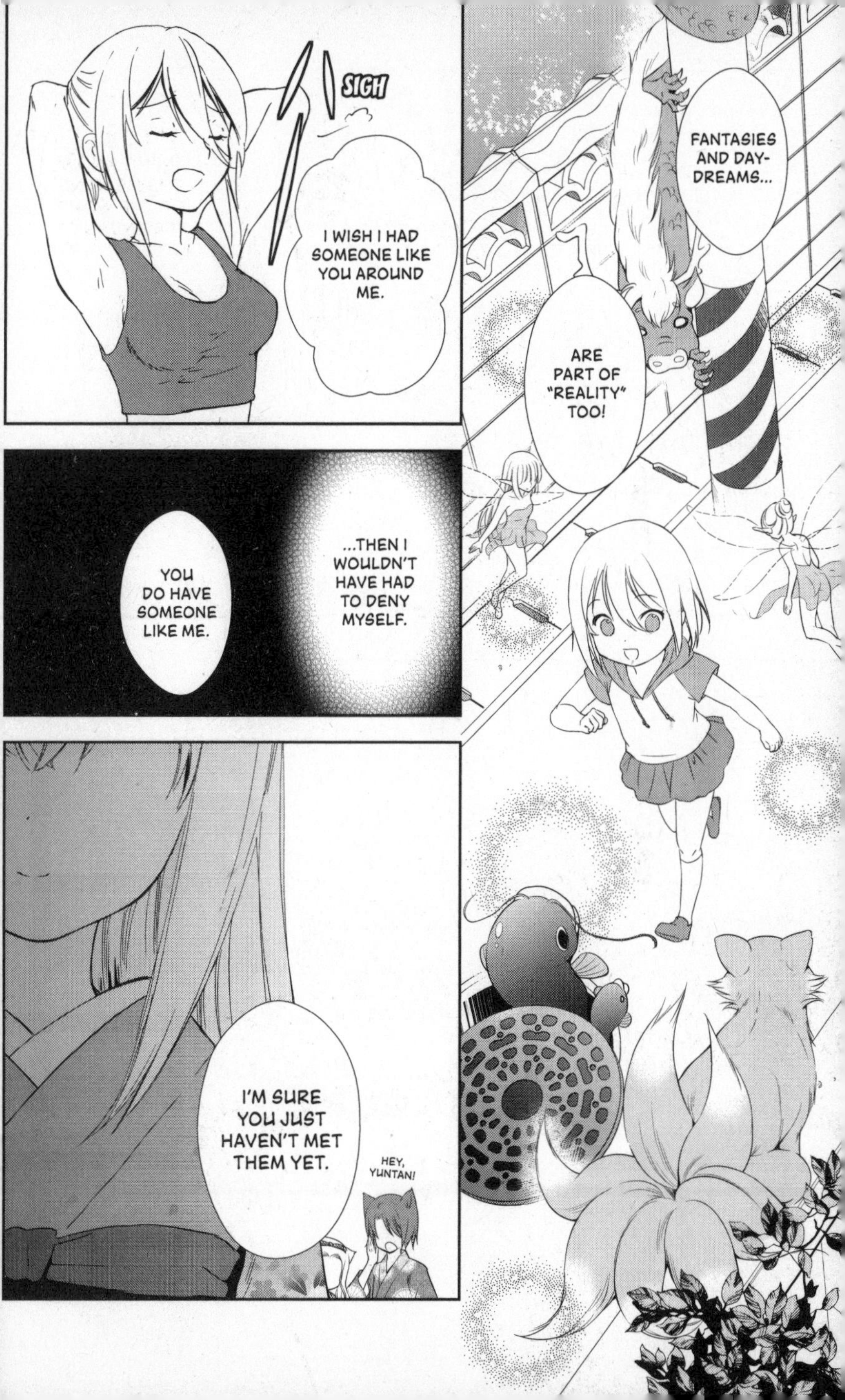
FANTASIES AND DAY-DREAMS...
ARE PART OF "REALITY" TOO!
SIGH
I WISH I HAD SOMEONE LIKE YOU AROUND ME.
...THEN I WOULDN'T HAVE HAD TO DENY MYSELF.
YOU DO HAVE SOMEONE LIKE ME.
I'M SURE YOU JUST HAVEN'T MET THEM YET.
HEY, YUNTAN!

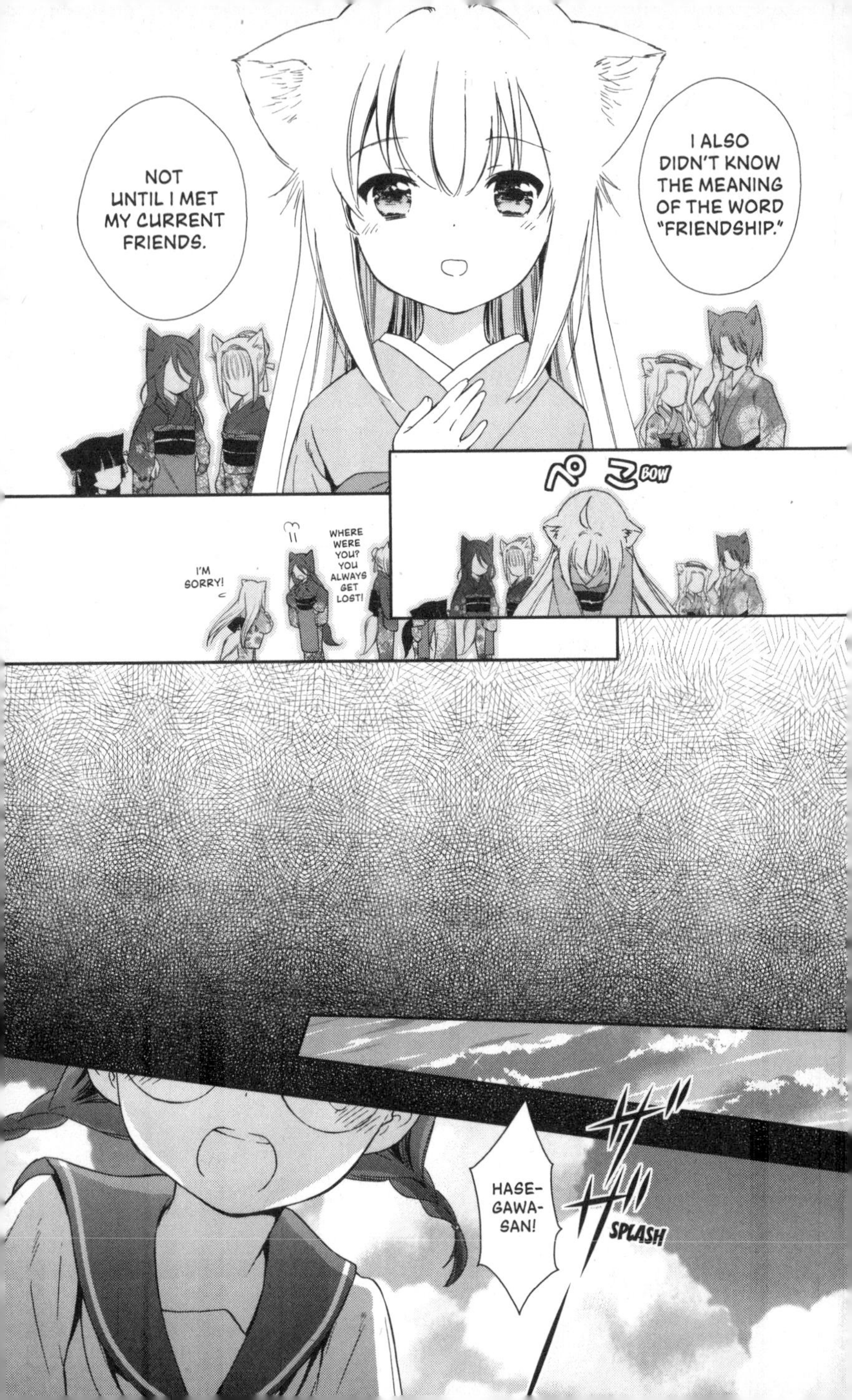
I ALSO DIDN'T KNOW THE MEANING OF THE WORD "FRIENDSHIP."
NOT UNTIL I MET MY CURRENT FRIENDS.
ぺこ BOW
WHERE WERE YOU? YOU ALWAYS GET LOST!
I'M SORRY!
ザザ SPLASH
HASE-GAWA-SAN!

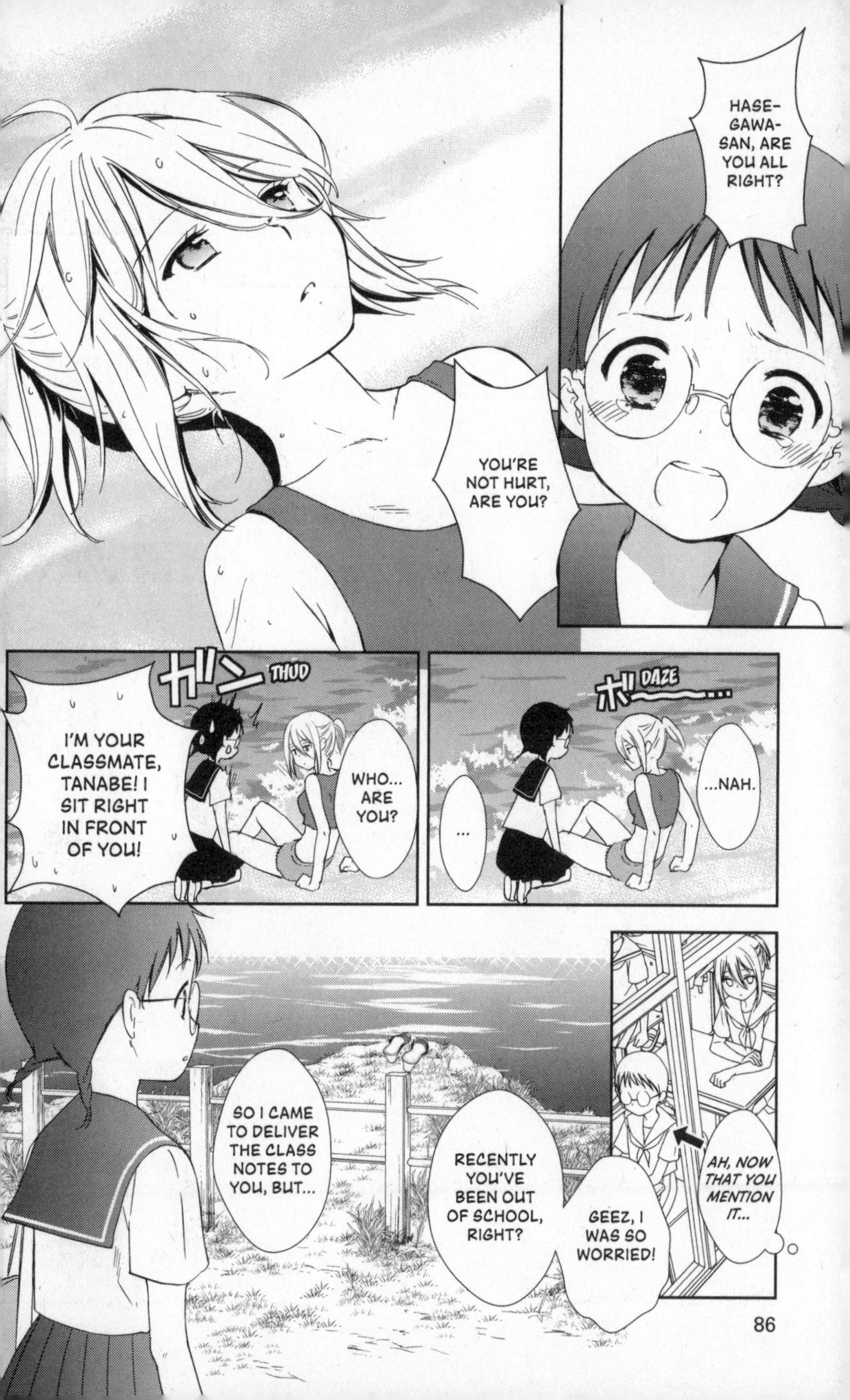
HASE-GAWA-SAN, ARE YOU ALL RIGHT?
YOU'RE NOT HURT, ARE YOU?
DAZE
...NAH.
...
THUD
WHO... ARE YOU?
I'M YOUR CLASSMATE, TANABE! I SIT RIGHT IN FRONT OF YOU!
AH, NOW THAT YOU MENTION IT...
GEEZ, I WAS SO WORRIED!
RECENTLY YOU'VE BEEN OUT OF SCHOOL, RIGHT?
SO I CAME TO DELIVER THE CLASS NOTES TO YOU, BUT...

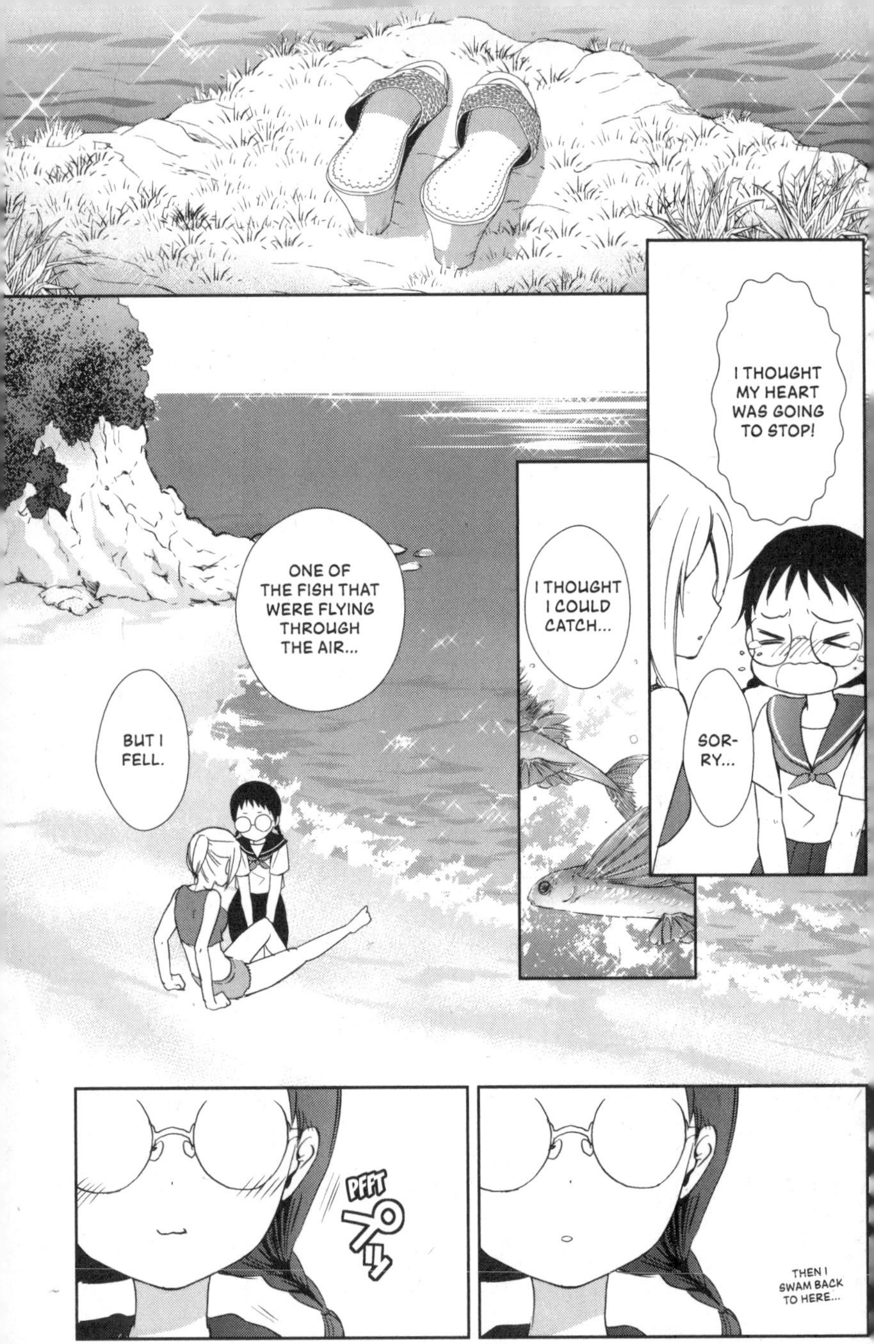
I THOUGHT MY HEART WAS GOING TO STOP!
SOR-RY...
I THOUGHT I COULD CATCH...
ONE OF THE FISH THAT WERE FLYING THROUGH THE AIR...
BUT I FELL.
THEN I SWAM BACK TO HERE...
PFFT

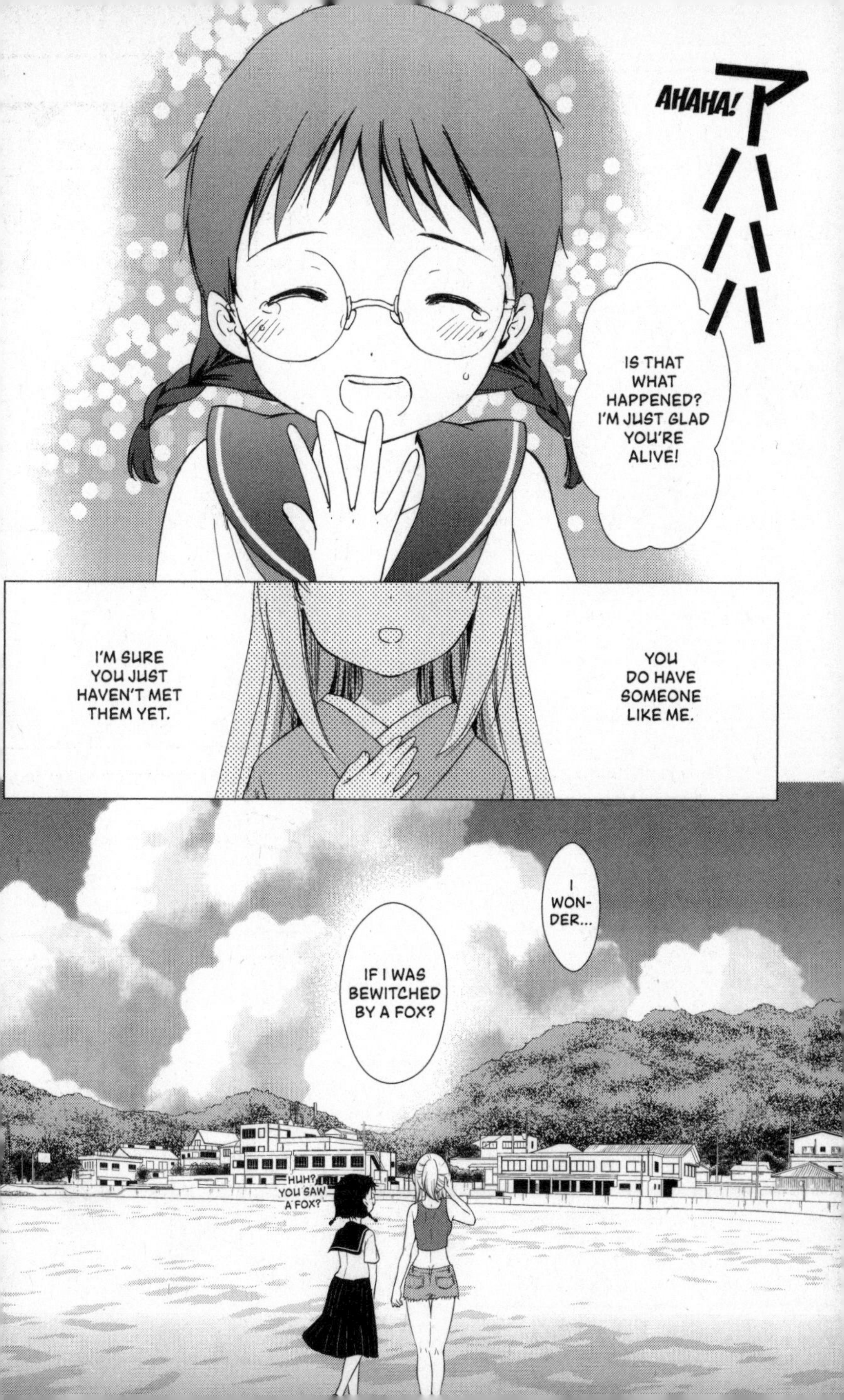
AHAHA!
IS THAT WHAT HAPPENED? I'M JUST GLAD YOU'RE ALIVE!
YOU DO HAVE SOMEONE LIKE ME.
I'M SURE YOU JUST HAVEN'T MET THEM YET.
I WONDER...
IF I WAS BEWITCHED BY A FOX?
HUH? YOU SAW A FOX?

The Sister Strikes

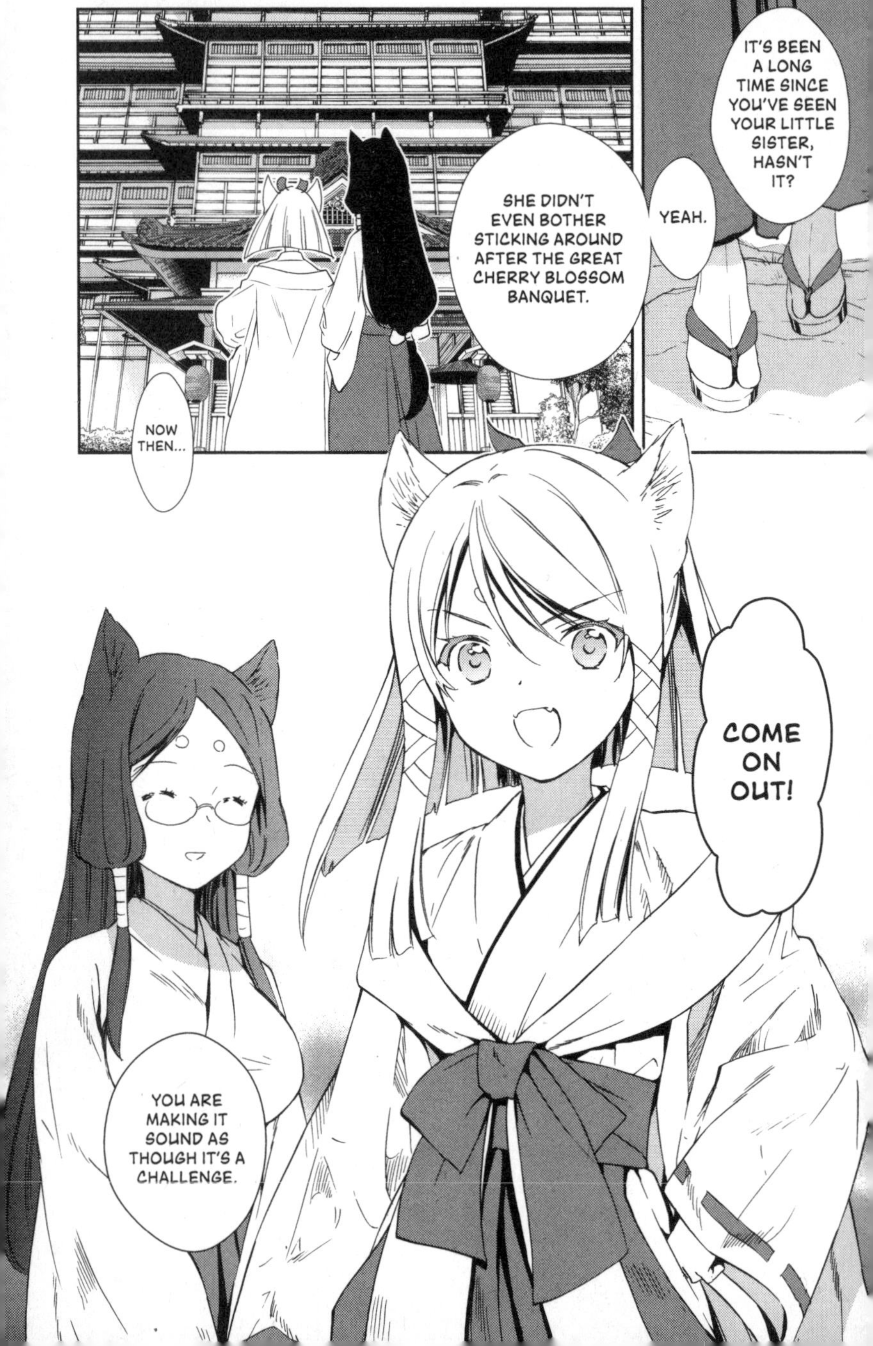
IT'S BEEN A LONG TIME SINCE YOU'VE SEEN YOUR LITTLE SISTER, HASN'T IT?
YEAH.
SHE DIDN'T EVEN BOTHER STICKING AROUND AFTER THE GREAT CHERRY BLOSSOM BANQUET.
NOW THEN...
COME ON OUT!
YOU ARE MAKING IT SOUND AS THOUGH IT'S A CHALLENGE.

The Sister Strikes

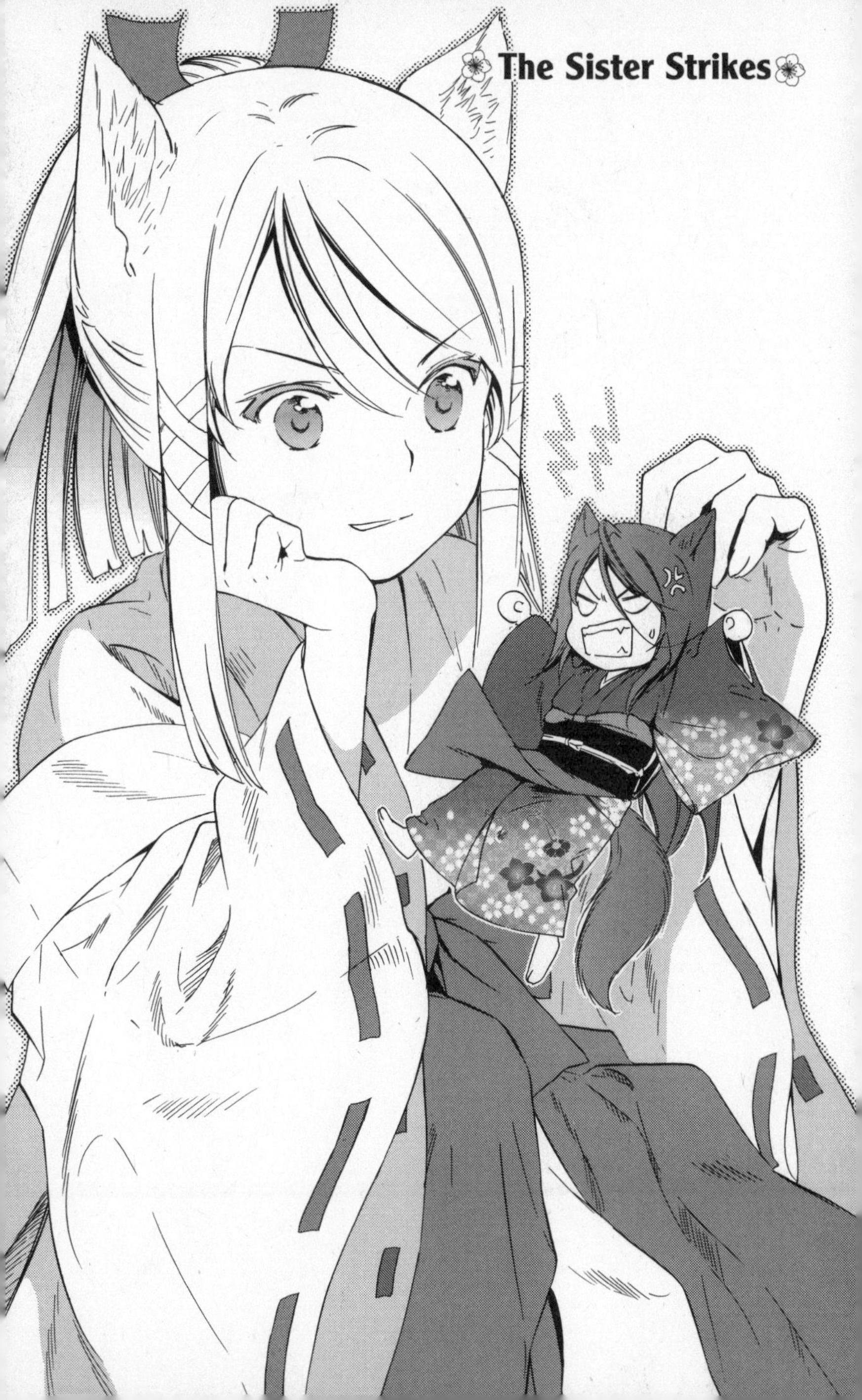

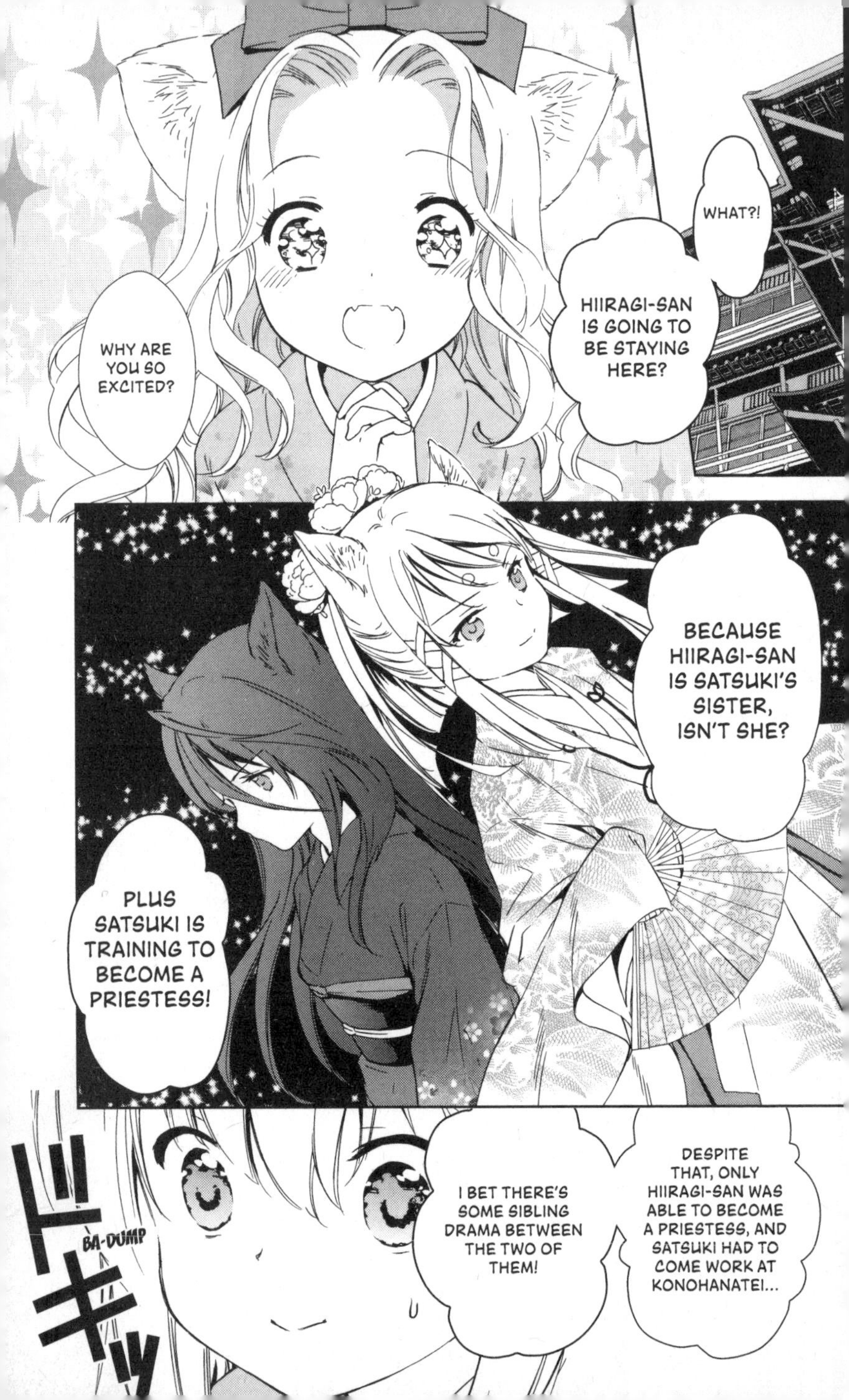
WHAT?!
HIIRAGI-SAN IS GOING TO BE STAYING HERE?
WHY ARE YOU SO EXCITED?
BECAUSE HIIRAGI-SAN IS SATSUKI'S SISTER, ISN'T SHE?
PLUS SATSUKI IS TRAINING TO BECOME A PRIESTESS!
DESPITE THAT, ONLY HIIRAGI-SAN WAS ABLE TO BECOME A PRIESTESS, AND SATSUKI HAD TO COME WORK AT KONOHANATEI...
I BET THERE'S SOME SIBLING DRAMA BETWEEN THE TWO OF THEM!
BA-DUMP

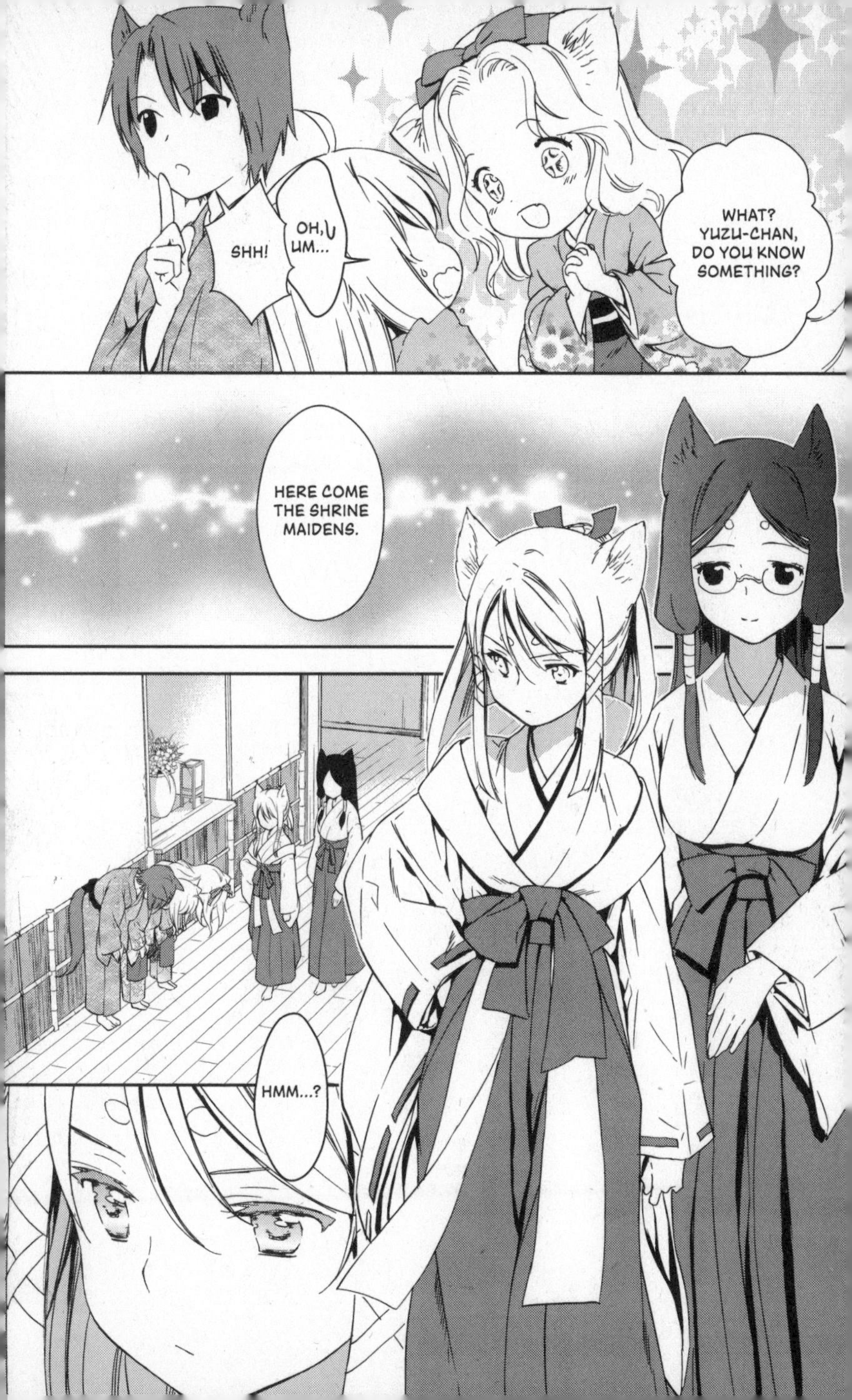
WHAT? YUZU-CHAN, DO YOU KNOW SOMETHING?
OH, UM...
SHH!
HERE COME THE SHRINE MAIDENS.
HMM...?

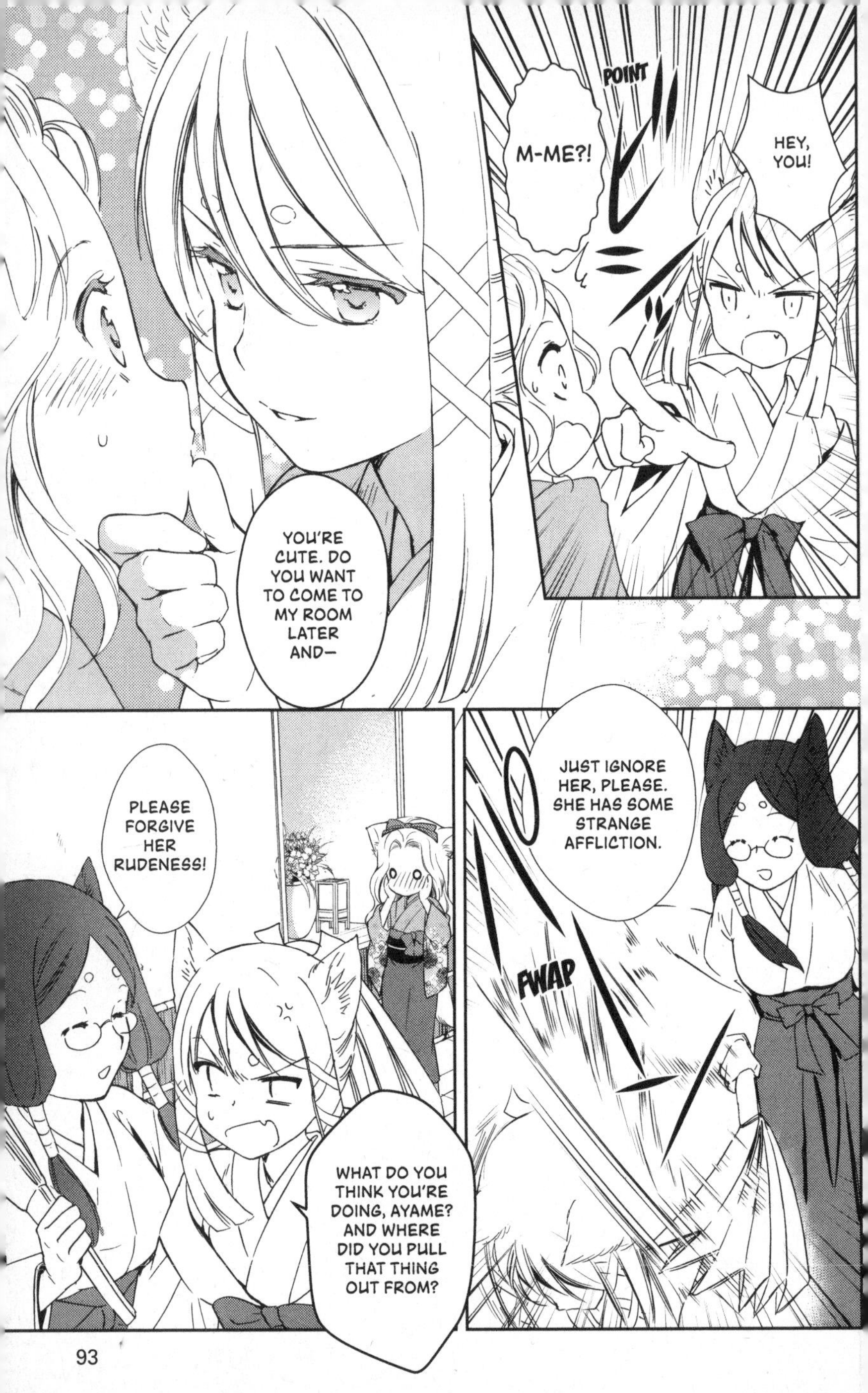
HEY, YOU!
POINT
M-ME?!
YOU'RE CUTE. DO YOU WANT TO COME TO MY ROOM LATER AND—
JUST IGNORE HER, PLEASE. SHE HAS SOME STRANGE AFFLICTION.
FWAP
PLEASE FORGIVE HER RUDENESS!
WHAT DO YOU THINK YOU'RE DOING, AYAME? AND WHERE DID YOU PULL THAT THING OUT FROM?

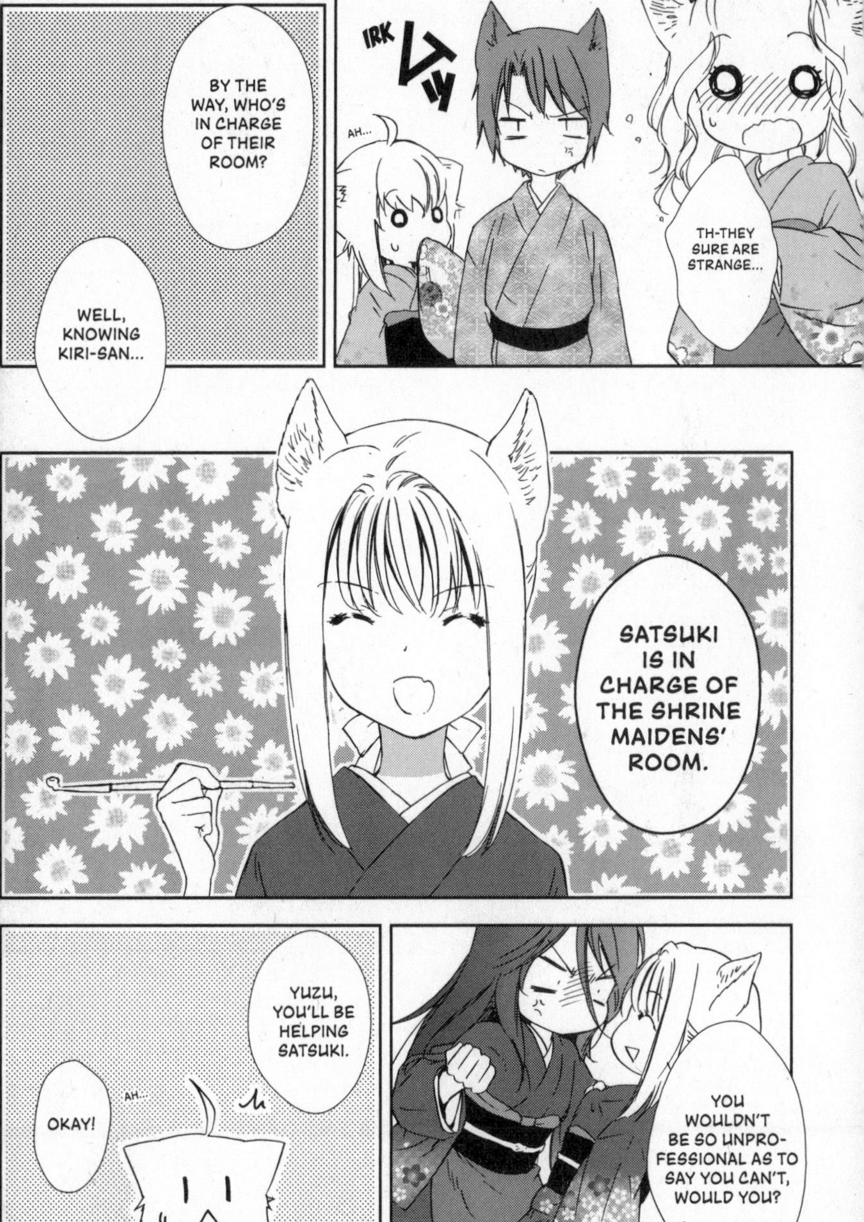
TH-THEY SURE ARE STRANGE...
IRK
AH...
BY THE WAY, WHO'S IN CHARGE OF THEIR ROOM?
WELL, KNOWING KIRI-SAN...
SATSUKI IS IN CHARGE OF THE SHRINE MAIDENS' ROOM.
YOU WOULDN'T BE SO UNPRO-FESSIONAL AS TO SAY YOU CAN'T, WOULD YOU?
RIGHT?
YUZU, YOU'LL BE HELPING SATSUKI.
AH...
OKAY!

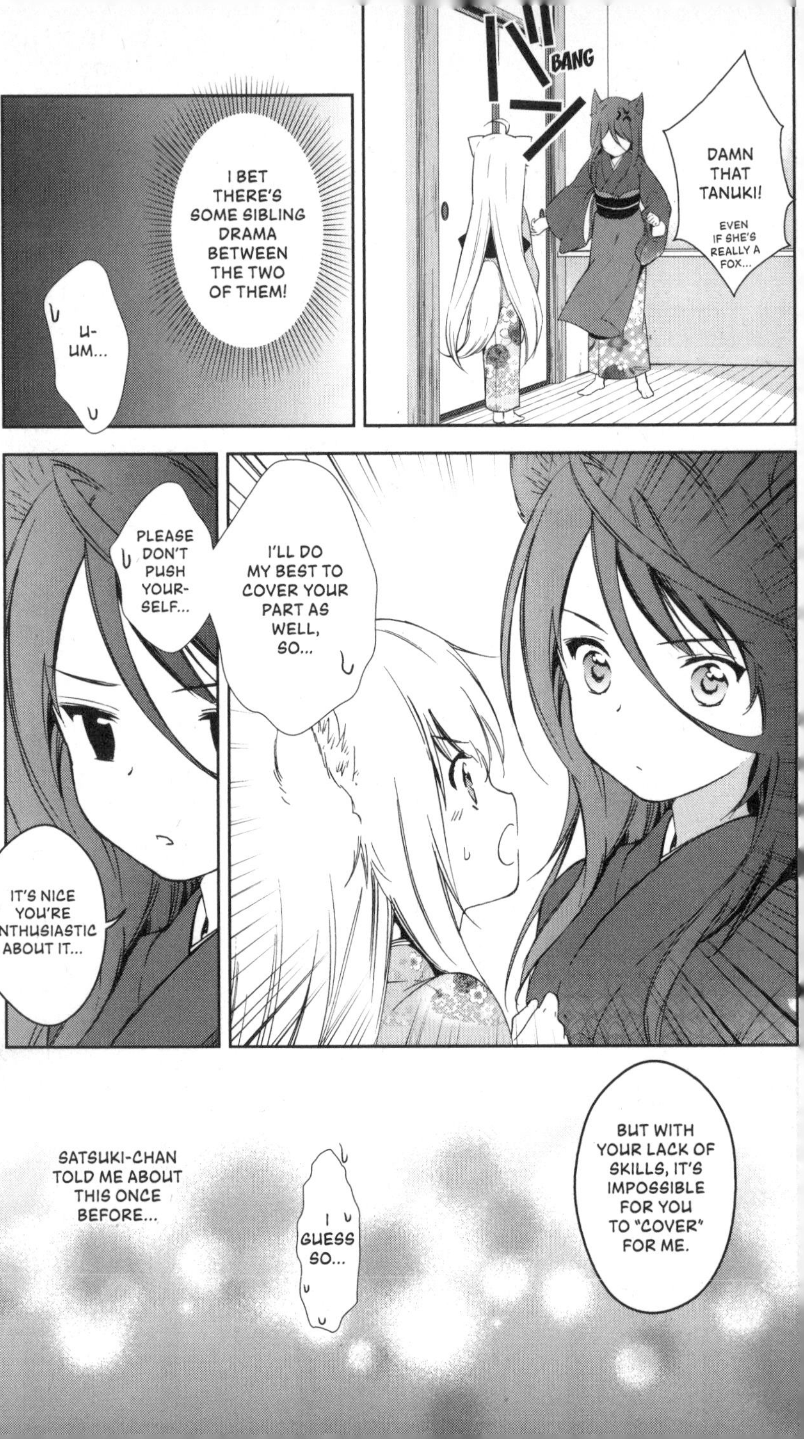
BANG
DAMN THAT TANUKI!
EVEN IF SHE'S REALLY A FOX...
I BET THERE'S SOME SIBLING DRAMA BETWEEN THE TWO OF THEM!
U-UM...
I'LL DO MY BEST TO COVER YOUR PART AS WELL, SO...
PLEASE DON'T PUSH YOURSELF...
IT'S NICE YOU'RE ENTHUSIASTIC ABOUT IT...
BUT WITH YOUR LACK OF SKILLS, IT'S IMPOSSIBLE FOR YOU TO "COVER" FOR ME.
I GUESS SO...
SATSUKI-CHAN TOLD ME ABOUT THIS ONCE BEFORE...

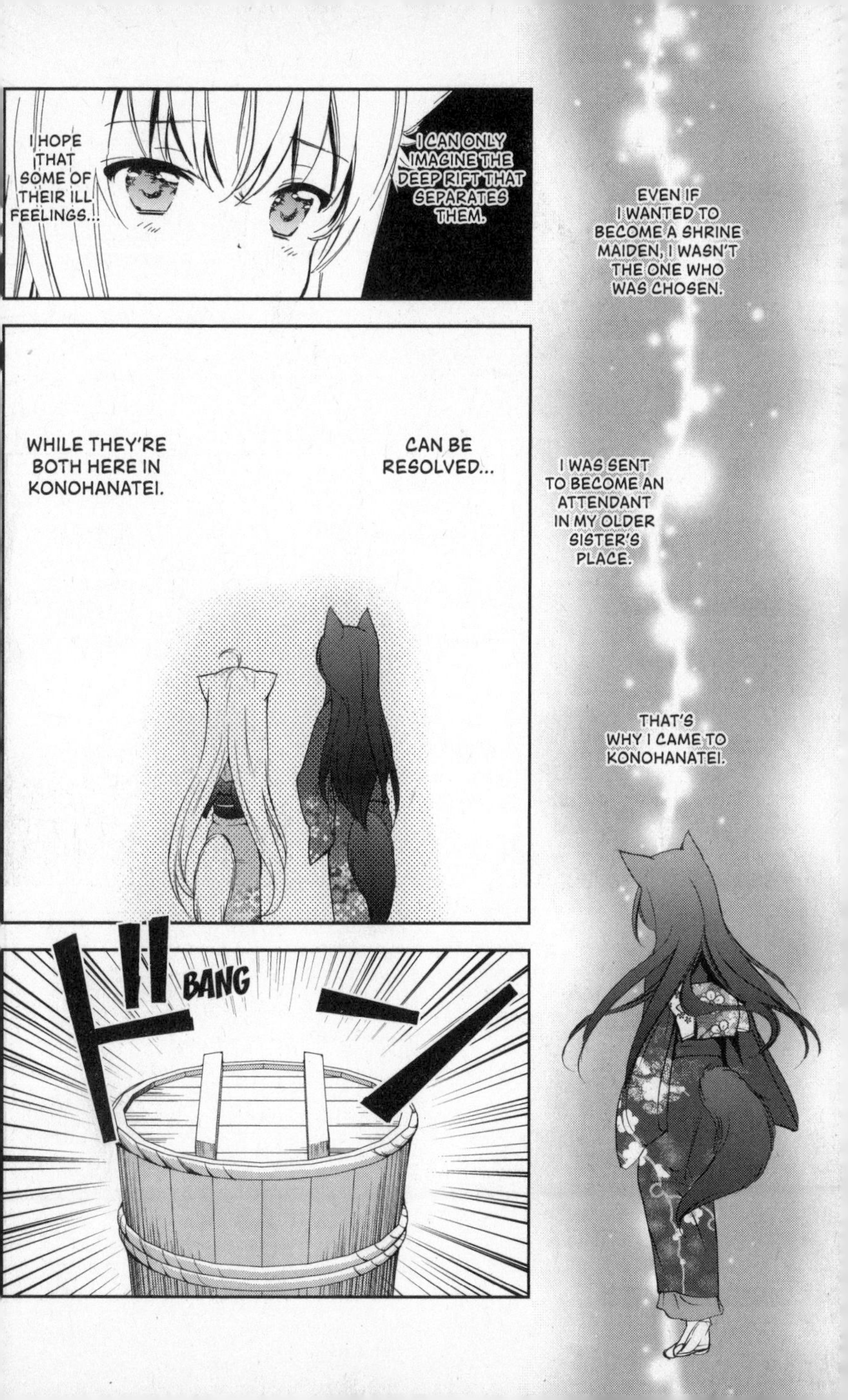
EVEN IF I WANTED TO BECOME A SHRINE MAIDEN, I WASN'T THE ONE WHO WAS CHOSEN.
I WAS SENT TO BECOME AN ATTENDANT IN MY OLDER SISTER'S PLACE.
THAT'S WHY I CAME TO KONOHANATEI.
I CAN ONLY IMAGINE THE DEEP RIFT THAT SEPARATES THEM.
I HOPE THAT SOME OF THEIR ILL FEELINGS...
CAN BE RESOLVED...
WHILE THEY'RE BOTH HERE IN KONOHANATEI.
BANG

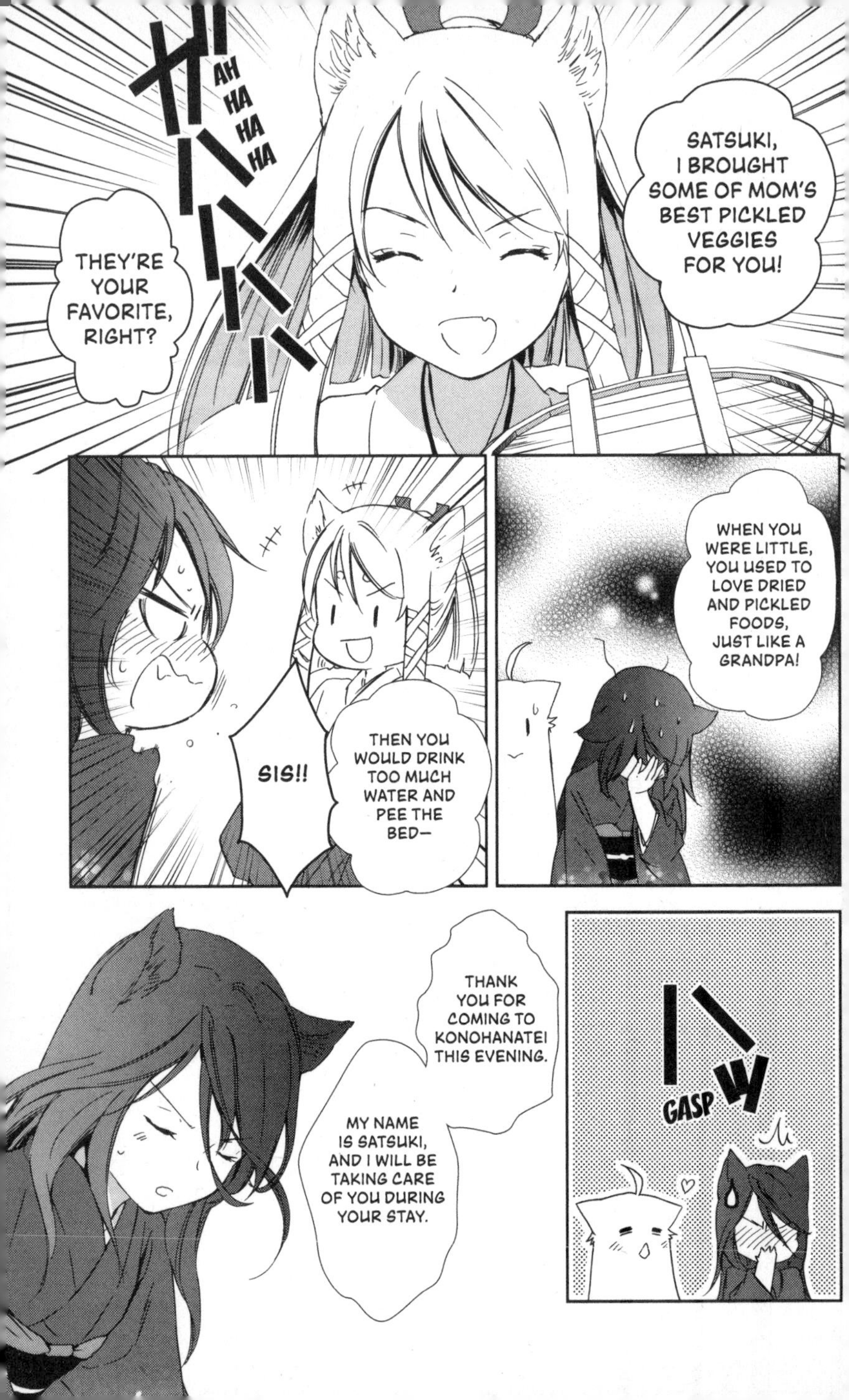
SATSUKI, I BROUGHT SOME OF MOM'S BEST PICKLED VEGGIES FOR YOU!
AH HA HA HA
THEY'RE YOUR FAVORITE, RIGHT?
WHEN YOU WERE LITTLE, YOU USED TO LOVE DRIED AND PICKLED FOODS, JUST LIKE A GRANDPA!
THEN YOU WOULD DRINK TOO MUCH WATER AND PEE THE BED—
SIS!!
GASP
THANK YOU FOR COMING TO KONOHANATEI THIS EVENING.
MY NAME IS SATSUKI, AND I WILL BE TAKING CARE OF YOU DURING YOUR STAY.

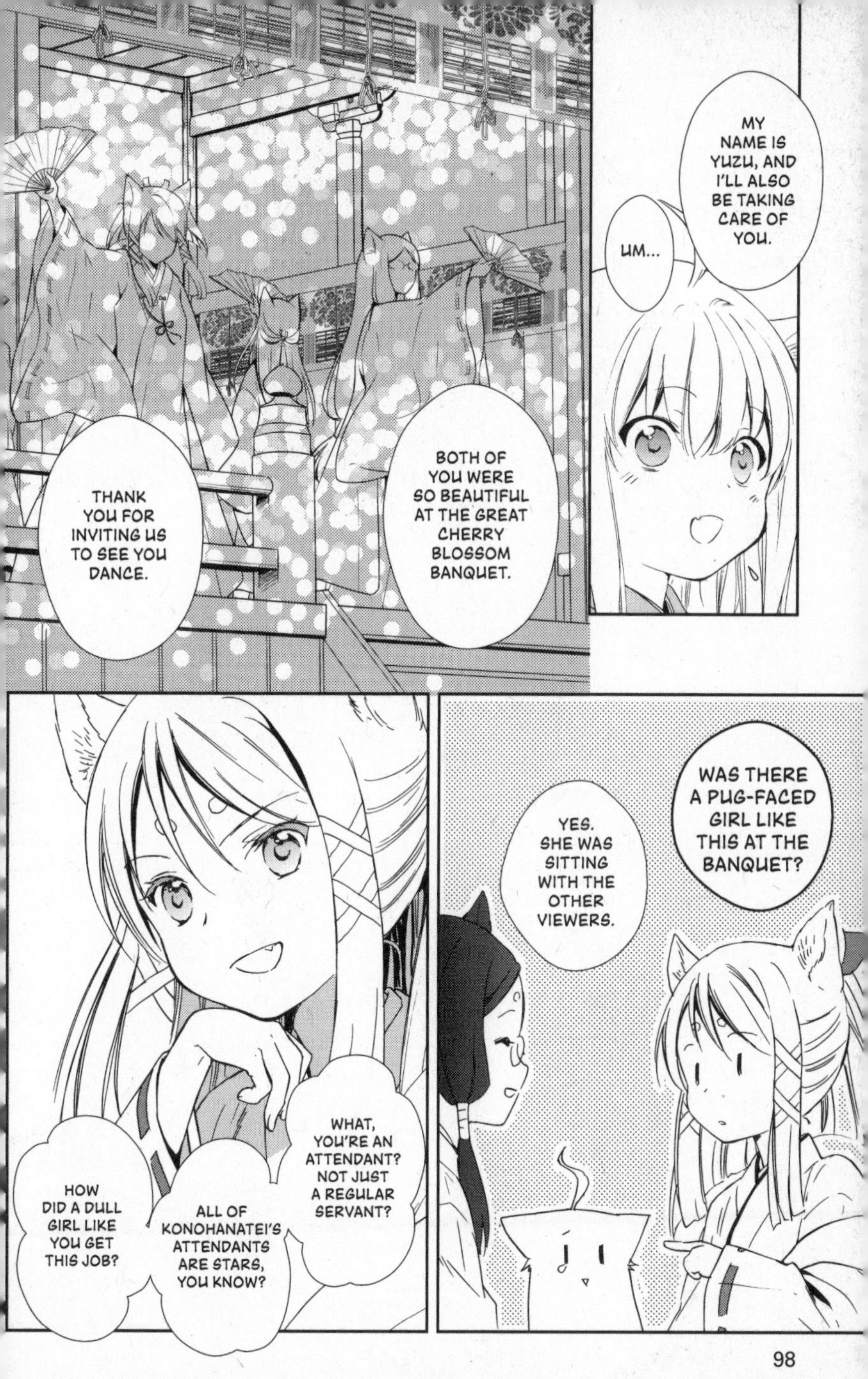
MY NAME IS YUZU, AND I'LL ALSO BE TAKING CARE OF YOU.
UM...
BOTH OF YOU WERE SO BEAUTIFUL AT THE GREAT CHERRY BLOSSOM BANQUET.
THANK YOU FOR INVITING US TO SEE YOU DANCE.
WAS THERE A PUG-FACED GIRL LIKE THIS AT THE BANQUET?
YES. SHE WAS SITTING WITH THE OTHER VIEWERS.
WHAT, YOU'RE AN ATTENDANT? NOT JUST A REGULAR SERVANT?
ALL OF KONOHANATEI'S ATTENDANTS ARE STARS, YOU KNOW?
HOW DID A DULL GIRL LIKE YOU GET THIS JOB?

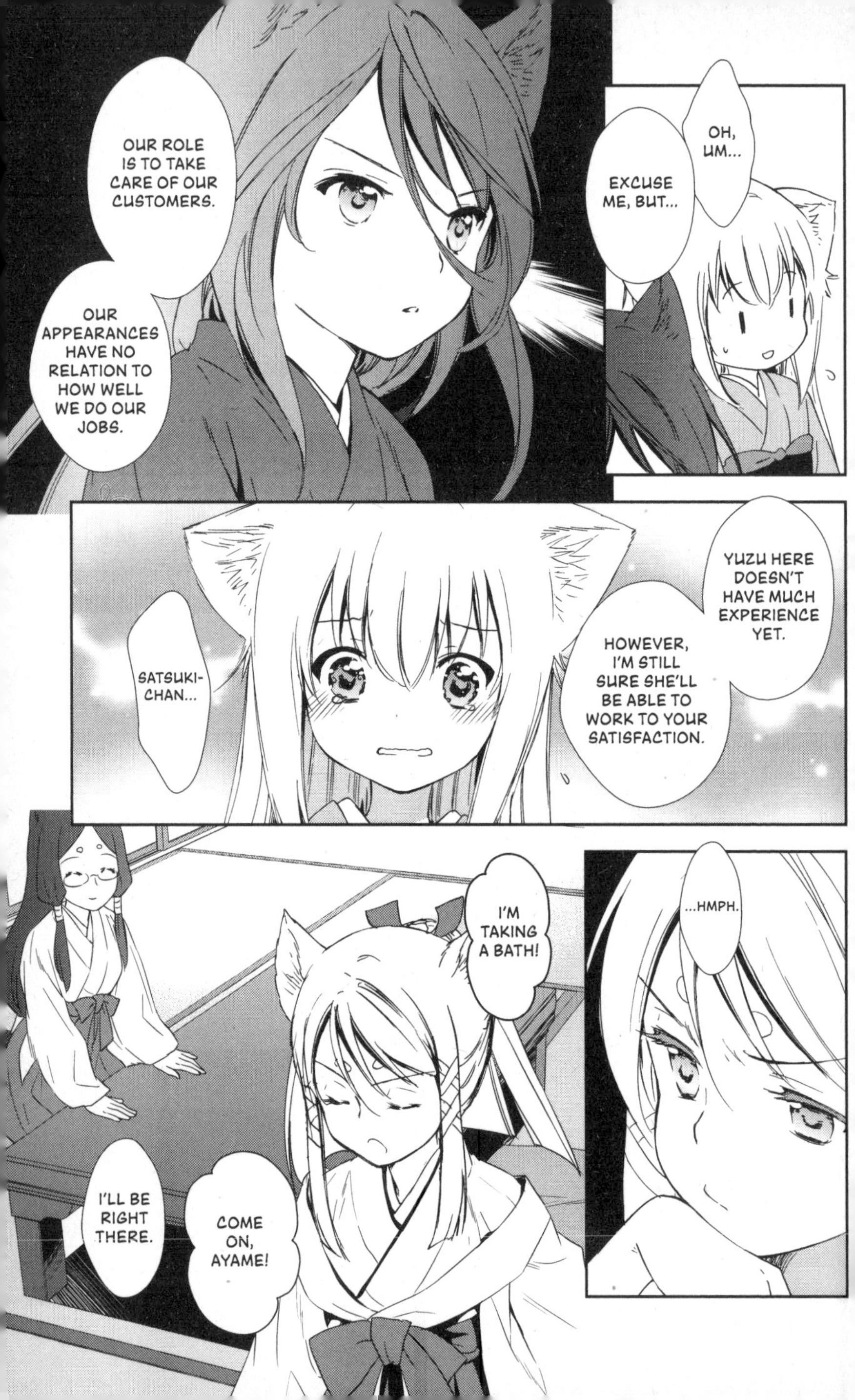
OH, UM...
EXCUSE ME, BUT...
OUR ROLE IS TO TAKE CARE OF OUR CUSTOMERS.
OUR APPEARANCES HAVE NO RELATION TO HOW WELL WE DO OUR JOBS.
YUZU HERE DOESN'T HAVE MUCH EXPERIENCE YET.
HOWEVER, I'M STILL SURE SHE'LL BE ABLE TO WORK TO YOUR SATISFACTION.
SATSUKI-CHAN...
...HMPH.
I'M TAKING A BATH!
COME ON, AYAME!
I'LL BE RIGHT THERE.

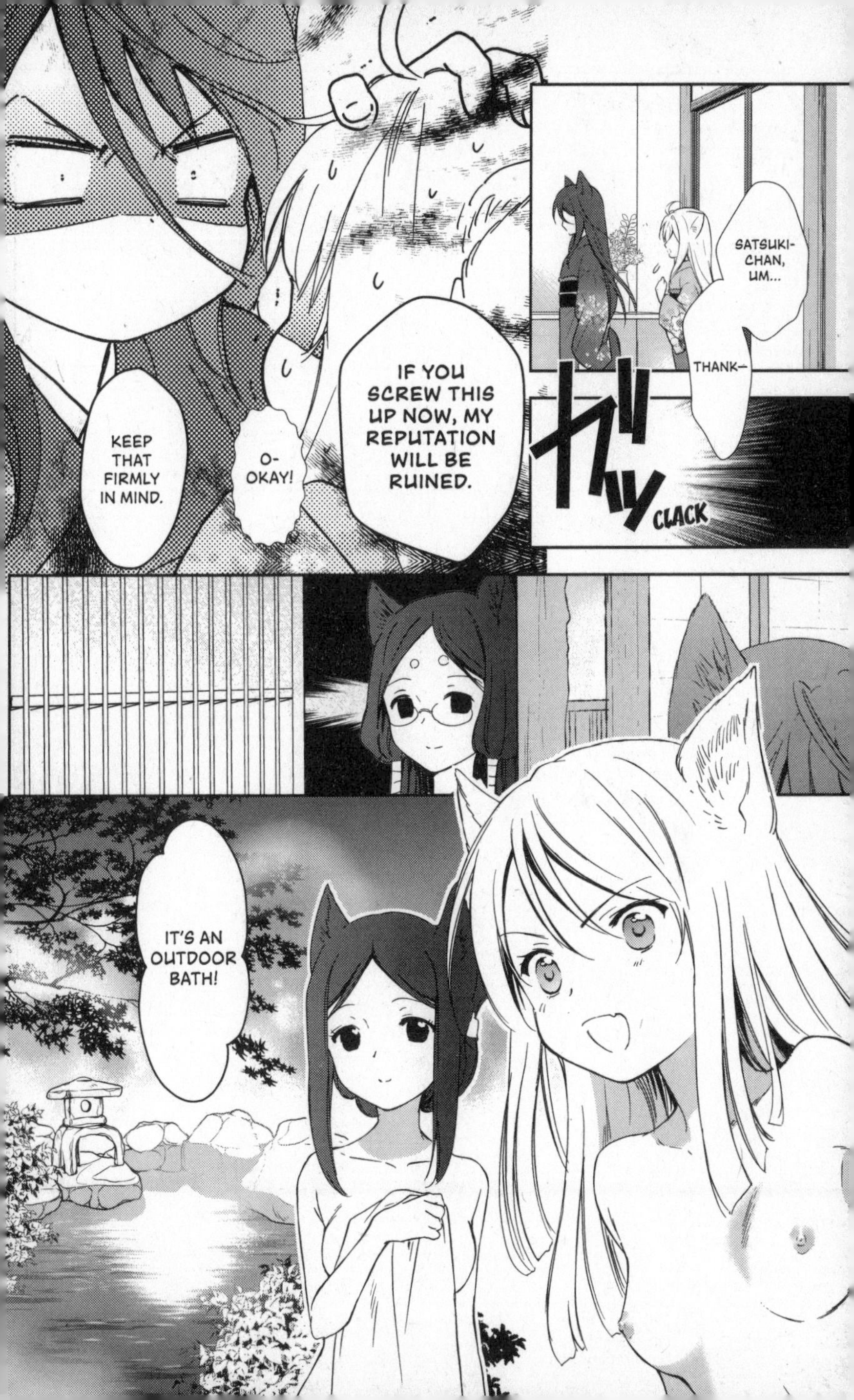
SATSUKI-CHAN, UM...
THANK—
CLACK
IF YOU SCREW THIS UP NOW, MY REPUTATION WILL BE RUINED.
O-OKAY!
KEEP THAT FIRMLY IN MIND.
IT'S AN OUTDOOR BATH!

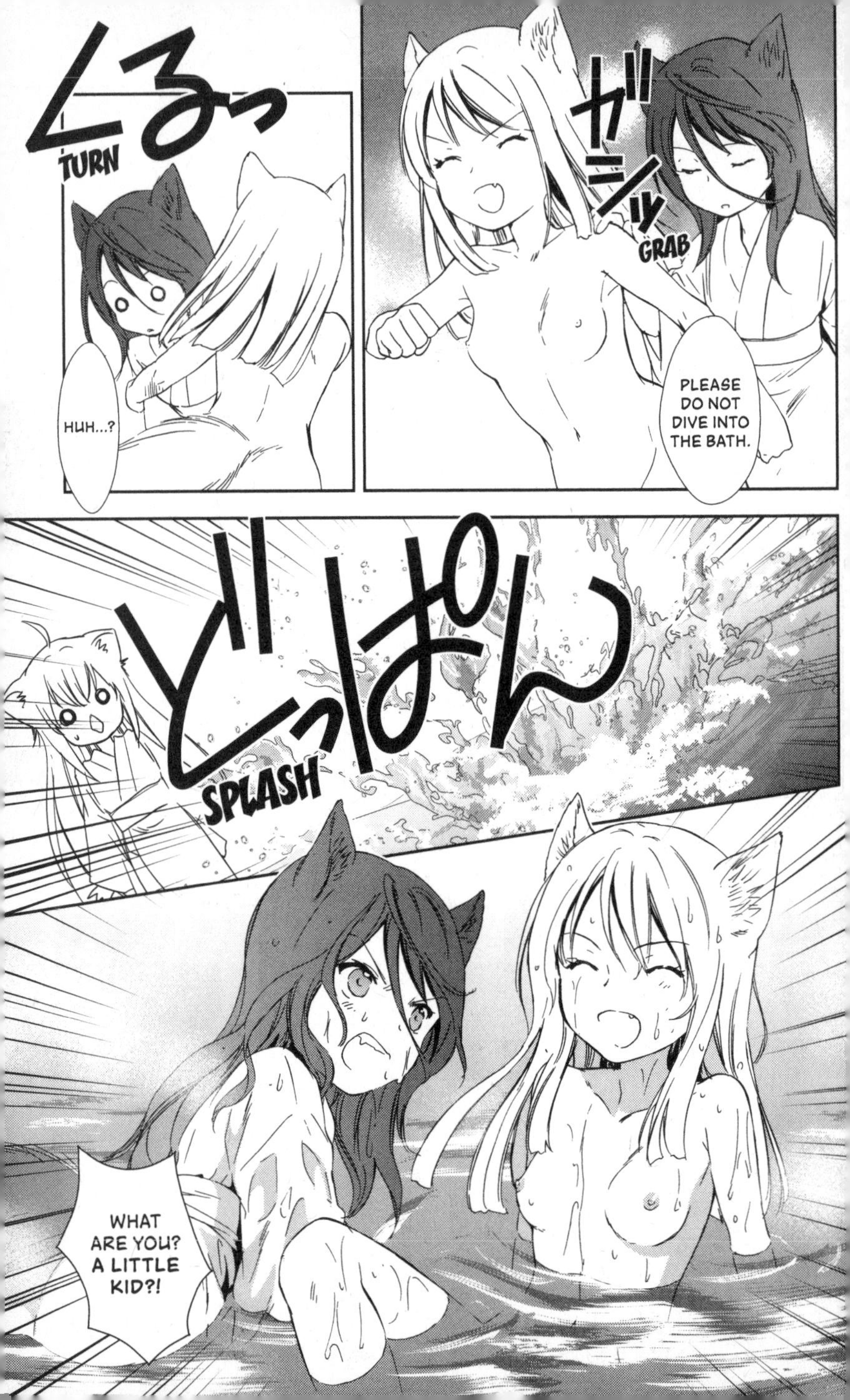
ガシッ
GRAB
PLEASE DO NOT DIVE INTO THE BATH.
くるっ
TURN
HUH...?
どっぽん
SPLASH
WHAT ARE YOU? A LITTLE KID?!

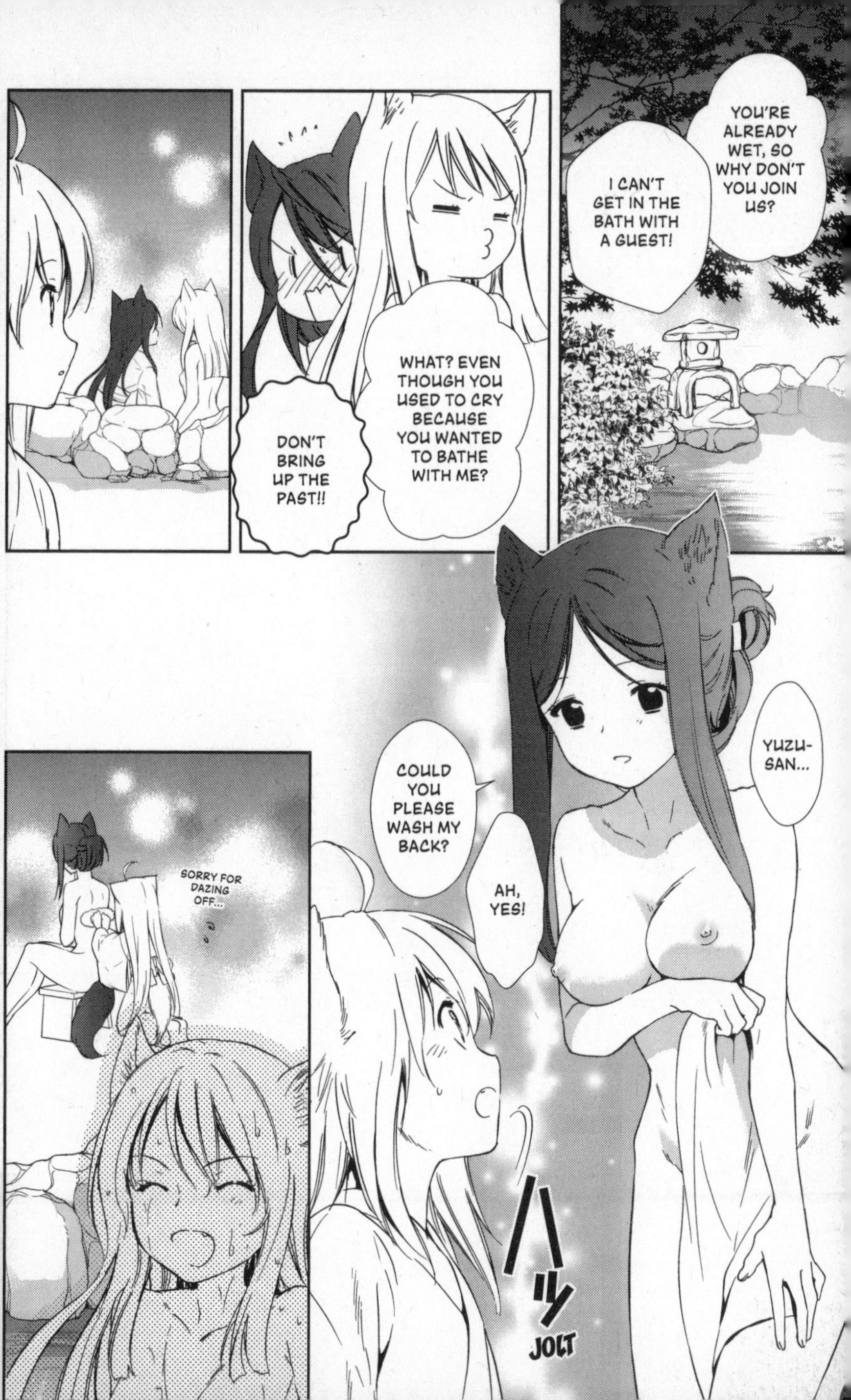
YOU'RE ALREADY WET, SO WHY DON'T YOU JOIN US?
I CAN'T GET IN THE BATH WITH A GUEST!
WHAT? EVEN THOUGH YOU USED TO CRY BECAUSE YOU WANTED TO BATHE WITH ME?
DON'T BRING UP THE PAST!!
YUZU-SAN...
COULD YOU PLEASE WASH MY BACK?
AH, YES!
JOLT
SORRY FOR DAZING OFF...

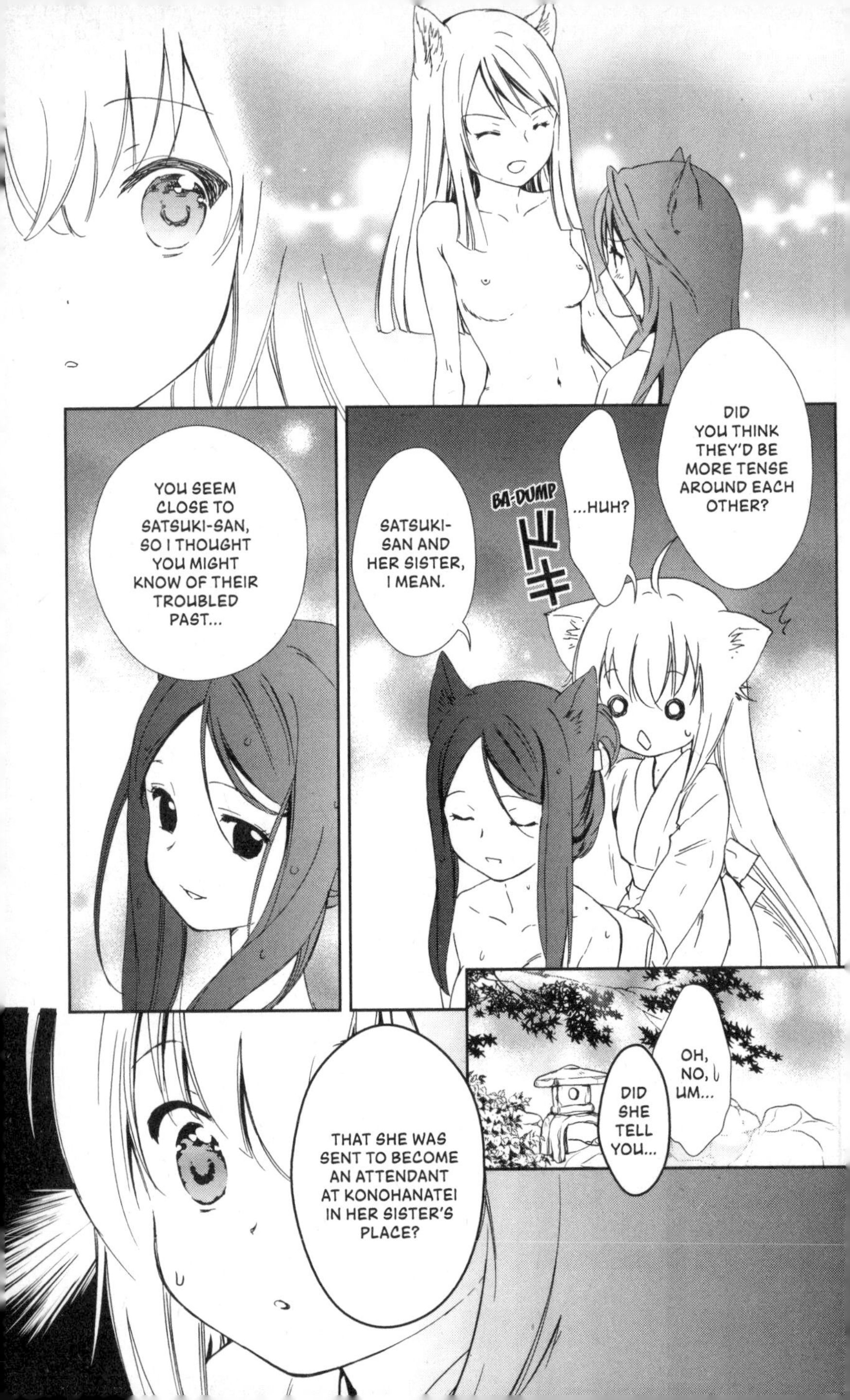
DID YOU THINK THEY'D BE MORE TENSE AROUND EACH OTHER?
...HUH?
BA-DUMP
SATSUKI-SAN AND HER SISTER, I MEAN.
YOU SEEM CLOSE TO SATSUKI-SAN, SO I THOUGHT YOU MIGHT KNOW OF THEIR TROUBLED PAST...
OH, NO, UM...
DID SHE TELL YOU...
THAT SHE WAS SENT TO BECOME AN ATTENDANT AT KONOHANATEI IN HER SISTER'S PLACE?

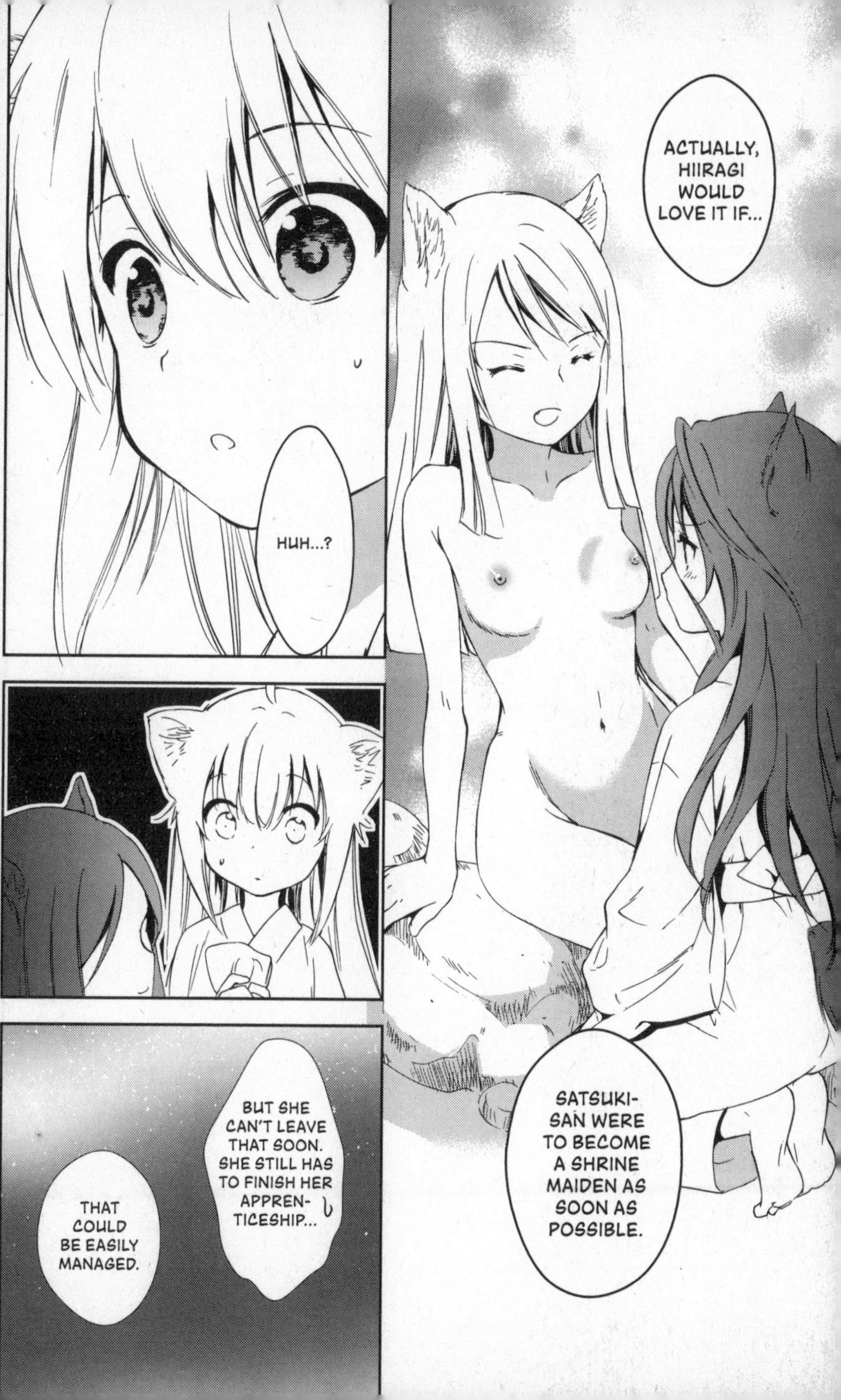
ACTUALLY, HIIRAGI WOULD LOVE IT IF...
SATSUKI-SAN WERE TO BECOME A SHRINE MAIDEN AS SOON AS POSSIBLE.
HUH...?
BUT SHE CAN'T LEAVE THAT SOON. SHE STILL HAS TO FINISH HER APPREN-TICESHIP...
THAT COULD BE EASILY MANAGED.

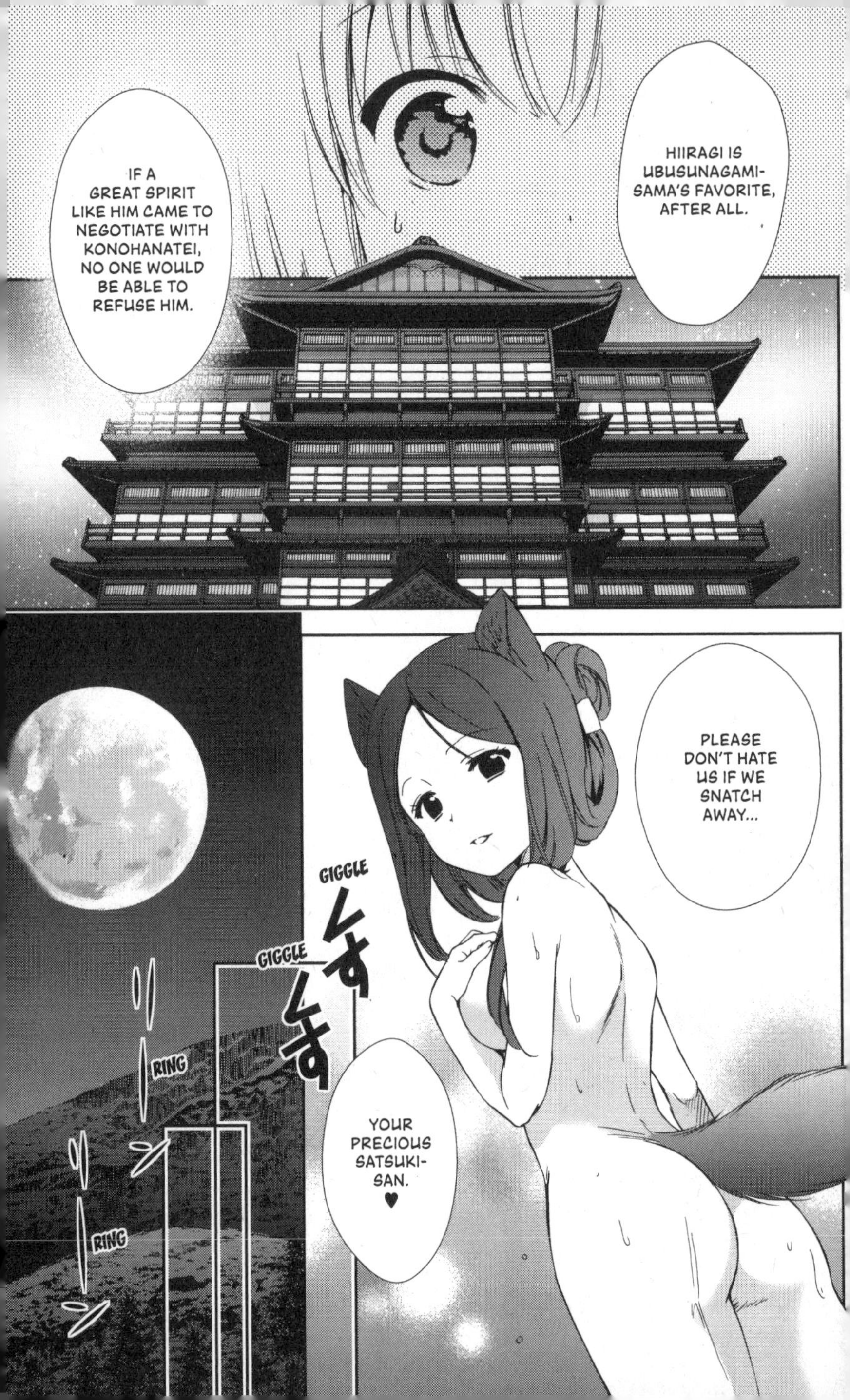

HIIRAGI IS UBUSUNAGAMI-SAMA'S FAVORITE, AFTER ALL.
IF A GREAT SPIRIT LIKE HIM CAME TO NEGOTIATE WITH KONOHANATEI, NO ONE WOULD BE ABLE TO REFUSE HIM.
PLEASE DON'T HATE US IF WE SNATCH AWAY...
GIGGLE
GIGGLE
YOUR PRECIOUS SATSUKI-SAN. ♥
RING
RING

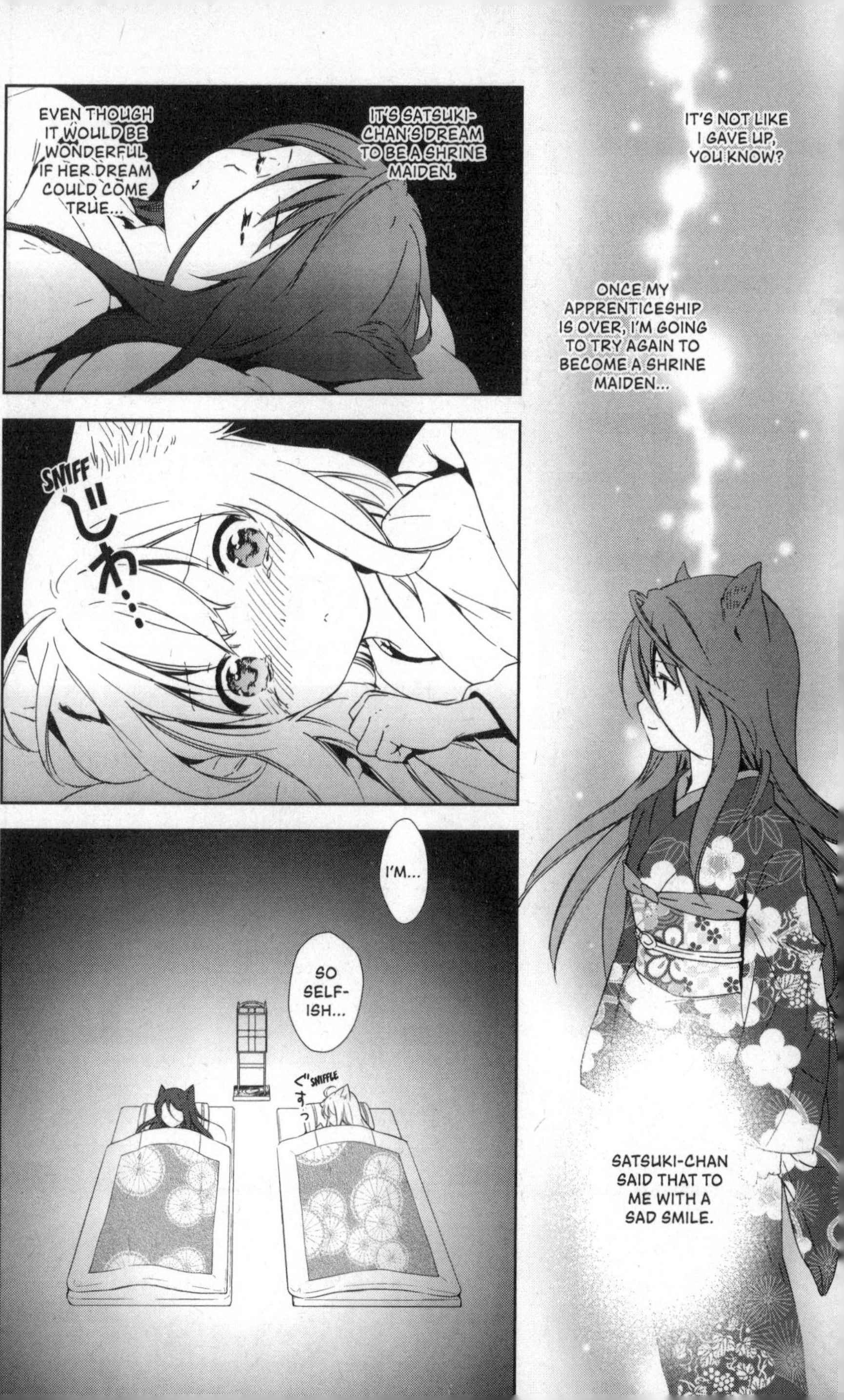
IT'S NOT LIKE I GAVE UP, YOU KNOW?
ONCE MY APPRENTICESHIP IS OVER, I'M GOING TO TRY AGAIN TO BECOME A SHRINE MAIDEN...
SATSUKI-CHAN SAID THAT TO ME WITH A SAD SMILE.
IT'S SATSUKI-CHAN'S DREAM TO BE A SHRINE MAIDEN.
EVEN THOUGH IT WOULD BE WONDERFUL IF HER DREAM COULD COME TRUE...
SNIFF
じわ…
I'M...
SO SELF-ISH...
ぐすっ
SNIFFLE

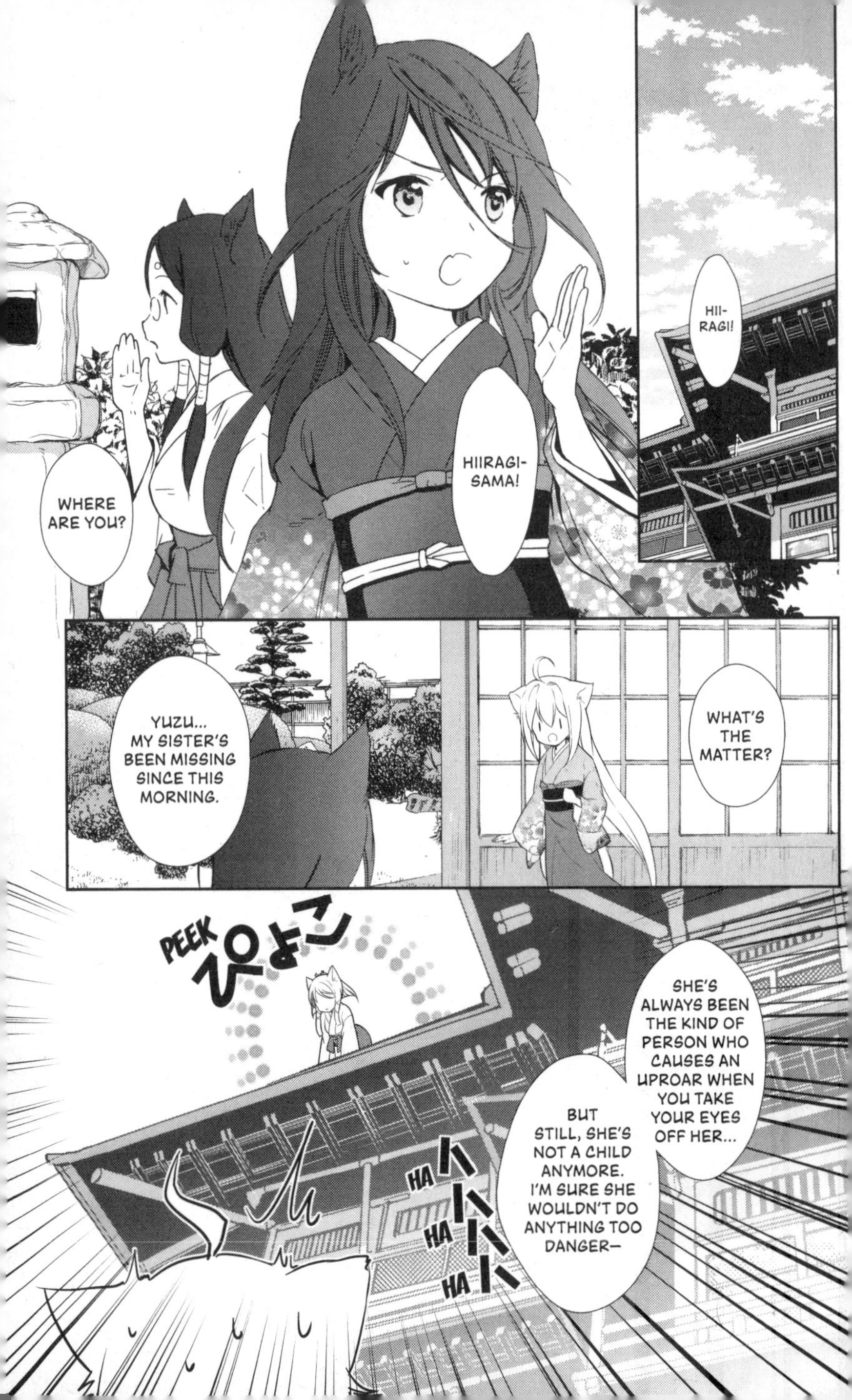
HII-RAGI!
HIIRAGI-SAMA!
WHERE ARE YOU?
WHAT'S THE MATTER?
YUZU... MY SISTER'S BEEN MISSING SINCE THIS MORNING.
SHE'S ALWAYS BEEN THE KIND OF PERSON WHO CAUSES AN UPROAR WHEN YOU TAKE YOUR EYES OFF HER...
BUT STILL, SHE'S NOT A CHILD ANYMORE. I'M SURE SHE WOULDN'T DO ANYTHING TOO DANGER—
PEEK
HA HA HA

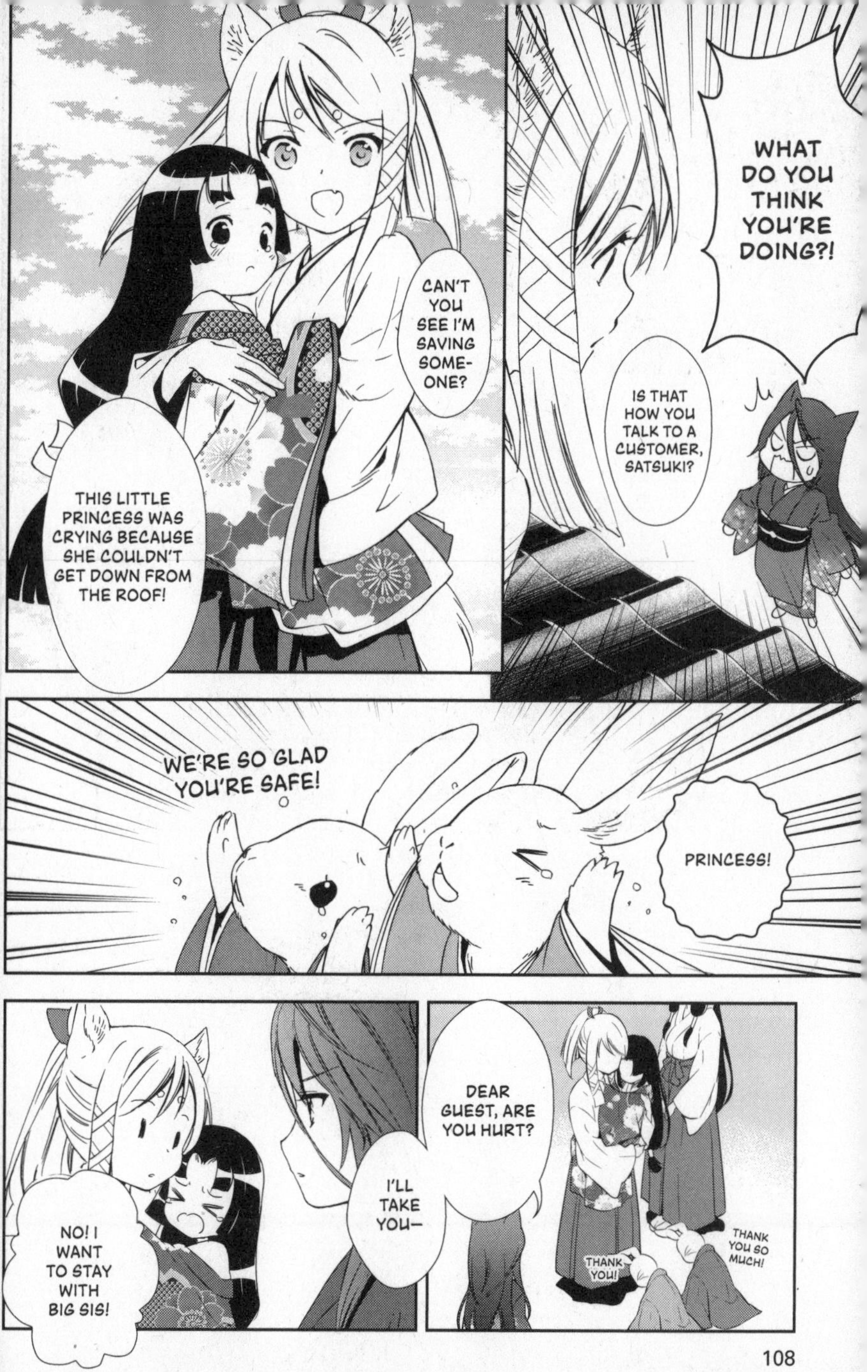
WHAT DO YOU THINK YOU'RE DOING?!
IS THAT HOW YOU TALK TO A CUSTOMER, SATSUKI?
CAN'T YOU SEE I'M SAVING SOME-ONE?
THIS LITTLE PRINCESS WAS CRYING BECAUSE SHE COULDN'T GET DOWN FROM THE ROOF!
PRINCESS!
WE'RE SO GLAD YOU'RE SAFE!
DEAR GUEST, ARE YOU HURT?
THANK YOU SO MUCH!
THANK YOU!
I'LL TAKE YOU—
NO! I WANT TO STAY WITH BIG SIS!

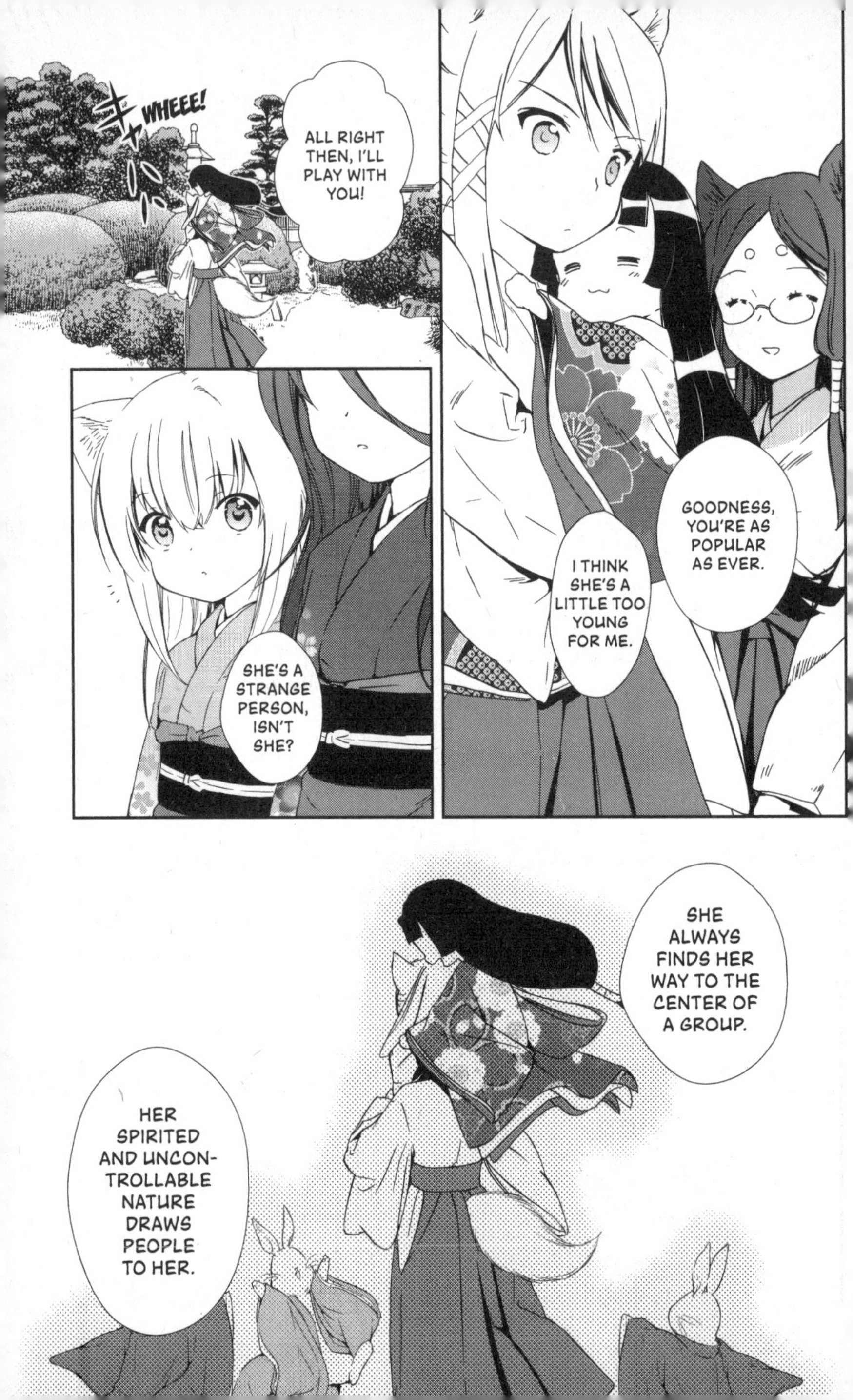
GOODNESS, YOU'RE AS POPULAR AS EVER.
I THINK SHE'S A LITTLE TOO YOUNG FOR ME.
WHEEE!
ALL RIGHT THEN, I'LL PLAY WITH YOU!
SHE'S A STRANGE PERSON, ISN'T SHE?
SHE ALWAYS FINDS HER WAY TO THE CENTER OF A GROUP.
HER SPIRITED AND UNCON-TROLLABLE NATURE DRAWS PEOPLE TO HER.

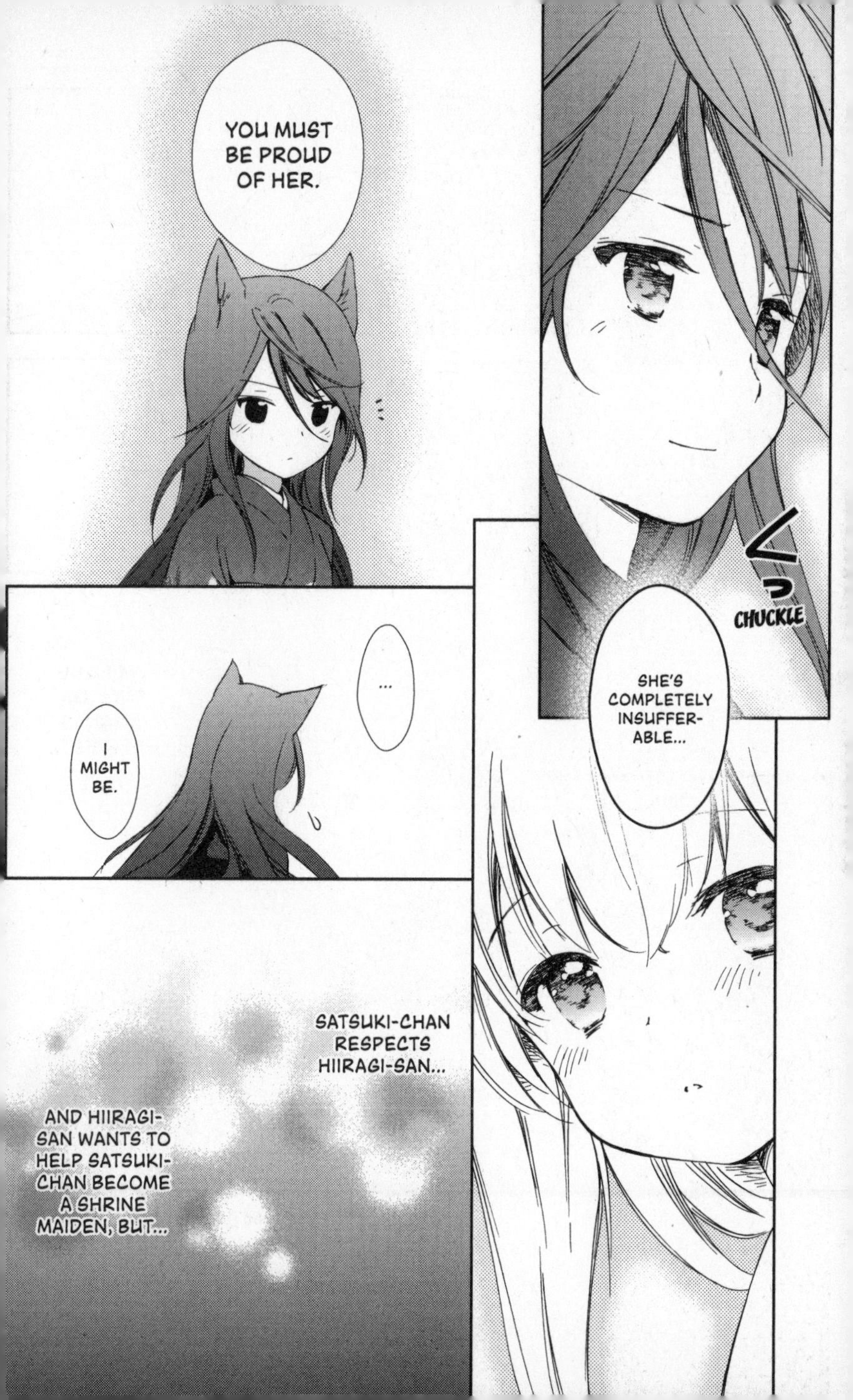
CHUCKLE
SHE'S COMPLETELY INSUFFER-ABLE...
YOU MUST BE PROUD OF HER.
...
I MIGHT BE.
SATSUKI-CHAN RESPECTS HIIRAGI-SAN...
AND HIIRAGI-SAN WANTS TO HELP SATSUKI-CHAN BECOME A SHRINE MAIDEN, BUT...

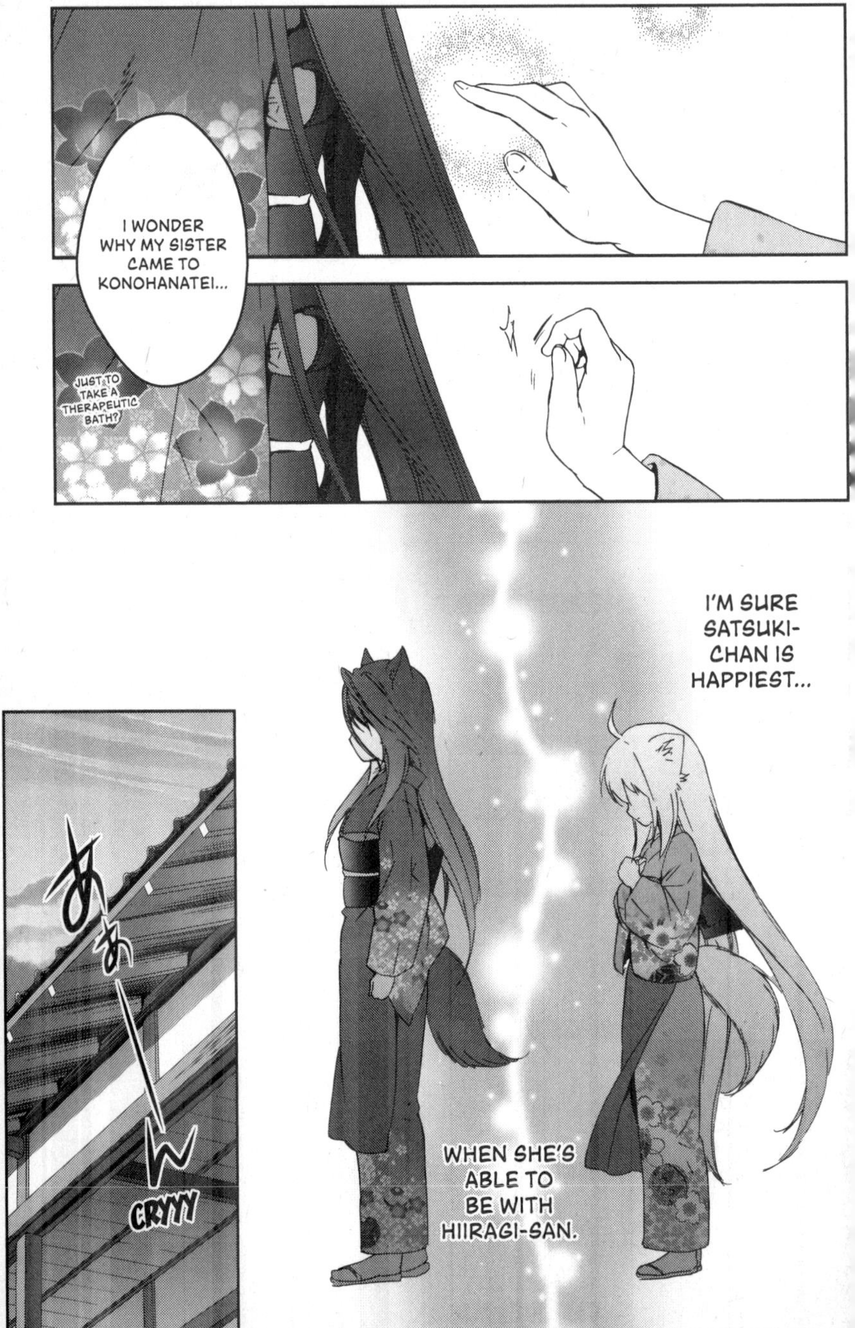
I WONDER WHY MY SISTER CAME TO KONOHANATEI...
JUST TO TAKE A THERAPEUTIC BATH?
I'M SURE SATSUKI-CHAN IS HAPPIEST...
WHEN SHE'S ABLE TO BE WITH HIIRAGI-SAN.
あぁ〜ん
CRYYY

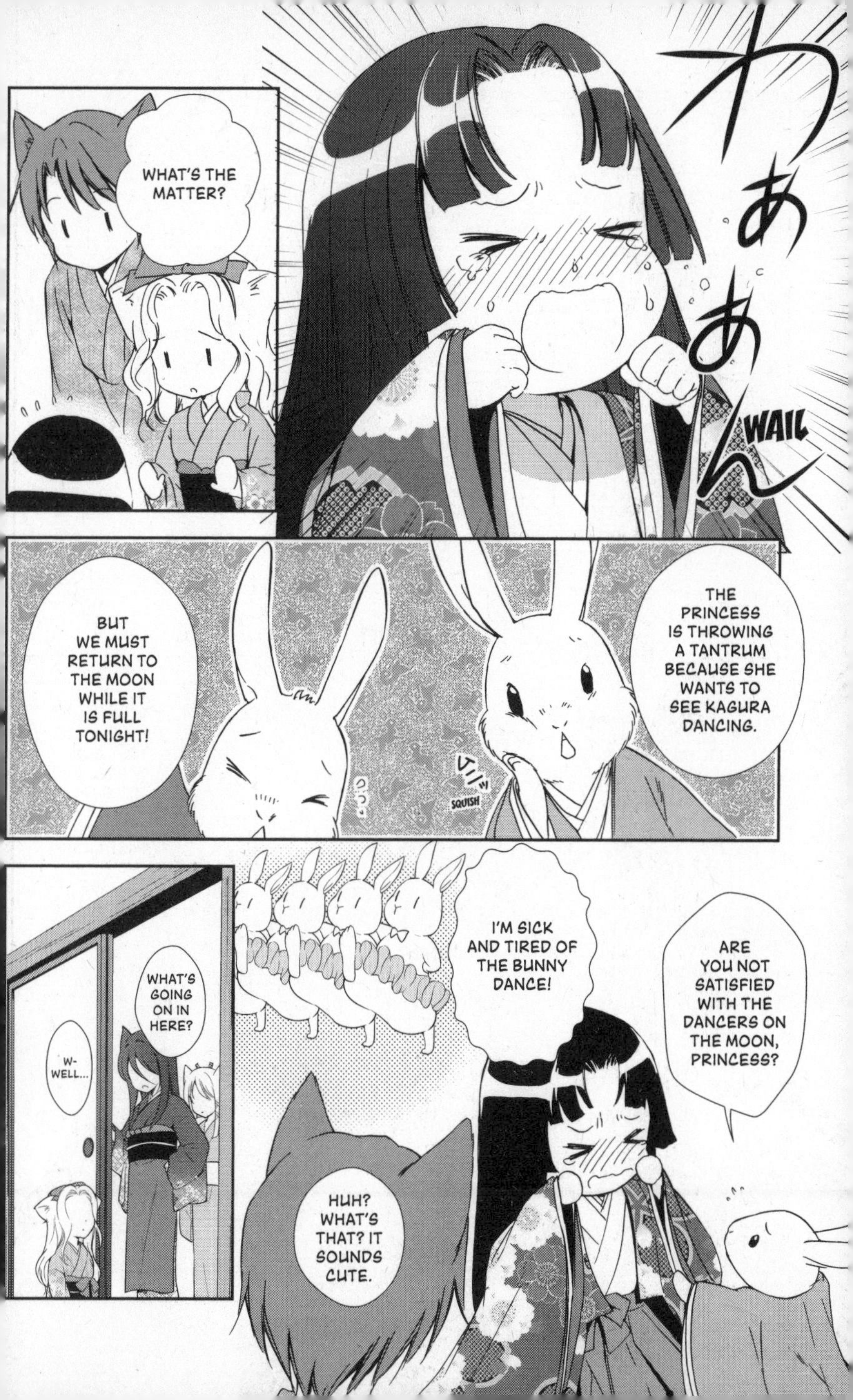
わああん
WAIL
WHAT'S THE MATTER?
THE PRINCESS IS THROWING A TANTRUM BECAUSE SHE WANTS TO SEE KAGURA DANCING.
ムニッ
SQUISH
BUT WE MUST RETURN TO THE MOON WHILE IT IS FULL TONIGHT!
ARE YOU NOT SATISFIED WITH THE DANCERS ON THE MOON, PRINCESS?
I'M SICK AND TIRED OF THE BUNNY DANCE!
WHAT'S GOING ON IN HERE?
W-WELL...
HUH? WHAT'S THAT? IT SOUNDS CUTE.

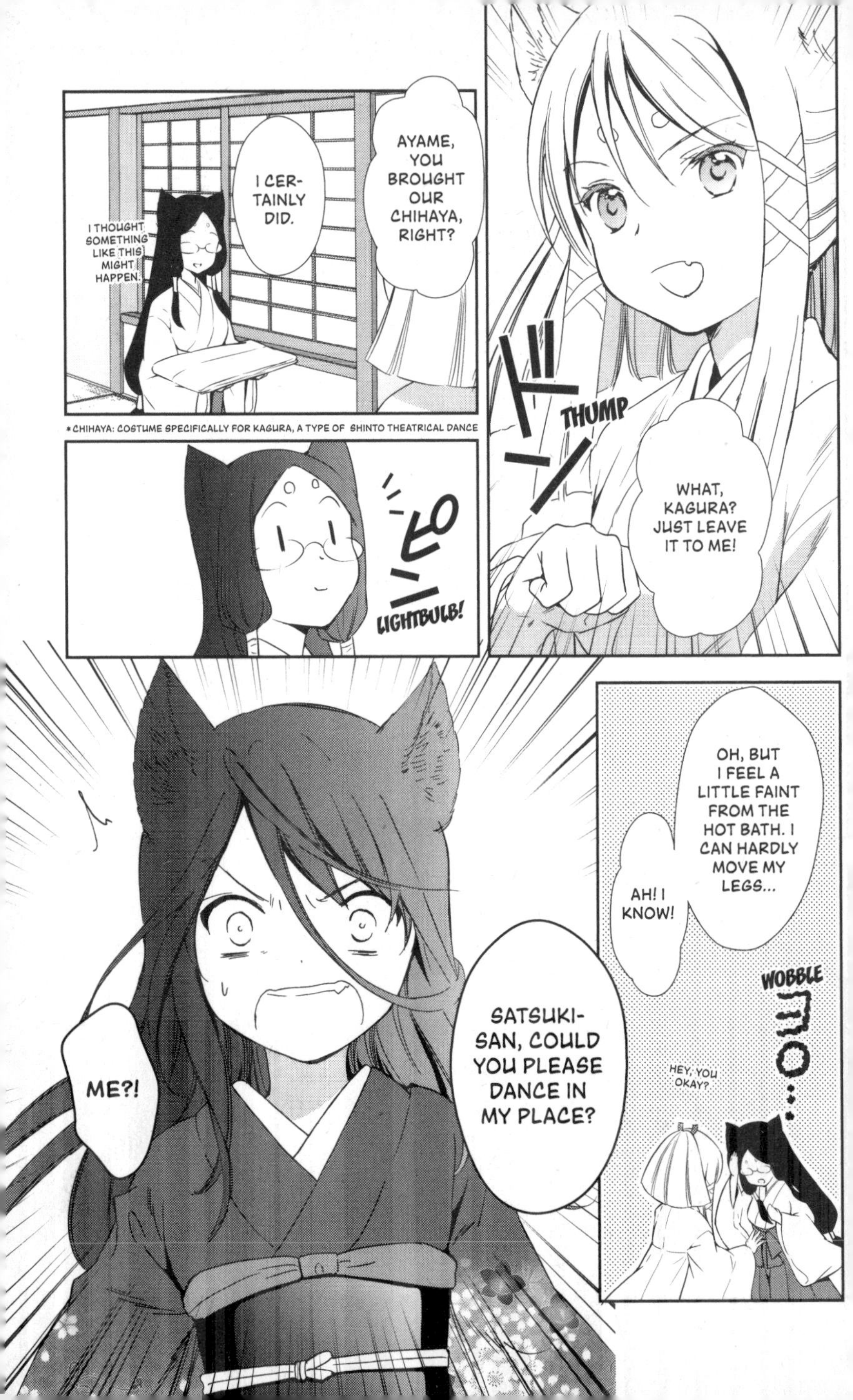
THUMP
WHAT, KAGURA? JUST LEAVE IT TO ME!
AYAME, YOU BROUGHT OUR CHIHAYA, RIGHT?
I CER-TAINLY DID.
I THOUGHT SOMETHING LIKE THIS MIGHT HAPPEN.
LIGHTBULB!
OH, BUT I FEEL A LITTLE FAINT FROM THE HOT BATH. I CAN HARDLY MOVE MY LEGS...
AH! I KNOW!
WOBBLE
HEY, YOU OKAY?
SATSUKI-SAN, COULD YOU PLEASE DANCE IN MY PLACE?
ME?!

* CHIHAYA: COSTUME SPECIFICALLY FOR KAGURA, A TYPE OF SHINTO THEATRICAL DANCE

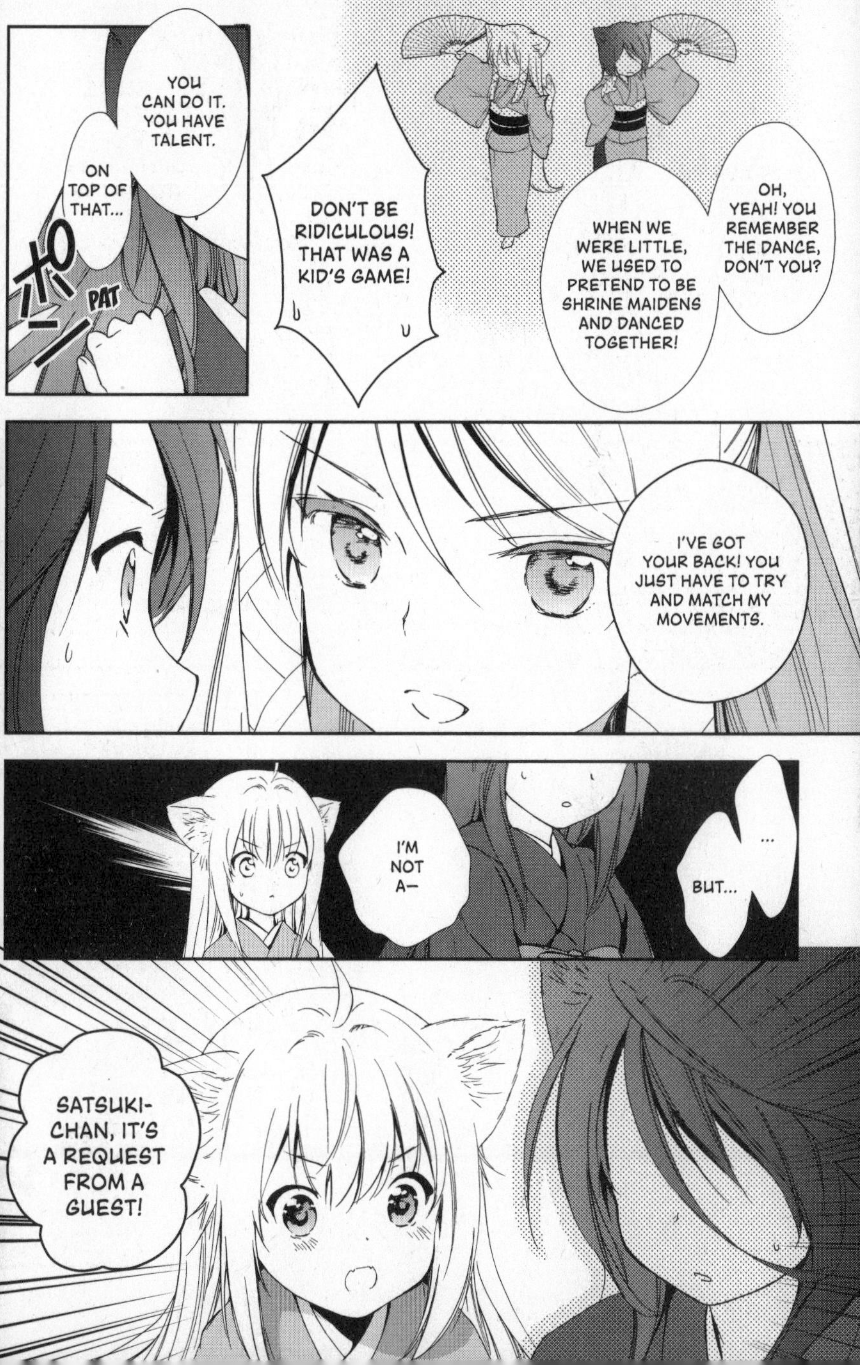
OH, YEAH! YOU REMEMBER THE DANCE, DON'T YOU?
WHEN WE WERE LITTLE, WE USED TO PRETEND TO BE SHRINE MAIDENS AND DANCED TOGETHER!
DON'T BE RIDICULOUS! THAT WAS A KID'S GAME!
YOU CAN DO IT. YOU HAVE TALENT.
ON TOP OF THAT...
PAT
I'VE GOT YOUR BACK! YOU JUST HAVE TO TRY AND MATCH MY MOVEMENTS.
...
BUT...
I'M NOT A—
SATSUKI-CHAN, IT'S A REQUEST FROM A GUEST!

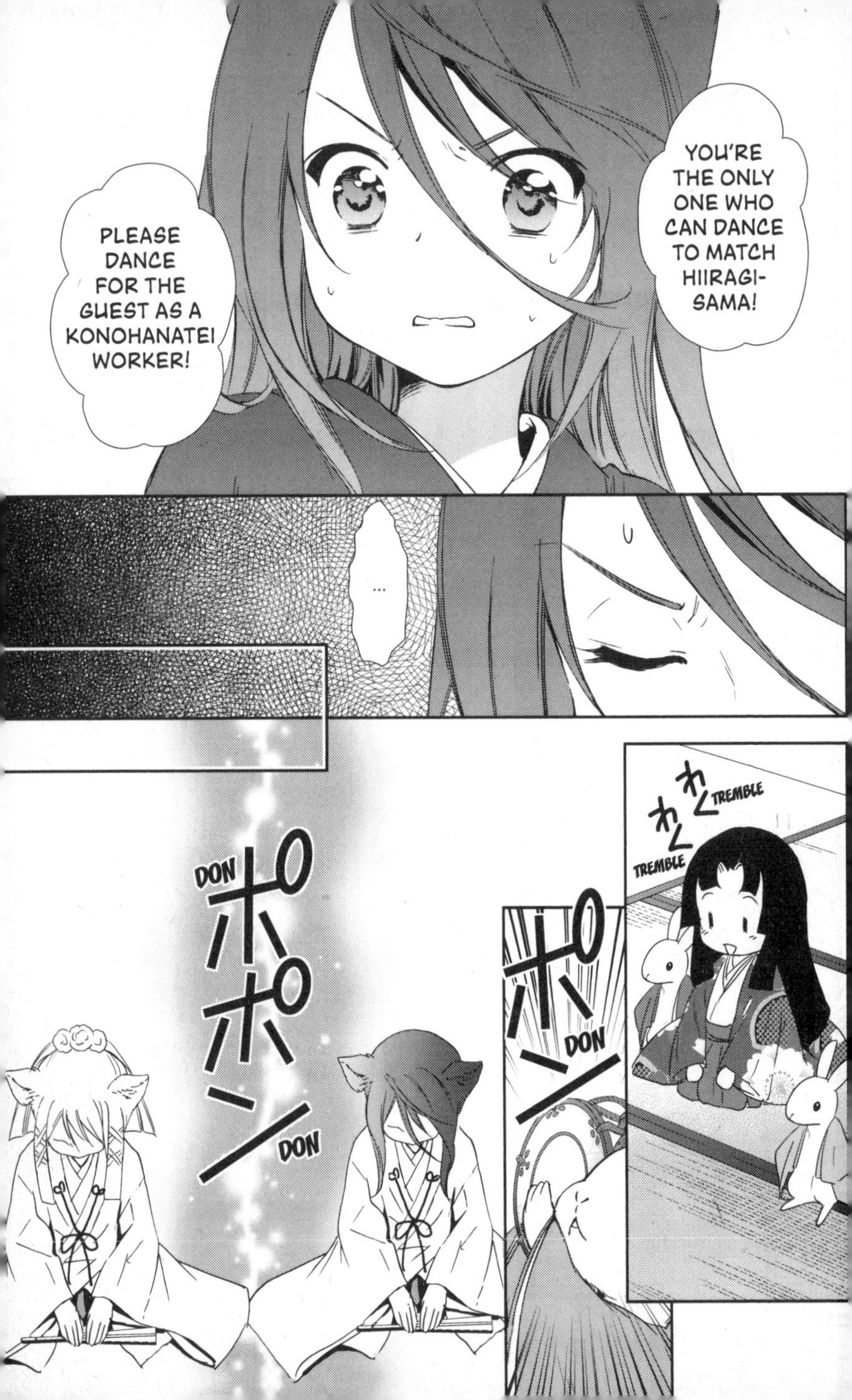
YOU'RE THE ONLY ONE WHO CAN DANCE TO MATCH HIIRAGI-SAMA!
PLEASE DANCE FOR THE GUEST AS A KONOHANATEI WORKER!
...
TREMBLE
TREMBLE
DON
DON
DON

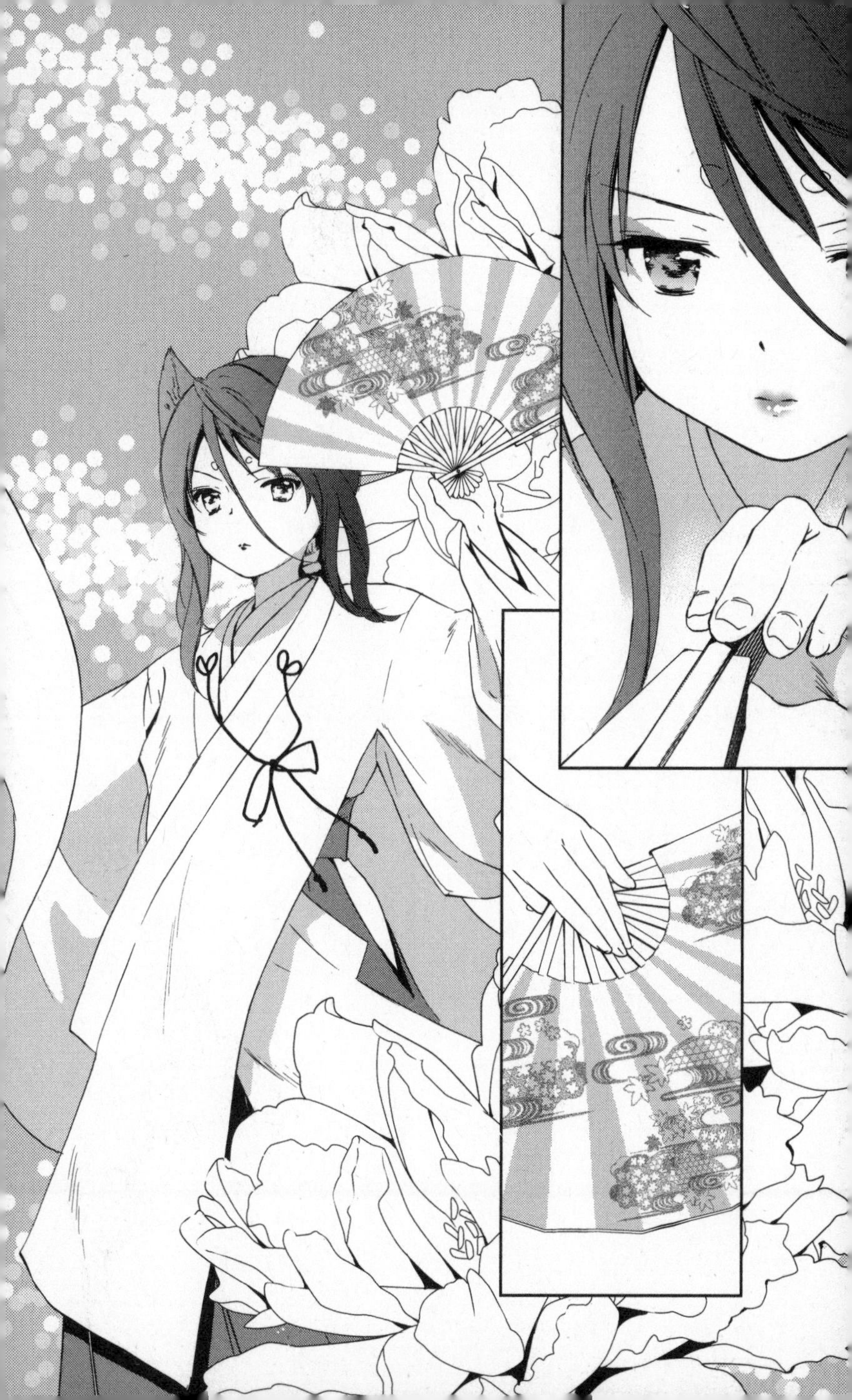

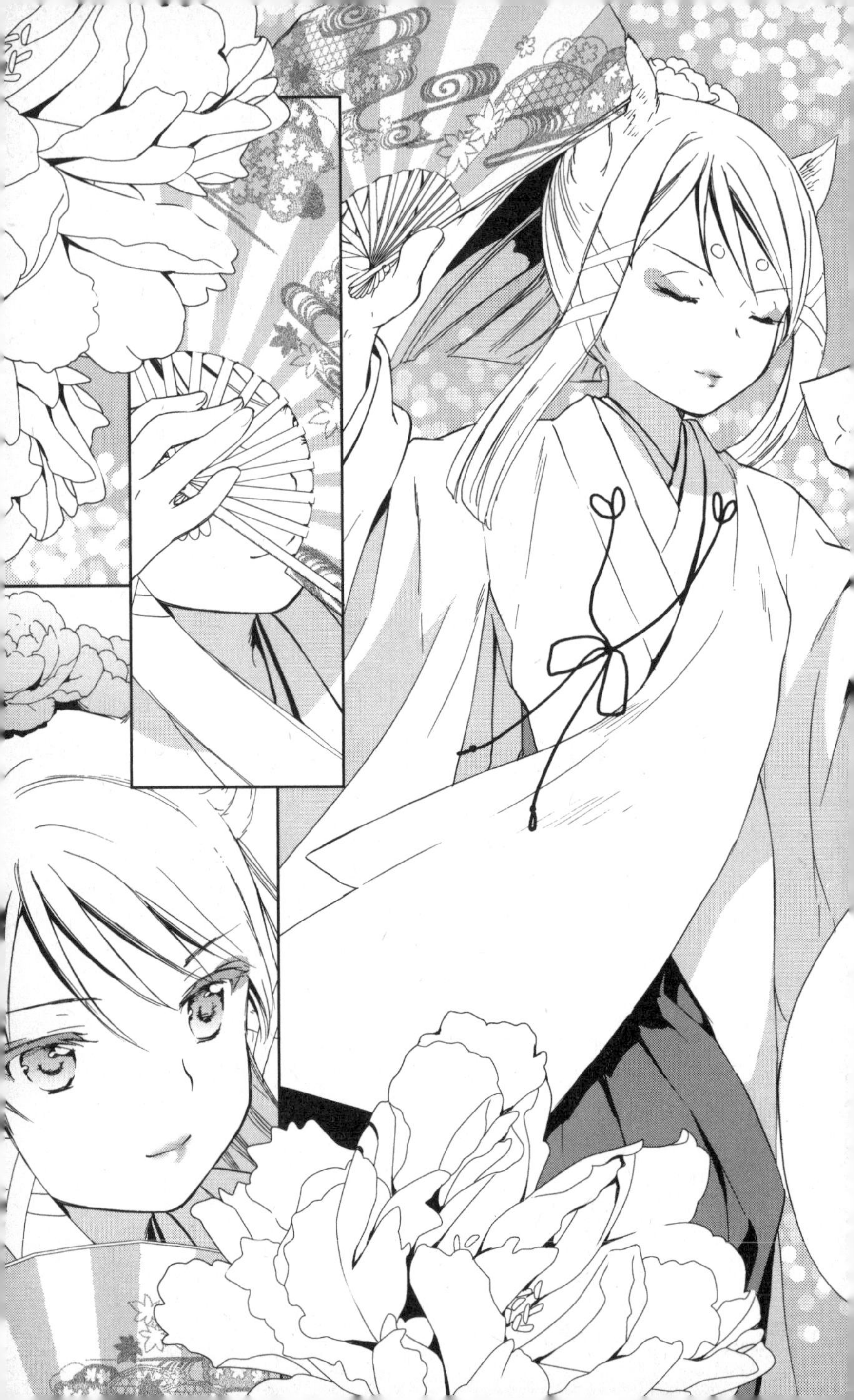

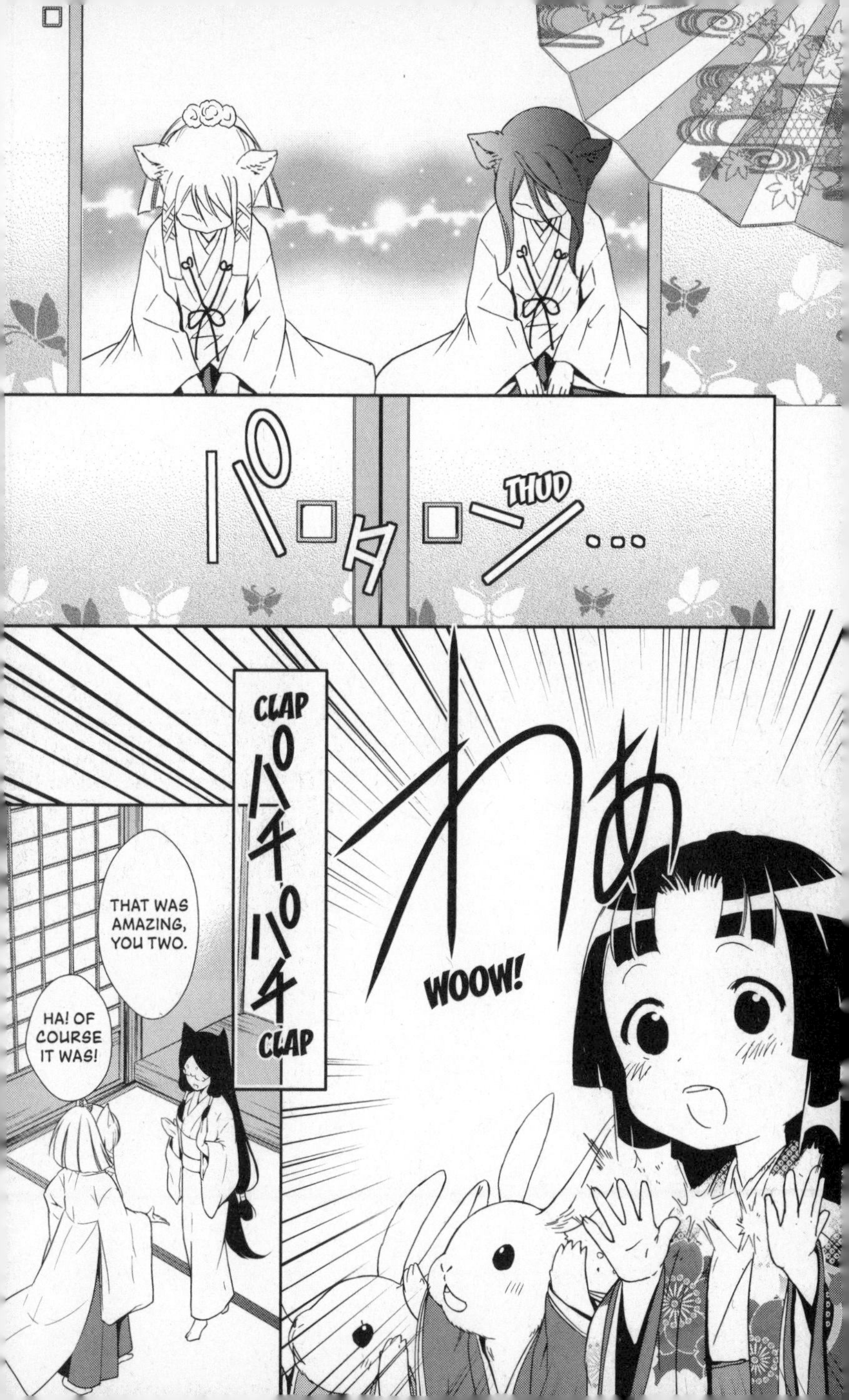
パロタロン…
THUD
わあ
WOOW!
CLAP
パチパチ
CLAP
THAT WAS AMAZING, YOU TWO.
HA! OF COURSE IT WAS!

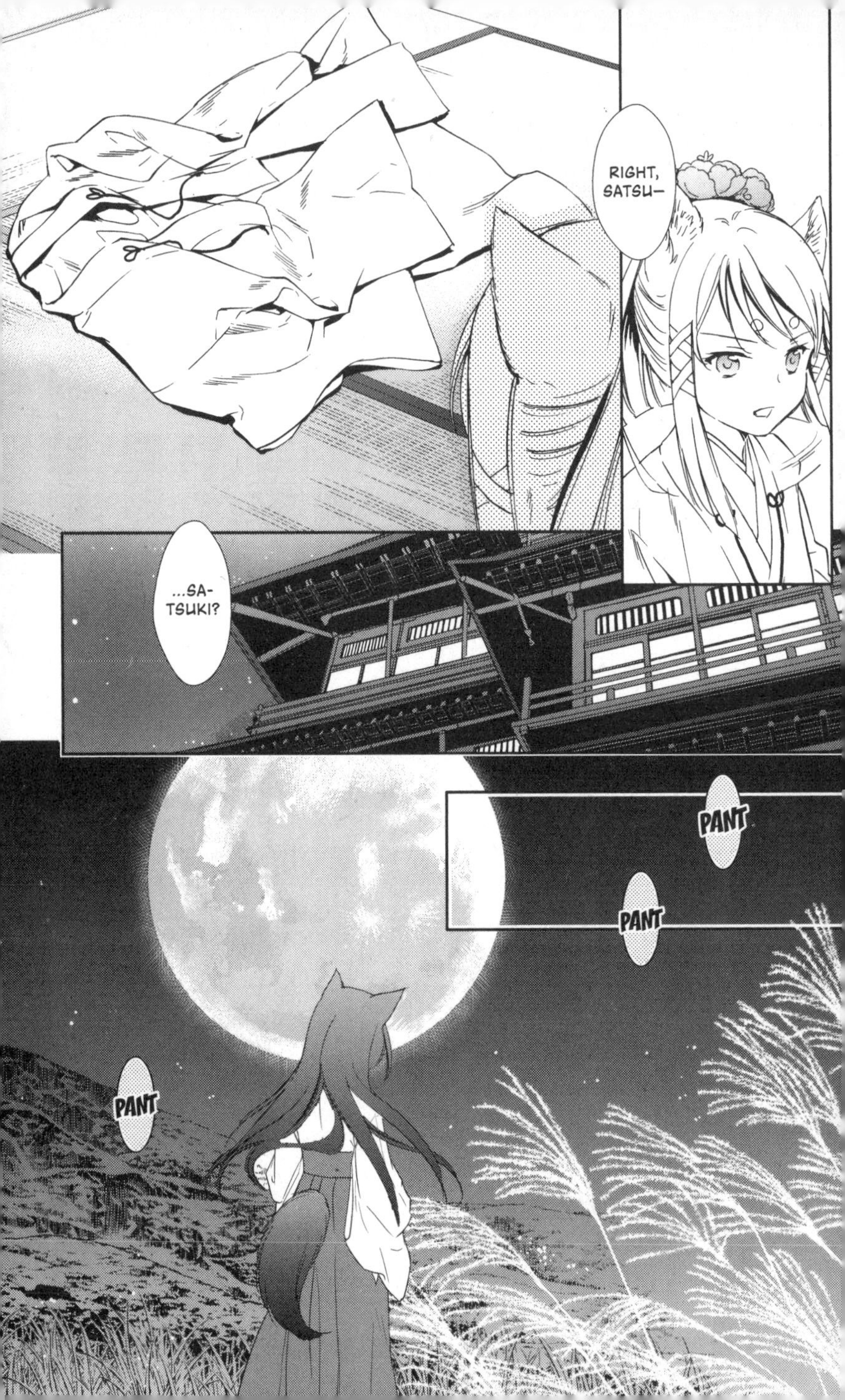
RIGHT, SATSU—
...SA-TSUKI?
PANT
PANT
PANT

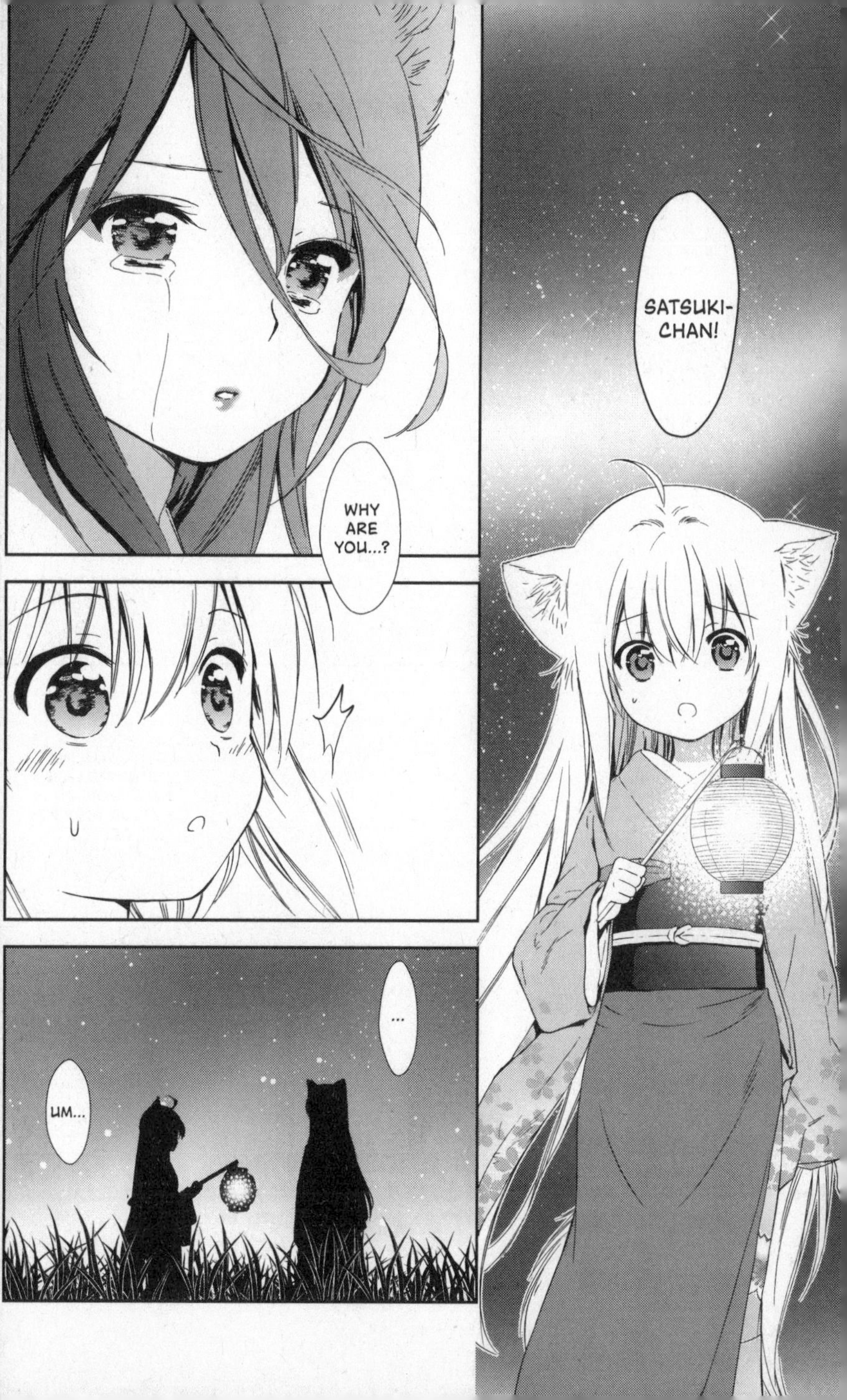
SATSUKI-CHAN!
WHY ARE YOU...?
...
UM...

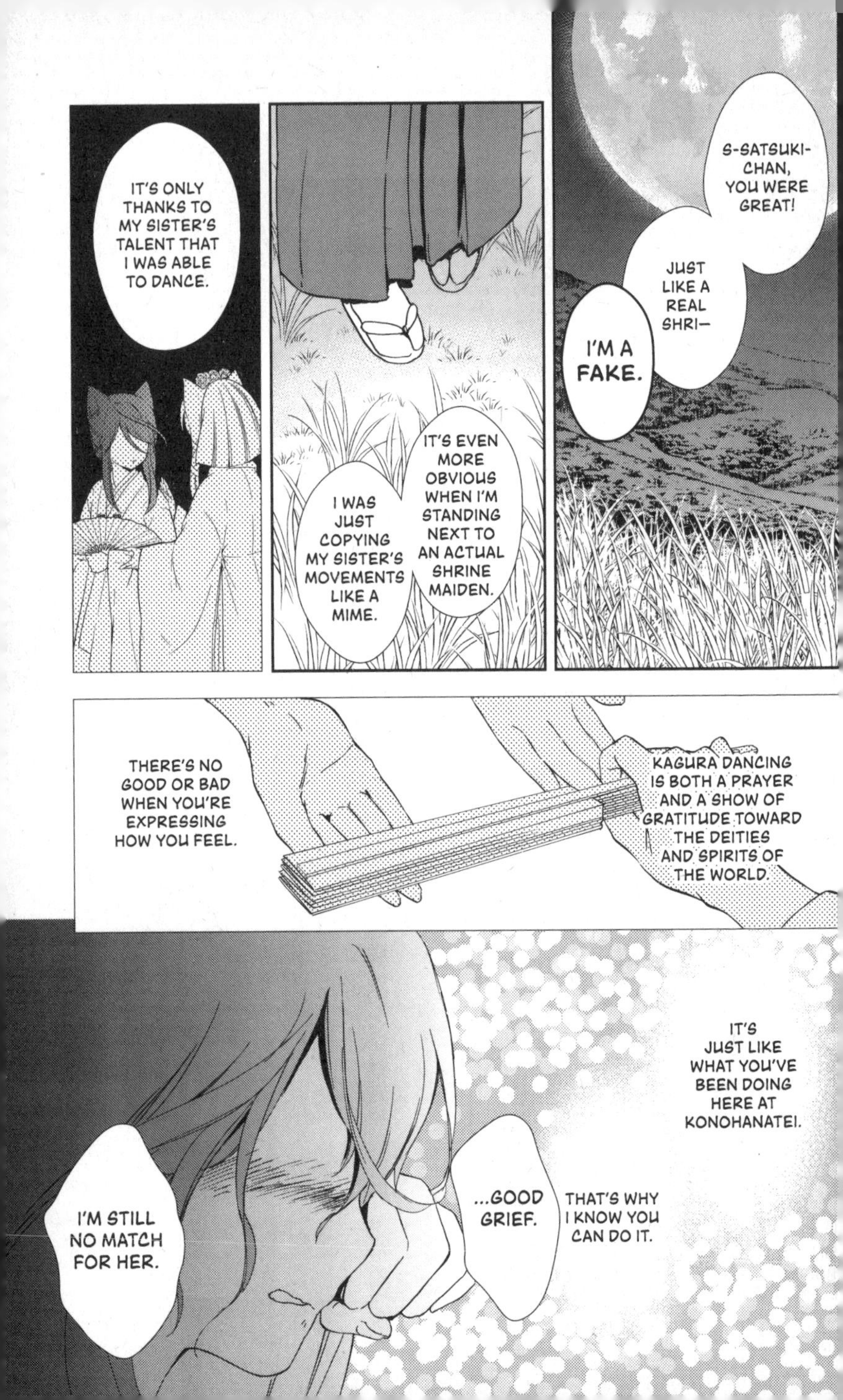
S-SATSUKI-CHAN, YOU WERE GREAT!
JUST LIKE A REAL SHRI—
I'M A FAKE.
IT'S EVEN MORE OBVIOUS WHEN I'M STANDING NEXT TO AN ACTUAL SHRINE MAIDEN.
I WAS JUST COPYING MY SISTER'S MOVEMENTS LIKE A MIME.
IT'S ONLY THANKS TO MY SISTER'S TALENT THAT I WAS ABLE TO DANCE.
KAGURA DANCING IS BOTH A PRAYER AND A SHOW OF GRATITUDE TOWARD THE DEITIES AND SPIRITS OF THE WORLD.
THERE'S NO GOOD OR BAD WHEN YOU'RE EXPRESSING HOW YOU FEEL.
IT'S JUST LIKE WHAT YOU'VE BEEN DOING HERE AT KONOHANATEI.
THAT'S WHY I KNOW YOU CAN DO IT.
...GOOD GRIEF.
I'M STILL NO MATCH FOR HER.

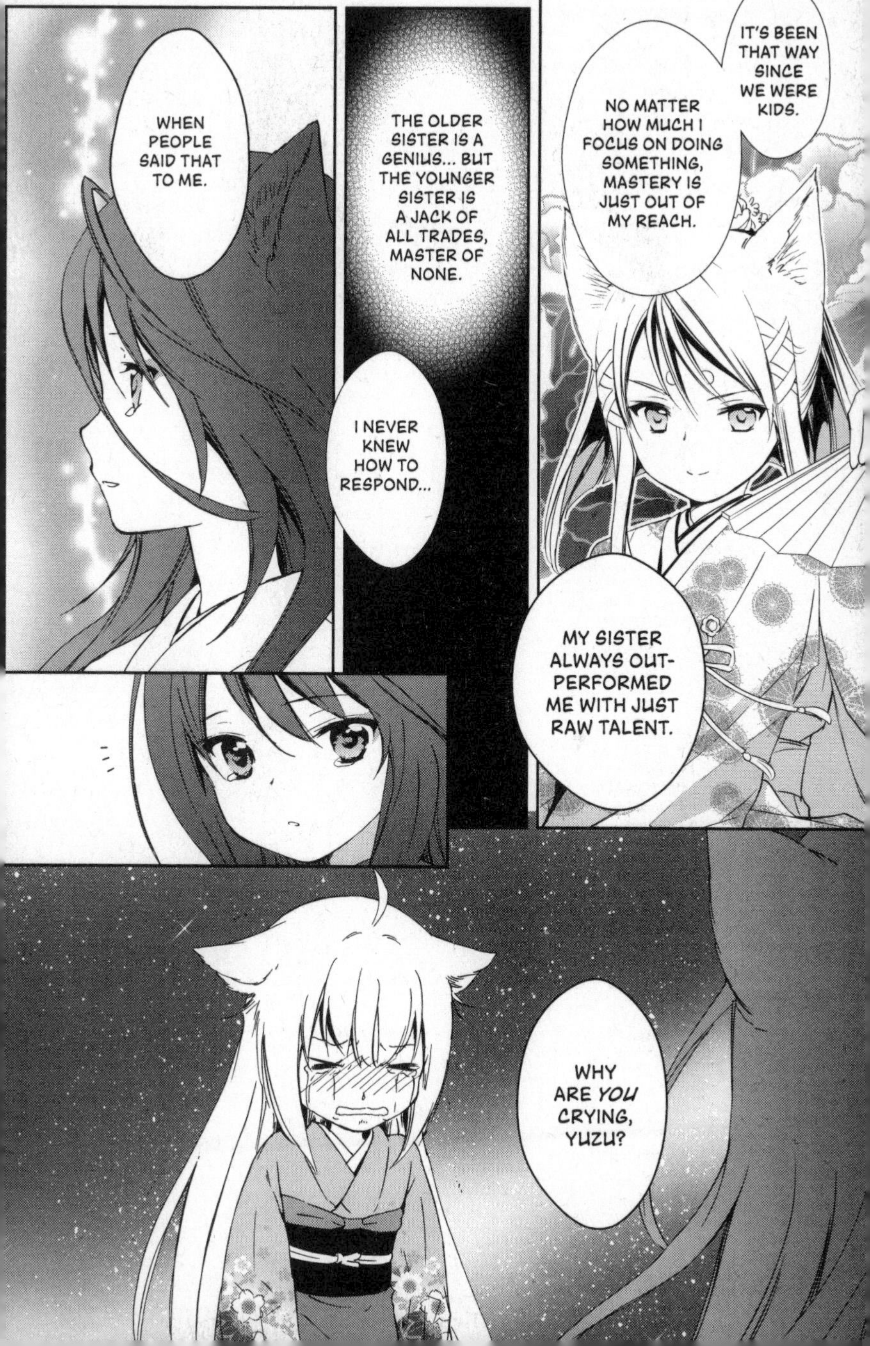
IT'S BEEN THAT WAY SINCE WE WERE KIDS.
NO MATTER HOW MUCH I FOCUS ON DOING SOMETHING, MASTERY IS JUST OUT OF MY REACH.
MY SISTER ALWAYS OUT-PERFORMED ME WITH JUST RAW TALENT.
THE OLDER SISTER IS A GENIUS... BUT THE YOUNGER SISTER IS A JACK OF ALL TRADES, MASTER OF NONE.
I NEVER KNEW HOW TO RESPOND...
WHEN PEOPLE SAID THAT TO ME.
WHY ARE *YOU* CRYING, YUZU?

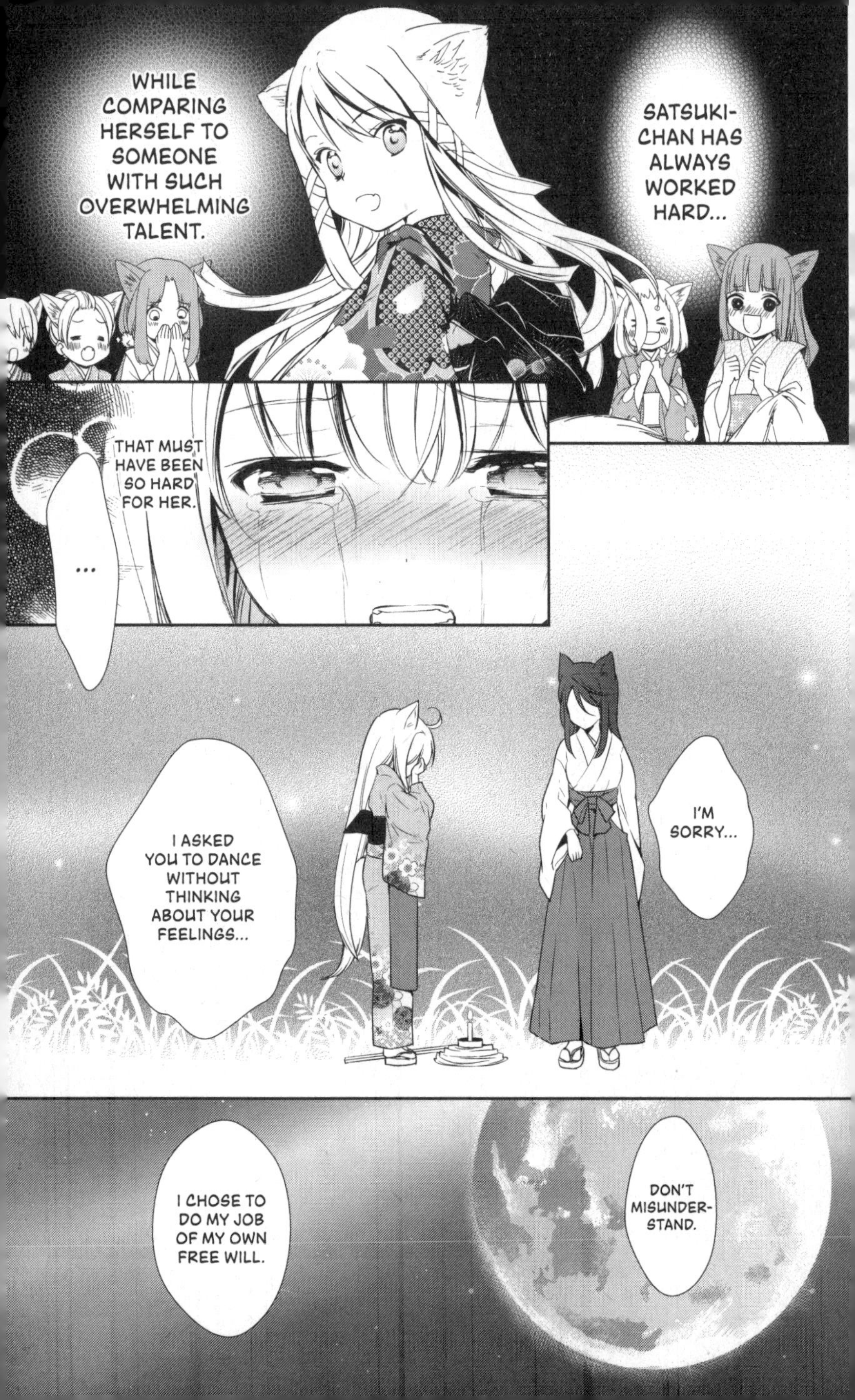
SATSUKI-CHAN HAS ALWAYS WORKED HARD...
WHILE COMPARING HERSELF TO SOMEONE WITH SUCH OVERWHELMING TALENT.
THAT MUST HAVE BEEN SO HARD FOR HER.
...
I'M SORRY...
I ASKED YOU TO DANCE WITHOUT THINKING ABOUT YOUR FEELINGS...
DON'T MISUNDERSTAND.
I CHOSE TO DO MY JOB OF MY OWN FREE WILL.

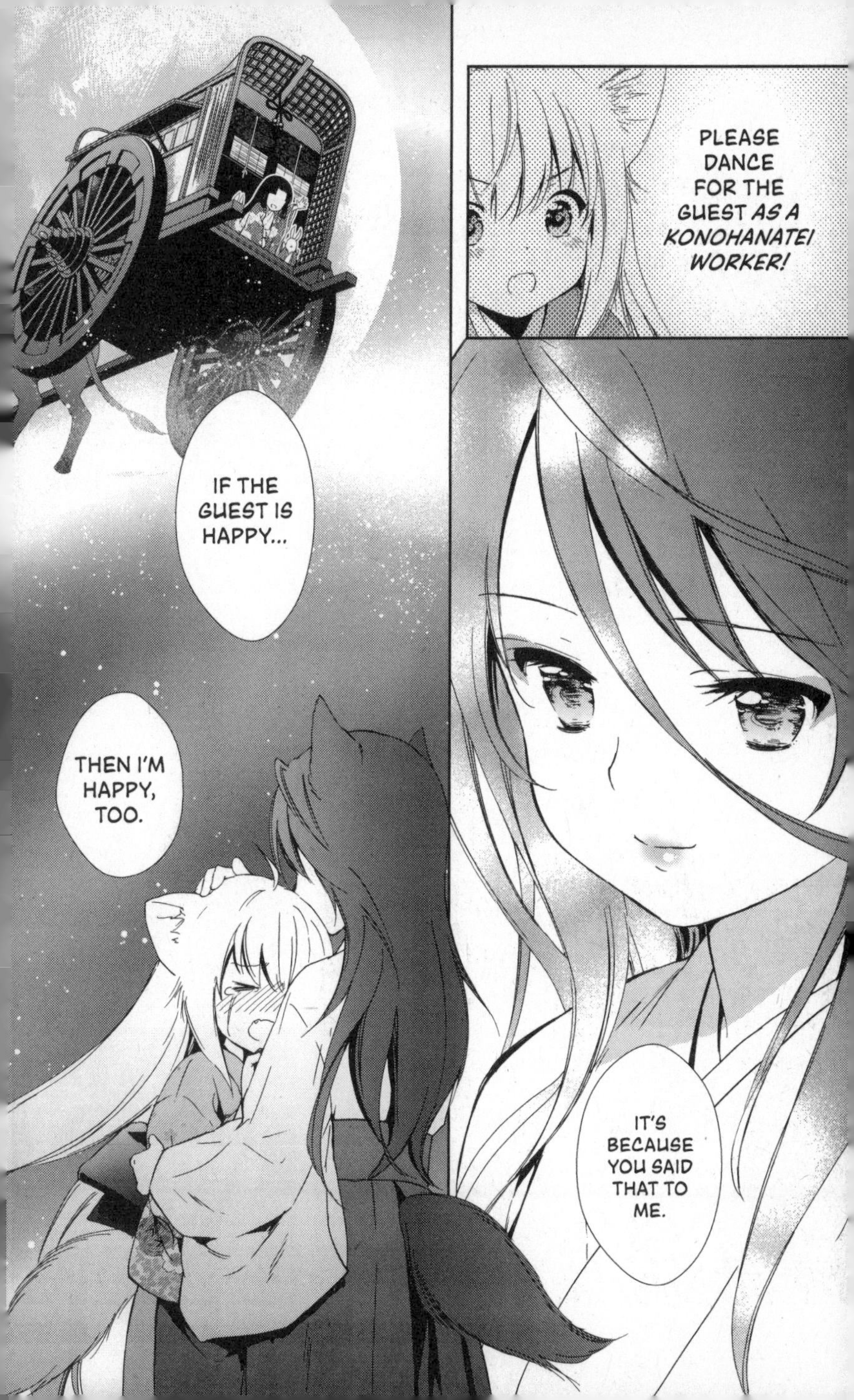
PLEASE DANCE FOR THE GUEST AS A KONOHANATEI WORKER!
IT'S BECAUSE YOU SAID THAT TO ME.
IF THE GUEST IS HAPPY...
THEN I'M HAPPY, TOO.

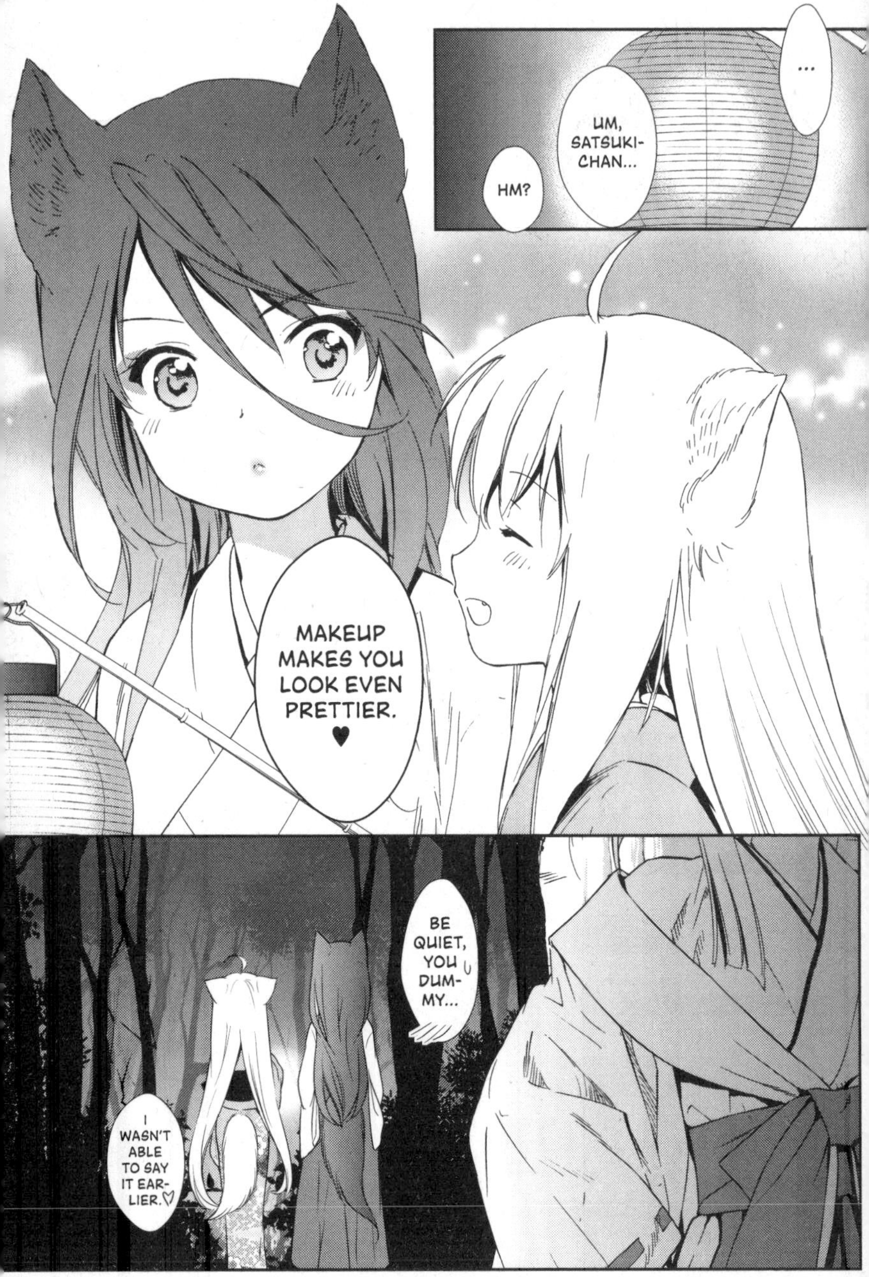
...
UM, SATSUKI-CHAN...
HM?
MAKEUP MAKES YOU LOOK EVEN PRETTIER. ♥
BE QUIET, YOU DUM-MY...
I WASN'T ABLE TO SAY IT EAR-LIER.♡

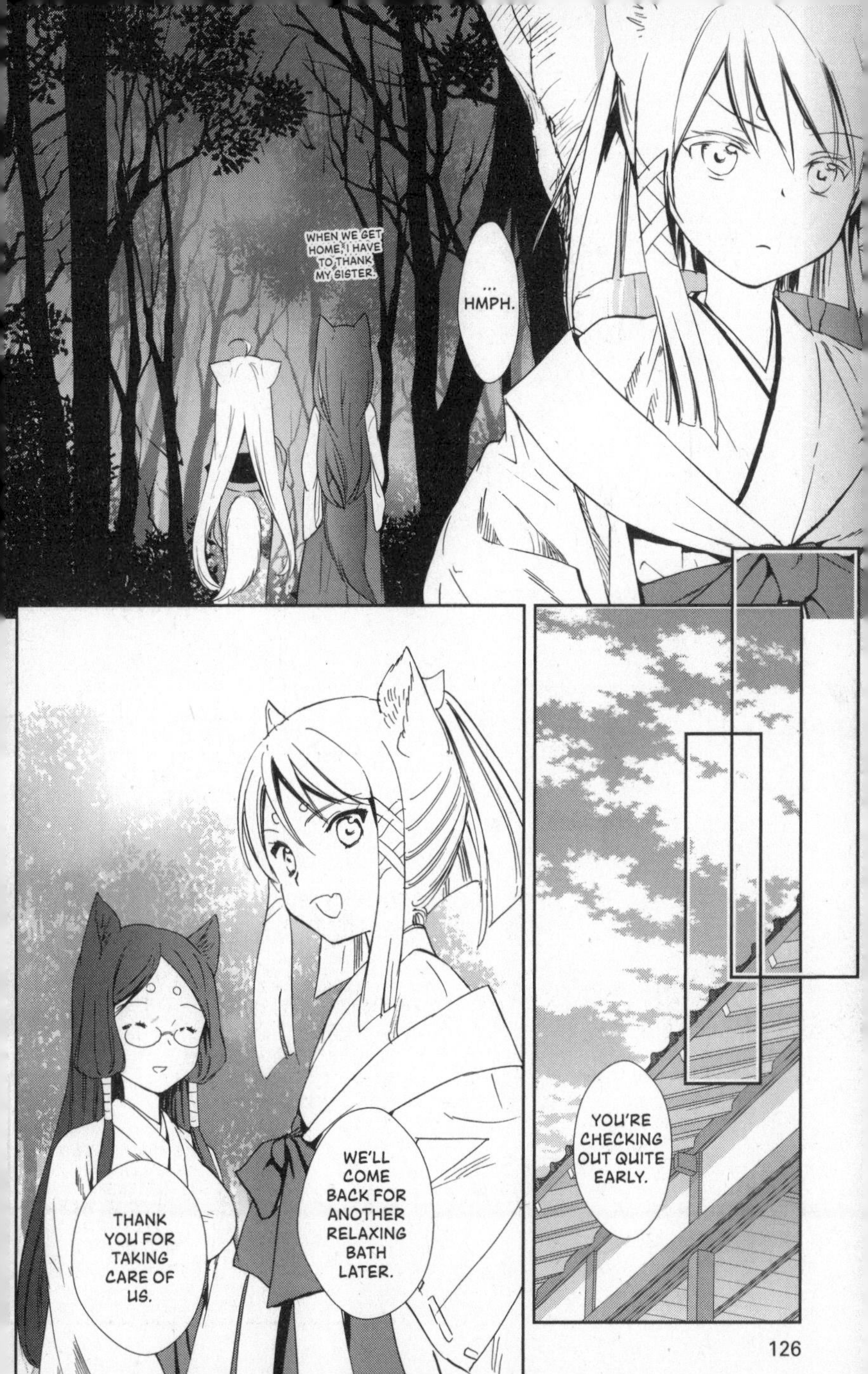

... HMPH.
WHEN WE GET HOME, I HAVE TO THANK MY SISTER.
YOU'RE CHECKING OUT QUITE EARLY.
WE'LL COME BACK FOR ANOTHER RELAXING BATH LATER.
THANK YOU FOR TAKING CARE OF US.

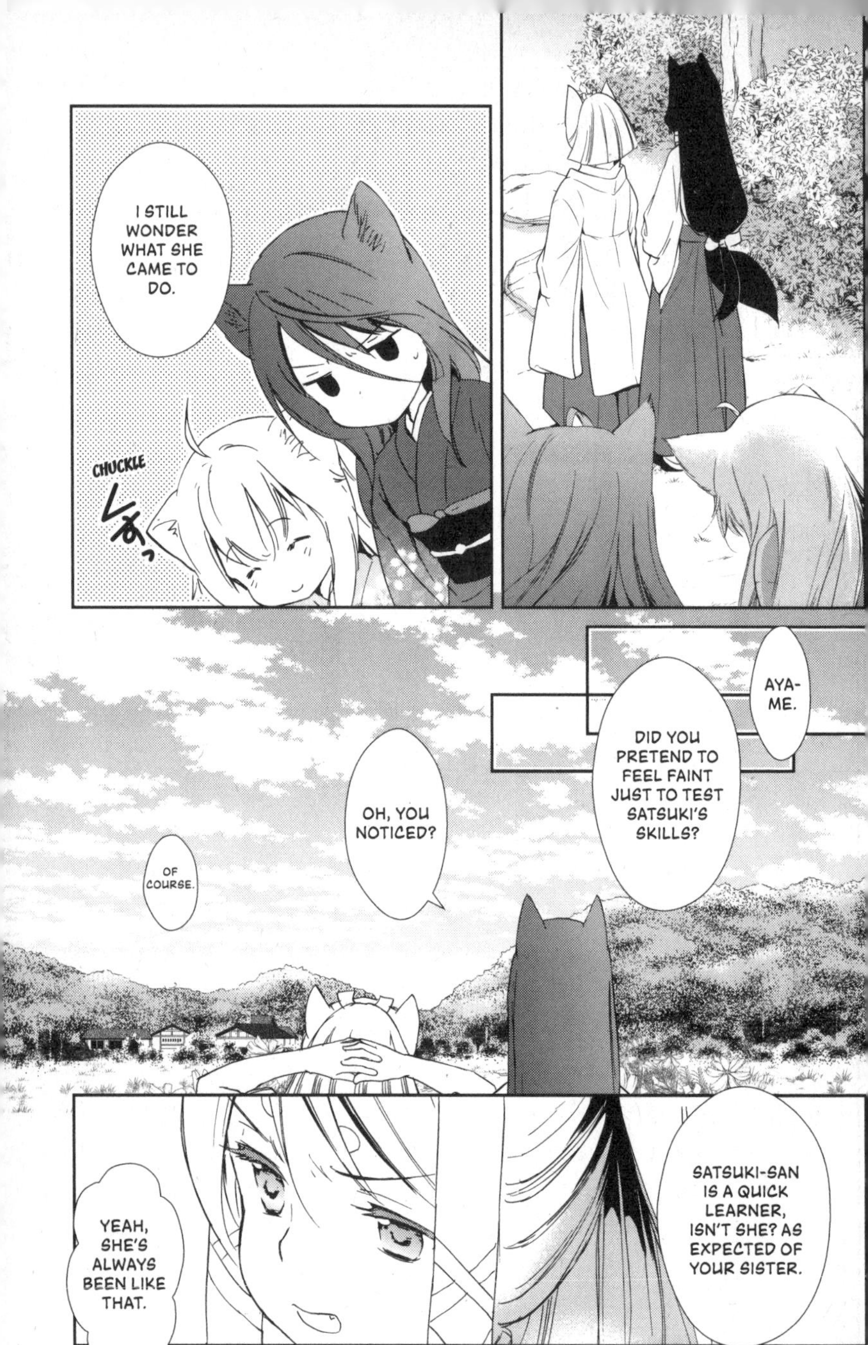
I STILL WONDER WHAT SHE CAME TO DO.
CHUCKLE
AYA-ME.
DID YOU PRETEND TO FEEL FAINT JUST TO TEST SATSUKI'S SKILLS?
OH, YOU NOTICED?
OF COURSE.
SATSUKI-SAN IS A QUICK LEARNER, ISN'T SHE? AS EXPECTED OF YOUR SISTER.
YEAH, SHE'S ALWAYS BEEN LIKE THAT.

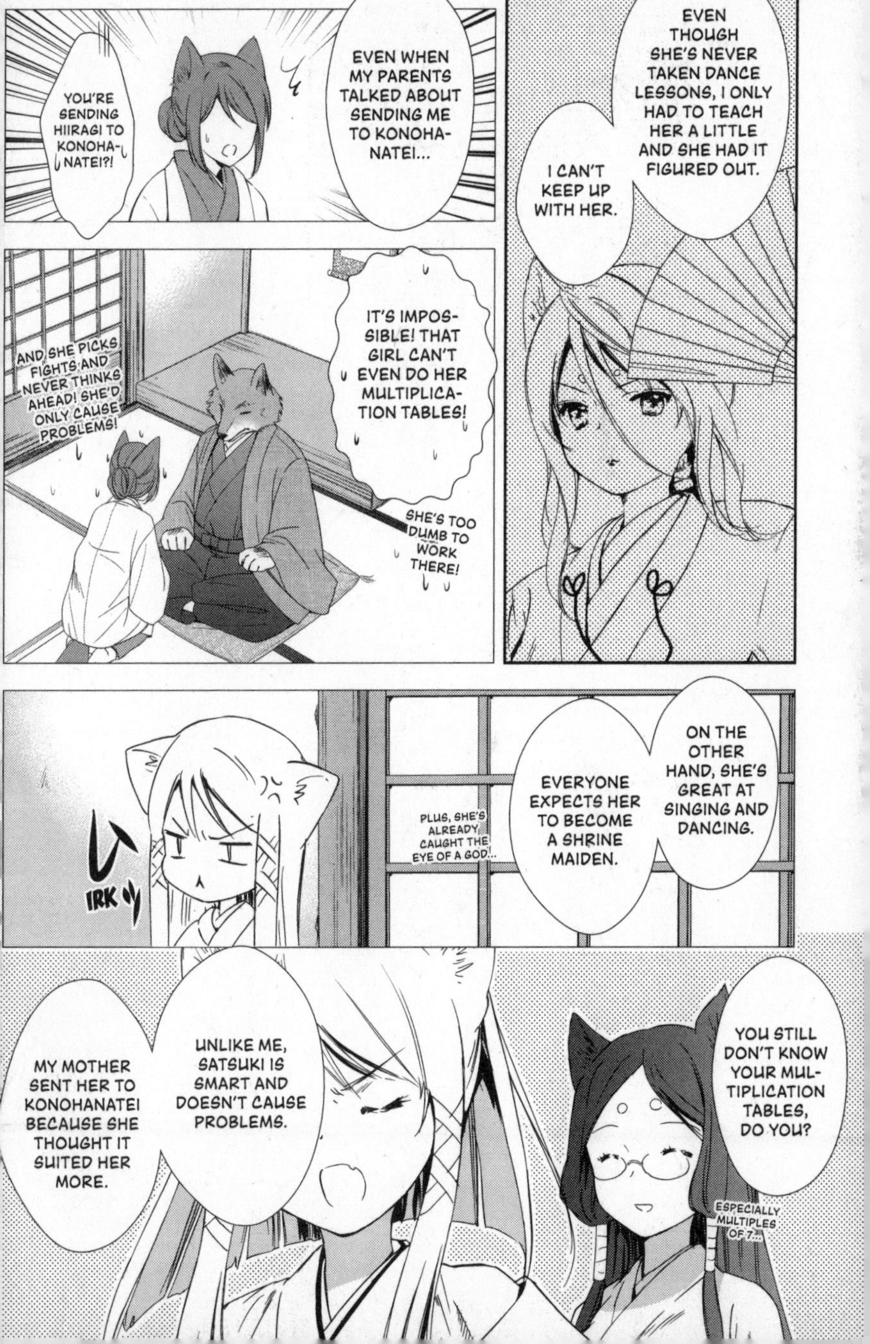
EVEN THOUGH SHE'S NEVER TAKEN DANCE LESSONS, I ONLY HAD TO TEACH HER A LITTLE AND SHE HAD IT FIGURED OUT.
I CAN'T KEEP UP WITH HER.
EVEN WHEN MY PARENTS TALKED ABOUT SENDING ME TO KONOHA-NATEI...
YOU'RE SENDING HIIRAGI TO KONOHA-NATEI?!
IT'S IMPOS-SIBLE! THAT GIRL CAN'T EVEN DO HER MULTIPLICA-TION TABLES!
AND SHE PICKS FIGHTS AND NEVER THINKS AHEAD! SHE'D ONLY CAUSE PROBLEMS!
SHE'S TOO DUMB TO WORK THERE!
ON THE OTHER HAND, SHE'S GREAT AT SINGING AND DANCING.
EVERYONE EXPECTS HER TO BECOME A SHRINE MAIDEN.
PLUS, SHE'S ALREADY CAUGHT THE EYE OF A GOD...
IRK
YOU STILL DON'T KNOW YOUR MUL-TIPLICATION TABLES, DO YOU?
ESPECIALLY MULTIPLES OF 7...
UNLIKE ME, SATSUKI IS SMART AND DOESN'T CAUSE PROBLEMS.
MY MOTHER SENT HER TO KONOHANATEI BECAUSE SHE THOUGHT IT SUITED HER MORE.

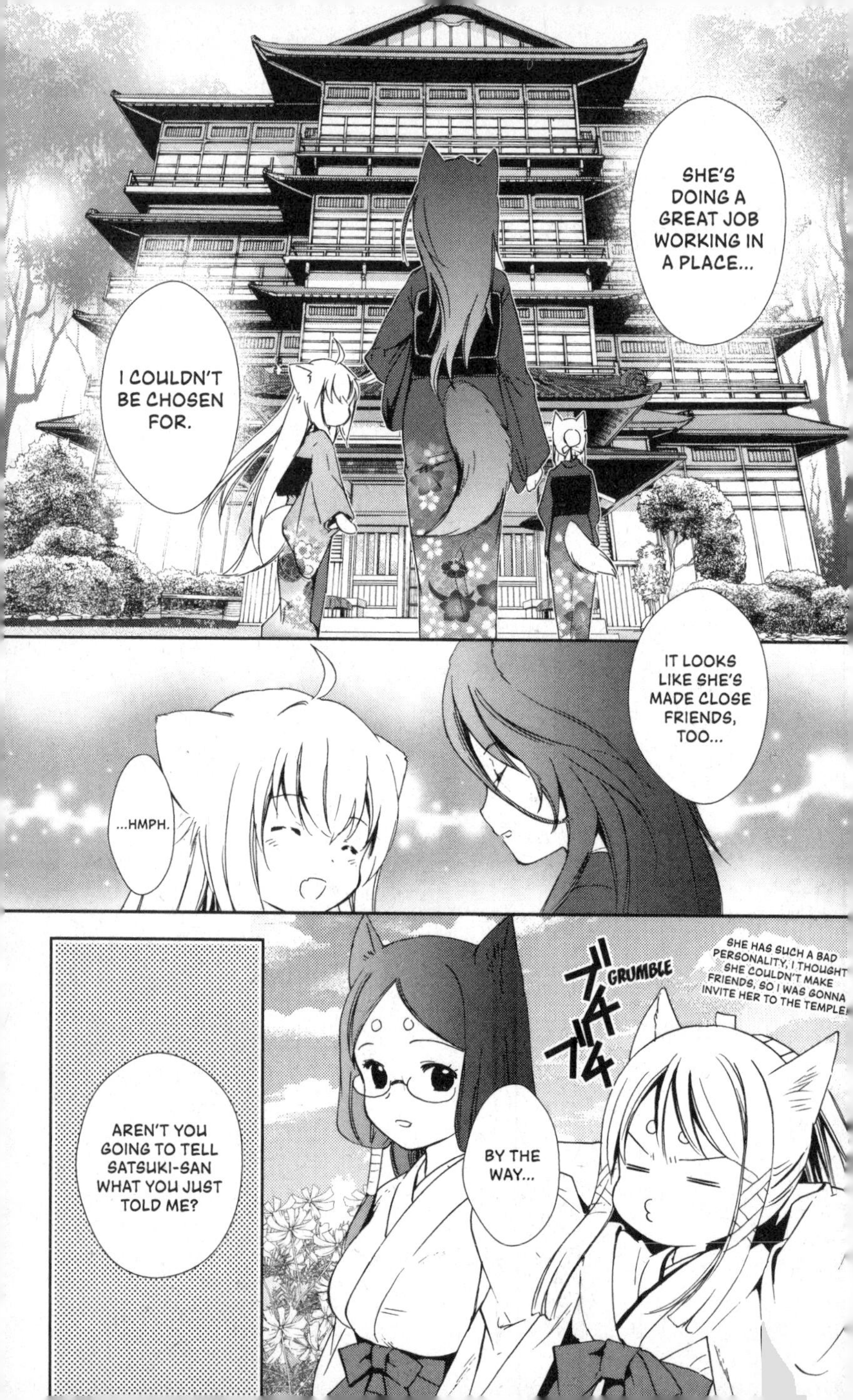
SHE'S DOING A GREAT JOB WORKING IN A PLACE...
I COULDN'T BE CHOSEN FOR.
IT LOOKS LIKE SHE'S MADE CLOSE FRIENDS, TOO...
...HMPH.
SHE HAS SUCH A BAD PERSONALITY, I THOUGHT SHE COULDN'T MAKE FRIENDS, SO I WAS GONNA INVITE HER TO THE TEMPLE!
GRUMBLE
BY THE WAY...
AREN'T YOU GOING TO TELL SATSUKI-SAN WHAT YOU JUST TOLD ME?

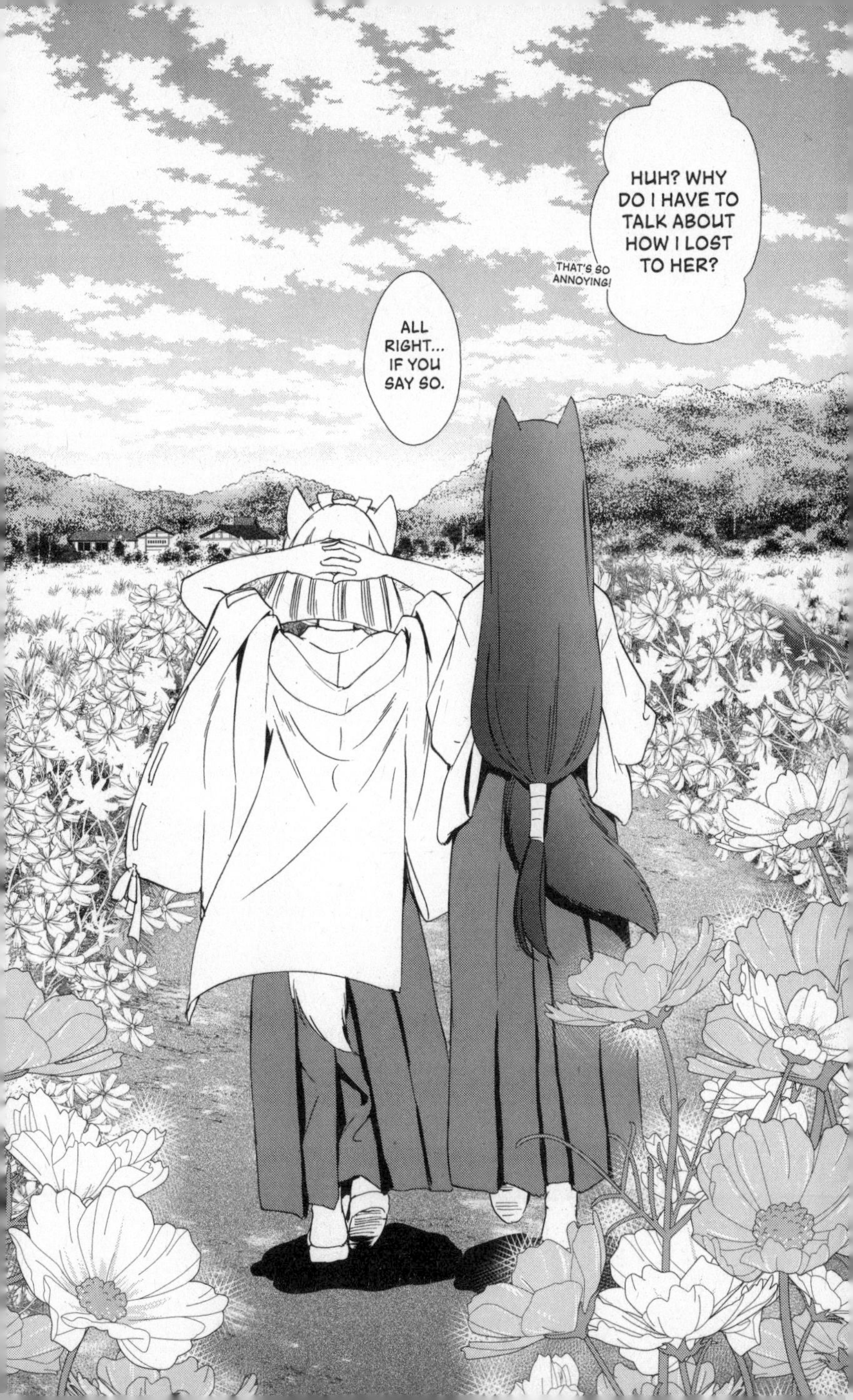
HUH? WHY DO I HAVE TO TALK ABOUT HOW I LOST TO HER?
THAT'S SO ANNOYING!
ALL RIGHT... IF YOU SAY SO.

KONOHANA KITAN

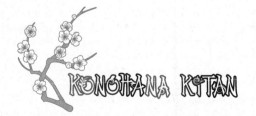

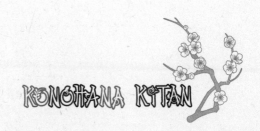
KONOHANA KITAN

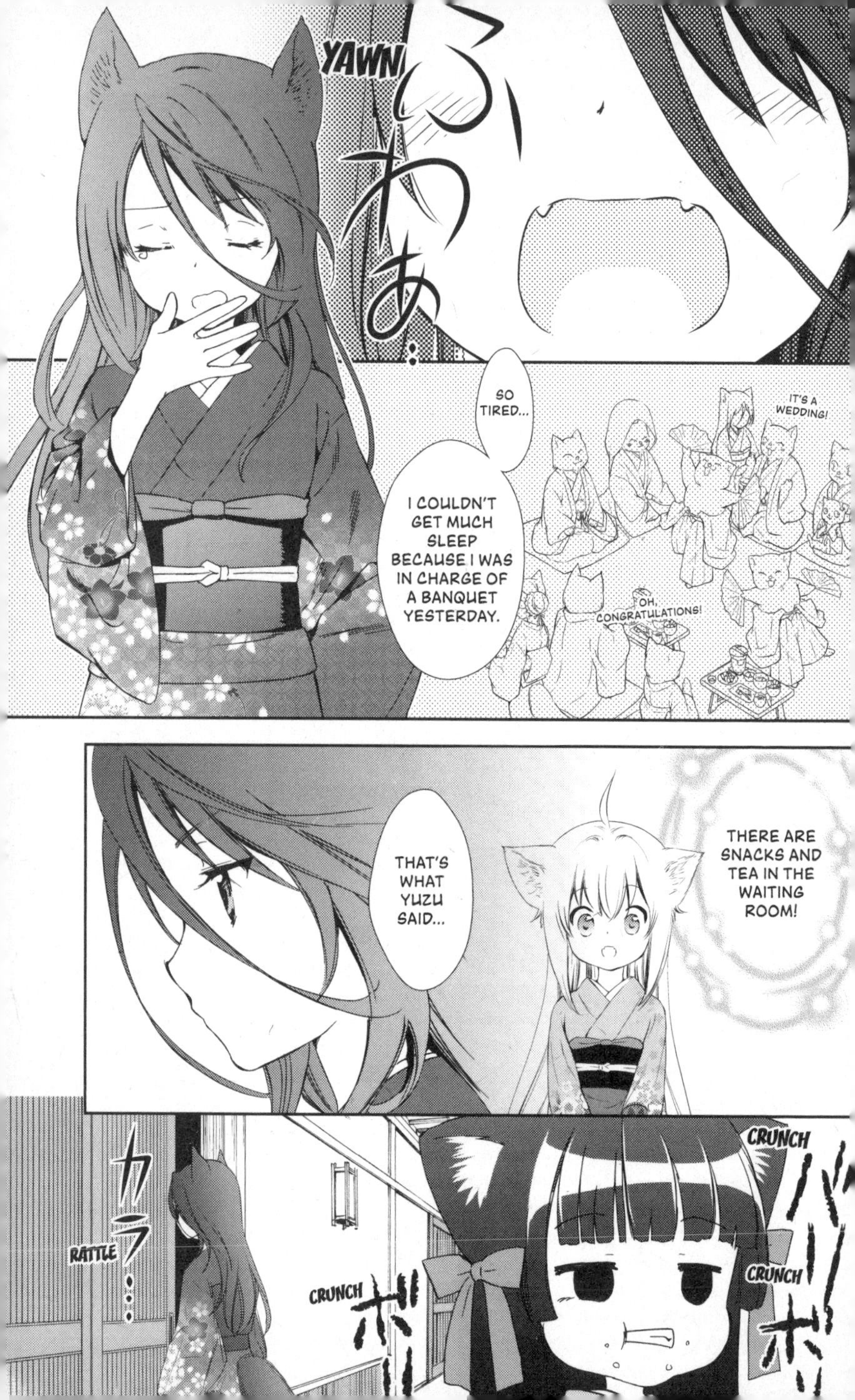

YAWN
ふわあ…
SO TIRED...
I COULDN'T GET MUCH SLEEP BECAUSE I WAS IN CHARGE OF A BANQUET YESTERDAY.
IT'S A WEDDING!
OH, CONGRATULATIONS!
THERE ARE SNACKS AND TEA IN THE WAITING ROOM!
THAT'S WHAT YUZU SAID...
CRUNCH
CRUNCH
CRUNCH
カラ…
RATTLE

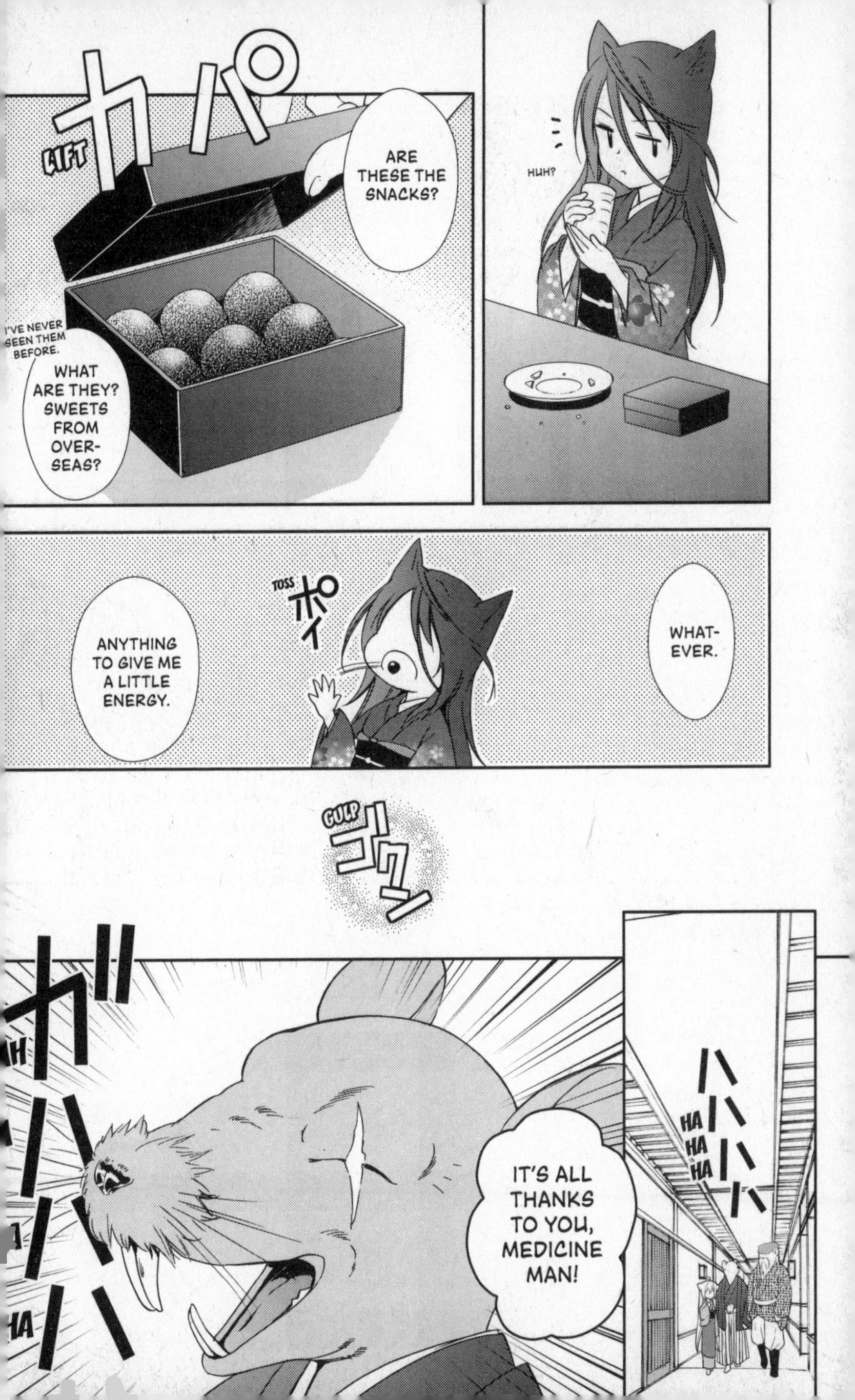
HUH?
LIFT
ARE THESE THE SNACKS?
I'VE NEVER SEEN THEM BEFORE.
WHAT ARE THEY? SWEETS FROM OVER-SEAS?
WHAT-EVER.
TOSS
ANYTHING TO GIVE ME A LITTLE ENERGY.
GULP
HA HA HA
IT'S ALL THANKS TO YOU, MEDICINE MAN!
HA

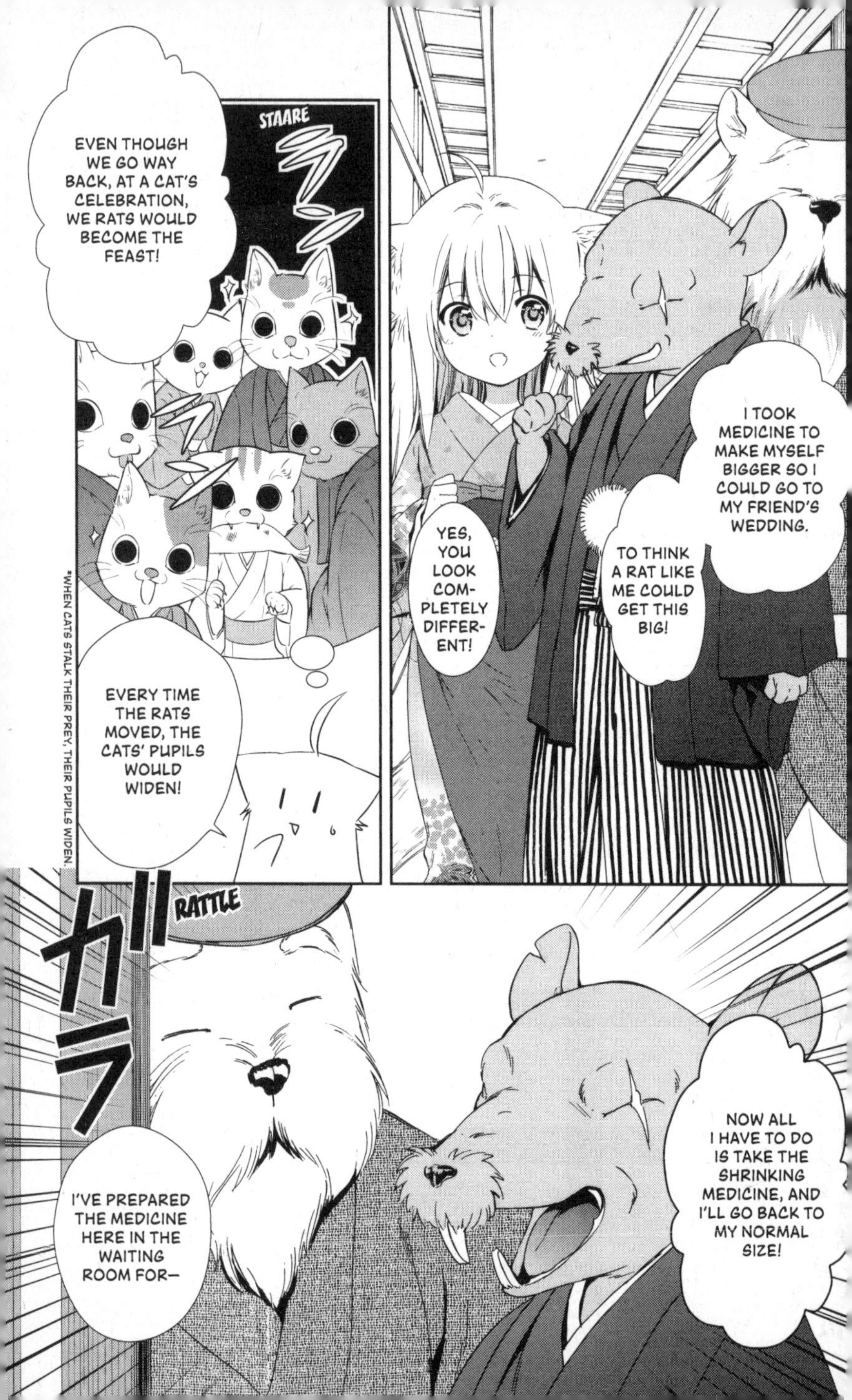
I TOOK MEDICINE TO MAKE MYSELF BIGGER SO I COULD GO TO MY FRIEND'S WEDDING.
TO THINK A RAT LIKE ME COULD GET THIS BIG!
YES, YOU LOOK COM-PLETELY DIFFER-ENT!
STAARE
EVEN THOUGH WE GO WAY BACK, AT A CAT'S CELEBRATION, WE RATS WOULD BECOME THE FEAST!
EVERY TIME THE RATS MOVED, THE CATS' PUPILS WOULD WIDEN!
*WHEN CATS STALK THEIR PREY, THEIR PUPILS WIDEN.
RATTLE
NOW ALL I HAVE TO DO IS TAKE THE SHRINKING MEDICINE, AND I'LL GO BACK TO MY NORMAL SIZE!
I'VE PREPARED THE MEDICINE HERE IN THE WAITING ROOM FOR—

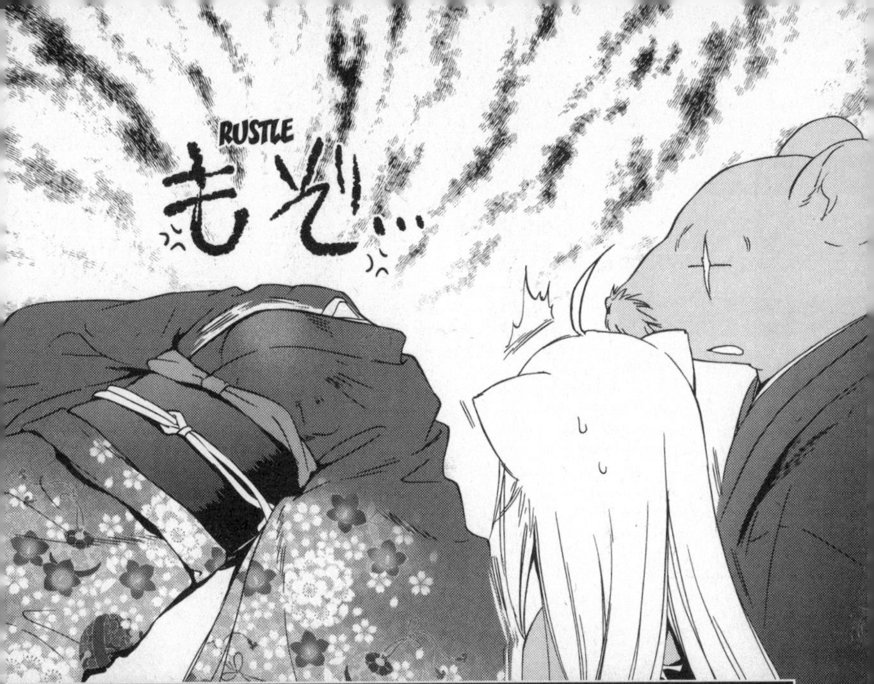
RUSTLE
もぞ…

Little Satsuki

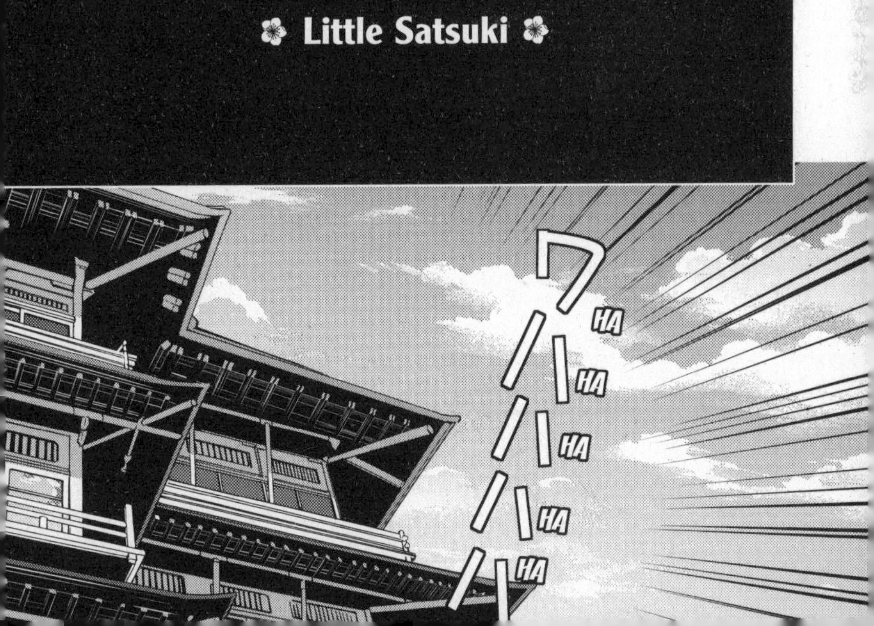
HA
HA
HA
HA
HA

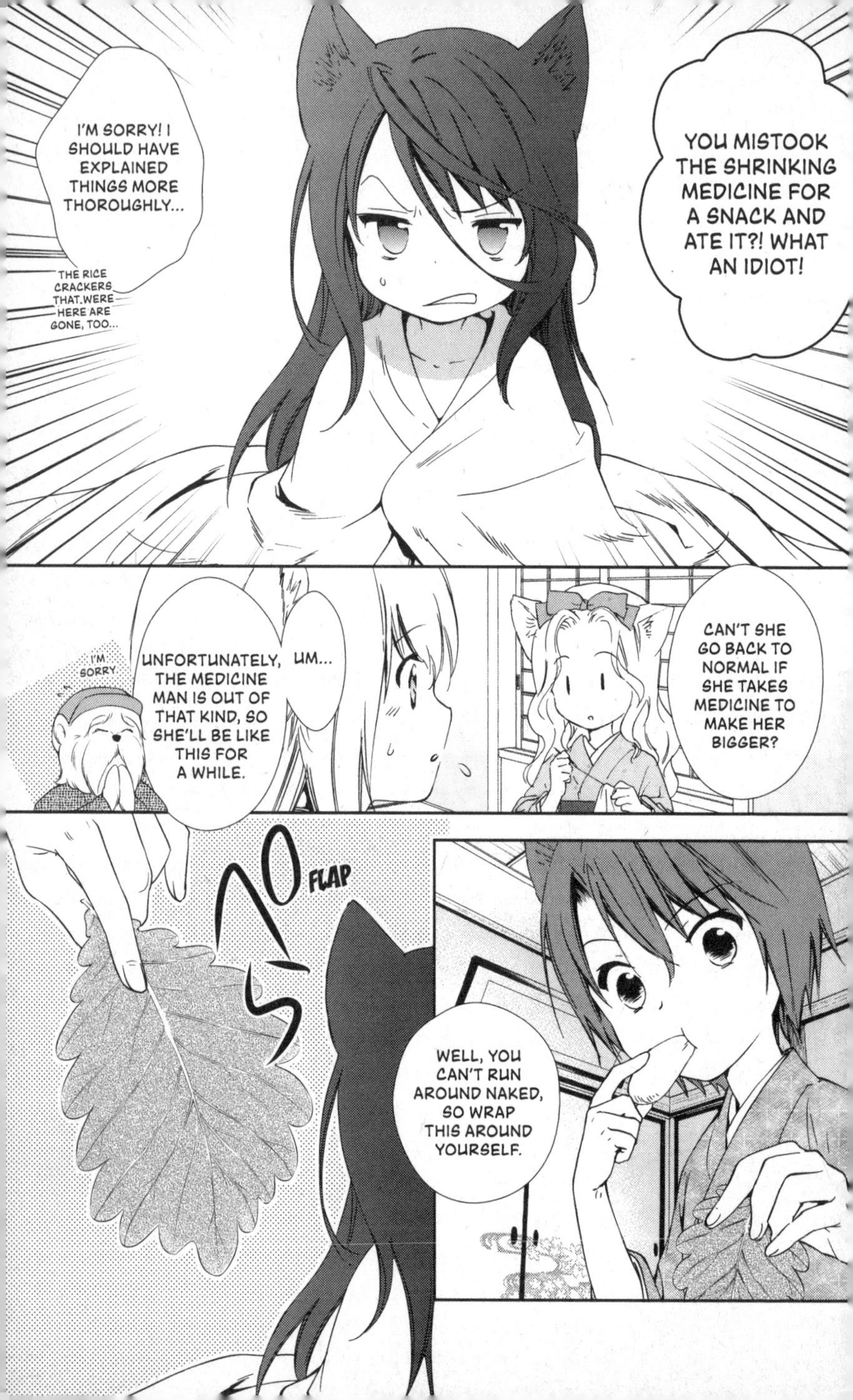
YOU MISTOOK THE SHRINKING MEDICINE FOR A SNACK AND ATE IT?! WHAT AN IDIOT!
I'M SORRY! I SHOULD HAVE EXPLAINED THINGS MORE THOROUGHLY...
THE RICE CRACKERS THAT WERE HERE ARE GONE, TOO...
CAN'T SHE GO BACK TO NORMAL IF SHE TAKES MEDICINE TO MAKE HER BIGGER?
UM...
UNFORTUNATELY, THE MEDICINE MAN IS OUT OF THAT KIND, SO SHE'LL BE LIKE THIS FOR A WHILE.
I'M SORRY
WELL, YOU CAN'T RUN AROUND NAKED, SO WRAP THIS AROUND YOURSELF.
FLAP

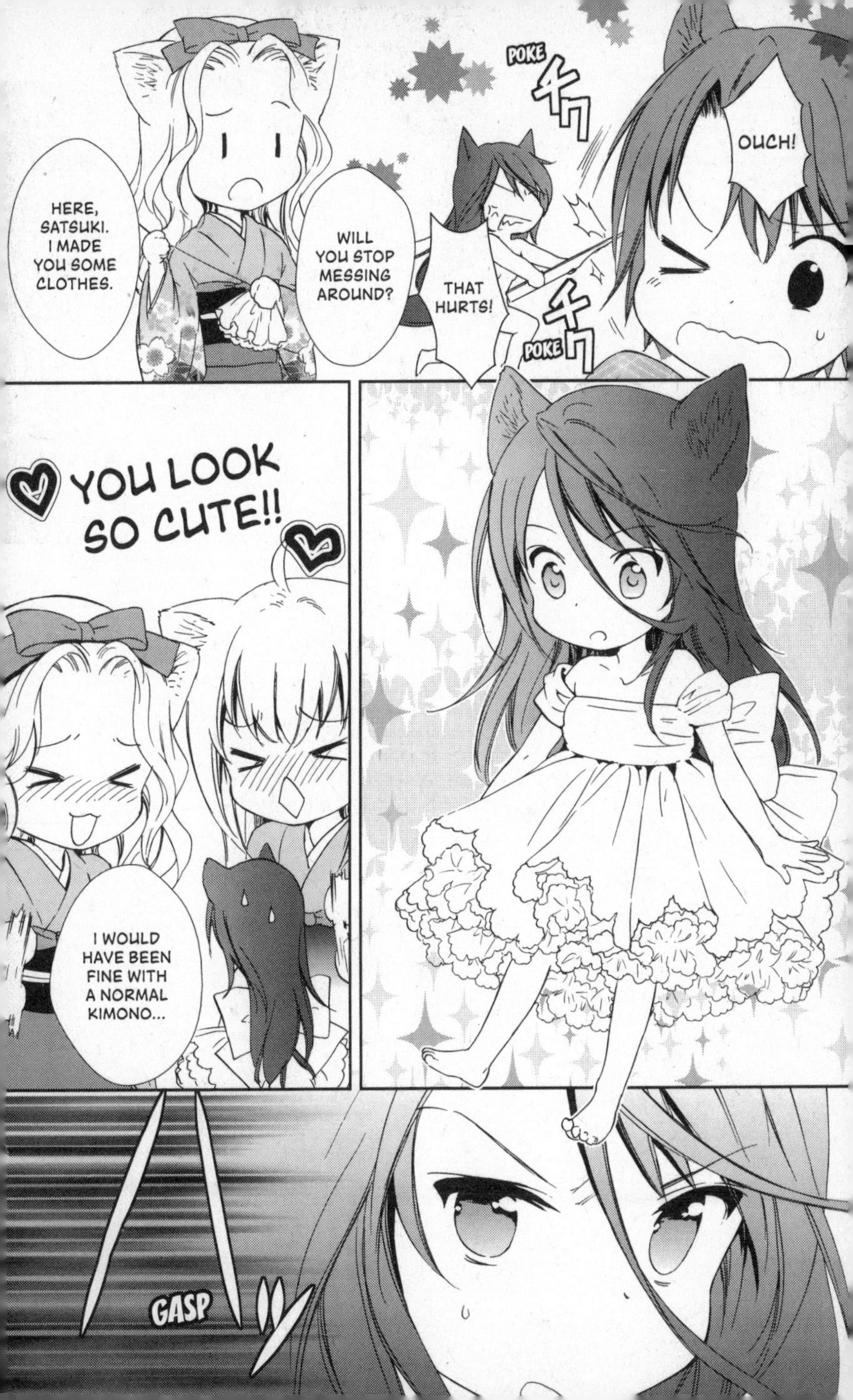
POKE
OUCH!
THAT HURTS!
POKE
WILL YOU STOP MESSING AROUND?
HERE, SATSUKI. I MADE YOU SOME CLOTHES.
YOU LOOK SO CUTE!!
I WOULD HAVE BEEN FINE WITH A NORMAL KIMONO...
GASP

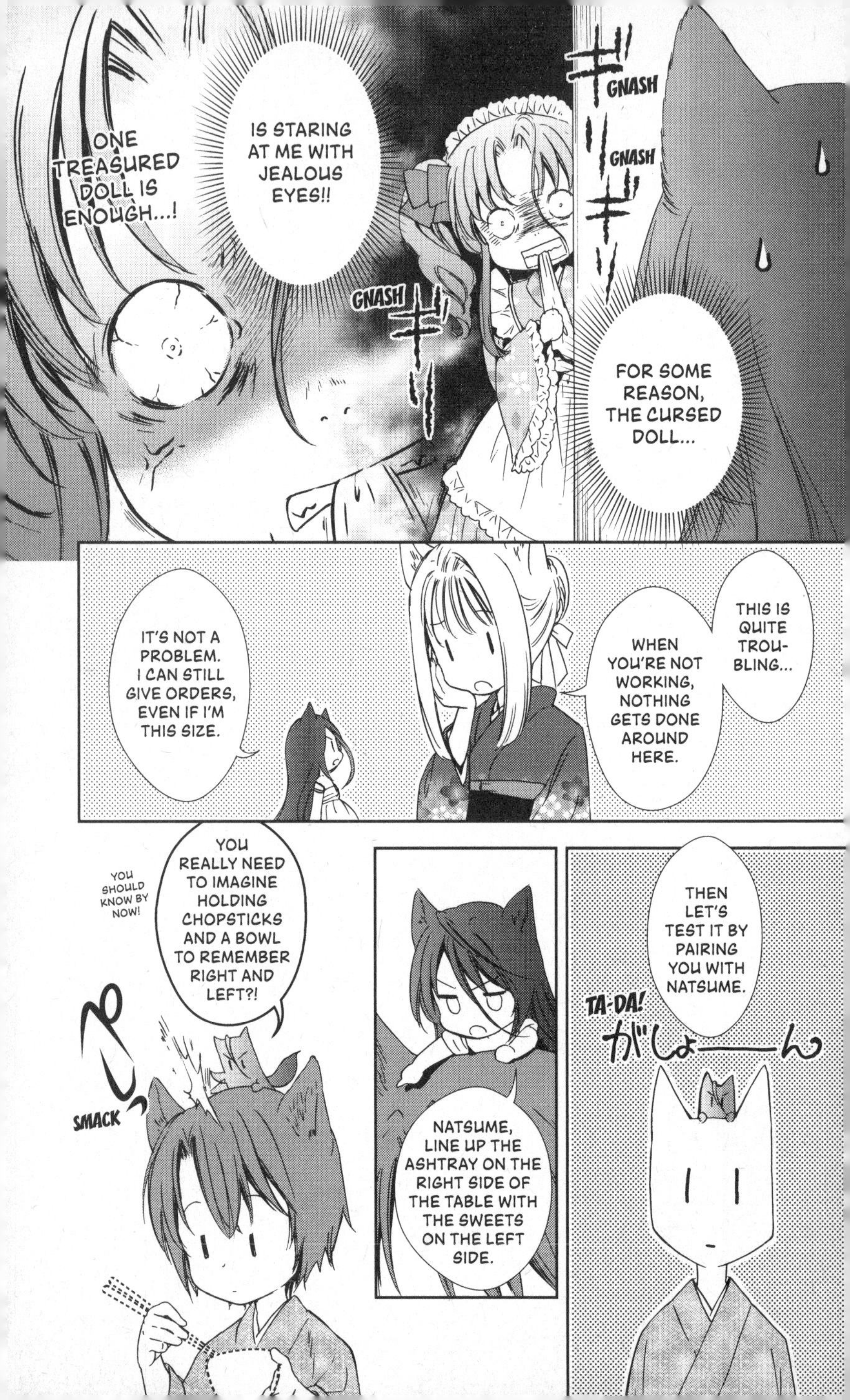
GNASH
GNASH
FOR SOME REASON, THE CURSED DOLL...
IS STARING AT ME WITH JEALOUS EYES!!
GNASH
ONE TREASURED DOLL IS ENOUGH...!
THIS IS QUITE TROU-BLING...
WHEN YOU'RE NOT WORKING, NOTHING GETS DONE AROUND HERE.
IT'S NOT A PROBLEM. I CAN STILL GIVE ORDERS, EVEN IF I'M THIS SIZE.
THEN LET'S TEST IT BY PAIRING YOU WITH NATSUME.
TA-DA!
がしょーーん
NATSUME, LINE UP THE ASHTRAY ON THE RIGHT SIDE OF THE TABLE WITH THE SWEETS ON THE LEFT SIDE.
YOU REALLY NEED TO IMAGINE HOLDING CHOPSTICKS AND A BOWL TO REMEMBER RIGHT AND LEFT?!
YOU SHOULD KNOW BY NOW!
SMACK

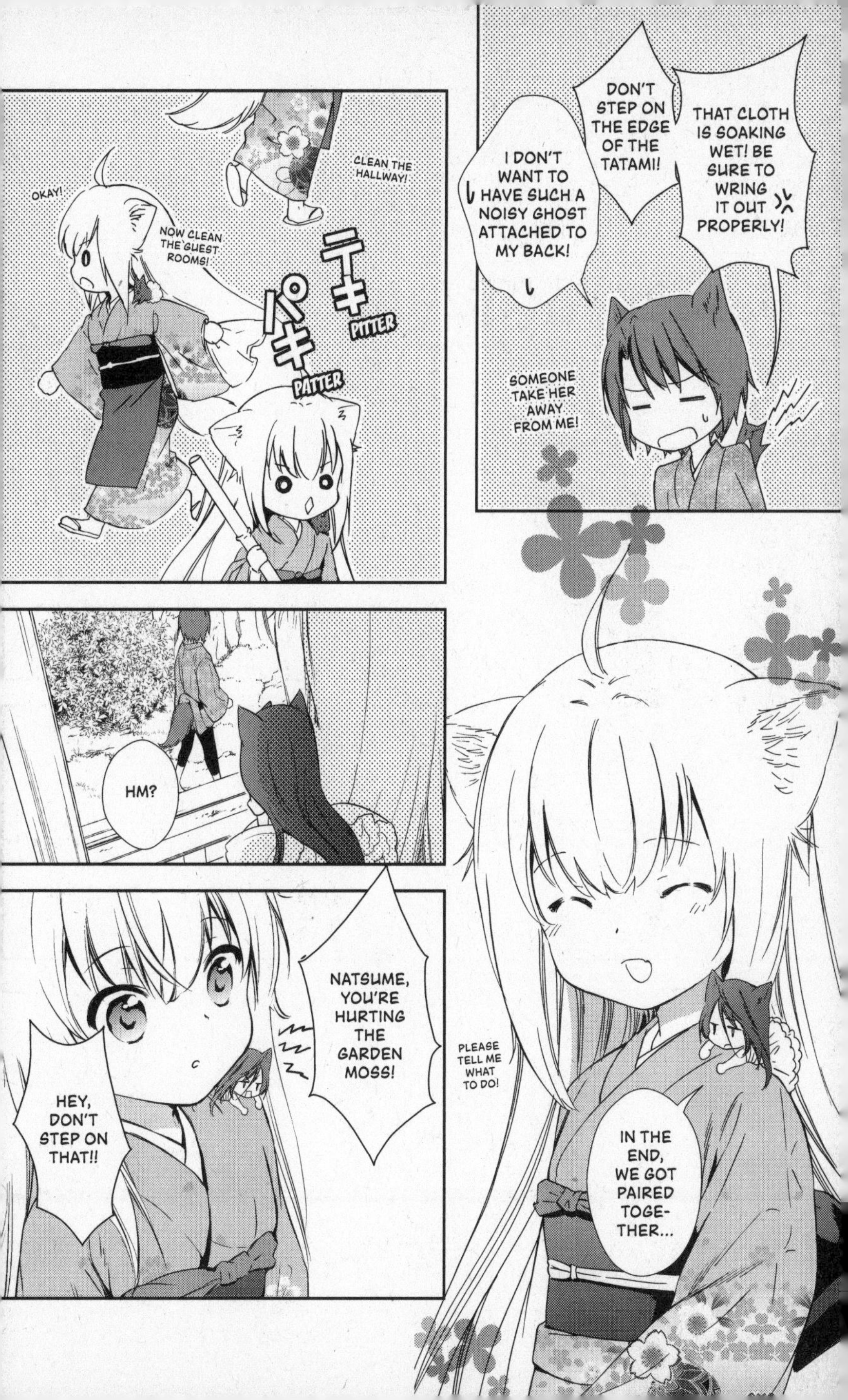
THAT CLOTH IS SOAKING WET! BE SURE TO WRING IT OUT PROPERLY!
DON'T STEP ON THE EDGE OF THE TATAMI!
I DON'T WANT TO HAVE SUCH A NOISY GHOST ATTACHED TO MY BACK!
SOMEONE TAKE HER AWAY FROM ME!
CLEAN THE HALLWAY!
OKAY!
NOW CLEAN THE GUEST ROOMS!
テキ
PITTER
パキ
PATTER
PLEASE TELL ME WHAT TO DO!
IN THE END, WE GOT PAIRED TOGE-THER...
HM?
NATSUME, YOU'RE HURTING THE GARDEN MOSS!
HEY, DON'T STEP ON THAT!!

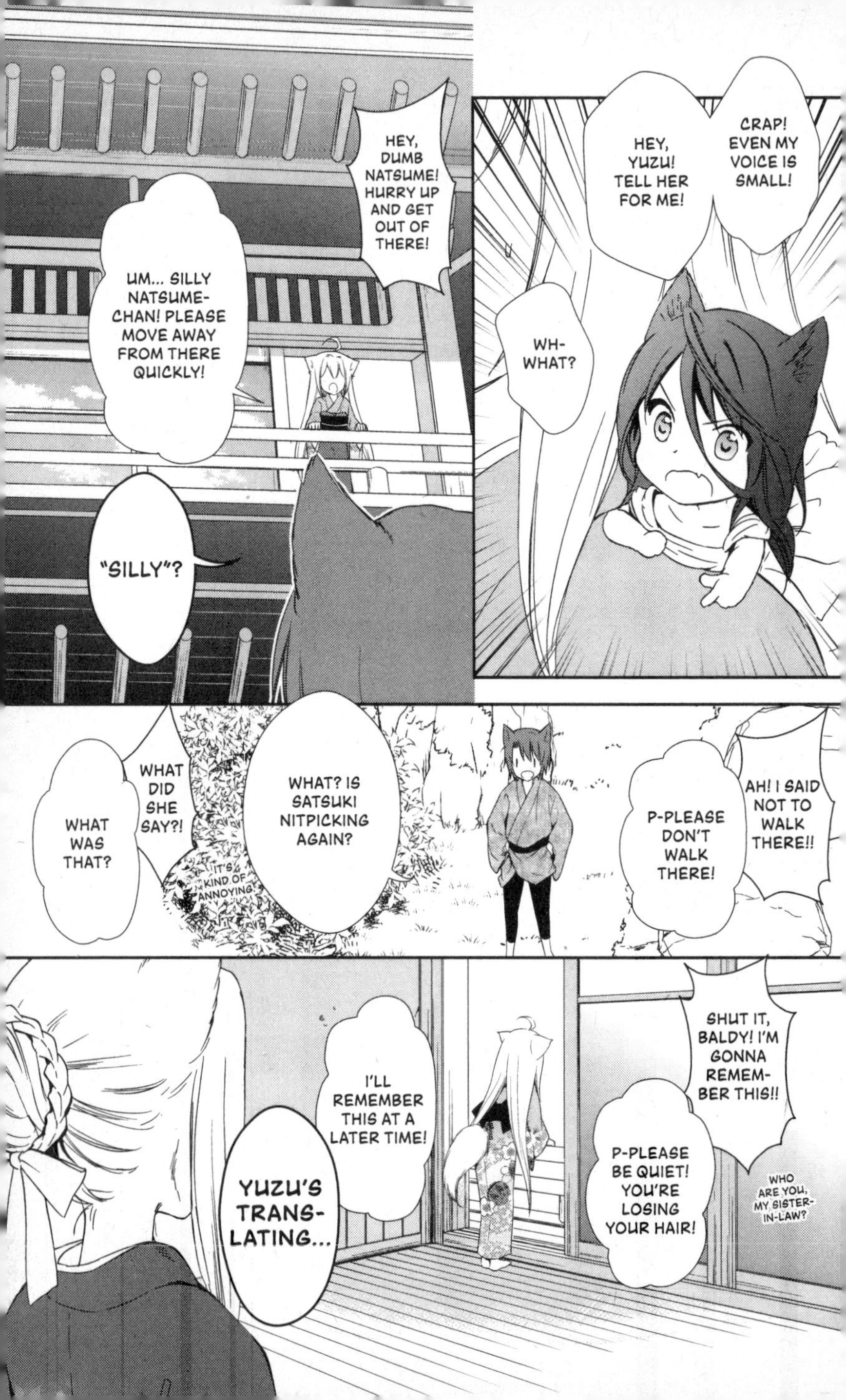
CRAP! EVEN MY VOICE IS SMALL!
HEY, YUZU! TELL HER FOR ME!
WH-WHAT?
HEY, DUMB NATSUME! HURRY UP AND GET OUT OF THERE!
UM... SILLY NATSUME-CHAN! PLEASE MOVE AWAY FROM THERE QUICKLY!
"SILLY"?
AH! I SAID NOT TO WALK THERE!!
P-PLEASE DON'T WALK THERE!
WHAT? IS SATSUKI NITPICKING AGAIN?
IT'S KIND OF ANNOYING
WHAT DID SHE SAY?!
WHAT WAS THAT?
SHUT IT, BALDY! I'M GONNA REMEMBER THIS!!
WHO ARE YOU, MY SISTER-IN-LAW?
P-PLEASE BE QUIET! YOU'RE LOSING YOUR HAIR!
I'LL REMEMBER THIS AT A LATER TIME!
YUZU'S TRANSLATING...

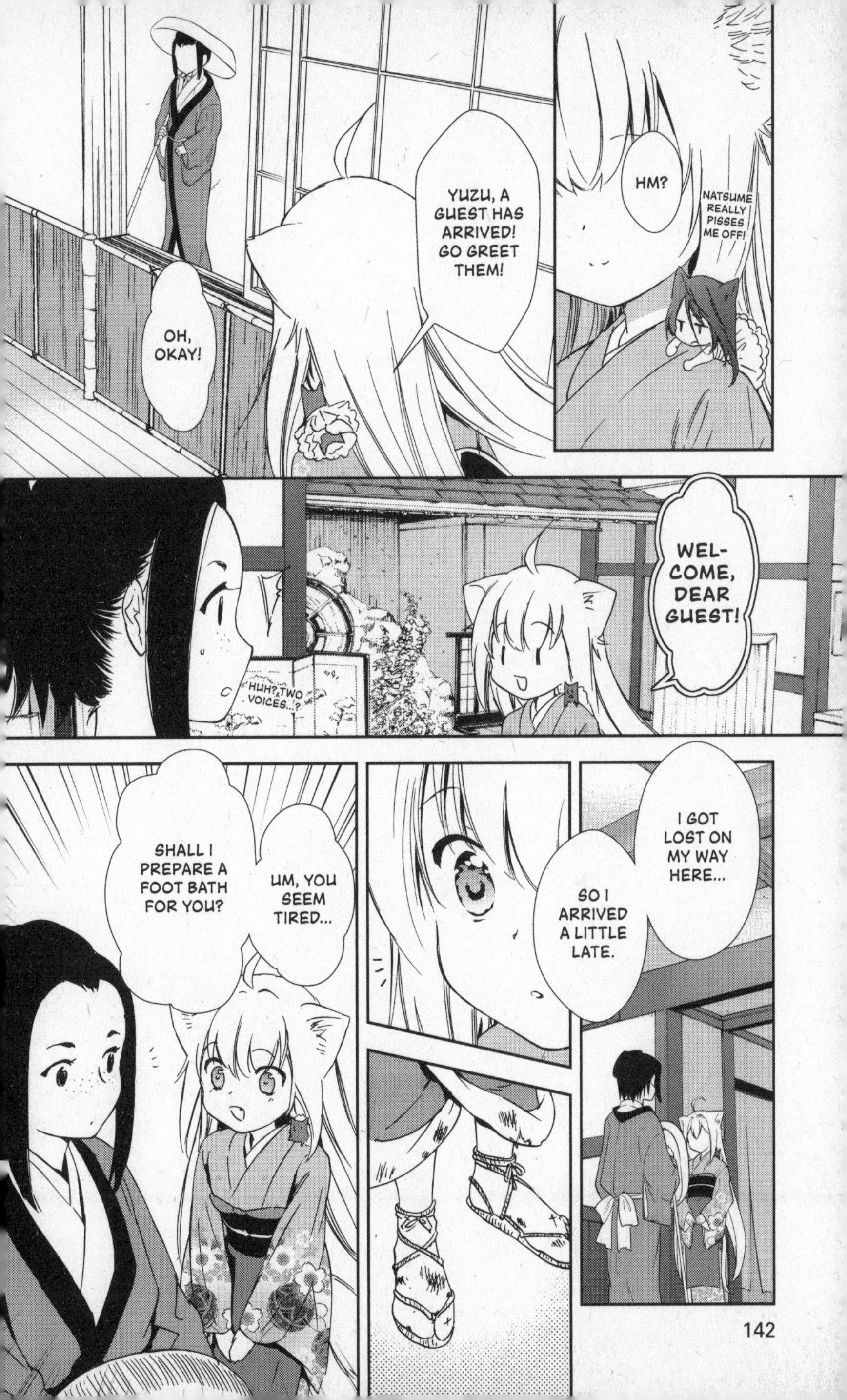
HM?
NATSUME REALLY PISSES ME OFF!
YUZU, A GUEST HAS ARRIVED! GO GREET THEM!
OH, OKAY!
WEL-COME, DEAR GUEST!
HUH? TWO VOICES...?
I GOT LOST ON MY WAY HERE...
SO I ARRIVED A LITTLE LATE.
UM, YOU SEEM TIRED...
SHALL I PREPARE A FOOT BATH FOR YOU?

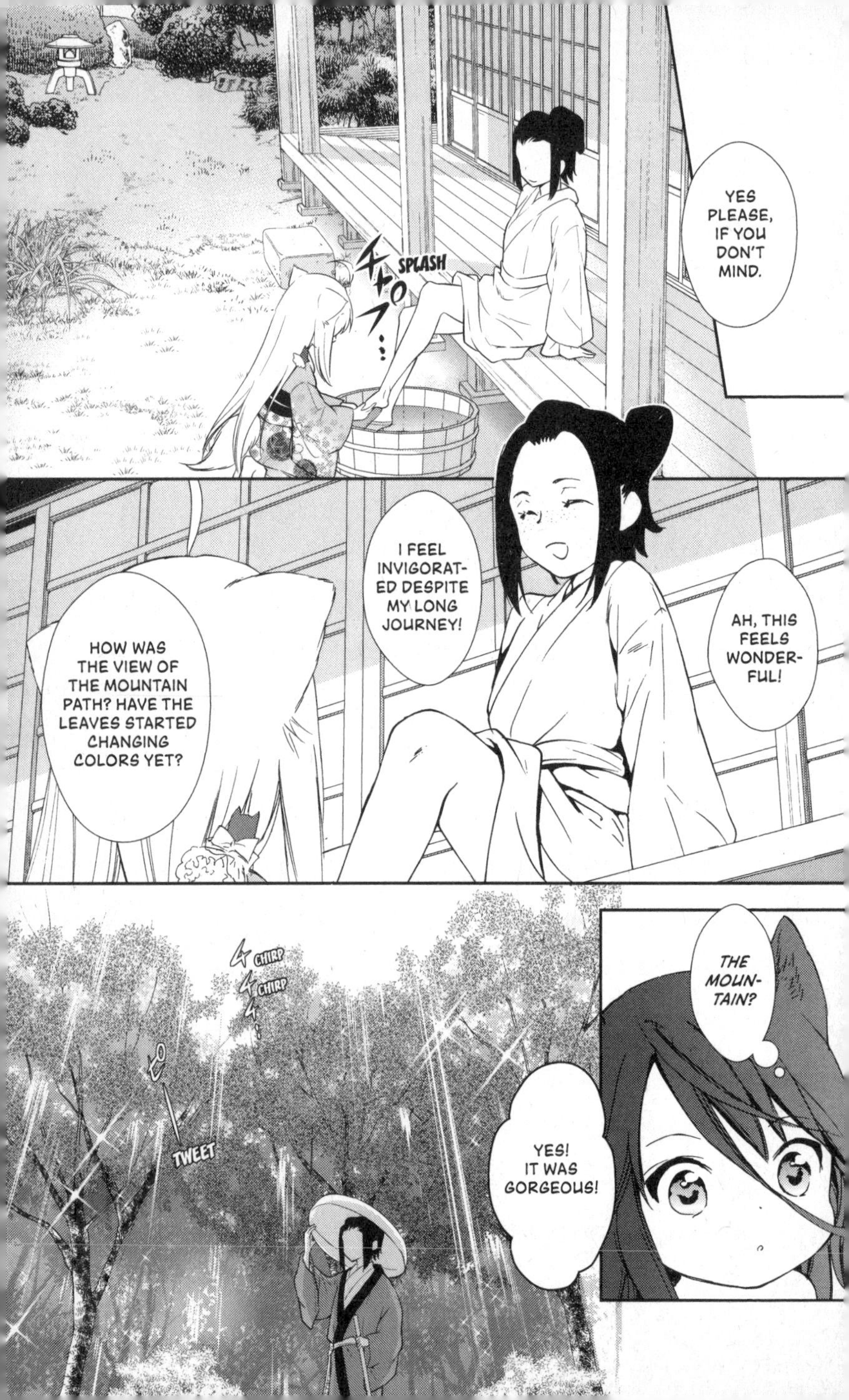
YES PLEASE, IF YOU DON'T MIND.
SPLASH
AH, THIS FEELS WONDER-FUL!
I FEEL INVIGORAT-ED DESPITE MY LONG JOURNEY!
HOW WAS THE VIEW OF THE MOUNTAIN PATH? HAVE THE LEAVES STARTED CHANGING COLORS YET?
THE MOUN-TAIN?
YES! IT WAS GORGEOUS!
CHIRP
CHIRP
TWEET

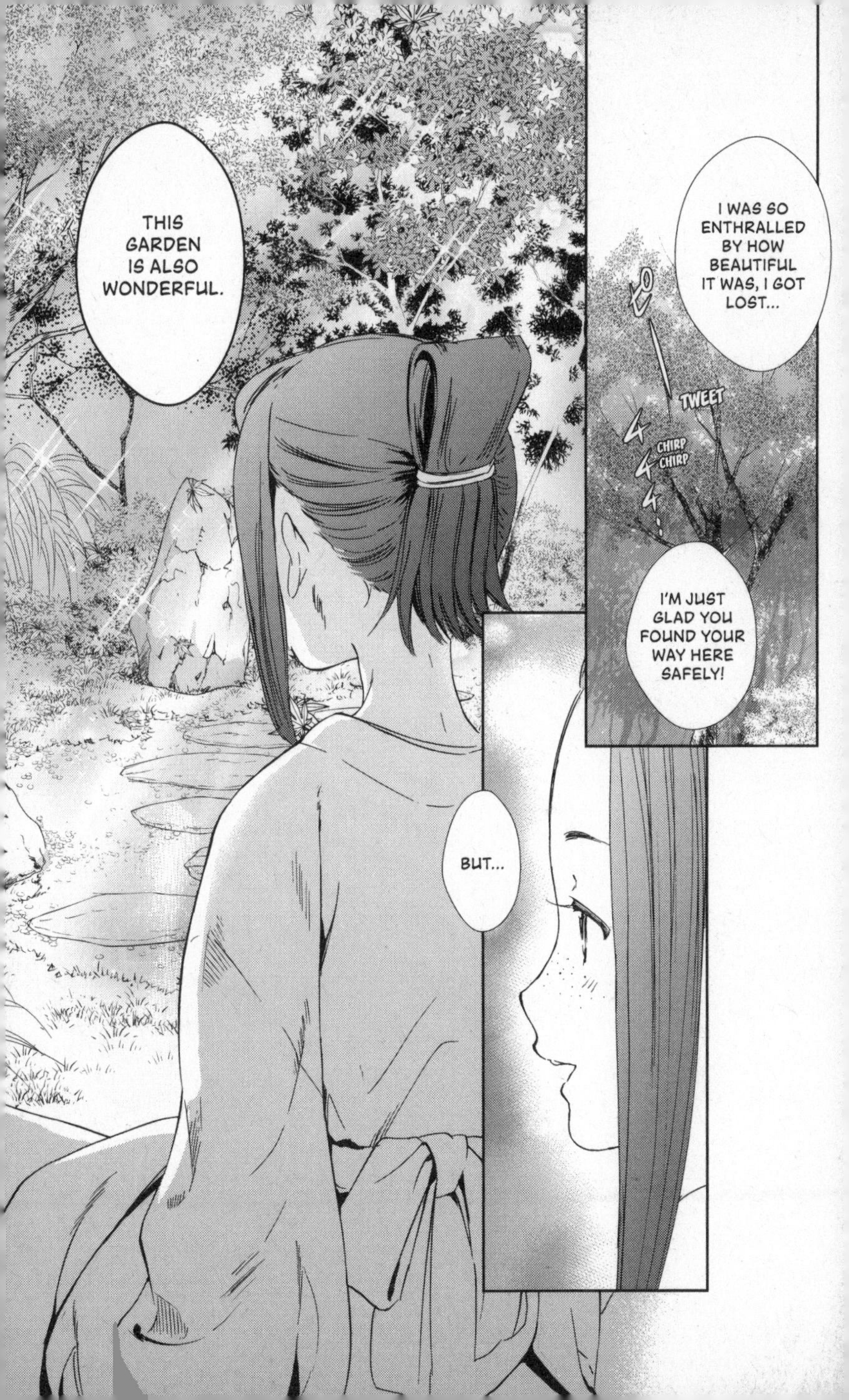
I WAS SO ENTHRALLED BY HOW BEAUTIFUL IT WAS, I GOT LOST...
TWEET
CHIRP CHIRP
I'M JUST GLAD YOU FOUND YOUR WAY HERE SAFELY!
THIS GARDEN IS ALSO WONDERFUL.
BUT...

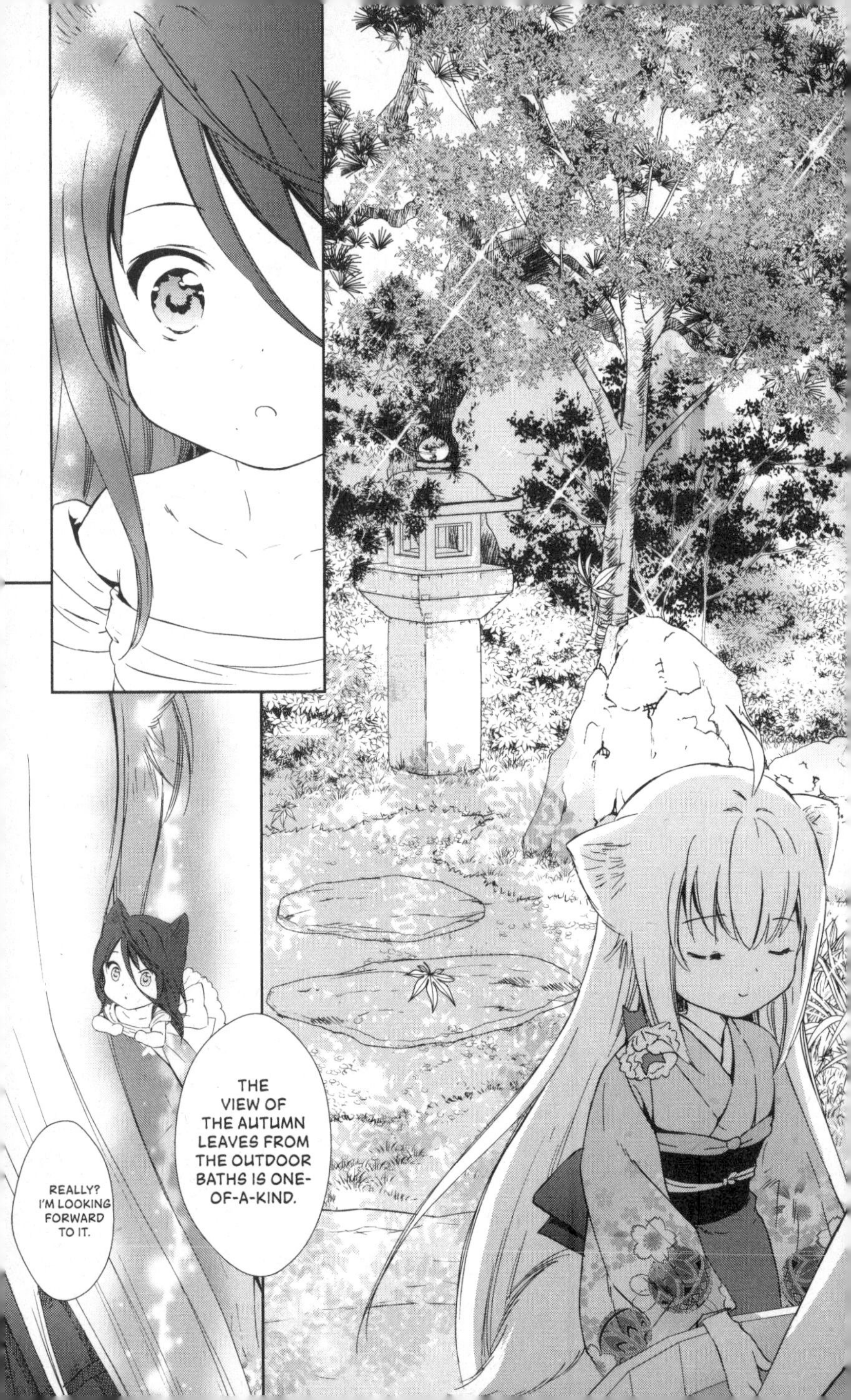
THE VIEW OF THE AUTUMN LEAVES FROM THE OUTDOOR BATHS IS ONE-OF-A-KIND.
REALLY? I'M LOOKING FORWARD TO IT.

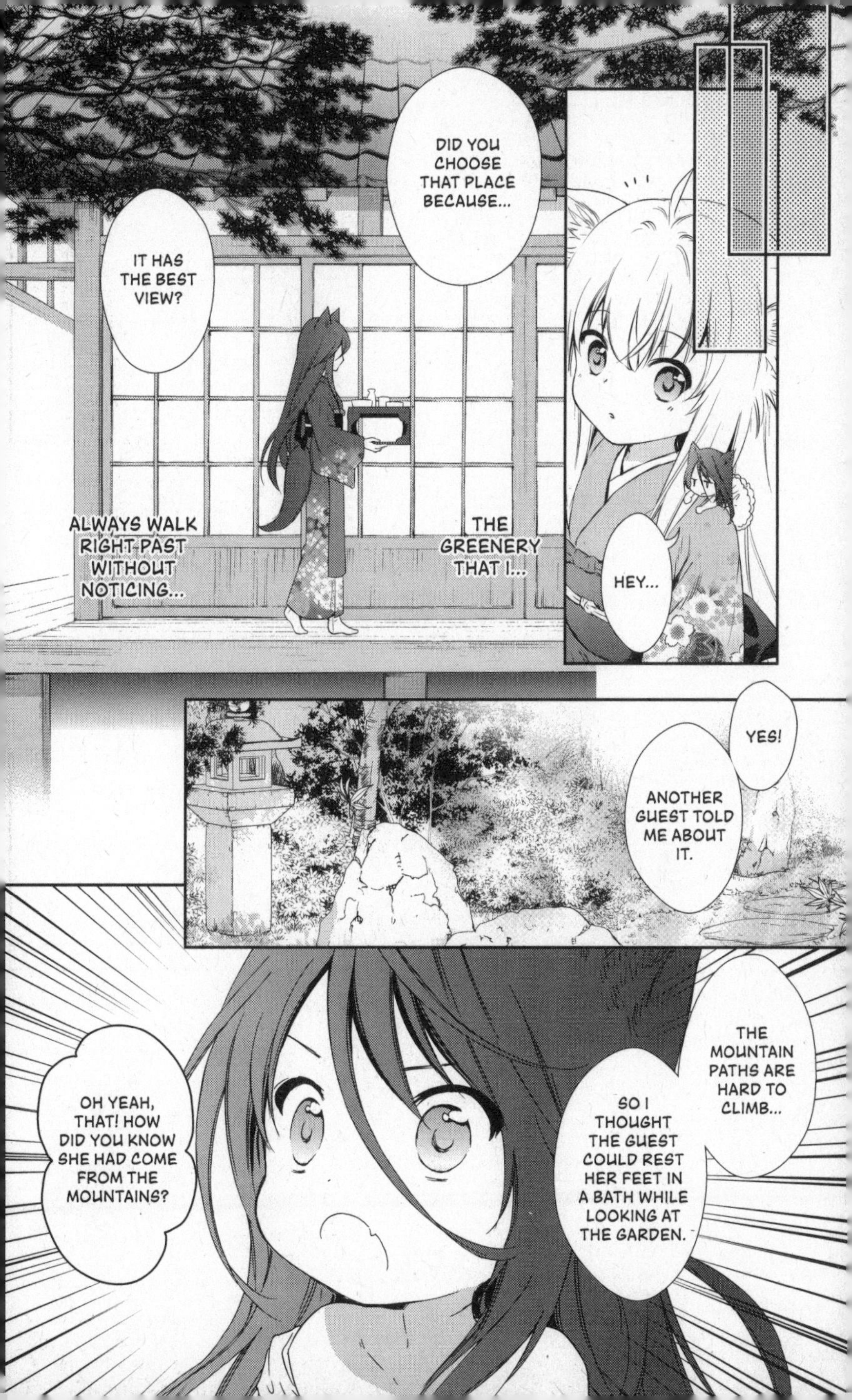
HEY...
DID YOU CHOOSE THAT PLACE BECAUSE...
IT HAS THE BEST VIEW?
THE GREENERY THAT I...
ALWAYS WALK RIGHT PAST WITHOUT NOTICING...
YES!
ANOTHER GUEST TOLD ME ABOUT IT.
THE MOUNTAIN PATHS ARE HARD TO CLIMB...
SO I THOUGHT THE GUEST COULD REST HER FEET IN A BATH WHILE LOOKING AT THE GARDEN.
OH YEAH, THAT! HOW DID YOU KNOW SHE HAD COME FROM THE MOUNTAINS?

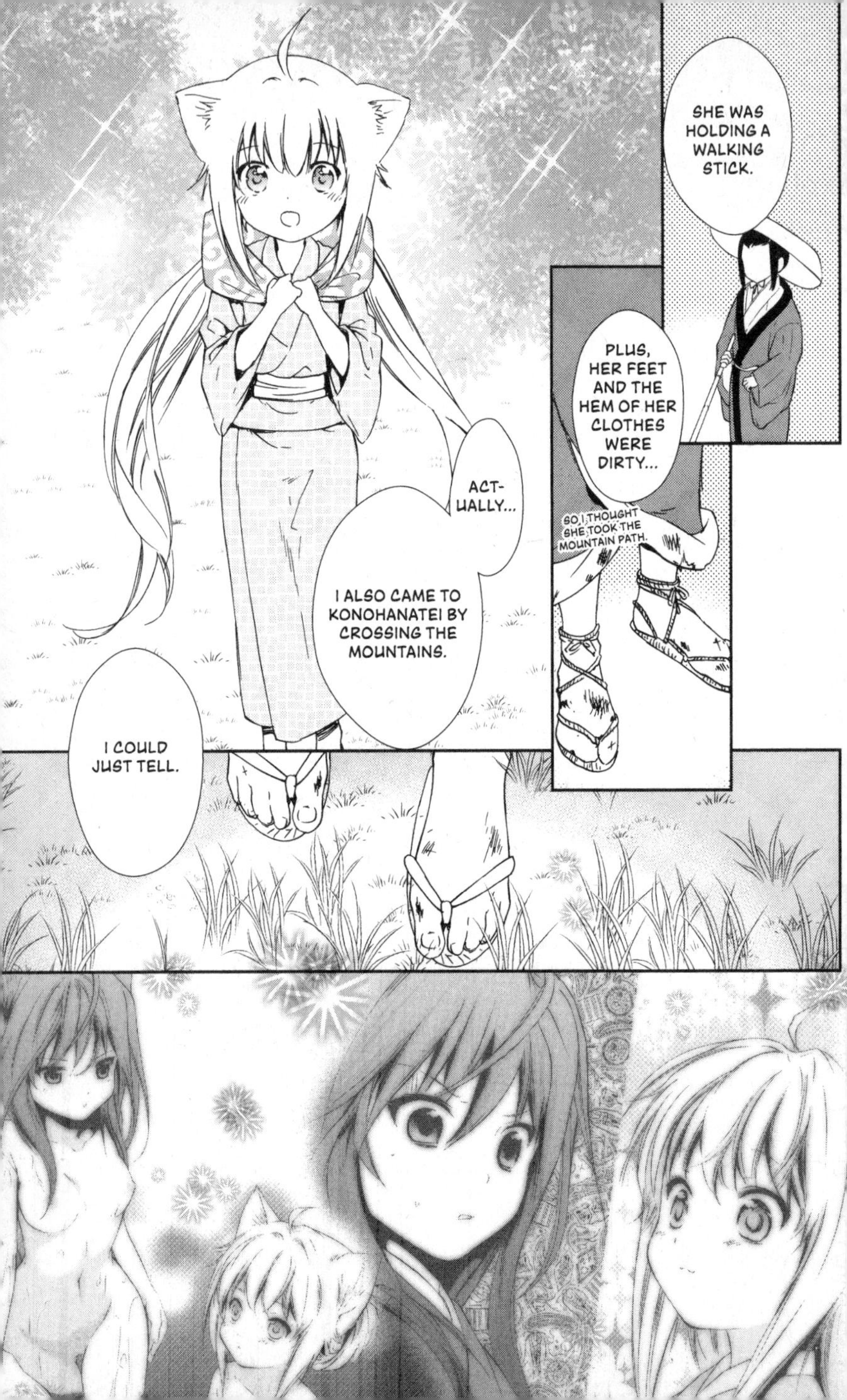

SHE WAS HOLDING A WALKING STICK.
PLUS, HER FEET AND THE HEM OF HER CLOTHES WERE DIRTY...
SO, I THOUGHT SHE TOOK THE MOUNTAIN PATH.
ACT-UALLY...
I ALSO CAME TO KONOHANATEI BY CROSSING THE MOUNTAINS.
I COULD JUST TELL.

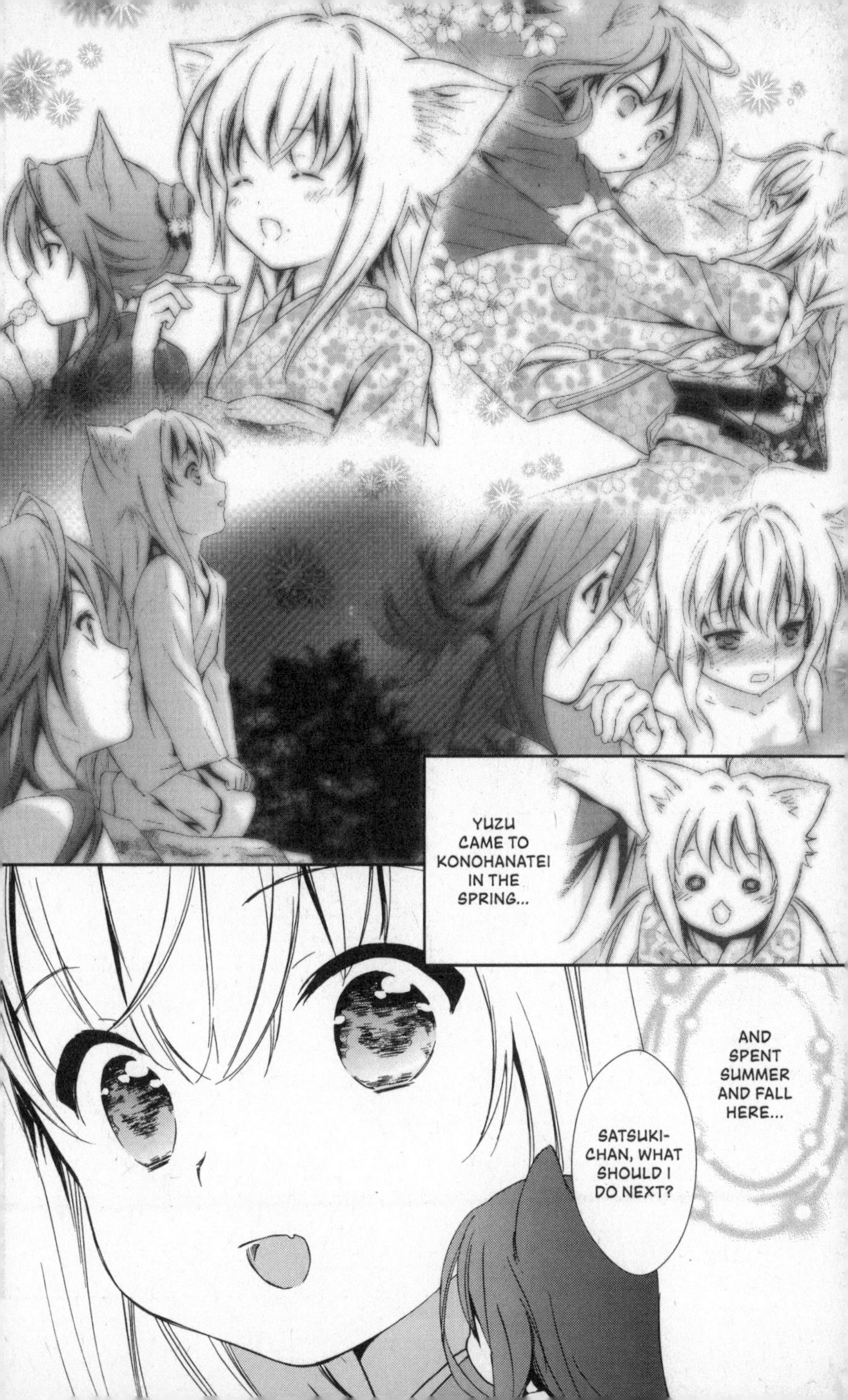
YUZU CAME TO KONOHANATEI IN THE SPRING...
AND SPENT SUMMER AND FALL HERE...
SATSUKI-CHAN, WHAT SHOULD I DO NEXT?

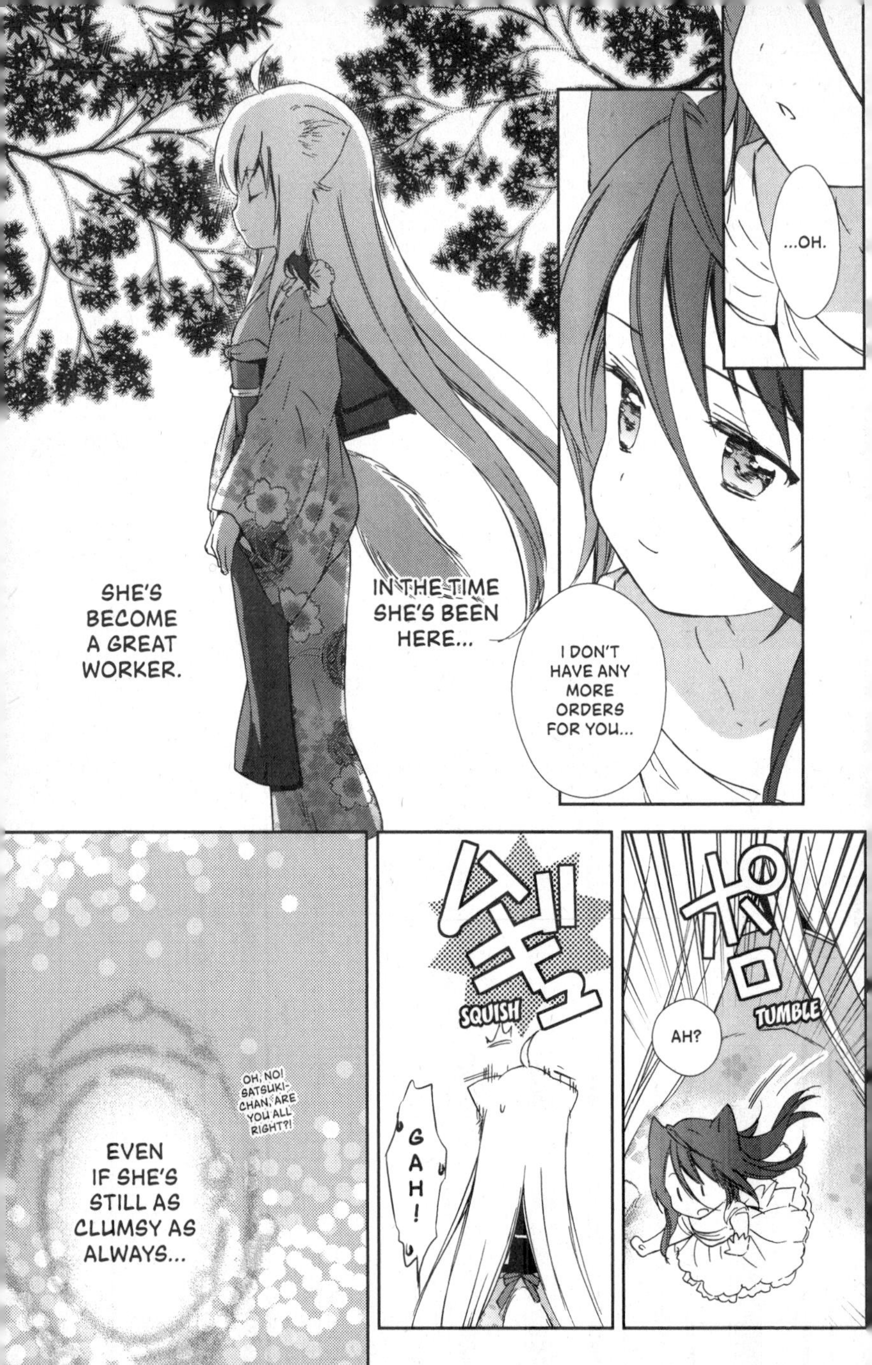
...OH.
I DON'T HAVE ANY MORE ORDERS FOR YOU...
IN THE TIME SHE'S BEEN HERE...
SHE'S BECOME A GREAT WORKER.
ポロ
TUMBLE
AH?
ムギュ
SQUISH
GAH!
OH, NO! SATSUKI-CHAN, ARE YOU ALL RIGHT?!
EVEN IF SHE'S STILL AS CLUMSY AS ALWAYS...

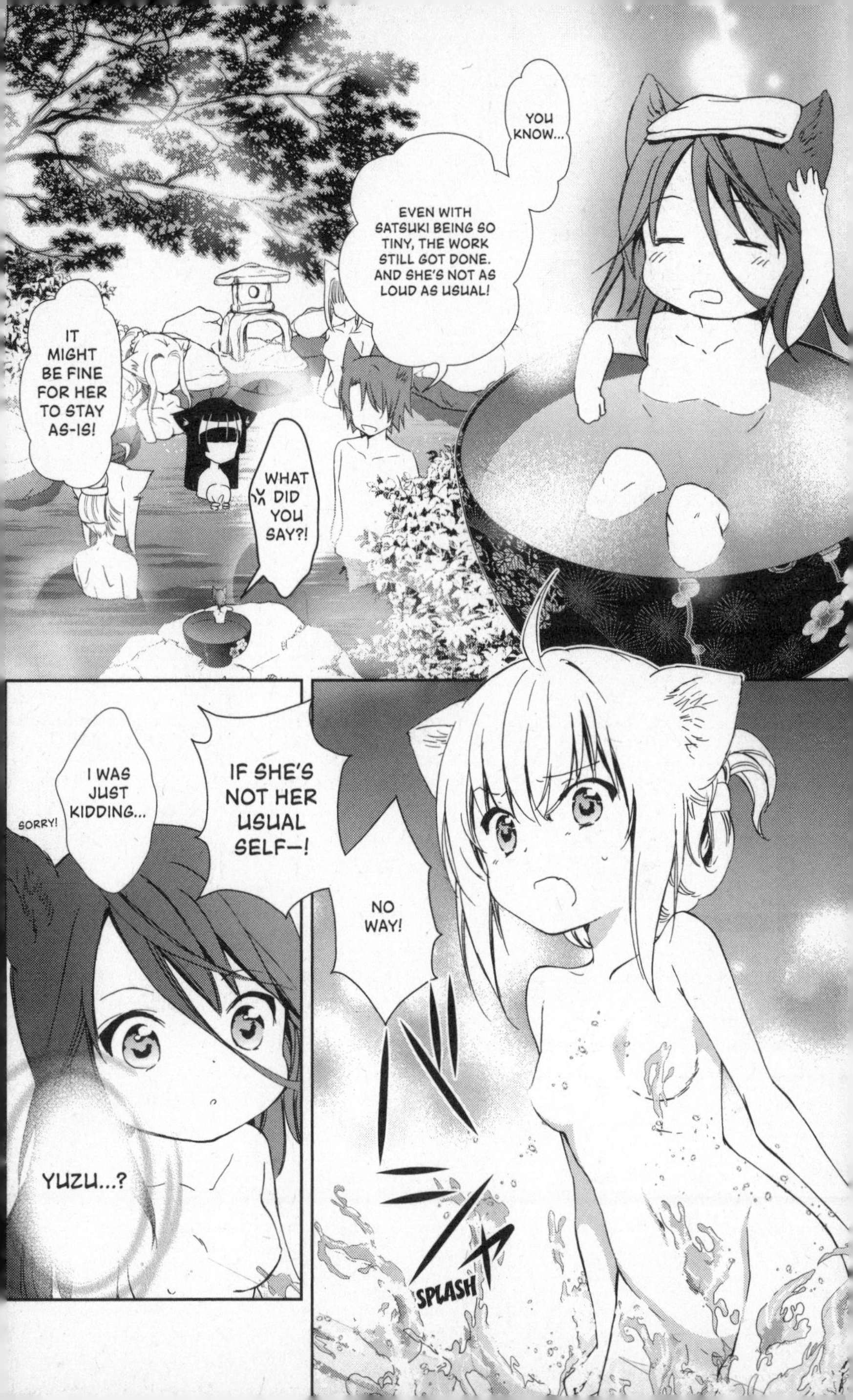

YOU KNOW...
EVEN WITH SATSUKI BEING SO TINY, THE WORK STILL GOT DONE. AND SHE'S NOT AS LOUD AS USUAL!
IT MIGHT BE FINE FOR HER TO STAY AS-IS!
WHAT DID YOU SAY?!
I WAS JUST KIDDING...
SORRY!
IF SHE'S NOT HER USUAL SELF—!
NO WAY!
SPLASH
YUZU...?

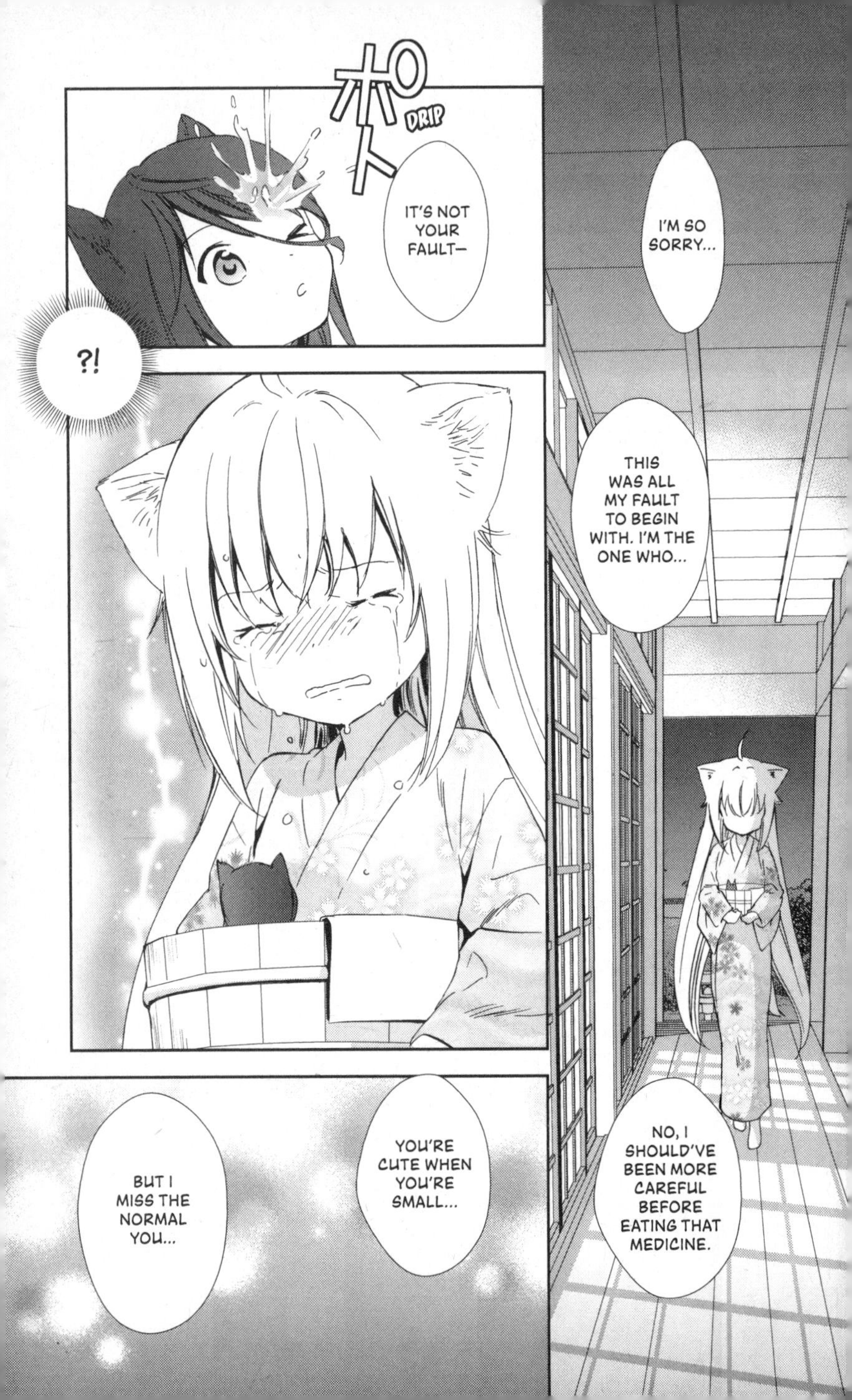
I'M SO SORRY...
THIS WAS ALL MY FAULT TO BEGIN WITH. I'M THE ONE WHO...
NO, I SHOULD'VE BEEN MORE CAREFUL BEFORE EATING THAT MEDICINE.
ポト
DRIP
IT'S NOT YOUR FAULT—
?!
YOU'RE CUTE WHEN YOU'RE SMALL...
BUT I MISS THE NORMAL YOU...

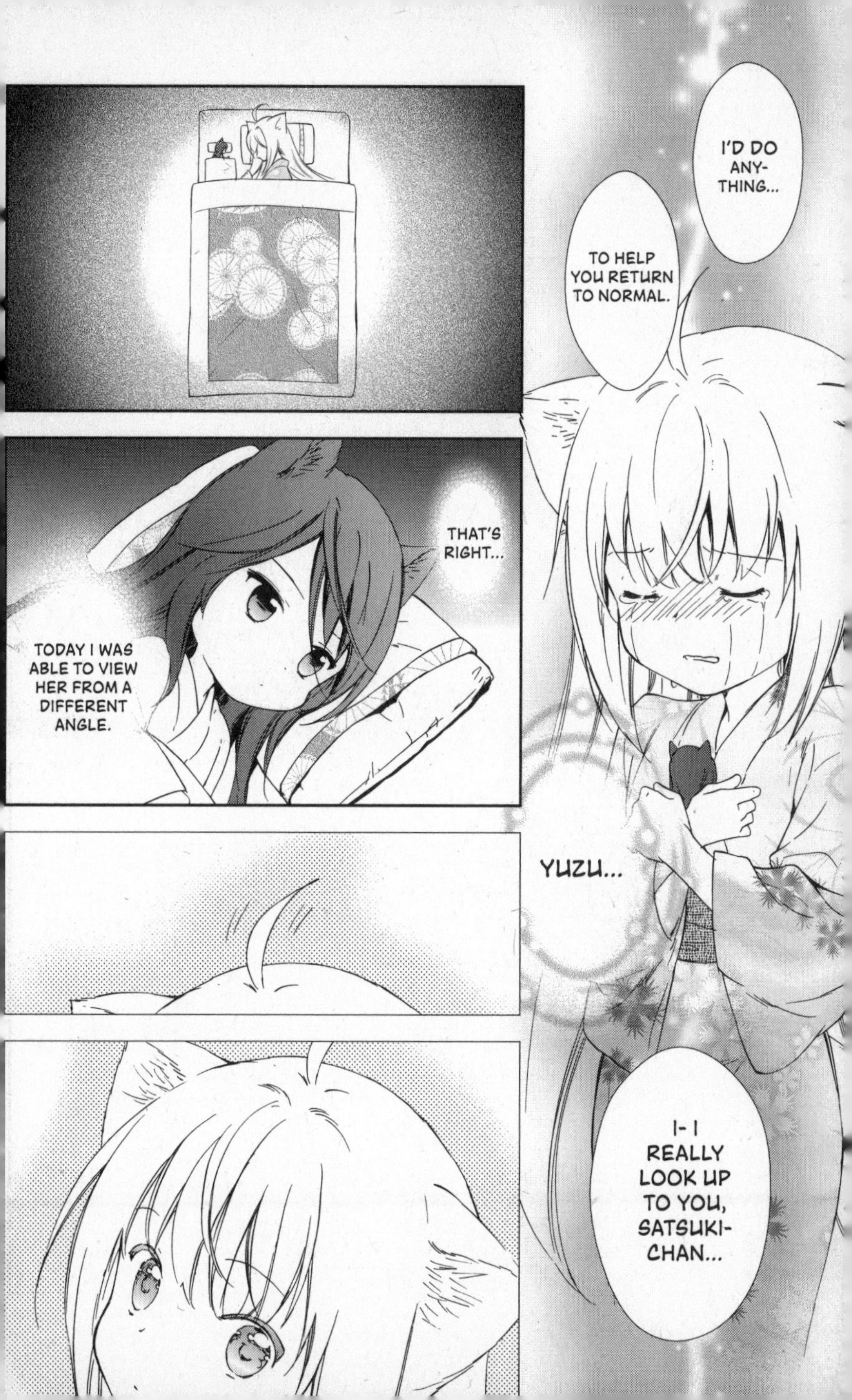
I'D DO ANY-THING...
TO HELP YOU RETURN TO NORMAL.
YUZU...
I- I REALLY LOOK UP TO YOU, SATSUKI-CHAN...
THAT'S RIGHT...
TODAY I WAS ABLE TO VIEW HER FROM A DIFFERENT ANGLE.

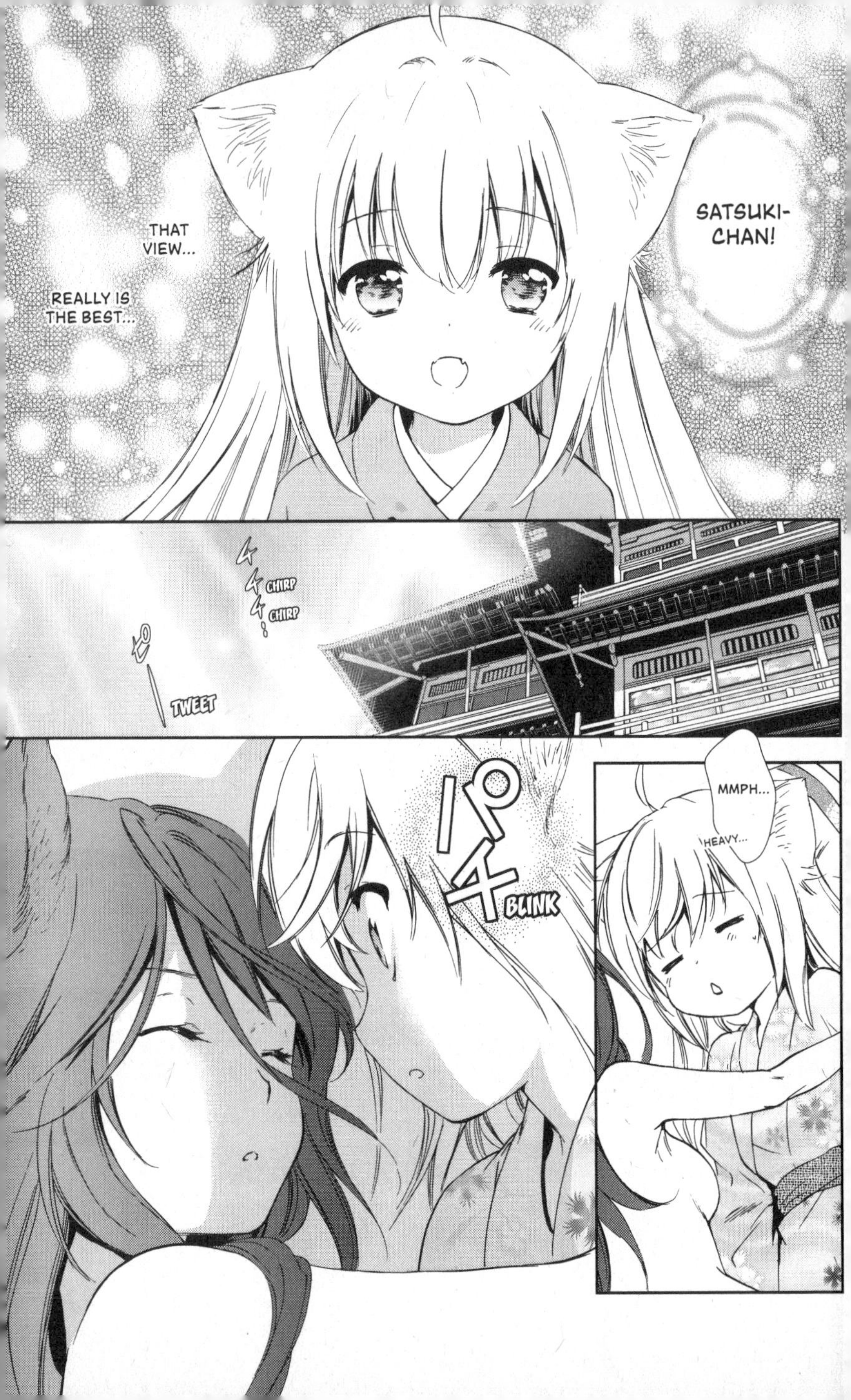
SATSUKI-CHAN!
THAT VIEW...
REALLY IS THE BEST...
CHIRP
CHIRP
TWEET
MMPH...
HEAVY...
BLINK

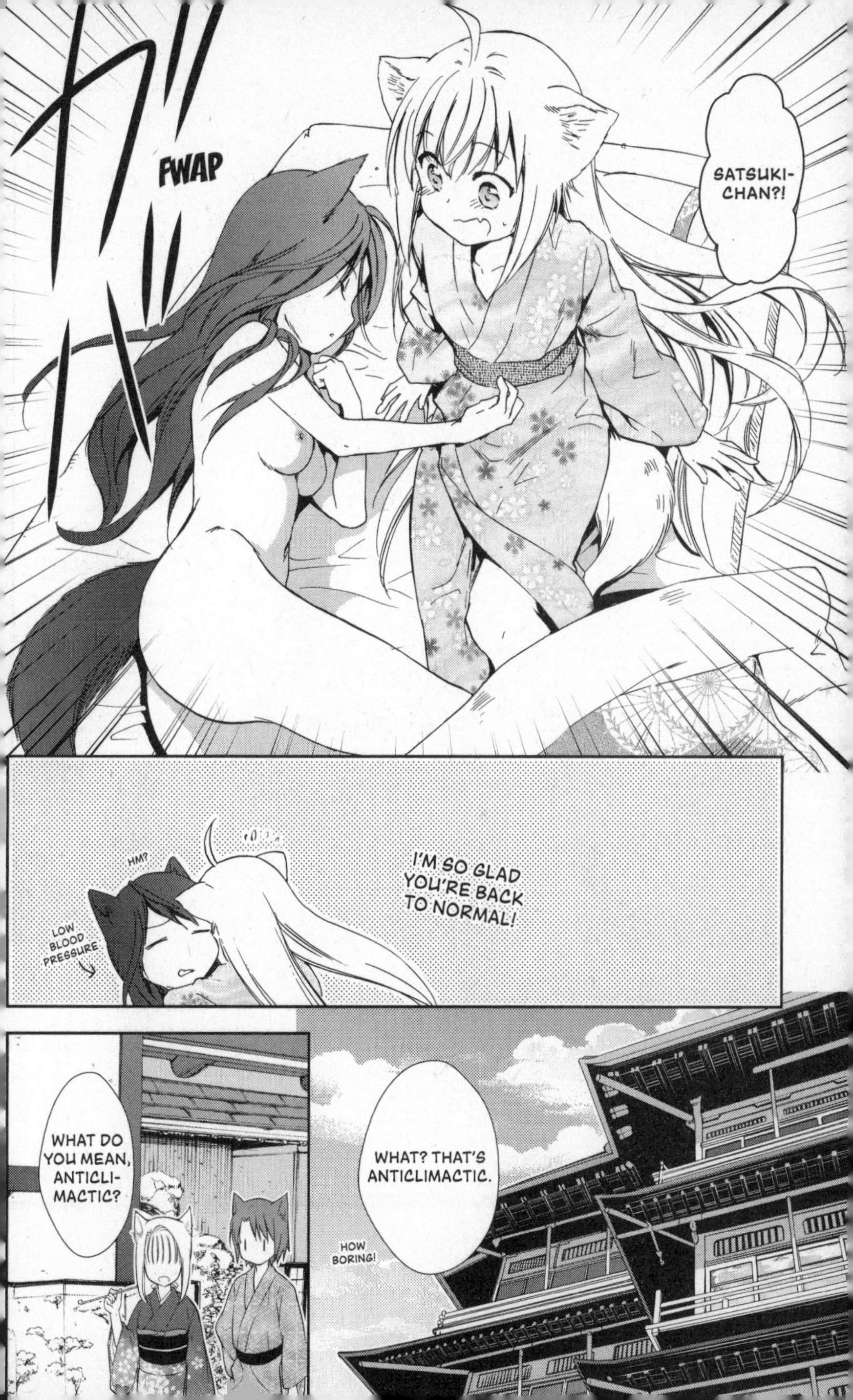
SATSUKI-CHAN?!
FWAP
I'M SO GLAD YOU'RE BACK TO NORMAL!
HM?
LOW BLOOD PRESSURE
WHAT? THAT'S ANTICLIMACTIC.
HOW BORING!
WHAT DO YOU MEAN, ANTICLIMACTIC?

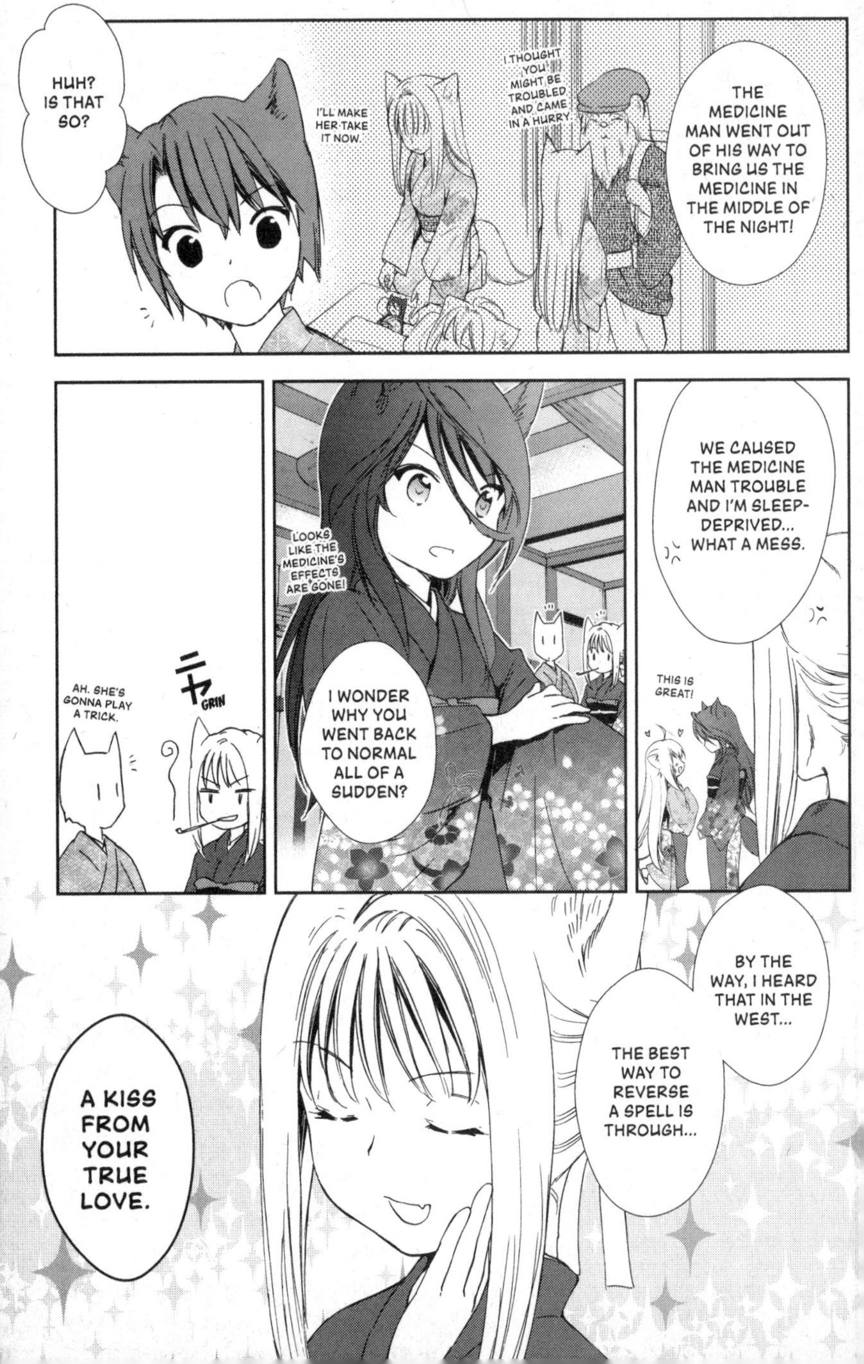
THE MEDICINE MAN WENT OUT OF HIS WAY TO BRING US THE MEDICINE IN THE MIDDLE OF THE NIGHT!
I THOUGHT YOU MIGHT BE TROUBLED AND CAME IN A HURRY.
I'LL MAKE HER TAKE IT NOW.
HUH? IS THAT SO?
WE CAUSED THE MEDICINE MAN TROUBLE AND I'M SLEEP-DEPRIVED... WHAT A MESS.
THIS IS GREAT!
LOOKS LIKE THE MEDICINE'S EFFECTS ARE GONE!
I WONDER WHY YOU WENT BACK TO NORMAL ALL OF A SUDDEN?
ニヤ GRIN
AH. SHE'S GONNA PLAY A TRICK.
BY THE WAY, I HEARD THAT IN THE WEST...
THE BEST WAY TO REVERSE A SPELL IS THROUGH...
A KISS FROM YOUR TRUE LOVE.

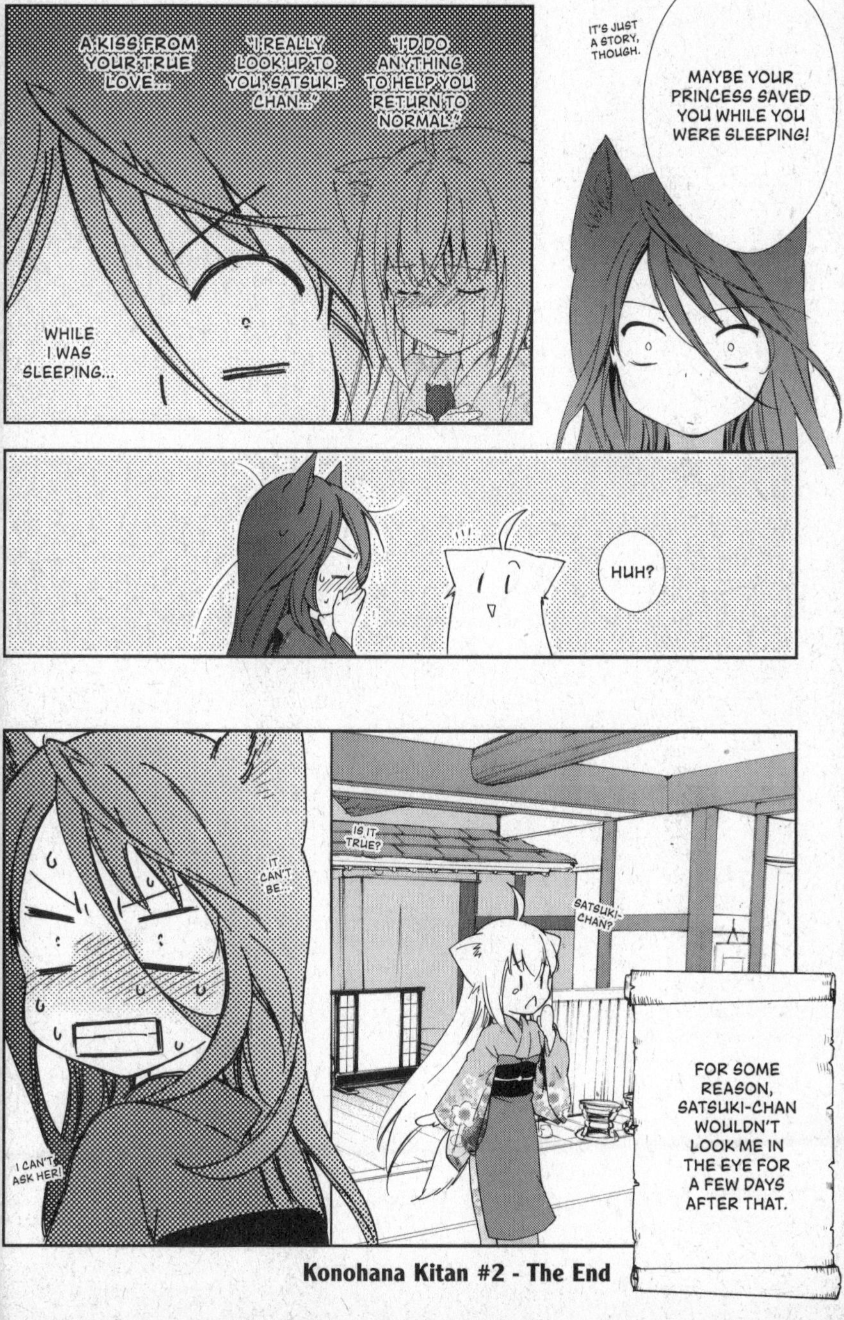
MAYBE YOUR PRINCESS SAVED YOU WHILE YOU WERE SLEEPING!
IT'S JUST A STORY, THOUGH.
"I'D DO ANYTHING TO HELP YOU RETURN TO NORMAL."
"I REALLY LOOK UP TO YOU, SATSUKI-CHAN..."
A KISS FROM YOUR TRUE LOVE...
WHILE I WAS SLEEPING...
HUH?
SATSUKI-CHAN?
FOR SOME REASON, SATSUKI-CHAN WOULDN'T LOOK ME IN THE EYE FOR A FEW DAYS AFTER THAT.
IS IT TRUE?
IT CAN'T BE...
I CAN'T ASK HER!

Konohana Kitan #2 - The End

❋ IN THE NEXT VOLUME OF ❋

KONOHANA KITAN

It's wintertime at Konohanatei, which
means all the foxes at the inn are getting ready
to celebrate the new year holiday together! But
when Yuzu accidentally gets separated from Satsuki
and her other friends on the way to the shrine, she
finds herself somewhere completely different... and
surrounded by strange foxes! Are these the foxes
who take care of New Year's wishes? Making
new friends is great, but there has to be
a way home... right?

Join Yuzu and all the other foxes of Konohanatei
as they greet the new year and new adventures
in the next installment of *Konohana Kitan*!

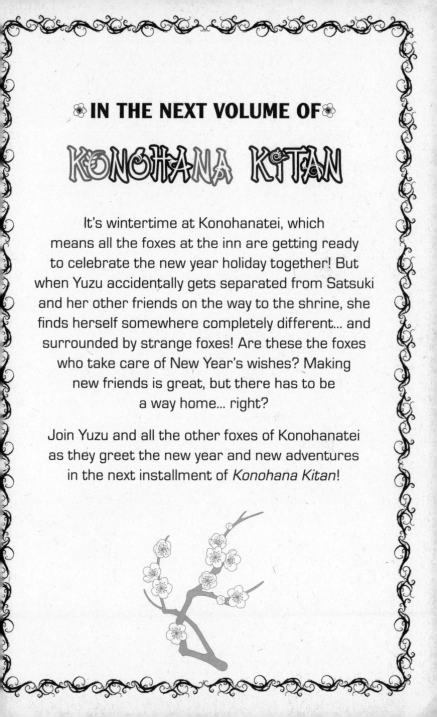

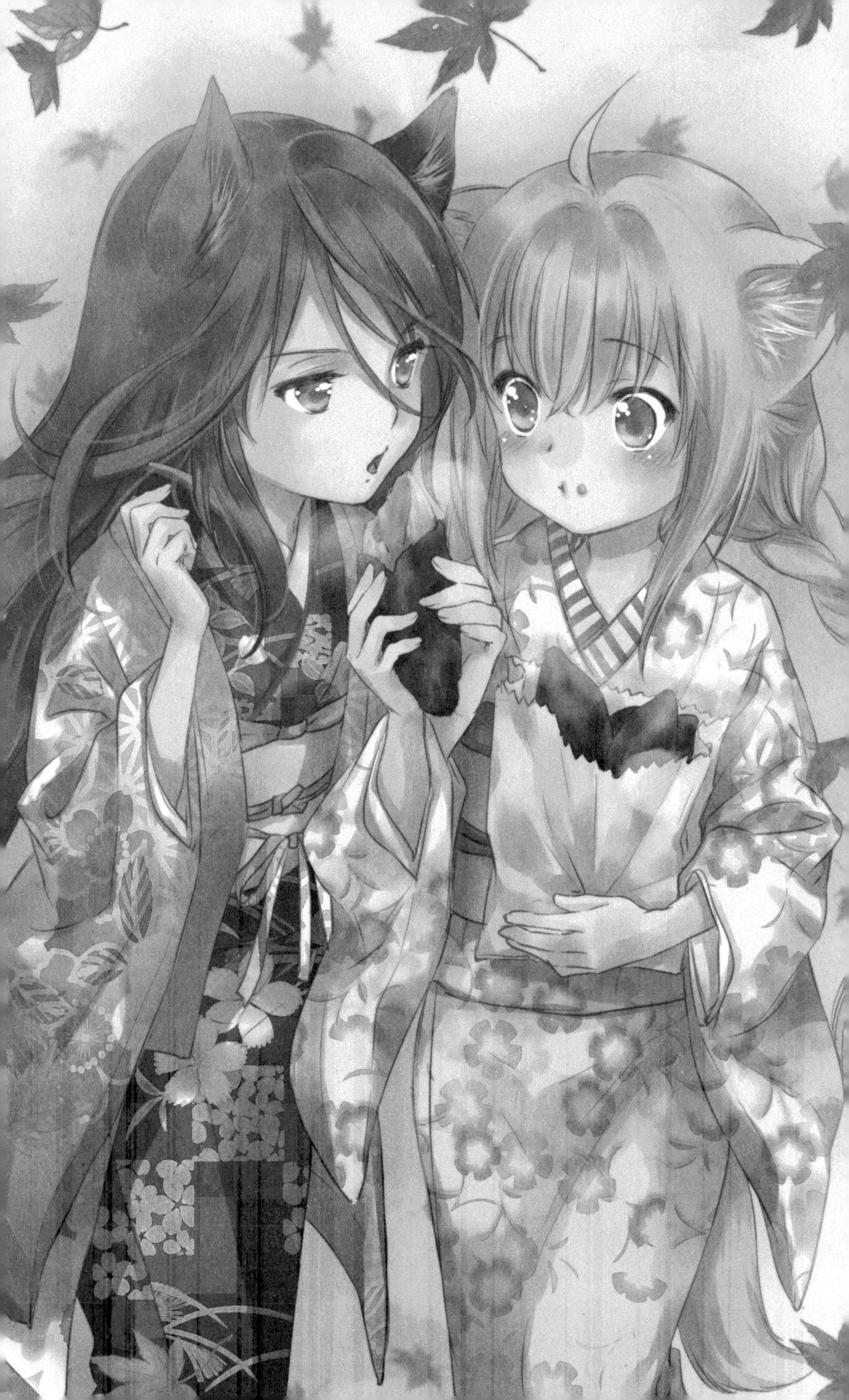

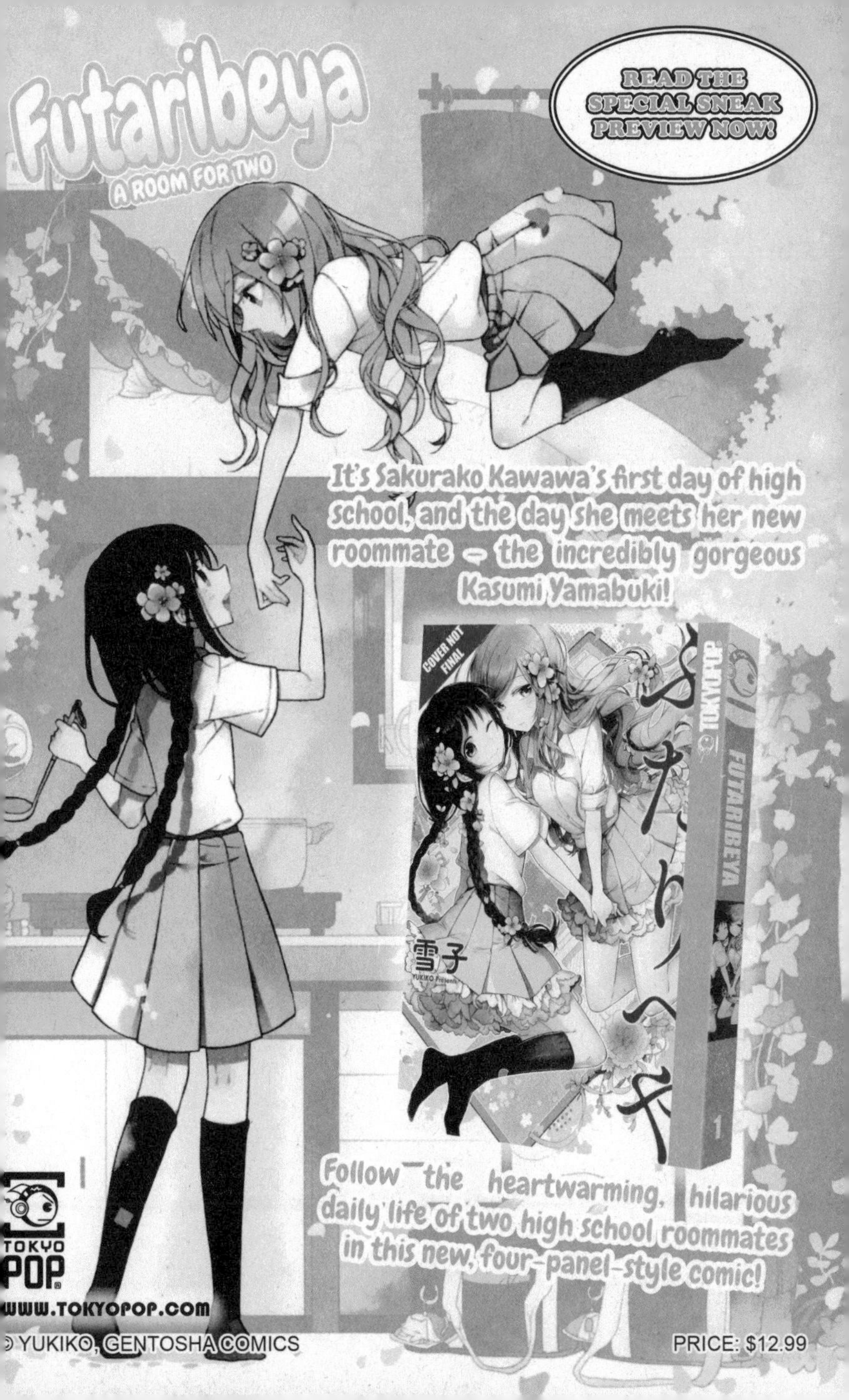

Futaribeya
A ROOM FOR TWO
READ THE SPECIAL SNEAK PREVIEW NOW!
It's Sakurako Kawawa's first day of high school, and the day she meets her new roommate – the incredibly gorgeous Kasumi Yamabuki!
COVER NOT FINAL
TOKYOPOP
FUTARIBEYA
1
雪子
YUKIKO Presents
Follow the heartwarming, hilarious daily life of two high school roommates in this new, four-panel-style comic!
TOKYO POP
WWW.TOKYOPOP.COM
© YUKIKO, GENTOSHA COMICS
PRICE: $12.99

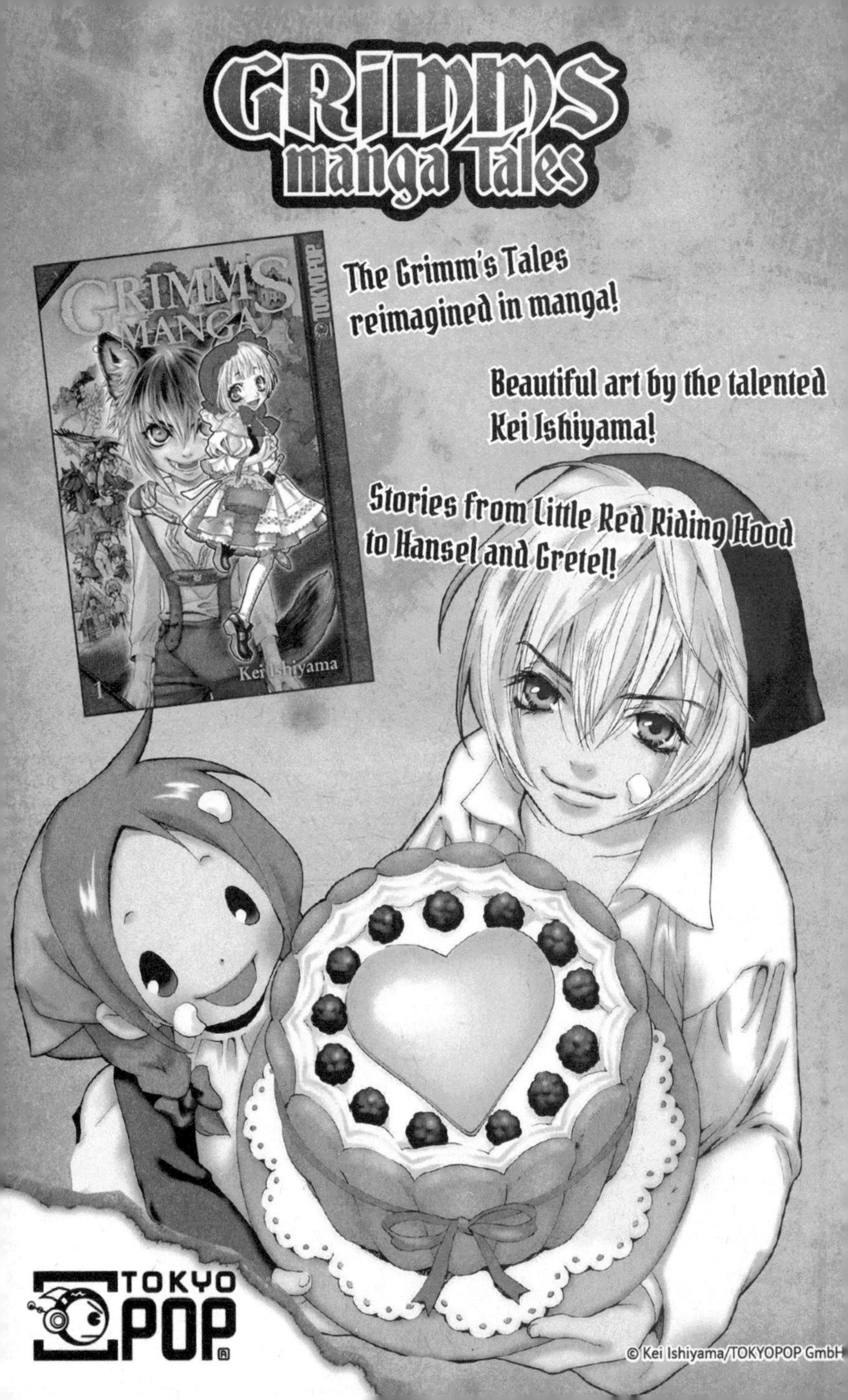
GRIMMS
manga Tales
The Grimm's Tales
reimagined in manga!
Beautiful art by the talented
Kei Ishiyama!
Stories from Little Red Riding Hood
to Hansel and Gretel!
GRIMMS MANGA
TOKYOPOP
Kei Ishiyama
1
TOKYO POP
© Kei Ishiyama/TOKYOPOP GmbH

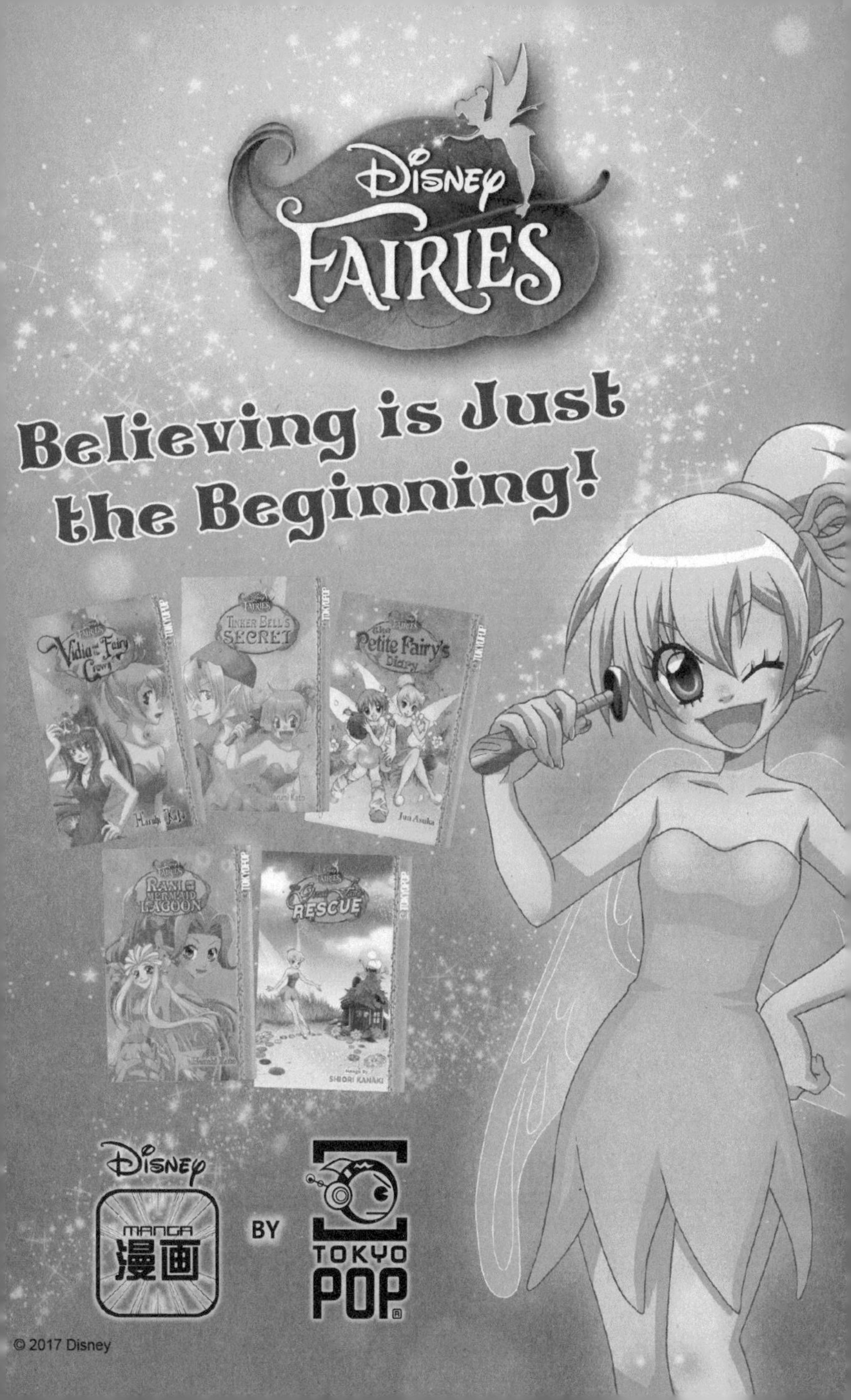
Disney
FAIRIES
Believing is Just the Beginning!
TINKER BELL'S SECRET
RESCUE
Disney
MANGA
漫画
BY
TOKYO POP
© 2017 Disney

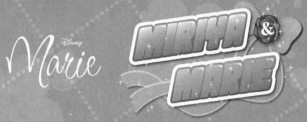

Disney *Marie* **MIRIYA & MARIE**

☆ **Inspired by the characters from Disney's The Aristocats**
  ☆ **Learn facts about Paris and Japan!**
    ☆ **Adorable original shojo story**
      ☆ **Full color manga**

Even though the wealthy young girl Miriya has almost everything she could ever need, what she really wants is the one thing money can't buy: her missing parents. But this year, she gets an extra special birthday gift when Marie, a magical white kitten, appears and whisks her away to Paris! Learning the art of magic is one thing, but getting to eat the tastiest French pastries and wear the most beautiful fashion takes Miriya and Marie's journey to a whole new level!

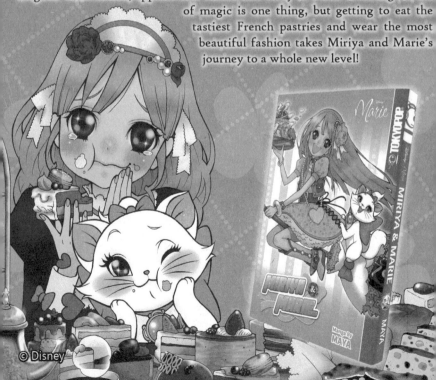

Manga by MAYA

© Disney

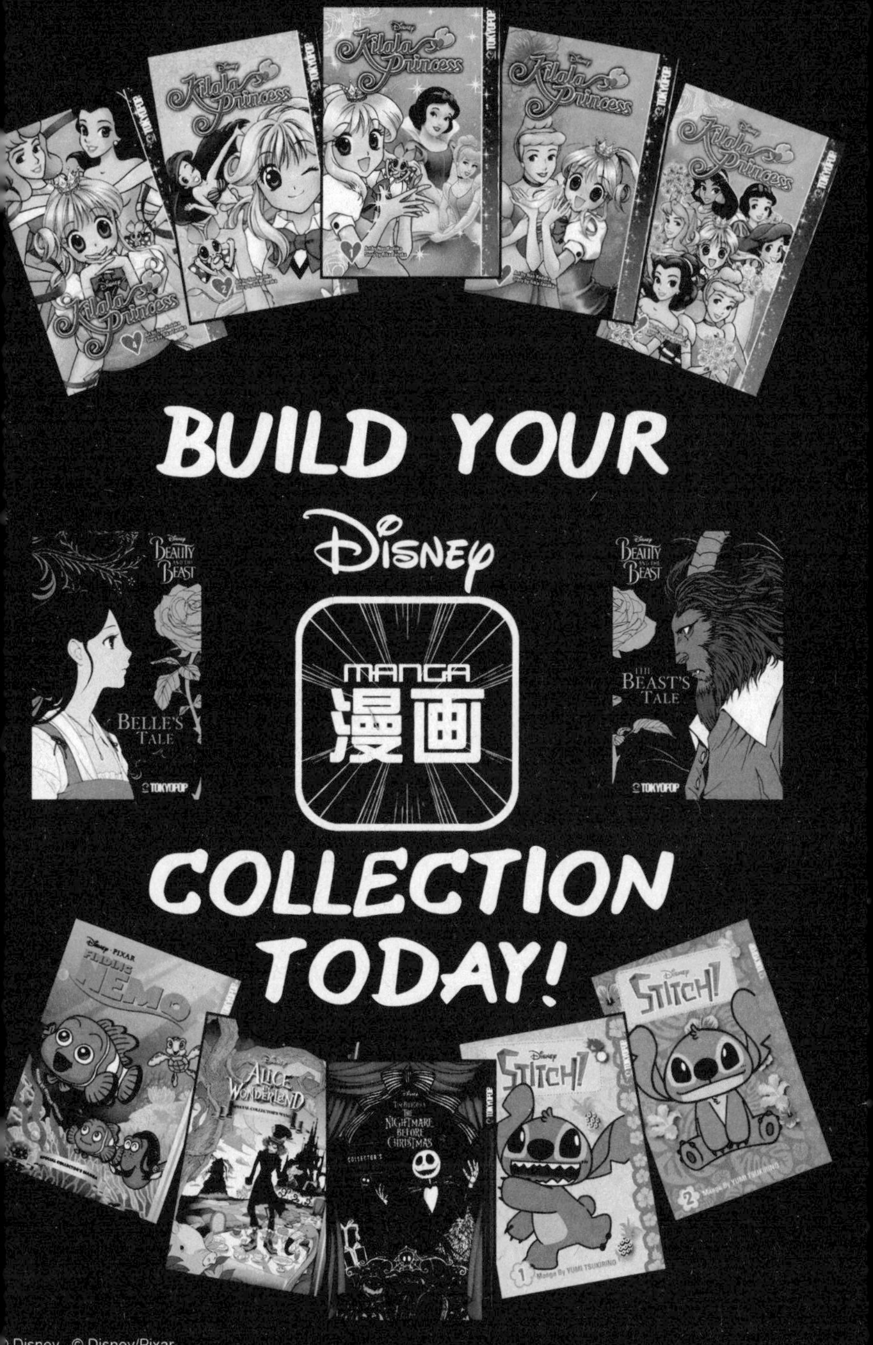
Kilala Princess
BUILD YOUR
Disney
Beauty and the Beast
Belle's Tale
The Beast's Tale
TOKYOPOP
MANGA
漫画
COLLECTION TODAY!
Finding Nemo
Alice in Wonderland
The Nightmare Before Christmas
Stitch!

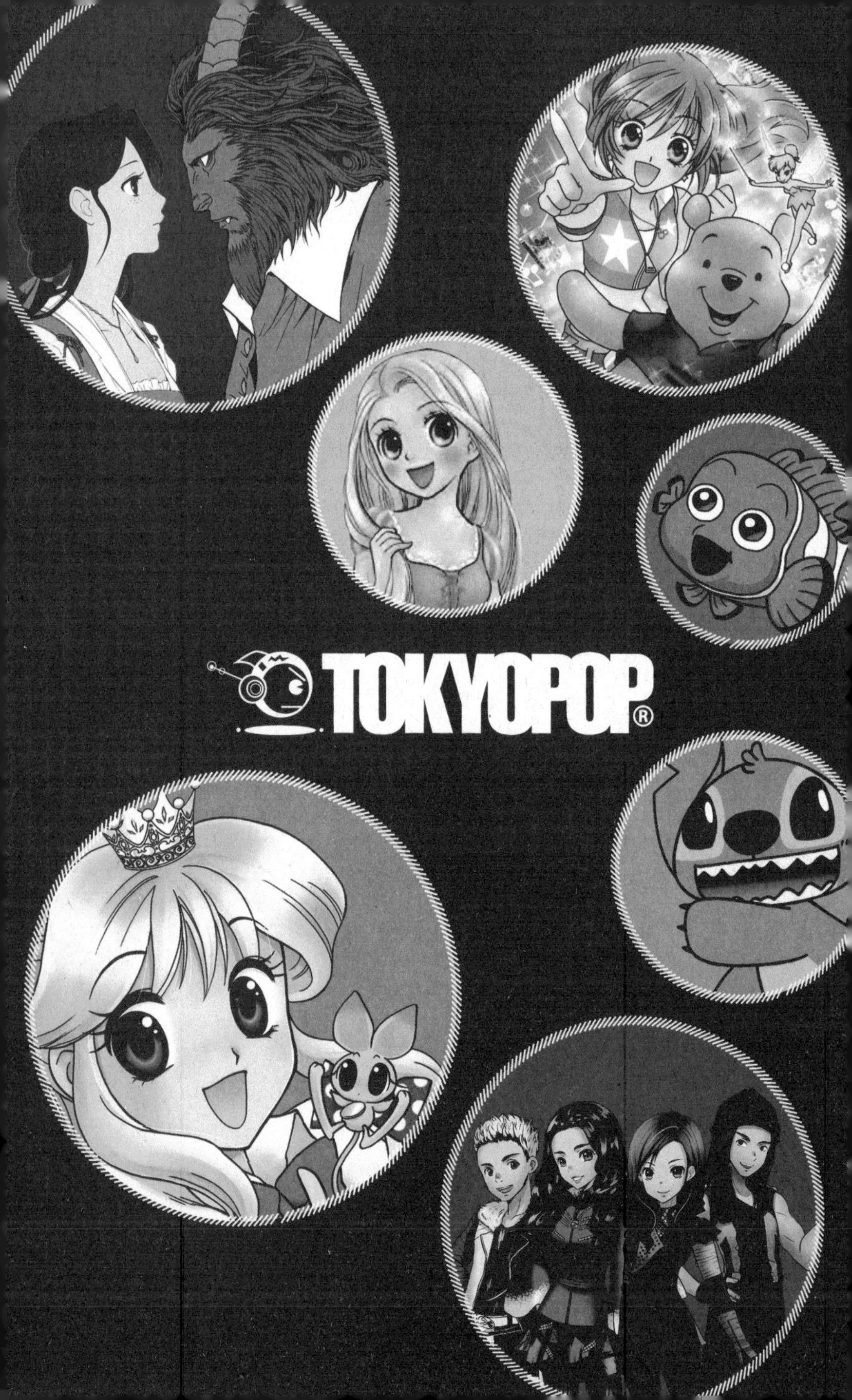
TOKYOPOP®

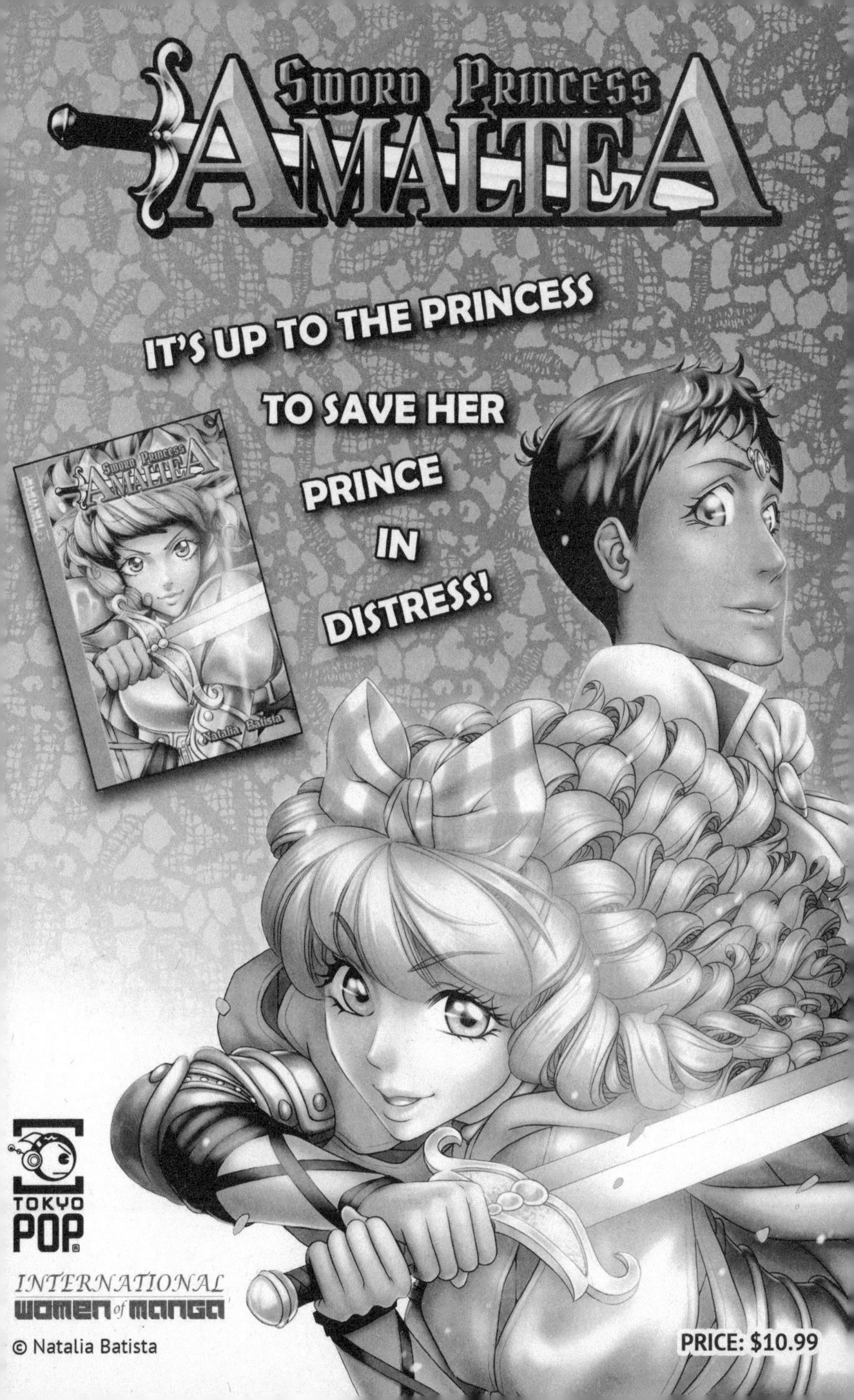
Sword Princess
AMALTEA
IT'S UP TO THE PRINCESS
TO SAVE HER
PRINCE
IN
DISTRESS!
Sword Princess
AMALTEA
Natalia Batista
TOKYO
POP
INTERNATIONAL
women of manga
© Natalia Batista
PRICE: $10.99

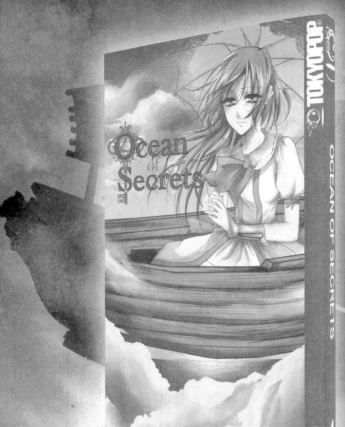

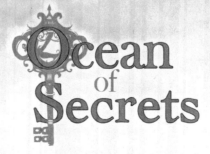

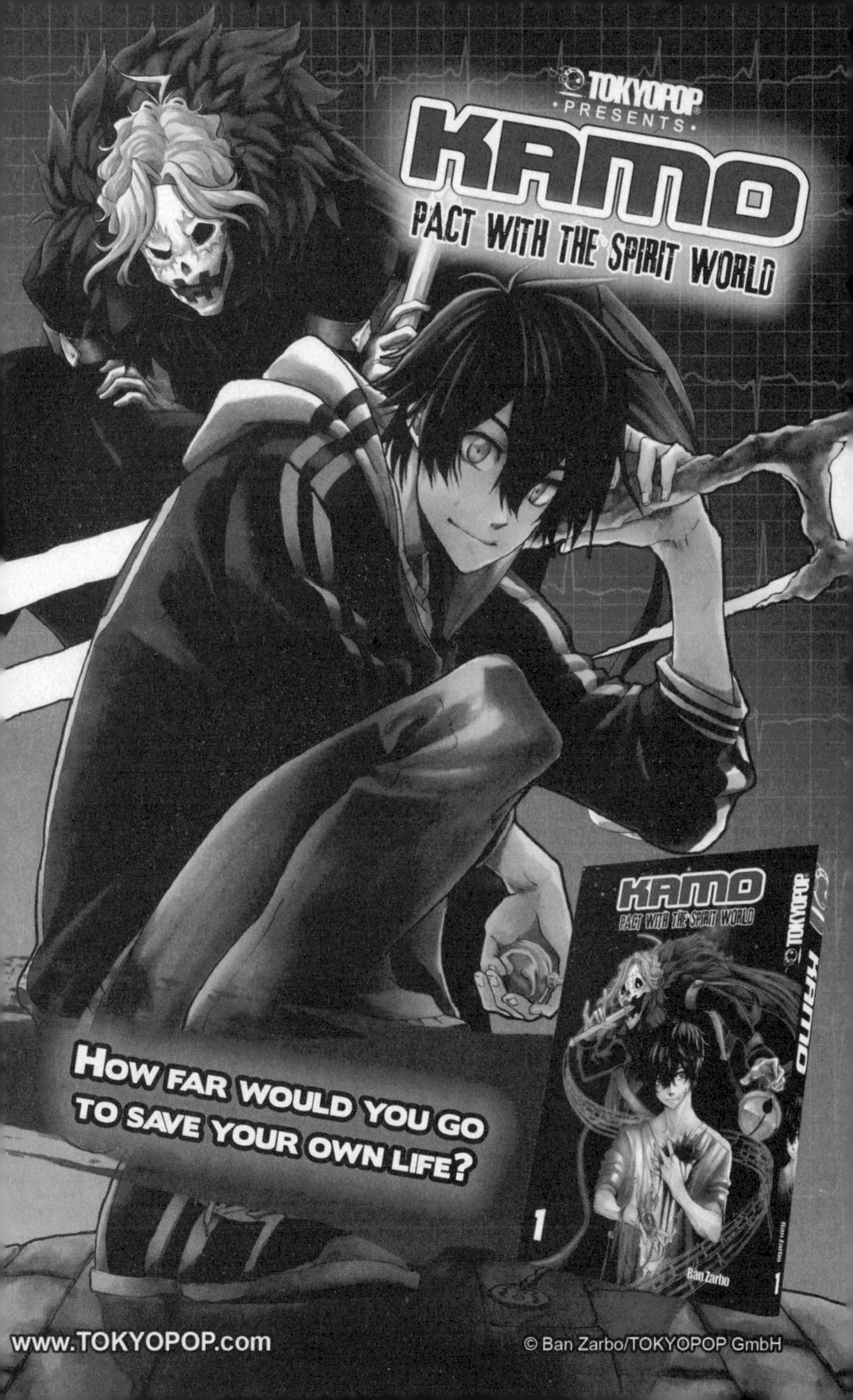
TOKYOPOP PRESENTS
KAMO
PACT WITH THE SPIRIT WORLD
HOW FAR WOULD YOU GO TO SAVE YOUR OWN LIFE?
KAMO
PACT WITH THE SPIRIT WORLD
1
Ban Zarbo
www.TOKYOPOP.com
© Ban Zarbo/TOKYOPOP GmbH

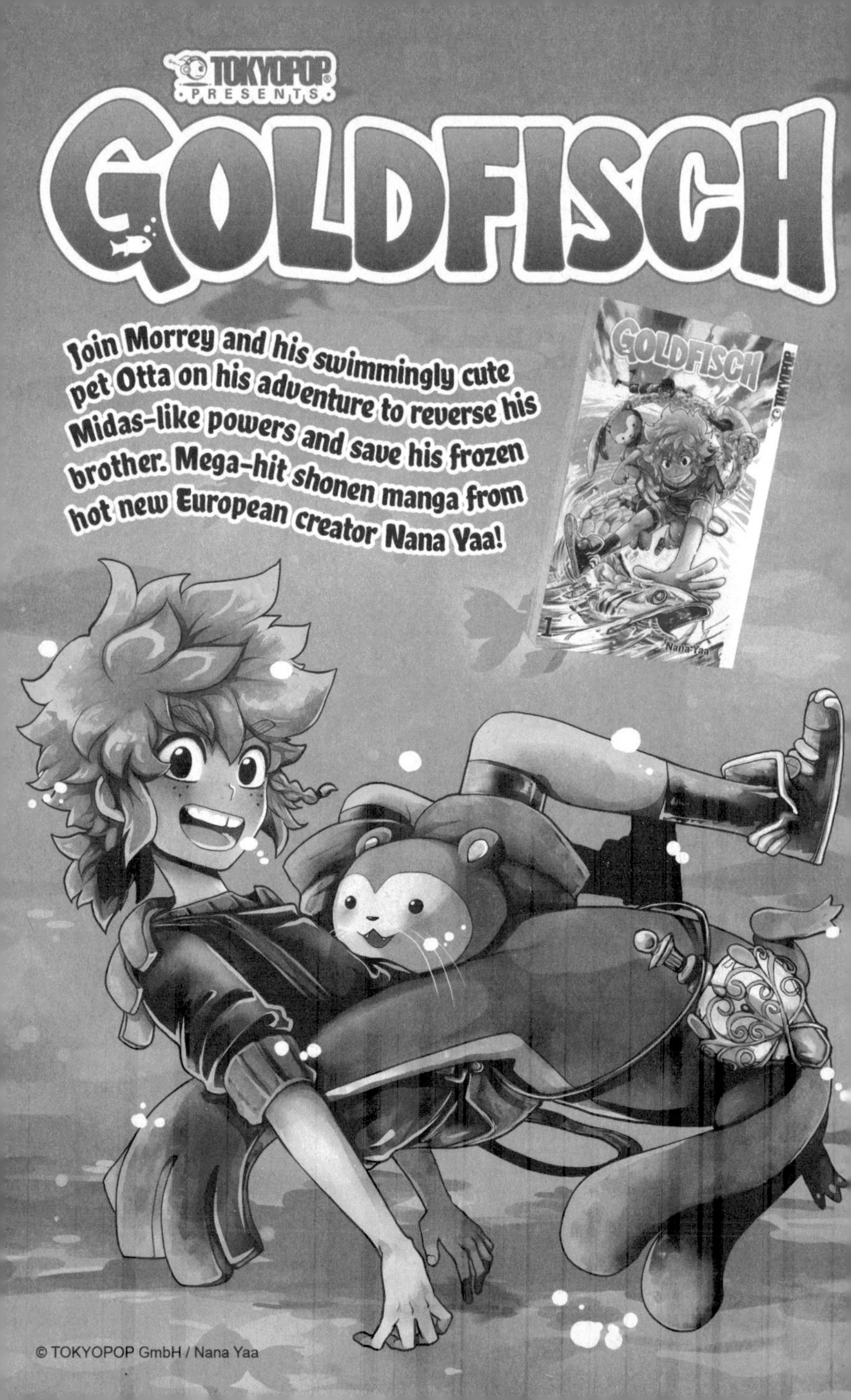
TOKYOPOP PRESENTS
GOLDFISCH
Join Morrey and his swimmingly cute pet Otta on his adventure to reverse his Midas-like powers and save his frozen brother. Mega-hit shonen manga from hot new European creator Nana Yaa!
GOLDFISCH
TOKYOPOP
1
Nana Yaa
© TOKYOPOP GmbH / Nana Yaa

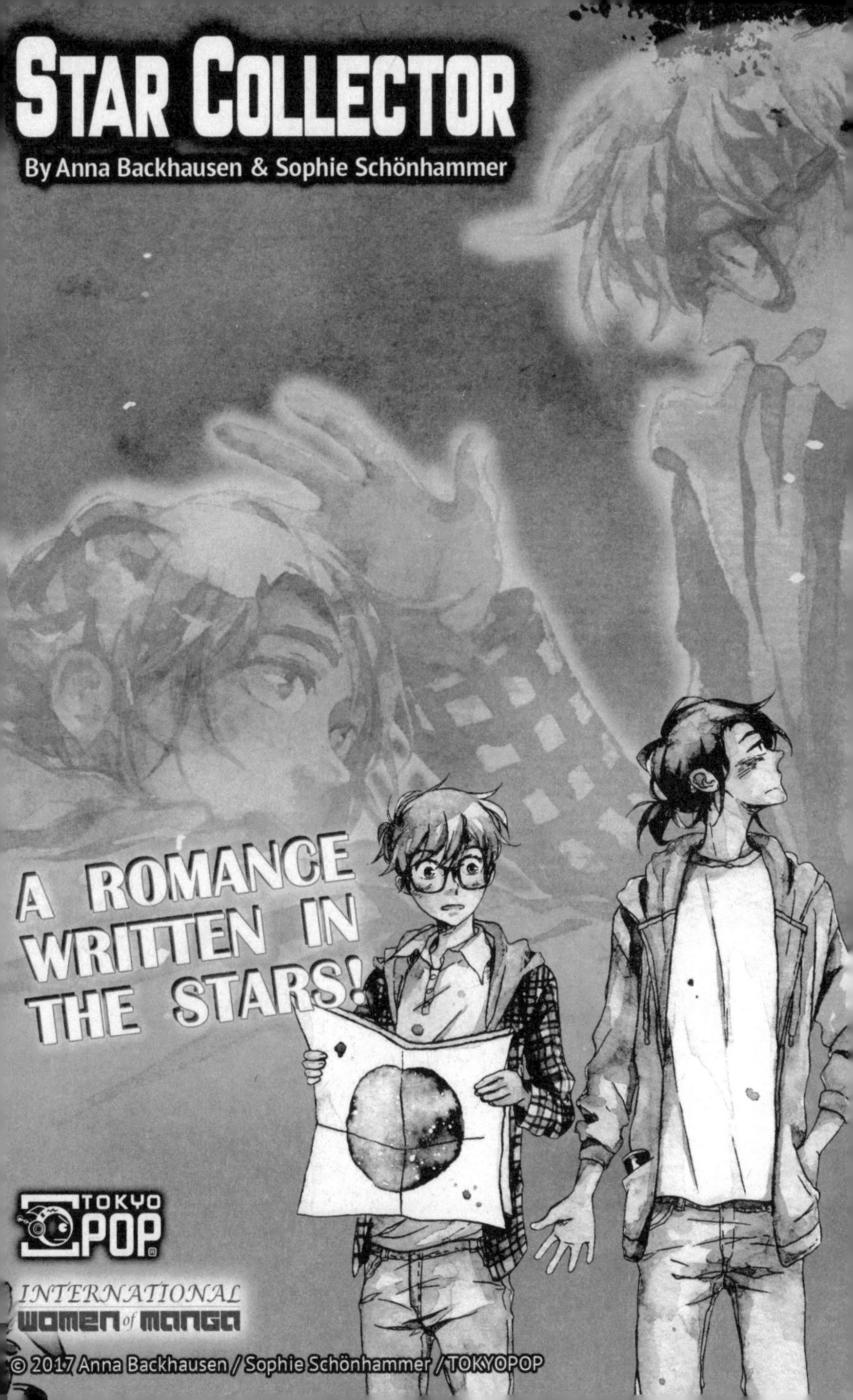
STAR COLLECTOR
By Anna Backhausen & Sophie Schönhammer
A ROMANCE WRITTEN IN THE STARS!
TOKYO POP
INTERNATIONAL Women of Manga
© 2017 Anna Backhausen / Sophie Schönhammer / TOKYOPOP

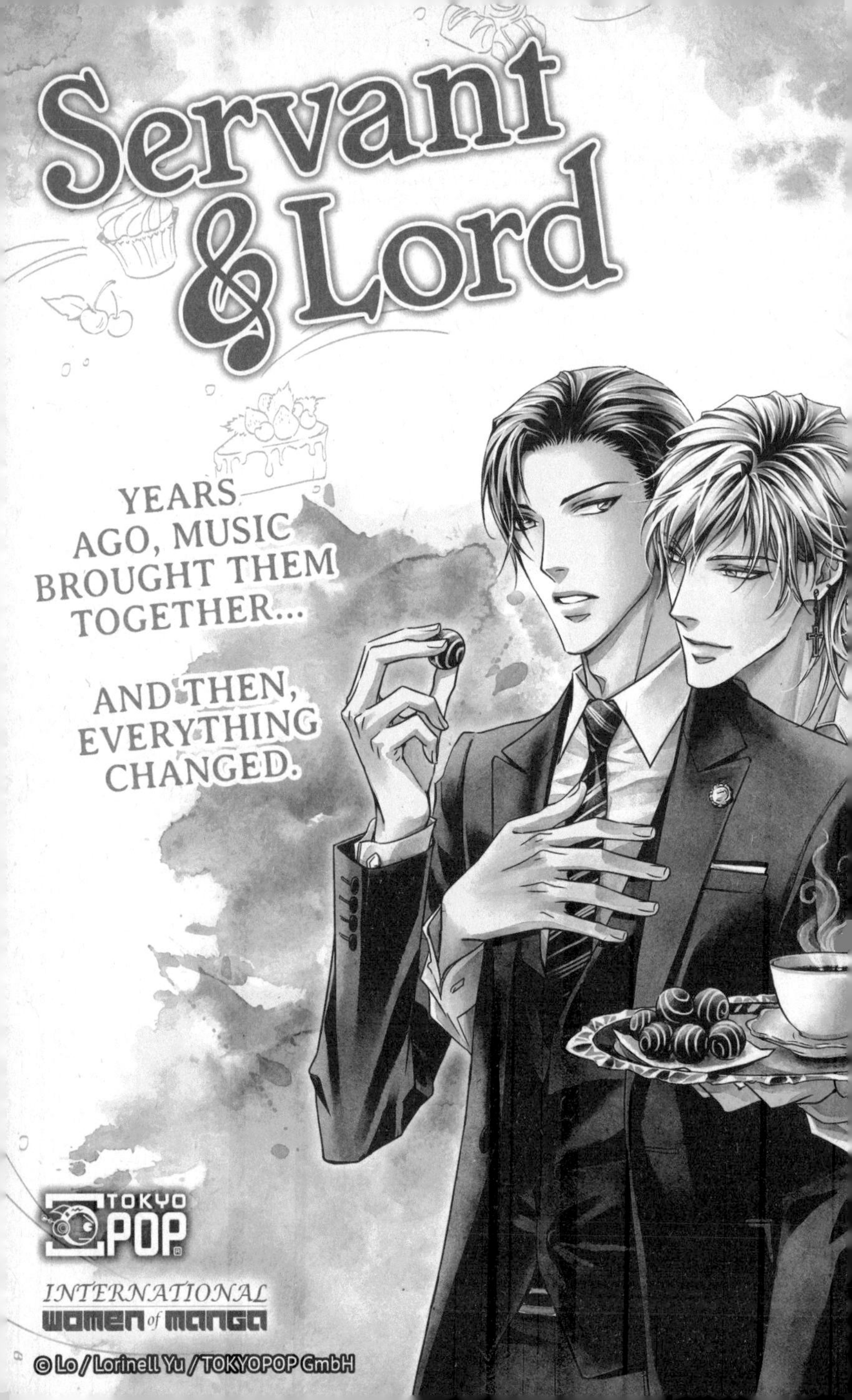
Servant & Lord
YEARS AGO, MUSIC BROUGHT THEM TOGETHER...
AND THEN, EVERYTHING CHANGED.
TOKYO POP
INTERNATIONAL
WOMEN of MANGA
© Lo / Lorinell Yu / TOKYOPOP GmbH

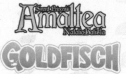

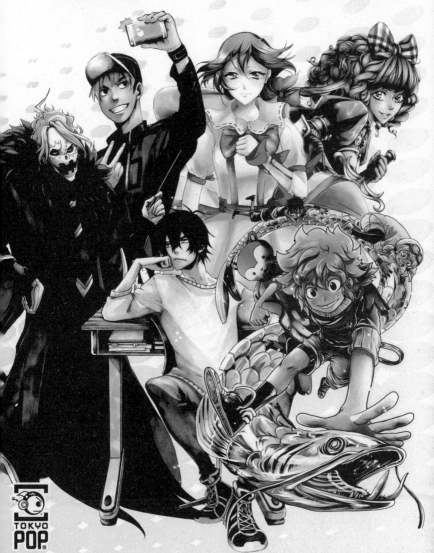

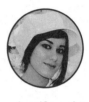

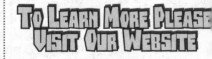

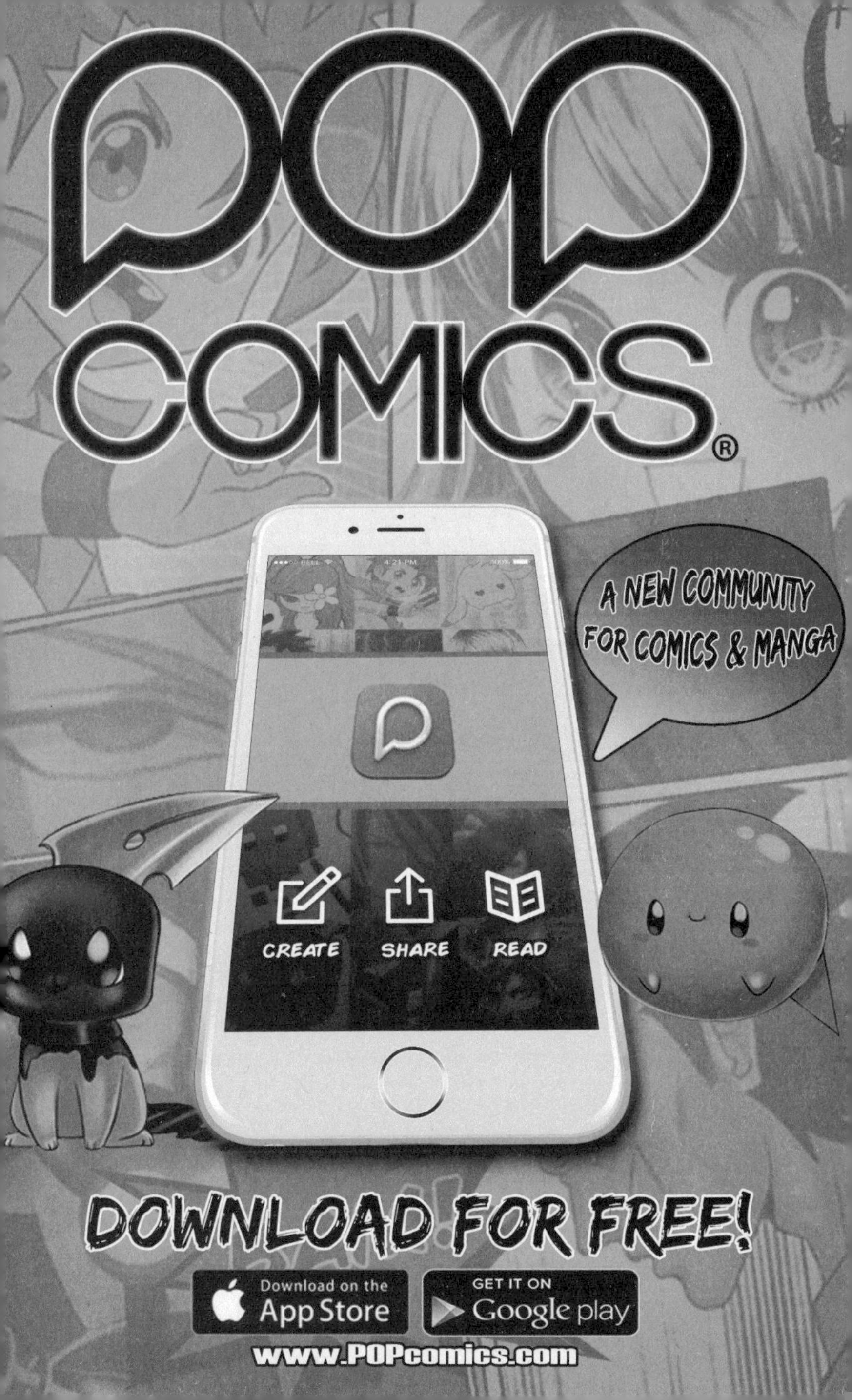
POP COMICS®
A NEW COMMUNITY FOR COMICS & MANGA
CREATE
SHARE
READ
DOWNLOAD FOR FREE!
Download on the App Store
GET IT ON Google play
www.POPcomics.com

Konohana Kitan Volume 2
Sakuya Amano

Editor - Lena Atanassova
Marketing Associate - Kae Winters
Technology and Digital Media Assistant - Phillip Hong
Translator - Katie McLendon
Copy Editor - Massiel Gutierrez
QC - Risa Otsuka
Graphic Designer - Phillip Hong
Retouching and Lettering - Vibrraant Publishing Studio
Editor-in-Chief & Publisher - Stu Levy

A 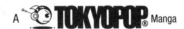 Manga

TOKYOPOP and 👁 are trademarks or registered trademarks of TOKYOPOP Inc.

TOKYOPOP Inc.
5200 W. Century Blvd. Suite 705
Los Angeles, 90045

E-mail: info@TOKYOPOP.com
Come visit us online at www.TOKYOPOP.com

f www.facebook.com/TOKYOPOP
🐦 www.twitter.com/TOKYOPOP
▶ www.youtube.com/TOKYOPOPTV
🅿 www.pinterest.com/TOKYOPOP
📷 www.instagram.com/TOKYOPOP

ISBN: 978-1-4278-5950-1
First TOKYOPOP Printing: October 2018
10 9 8 7 6 5 4 3 2 1
Printed in CANADA

STO

THIS IS THE BACK OF THE BOOK!

How do you read manga-style? It's simple! To learn, just start in the top right panel and follow the numbers:

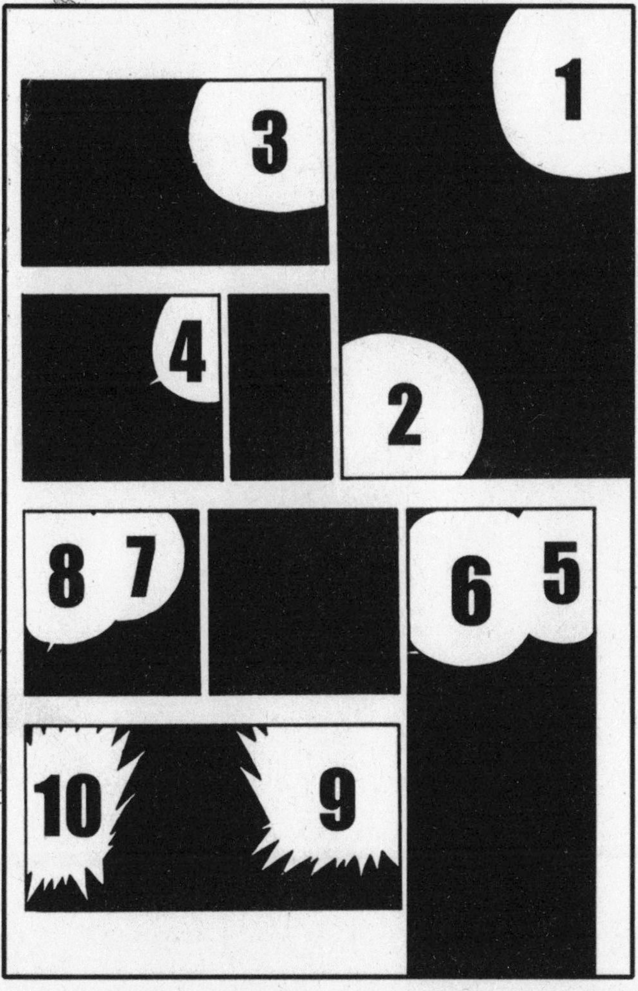
1
2
3
4
5
6
7
8
9
10